T0122791

Get the eBook FREE!

(PDF, ePub, Kindle, and liveBook all included)

We believe that once you buy a book from us, you should be able to read it in any format we have available. To get electronic versions of this book at no additional cost to you, purchase and then register this book at the Manning website.

Go to https://www.manning.com/freebook and follow the instructions to complete your pBook registration.

That's it!
Thanks from Manning!

Effective Data
Science Infrastructure

HOW TO MAKE DATA SCIENTISTS PRODUCTIVE

VILLE TUULOS
FOREWORD BY TRAVIS OLIPHANT

MANNING
SHELTER ISLAND

For online information and ordering of this and other Manning books, please visit
www.manning.com. The publisher offers discounts on this book when ordered in quantity.
For more information, please contact

Special Sales Department
Manning Publications Co.
20 Baldwin Road
PO Box 761
Shelter Island, NY 11964
Email: orders@manning.com

Manning Publications Co.
20 Baldwin Road
PO Box 761
Shelter Island, NY 11964

Development editor:	Doug Rudder
Technical development editor:	Nick Watts
Review editor:	Mihaela Batinić
Production editor:	Andy Marinkovich
Copy editor:	Pamela Hunt
Proofreader:	Keri Hales
Technical proofreader:	Al Krinker
Typesetter:	Gordan Salinovic
Cover designer:	Marija Tudor

ISBN 9781617299193
Printed in the United States of America

contents

foreword

I first met the author, Ville Tuulos, in 2012 when I was trying to understand the hype around Hadoop. At the time, Ville was working on Disco, an Erlang-based solution to map-reduce that made it easy to interact with Python. Peter Wang and I had just started Continuum Analytics Inc., and Ville's work was a big part of the motivation for releasing Anaconda, our distribution of Python for Big Data.

As a founder of NumPy and Anaconda, I've watched with interest as the explosion of ML Ops tools emerged over the past six to seven years in response to the incredible opportunities that machine learning presents. There are an incredible variety of choices and many marketing dollars are spent to convince you to choose one tool over another. My teams at Quansight and OpenTeams are constantly evaluating new tools and approaches to recommend to our customers.

It is comforting to have trusted people like Ville and the teams at Netflix and outerbounds.co that created and maintain Metaflow. I am excited by this book because it covers Metaflow in some detail and provides an excellent overview of why data infrastructure and machine learning operations are so important in a data-enriched world. Whatever MLOps framework you use, I'm confident you will learn how to make your machine learning operations more efficient and productive by reading and referring to this book.

—TRAVIS OLIPHANT
author of NumPy,
founder of Anaconda,
PyData, and NumFocus

preface

As a teenager, I was deeply intrigued by artificial intelligence. I trained my first artificial neural network at 13. I hacked simple training algorithms in C and C++ from scratch, which was the only way to explore the field in the 1990s. I went on to study computer science, mathematics, and psychology to better understand the underpinnings of this sprawling topic. Often, the way machine learning (the term *data science* didn't exist yet) was applied seemed more like alchemy than real science or principled engineering.

My journey took me from academia to large companies and startups, where I kept building systems to support machine learning. I was heavily influenced by open source projects like Linux and the then-nascent Python data ecosystem, which provided packages like NumPy that made it massively easier to build high-performance code compared to C or C++. Besides the technical merits of open source, I observed how incredibly innovative, vibrant, and welcoming communities formed around these projects.

When I joined Netflix in 2017 with a mandate to build new machine learning infrastructure from scratch, I had three tenets in mind. First, we needed a principled understanding of the full stack—data science and machine learning needed to become a real engineering discipline, not alchemy. Second, I was convinced that Python was the right foundation for the new platform, both technically as well as due to its massive, inclusive community. Third, ultimately data science and machine learning are tools to be used by human beings. The sole purpose of a tool is to make its users more effective and, in success, provide a delightful user experience.

Tools are shaped by the culture that creates them. Netflix's culture was highly influential in shaping Metaflow, an open source tool that I started, which has since become a vibrant open source project. The evolutionary pressure at Netflix made sure that Metaflow, and our understanding of the full stack of data science, was grounded on the pragmatic needs of practicing data scientists.

Netflix grants a high degree of autonomy to its data scientists, who are typically not software engineers by training. This forced us to think carefully about all challenges, small and large, that data scientists face as they develop projects and eventually deploy them to production. Our understanding of the stack was also deeply influenced by top-notch engineering teams at Netflix who had been using cloud computing for over a decade, forming a massive body of knowledge about its strengths and weaknesses.

I wanted to write this book to share these experiences with the wider world. I have learned so much from open source communities, amazingly insightful and selfless individuals, and wicked smart data scientists that I feel obliged to try to give back. This book is surely not the end of my learning journey but merely a milestone. Hence, I would love to hear from you. Don't hesitate to reach out to me and share your experiences, ideas, and feedback!

acknowledgments

This book wouldn't be possible without all the data scientists and engineers at Netflix and many other companies who have patiently explained their pain points, shared feedback, and allowed me to peek into their projects. Thank you! Keep the feedback coming.

Metaflow was influenced and continues to be developed by a talented, passionate, and empathetic group of engineers: Savin Goyal, Romain Cledat, David Berg, Oleg Avdeev, Ravi Kiran Chirravuri, Valay Dave, Ferras Hamad, Jason Ge, Rob Hilton, Brett Rose, Abhishek Kapatkar, and many others. Your handprints are all over this book! It has been a privilege and a ton of fun to work with all of you. Also, I want to thank Kurt Brown, Julie Amundson, Ashish Rastogi, Faisal Siddiqi, and Prasanna Padmanabhan who have supported the project since its inception.

I wanted to write this book with Manning because they have a reputation for publishing high-quality technical books. I wasn't disappointed! I was lucky to get to work with an experienced editor, Doug Rudder, who made me a better author and turned the 1.5-year-long writing process into an enjoyable experience. A huge thanks goes to Nick Watts and Al Krinker for their insightful technical comments, as well as to all readers and reviewers who provided feedback during Early Access.

To all the reviewers: Abel Alejandro Coronado Iruegas, Alexander Jung, David Patschke, David Yakobovitch, Edgar Hassler, Fibinse Xavier, Hari Ravindran, Henry Chen, Ikechukwu Okonkwo, Jesús A. Juárez Guerrero, Matthew Copple, Matthias Busch, Max Dehaut, Mikael Dautrey, Ninoslav Cerkez, Obiamaka Agbaneje, Ravikanth

Kompella, Richard Vaughan, Salil Athalye, Sarah Catanzaro, Sriram Macharla, Tuomo Kalliokoski, and Xiangbo Mao, your suggestions helped make this a better book.

Finally, I want to thank my wife and kids for being infinitely patient and supportive. Kids—if you ever read this sentence, I owe you an ice cream!

about this book

Machine learning and data science applications are some of the most complex engineering artifacts built by humankind, if you consider the full stack of software and hardware that powers them. In this light, it is no surprise that today, in the early 2020s, building such applications doesn't exactly feel easy.

Machine learning and data science are here to stay. Applications powered by advanced data-driven techniques are only becoming more ubiquitous across industries. Hence, there is a clear need to make building and operating such applications a more painless and disciplined process. To quote Alfred Whitehead: "Civilization advances by extending the number of important operations which we can perform without thinking about them."

This book teaches you how to build an effective data science infrastructure that allows its users to experiment with innovative applications, deploy them to production, and improve them continuously without thinking about the technical details too much. There isn't a single cookie-cutter approach that works for all use cases. Hence, this book focuses on general, foundational principles and components that you can implement in a way that makes sense in your environment.

Who should read this book?

This book has the following two primary audiences:

- *Data scientists* who want to understand the full stack of systems that make it possible to develop and deploy data science applications effectively in real-world business environments. Even if you don't have a background in infrastructure engineering, DevOps, or software engineering in general, you can use this book to get a comprehensive idea of all the moving parts and learn something new.

- *Infrastructure engineers* who are tasked to set up infrastructure to help data scientists. Even if you are experienced in DevOps or systems engineering, you can use this book to get a comprehensive idea of how the needs of data science differ from traditional software engineering, and correspondingly, how and why a different infrastructure stack is required to make data scientists productive.

In addition, leaders of data science and platform engineering organizations can quickly scan through the book, because infrastructure shapes organizations and vice versa.

How this book is organized: A road map

This book is organized around the full stack of data science infrastructure, which you can find printed on the inside front cover of the book. The stack is structured so that the most foundational, engineering-oriented layers are at the bottom and higher-level concerns related to data science are at the top. We will go through the stack roughly from the bottom up as follows:

- Chapter 1 explains why data science infrastructure is needed in the first place. It will also motivate our human-centric approach to infrastructure.
- Chapter 2 starts with the basics: what activities data scientists perform on a daily basis and how to optimize the ergonomics of their working environment.
- Chapter 3 introduces Metaflow, an open source framework that we will use to demonstrate the concepts of effective infrastructure.
- Chapter 4 focuses on scalable compute: all data science applications need to perform computation, sometimes at small scale, sometimes at large scale. We will make this possible using the cloud.
- Chapter 5 focuses on performance: it is widely known that premature optimization is not a good idea. A better approach is to optimize code gradually, adding complexity only when needed.
- Chapter 6 talks about production deployments: several crucial differences exist between prototyping and production environments, but moving between them shouldn't be too hard.
- Chapter 7 dives deep into another foundational concern of data science: data. We will investigate effective ways to integrate with modern data warehouses and data engineering teams.
- Chapter 8 discusses data science applications in the context of surrounding business systems. Data science shouldn't be an island—we will learn how to connect it to other systems to produce real business value.
- Chapter 9 ties together all the layers of the stack by walking through a realistic, end-to-end deep learning application.
- The appendix includes instructions for installing and configuring the Conda package manager for Metaflow.

From chapter 3 onward, the chapters include small but realistic machine learning applications to demonstrate the concepts. No previous knowledge of machine learning or data science is required—we will just use these techniques for illustration. This book won't teach you machine learning and data science techniques in depth—many excellent books already do that. Our focus is solely on the infrastructure that enables these applications.

After you are done with the first three chapters, feel free to skip chapters that are not relevant for you. For instance, if you deal only with small-scale data, you can focus on chapters 3, 6, and 8.

About the code

This book uses an open-source Python framework, Metaflow (https://metaflow.org), in all examples. However, the concepts and principles presented in this book are not specific to Metaflow. In particular, chapters 4–8 can be easily adapted to other frameworks, too. You can find all the source code presented in this book at https://github.com/outerbounds/dsbook.

You can execute examples on an OS X or Linux laptop. You will just need a code editor and a terminal window. Lines that start with # python like this

```
# python taxi_regression_model.py --environment=conda run
```

are meant to be executed on a terminal. Optionally, many examples benefit from an AWS account, as instructed in chapter 4.

liveBook discussion forum

Purchase of *Effective Data Science Infrastructure* includes free access to liveBook, Manning's online reading platform. Using liveBook's exclusive discussion features, you can attach comments to the book globally or to specific sections or paragraphs. It's a snap to make notes for yourself, ask and answer technical questions, and receive help from the author and other users. To access the forum, go to https://livebook.manning.com/book/effective-data-science-infrastructure/discussion. You can also learn more about Manning's forums and the rules of conduct at https://livebook.manning.com/discussion.

Manning's commitment to our readers is to provide a venue where a meaningful dialogue between individual readers and between readers and the author can take place. It is not a commitment to any specific amount of participation on the part of the author, whose contribution to the forum remains voluntary (and unpaid). We suggest you try asking the author some challenging questions lest his interest stray! The forum and the archives of previous discussions will be accessible from the publisher's website as long as the book is in print.

Other online resources

If you get stuck, need additional help, or have feedback or ideas related to the topics of this book, you are very welcome to join our beginner-friendly online community at http://slack.outerbounds.co. You can also contact the author via LinkedIn (https://www.linkedin.com/in/villetuulos/) or on Twitter (@vtuulos). If you think you have found a bug in Metaflow, please open an issue at https://github.com/Netflix/metaflow/issues.

about the author

 VILLE TUULOS has been developing infrastructure for machine learning for more than two decades. His journey includes academia, startups focusing on data and machine learning, as well as two global enterprises. He led the machine learning infrastructure team at Netflix, where he started Metaflow, an open source framework featured in this book. He is the CEO and co-founder of Outerbounds, a startup focusing on human-centric data science infrastructure.

about the cover illustration

The figure on the cover of *Effective Data Science Infrastructure* is "Dame d'ausbourg," or "Lady of Augsburg," taken from a collection by Jacques Grasset de Saint-Sauveur, published in 1797. Each illustration is finely drawn and colored by hand.

In those days, it was easy to identify where people lived and what their trade or station in life was just by their dress. Manning celebrates the inventiveness and initiative of the computer business with book covers based on the rich diversity of regional culture centuries ago, brought back to life by pictures from collections such as this one.

Introducing data science infrastructure

This chapter covers

- Why companies need data science infrastructure in the first place
- Introducing the infrastructure stack for data science and machine learning
- Elements of successful data science infrastructure

Machine learning and artificial intelligence were born in academia in the 1950s. Technically, everything presented in this book has been possible to implement for decades, if time and cost were not a concern. However, for the past seven decades, nothing in this problem domain has been easy.

As many companies have experienced, building applications powered by machine learning has required large teams of engineers with specialized knowledge, often working for years to deliver a well-tuned solution. If you look back on the history of computing, most society-wide shifts have happened not when impossible things have become possible but when possible things have become easy. Bridging the gap between possible and easy requires effective infrastructure, which is the topic of this book.

A dictionary defines infrastructure as "the basic equipment and structures (such as roads and bridges) that are needed for a country, region, or organization to function properly." This book covers the basic stack of equipment and structures needed for data science applications to function properly. After reading this book, you will be able to set up and customize an infrastructure that helps your organization to develop and deliver data science applications faster and more easily than ever before.

A WORD ABOUT TERMINOLOGY

The phrase *data science* in its modern form was coined in the early 2000s. As noted earlier, the terms *machine learning* and *artificial intelligence* have been used for decades prior to this, alongside other related terms such as *data mining* or *expert systems*, which was trendy at one time.

No consensus exists on what these terms mean exactly, which is a challenge. Professionals in these fields recognize nuanced differences between data science, machine learning, and artificial intelligence, but the boundaries between these terms are contentious and fuzzy, which must delight those who were excited about the term *fuzzy logic* in the 1970s and '80s!

This book is targeted at the union of the modern fields of data science, machine learning, and artificial intelligence. For brevity, we have chosen to use the term *data science* to describe the union. The choice of term is meant to be inclusive: we are not excluding any particular approach or set of methods.

For the purposes of this book, the differences between these fields are not significant. In a few specific cases where we want to emphasize the differences, we will use more specific terms, such as *deep neural networks*. To summarize, whenever this book uses the term, you can substitute it with your preferred term if it makes the text more meaningful to you.

If you ask someone in the field what the job of a data scientist is, you might get a quick answer: their job is to build models. Although that answer is not incorrect, it is a bit narrow. Increasingly, data scientists and engineers are expected to build end-to-end solutions to business problems, of which models are a small but important part. Because this book focuses on end-to-end solutions, we say that the data scientist's job is to build *data science applications*. Hence, when you see the phrase used in this book, consider that it means "models and everything else required by an end-to-end solution."

1.1   *Why data science infrastructure?*

Many great books have been written about what data science is, why it is beneficial, and how to apply it in various contexts. This book focuses on questions related to *infrastructure*. Before we go into details on why we need infrastructure specifically for data science, let's discuss briefly why any infrastructure exists at all.

Consider how milk has been produced and consumed for millennia prior to the advent of industrial-scale farming in the 20th century. Many households had a cow or two, producing milk for the immediate needs of the family. Sustaining a cow required some expertise but not much technical infrastructure. If the family wanted to expand their dairy operation, it would have been challenging without investing in larger-scale feed production, head count, and storage mechanisms. In short, they were able to operate a small-scale dairy business with minimal infrastructure, but scaling up the *volume* of production would have required deeper investments than just acquiring another cow.

Even if the farm could have supported a larger number of cows, they would have needed to distribute the extra milk outside the household for sale. This presents a *velocity* problem: if the farmer can't move the milk fast enough, other farmers may sell their produce first, saturating the market. Worse, the milk may spoil, which undermines the *validity* of the product.

Maybe a friendly neighbor is able to help with distribution and transports the milk to a nearby town. Our enterprising farmer may find that the local marketplace has an oversupply of raw milk. Instead, customers demand a *variety* of refined dairy products, such as yogurt, cheese, or maybe even ice cream. The farmer would very much like to serve the customers (and get their money), but it is clear that their operation isn't set up to deal with this level of complexity.

Over time, a set of interrelated systems emerged to address these needs, which today form the modern dairy infrastructure: industrial-scale farms are optimized for volume. Refrigeration, pasteurization, and logistics provide the velocity needed to deliver high-quality milk to dairy factories, which then churn out a wide variety of products that are distributed to grocery markets. Note that the dairy infrastructure didn't displace all small-scale farmers: there is still a sizable market for specialized produce from organic, artisanal, family farms, but it wouldn't be feasible to satisfy all demand in this labor-intensive manner.

The three Vs—volume, velocity, and variety—were originally used by Professor Michael Stonebraker to classify database systems for big data. We added validity as the fourth dimension because it is highly relevant for data science. As a thought exercise, consider which of these dimensions matter the most in your business context. In most cases, the effective data science infrastructure should strike a healthy balance between the four dimensions.

1.1.1 *The life cycle of a data science project*

For the past seven decades, most data science applications have been produced in a manner that can be described as artisanal, by having a team of senior software engineers to build the whole application from the ground up. As with dairy products, artisanal doesn't imply "bad"—often quite the opposite. The artisanal way is often the right way to experiment with bleeding-edge innovations or to produce highly specialized applications.

However, as with dairy, as the industry matures and needs to support a higher volume, velocity, validity, and variety of products, it becomes rational to build many, if not most, applications on a common infrastructure. You may have a rough idea of how raw milk turns into cheese and what infrastructure is required to support industrial-scale cheese production, but what about data science? Figure 1.1 illustrates a typical data science project.

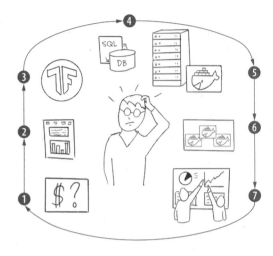

Figure 1.1   Life cycle of a data science project

1   At the center, we have a data scientist who is asked to solve a business problem, for instance, to create a model to estimate the lifetime value of a customer or to create a system that generates personalized product recommendations in an email newsletter.

2   The data scientist starts the project by coming up with hypotheses and experiments. They can start testing ideas using their favorite tools of the trade: Jupyter notebooks, specialized languages like R or Julia, or software packages like MAT-LAB or Mathematica.

3   When it comes to prototyping machine learning or statistical models, excellent open source packages are available, such as Scikit-Learn, PyTorch, TensorFlow, Stan, and many others. Thanks to excellent documentation and tutorials available online, in many cases it doesn't take long to put together an initial prototype using these packages.

4   However, every model needs data. Maybe suitable data exists in a database. Extracting a static sample of data for a prototype is often quite straightforward, but handling a larger dataset, say, tens of gigabytes, may get more complicated. At this point, the data scientist is not even worrying how to get the data to update automatically, which would require more architecture and engineering.

5   Where does the data scientist run the notebook? Maybe they can run it on a laptop, but how are they going to share the results? What if their colleagues want to test the prototype, but they don't have a sufficiently powerful laptop? It might be convenient to execute the experiment on a shared server—in the cloud—where all collaborators can access it easily. However, someone needs to set up this environment first and make sure that the required tools and libraries, as well as data, are available on the server.

6   The data scientist was asked to solve a business problem. Very few companies conduct their business in notebooks or other data science tools. To prove the

value of the prototype, it is not sufficient that the prototype exists in a notebook or other data science environment. It needs to be integrated into the surrounding business infrastructure. Maybe those systems are organized as microservices, so it would be beneficial if the new model could be deployed as a microservice, too. Doing this may require quite a bit of experience and knowledge in infrastructure engineering.

7 Finally, after the prototype has been integrated to surrounding systems, stakeholders—product managers and business owners—evaluate the results and give feedback to the data scientist. Two outcomes can occur: either the stakeholders are optimistic with the results and shower the data scientist with further requests for improvement, or they deem that the scientist's time is better spent on other, more promising business problems. Remarkably, both outcomes lead to the same next step: the whole cycle starts again from the beginning, either focusing on refining the results or working on a new problem.

Details of the life cycle will naturally vary between companies and projects: How you develop a predictive model for customer lifetime value differs greatly from building self-driving cars. However, all data science and machine learning projects have the following key elements in common:

1 In the technical point of view, all projects involve *data and computation* at their foundation.

2 This book focuses on practical applications of these techniques instead of pure research, so we expect that all projects will eventually need to address the question of *integrating results into production systems,* which typically involves a great deal of software engineering.

3 Finally, from the human point of view, all projects involve *experimentation and iteration,* which many consider to be the central activity of data science.

Although it is certainly possible for individuals, companies, or teams to come up with their own bespoke processes and practices to conduct data science projects, a common infrastructure can help to increase the number of projects that can be executed simultaneously (*volume*), speed up the time to market (*velocity*), ensure that the results are robust (*validity*), and make it possible to support a larger *variety* of projects.

Note that the scale of the project, that is, the size of the data set or model, is an orthogonal concern. In particular, it would be a mistake to think that only large-scale projects require infrastructure. Often the situation is quite the opposite.

IS THIS BOOK FOR ME?

If the questions and potential solutions related to the life cycle of a data science project resonate with you, you should find this book useful. If you are a data scientist, you may have experienced some of the challenges firsthand. If you are an infrastructure engineer looking to design and build systems to help data scientists, you probably want to find scalable, robust solutions to these questions, so you don't have to wake up at night when something breaks.

We will systematically go through the stack of systems that make a modern, effective infrastructure for data science. The principles covered in this book are not specific to any particular implementation, but we will use an open source framework, *Metaflow*, to show how the ideas can be put into practice. Alternatively, you can customize your own solution by using other off-the-shelf libraries. This book will help you to choose the right set of tools for the job.

It is worth noting that perfectly valid, important scenarios exist where this book does not apply. This book, and data science infrastructure in general, is probably not relevant for you if you are in the following situations:

- You are focusing on theoretical research and not applying the methods and results in practical use cases.
- You are in the early phases (steps 1–4 as described earlier) of your first applied data science project, and everything is going smoothly.
- You are working on a very specific, mature application, so optimizing the volume, velocity, and variety of projects doesn't concern you.

In these cases, you can return to this book later when more projects start coming up or you start hitting tough questions like the ones faced by our data scientist earlier. Otherwise, keep on reading! In the next section, we introduce an infrastructure stack that provides the overall scaffolding for everything that we will discuss in the later chapters.

1.2   What is data science infrastructure?

How does new infrastructure emerge? In the early days of the World Wide Web in the 1990s, no infrastructure existed besides primordial web browsers and servers. During the dot-com boom, setting up an e-commerce store was a major technical feat, involving teams of people, lots of custom C or C++ code, and a deep-pocketed venture capitalist.

Over the next decade, a Cambrian explosion of web frameworks started to converge to common infrastructure stacks like LAMP (Linux, Apache, MySQL, PHP/Perl/Python). By 2020, a number of components, such as the operating system, the web server, and databases, have become commodities that few people have to worry about, allowing most developers to focus on the user-facing application layer using polished high-level frameworks like ReactJS.

The infrastructure for data science is going through a similar evolution. Primordial machine learning and optimization libraries have existed for decades without much other infrastructure. Now, in the early 2020s, we are experiencing an explosion of data science libraries, frameworks, and infrastructures, often driven by commercial interests, similar to what happened during and immediately after the dot-com boom. If history is any proof, widely shared patterns will emerge from this fragmented landscape that will form the basis of a common, open source infrastructure stack for data science.

When building any infrastructure, it is good to remember that infrastructure is just a means to an end, not an end in itself. In our case, we want to build infrastructure to make data science projects—and data scientists who are responsible for them, more successful—as illustrated in figure 1.2.

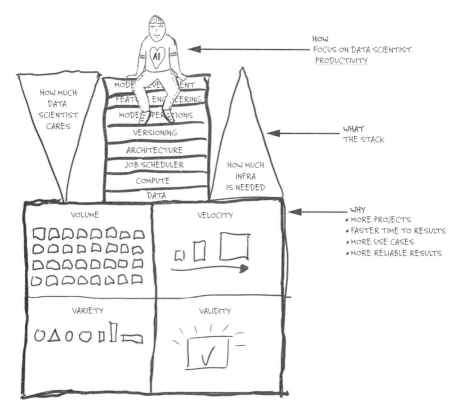

Figure 1.2 Summarizing the key concerns of this book

The goal of the stack, which is introduced in the next section, is to unlock the four Vs: it should enable a greater volume and variety of projects, delivered with a higher velocity, without compromising validity of results. However, the stack doesn't deliver projects by itself—successful projects are delivered by data scientists whose productivity is hopefully greatly improved by the stack.

1.2.1 The infrastructure stack for data science

What exactly are the elements of the infrastructure stack for data science? Thanks to the culture of open source and relatively free technical information sharing between companies in Silicon Valley and globally, we have been able to observe and collect common patterns in data science projects and infrastructure components. Though implementation details vary, the major infrastructural layers are relatively uniform across a large number of projects. The purpose of this book is to distill and describe these layers and the infrastructure stack that they form for data science.

The stack presented in figure 1.3 is not the only valid way to build infrastructure for data science. However, it should be a well-justified one: if you start from first principles, it is rather hard to see how you could execute data science projects successfully without addressing all layers of the stack somehow. As an exercise, you can challenge any layer of the stack and ask what would happen if that layer didn't exist.

Each layer can be implemented in various ways, driven by the specific needs of its environment and use cases but the big picture is remarkably consistent.

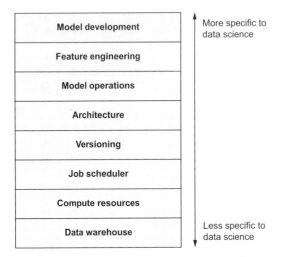

Figure 1.3   **The infrastructure stack for data science**

This infrastructure stack for data science is organized so that the most fundamental, generic components are at the bottom of the stack. The layers become more specific to data science toward the top of the stack.

The stack is the key mental model that binds together the chapters of this book. By the time you get to the last chapter, you will be able to answer questions like why the stack is needed, what purpose each layer serves, and how to make appropriate technical choices at each layer of the stack. Because you will be able to build infrastructure with a coherent vision and architecture, it will provide a seamless, delightful experience to data scientists using it. To give you a high-level idea what the layers mean, let's go through them one by one from the bottom up.

DATA WAREHOUSE

The data warehouse stores input data used by applications. In general, it is beneficial to rely on a single centralized data warehouse that acts as a common source of truth, instead of building a separate warehouse specifically for data science, which can easily lead to diverging data and definitions. Chapter 7 is dedicated to this broad and deep topic.

COMPUTE RESOURCES

Raw data doesn't do anything by itself—you need to run computations, such as data transformations or model training, to turn it into something more valuable. Compared to other fields of software engineering, data science tends to be particularly compute-hungry. Algorithms used by data scientists come in many shapes and sizes. Some need many CPU cores, some GPUs, and some a lot of memory. We need a compute layer that can smoothly scale to handle many different types of workloads. We cover these topics in chapters 4 and 5.

JOB SCHEDULER

Arguably, nothing in data science is a one-time operation: models should be retrained regularly and predictions produced on demand. Consider a data science application as a continuously humming engine that pushes a never-ending stream of data through models. It is the job of the scheduling layer to keep the machine running at the desired cadence. Also, the scheduler helps to structure and execute applications as workflows of interrelated steps of computation. The topics of job scheduling and workflow orchestration are discussed in chapters 2, 3, and 6.

VERSIONING

Experimentation and iteration are defining features of data science projects. As a result, applications are always subject to change. However, progress is seldom linear. Often, we don't know upfront which version of the application is an improvement over others. To judge the versions properly, you need to run multiple versions side by side, as an A/B experiment. To enable rapid but disciplined development and experimentation, we need a robust versioning layer to keep the work organized. Topics related to versioning are discussed in chapters 3 and 6.

ARCHITECTURE

In addition to core data science work, it takes a good amount of software engineering to build a robust, production-ready data science application. Increasingly many companies find it beneficial to empower data scientists, who are not software engineers by training, to build these applications autonomously while supporting them with a robust infrastructure. The infrastructure stack must provide software scaffolding and guide rails for data scientists, ensuring that the code they produce follows architectural best practices. We introduce Metaflow, an open source framework that codifies many such practices, in chapter 3.

MODEL OPERATIONS

Data science applications don't have inherent value—they become valuable only when connected to other systems, such as product UIs or decision support systems. Once the application is deployed, to be a critical part of a product experience or business operations, it is expected to stay up and deliver correct results under varying conditions. If and when the application fails, as all production systems occasionally do, systems must be in place to allow quick detection, troubleshooting, and fixing of errors. We can learn a lot from the best practices of traditional software engineering, but the changing nature of data and probabilistic models give data science operations a special flavor, which we discuss in chapters 6 and 8.

FEATURE ENGINEERING

On top of the engineering-oriented layers sit the core concerns of data science. First, the data scientist must discover suitable raw data, determine desirable subsets of it, develop transformations, and decide how to feed the resulting features into models. Designing pipelines like this is a major part of the data scientist's daily work. We should strive to make the process as efficient as possible, both in the point of view of human productivity as well as computational complexity. Effective solutions are often quite specific to each problem domain, so our infrastructure should be capable of supporting various approaches to feature engineering as discussed in chapters 7 and 9.

MODEL DEVELOPMENT

Finally, at the very top of the stack is the layer of model development: the quest for finding and describing a mathematical model that transforms features into desired outputs. We expect this layer to be solidly in the domain of expertise of a data scientist, so the infrastructure doesn't need to get too opinionated about the modeling approach. We should be able to support a wide variety of off-the-shelf libraries, so the scientist has the flexibility to choose the best tool for the job.

If you are new to the field, it may come as a surprise to many that model development occupies only a tiny part of the end-to-end machinery that makes an effective data science application. Compare the model development layer to the human brain, which makes up only 2–3% of one's total body weight.

1.2.2   *Supporting the full life cycle of a data science project*

The goal of the infrastructure stack is to support a typical data science project throughout its life cycle, from its inception and initial deployment to countless iterations of incremental improvement. Earlier, we identified the following three common themes that are common to most data science projects. Figure 1.4 shows how the themes map to the stack.

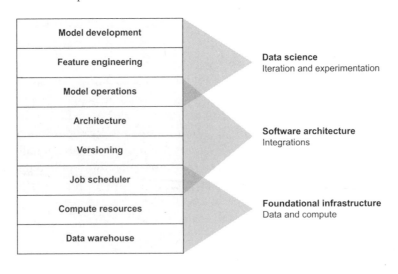

Figure 1.4
Concerns of a data science project mapped to the infrastructure layers

1. It is easy to see that every data science project regardless of the problem domain needs to deal with data and compute, so these layers form *the foundational infrastructure*. These layers are agnostic of what exactly gets executed.

2. The middle layers define *the software architecture* of an individual data science application: what gets executed and how—the algorithms, data pipelines, deployment strategies, and distribution of the results. Much about the work is about integrating existing software components.

3. The top of the stack is the realm of *data science*: defining a mathematical model and how to transform raw input to something that the model can process. In a typical data science project, these layers can evolve quickly as the data scientist experiments with different approaches.

Note that there isn't a one-to-one mapping between the layers and the themes. The concerns overlap. We use the stack as a blueprint for designing and building the infrastructure, but the user shouldn't have to care about it. In particular, they shouldn't hit the seams between the layers, but they should use the stack as one effective data science infrastructure.

In the next chapter, we will introduce Metaflow, a framework that provides an example of how this can be achieved in practice. Alternatively, you can customize your own solution by combining frameworks that address different parts of the stack by following the general principles laid out in the coming chapters.

1.2.3 One size doesn't fit all

What if your company needs a highly specialized data science application—a self-driving car, a high-frequency trading system, or a miniaturized model that can be deployed on resource constrained Internet of Things devices? Surely the infrastructure stack would need to look very different for such applications. In many such cases, the answer is yes—at least initially.

Let's say your company wants to deliver the most advanced self-flying drone to the market. The whole company is rallied around developing one data science application: a drone. Naturally, such a complex project involves many subsystems, but ultimately the end result is to produce one application, and hence, volume or variety are not the top concerns. Unquestionably, velocity and validity matter, but the company may feel that a core business concern requires a highly customized solution.

You can use the quadrants depicted in figure 1.5 to evaluate whether your company needs a highly customized solution or a generalized infrastructure.

A drone company has one special application, so they may focus on building a single *custom application* because they don't have the variety and the volume that would necessitate a generalized infrastructure. Likewise, a small startup pricing used cars using a predictive model can quickly put together *a basic application* to get the job done—again, no need to invest in infrastructure initially.

In contrast, a large multinational bank has hundreds of data science applications from credit rating to risk analysis and trading, each of which can be solved using

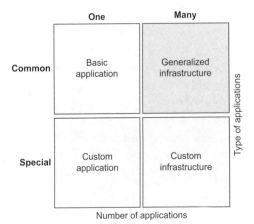

Figure 1.5   Types of infrastructure

well-understood (albeit sophisticated—"common" doesn't imply simple or unadvanced in this context) models, so a *generalized infrastructure* is well justified. A research institute for bioinformatics may have many highly specialized applications, which require very *custom infrastructure*.

Over time, companies tend to gravitate toward *generalized infrastructure*, no matter where they start. A drone company that initially had a custom application will eventually need other data science applications to support sales, marketing, customer service, or maybe another line of products. They may keep a specialized application or even custom infrastructure for their core technology while employing generalized infrastructure for the rest of the business.

> **NOTE**   When deciding on your infrastructure strategy, consider the broadest set of use cases, including new and experimental applications. It is a common mistake to design the infrastructure around the needs of a few most visible applications, which may not represent the needs of the majority of (future) use cases. In fact, the most visible applications may require a custom approach that can coexist alongside generalized infrastructure.

Custom applications may have unique needs when it comes to scale (think Google Search) or performance (think high-frequency trading applications that must provide predictions in microseconds). Applications like this often necessitate an artisanal approach: they need to be carefully crafted by experienced engineers, maybe using specialized hardware. A downside is that specialized applications often have hard time optimizing for velocity and volume (special skills required limit the number of people who can work on the app), and they can't support a variety of applications by design.

Consider carefully what kind of applications you will need to build or support. Today, most data science applications can be supported by generalized infrastructure, which is the topic of this book. This is beneficial because it allows you to optimize for volume, velocity, variety, and validity. If one of your applications has special needs, it may require a more custom approach. In this case, it might make sense to treat the special application as a special case while letting the other applications benefit from generalized infrastructure.

1.3 Why good infrastructure matters

As we went through the eight layers of the infrastructure stack, you got a glimpse of the wide array of technical components that are needed to build modern data science applications. In fact, large-scale machine learning applications like personalized recommendations for YouTube or sophisticated models that optimize banner ads in real time—a deliberately mundane example—are some of the most complex machines ever built by humankind, considering the hundreds of subsystems and tens of millions of lines of code involved.

Building infrastructure for the dairy industry, following our original example, probably involves an order of magnitude less complexity than many production-grade data science applications. Much of the complexity is not visible on the surface, but it surely becomes visible when things fail.

To illustrate the complexity, imagine having the aforementioned eight-layer stack powering a data science project. Remember how a single project can involve many interconnected machines, with each machine representing a sophisticated model. A constant flow of fresh data, potentially large amounts of it, goes through these machines. The machines are powered by a compute platform that needs to manage thousands of machines of various sizes executing concurrently. The machines are orchestrated by a job scheduler, which makes sure that data flows between the machines correctly and each machine executes at the right moment.

We have a team of data scientists working on these machines, each of them experimenting with various versions of the machine that is allocated for them in rapid iterations. We want to ensure that each version produces valid results, and we want to evaluate them in real time by executing them side by side. Every version needs its own isolated environment to ensure that no interference occurs between the versions.

This scenario should evoke a picture of a factory, employing teams of people and hundreds of incessantly humming machines. In contrast to an industrial-era factory, this factory isn't built only once but it is constantly evolving, slightly changing its shape multiple times a day. Software isn't bound by the limitations of the physical world, but it is bound to produce ever-increasing business value.

The story doesn't end here. A large or midsize modern company doesn't have only a single factory, a single data science application, but can have any number of them. The sheer volume of applications causes operational burden, but the main challenge is variety: every real-world problem domain requires a different solution, each with its own requirements and characteristics, leading to a diverse set of applications that need to be supported. As a cherry on top of the complexity cake, the applications are often interdependent.

For a concrete example, consider a hypothetical midsize e-commerce store. They have a custom recommendation engine ("These products are recommended to you!");

a model to measure the effectiveness of marketing campaigns ("Facebook ads seem to be performing better than Google Ads in Connecticut."); an optimization model for logistics ("It is more efficient to dropship category B versus keeping them in stock."); and a financial forecasting model for estimating churn ("Customers buying X seem to churn less."). Each of these four applications is a factory in itself. They may involve multiple models, multiple data pipelines, multiple people, and multiple versions.

1.3.1   *Managing complexity*

This complexity of real-life data science applications poses a number of challenges to the infrastructure. There isn't a simple, nifty technical solution to the problem. Instead of treating complexity as a nuisance that can be swept or abstracted away, we make managing complexity a key goal of effective infrastructure. We address the challenge on multiple fronts, as follows:

- *Implementation*—Designing and implementing infrastructure that deals with this level of complexity is a nontrivial task. We will discuss strategies to address the engineering challenge later.
- *Usability*—It is a key challenge of *effective* infrastructure to make data scientists productive despite the complexities involved, which is a key motivation for *human-centric infrastructure* introduced later.
- *Operations*—How do we keep the machines humming with minimal human intervention? Reducing the operational burden of data science applications is another key goal of the infrastructure, which is a common thread across chapters of this book.

In all these cases, we must avoid introducing *incidental complexity*, or complexity that is not necessitated by the problem itself but is an unwanted artifact of a chosen approach. Incidental complexity is a huge problem for real-world data science because we have to deal with such a high level of *inherent complexity* that distinguishing between real problems and imaginary problems becomes hard.

You may have heard of *boilerplate code* (code that exists just to make a framework happy), *spaghetti pipelines* (poorly organized relationships between systems), or *dependency hells* (managing a constantly evolving graph of third-party libraries is hard). On top of these technical concerns, we have incidental complexity caused by human organizations: sometimes we have to introduce complex interfaces between systems, not because they are necessary technically, but because they follow the organizational boundaries, for example, between data scientists and data engineers. You can read more about these issues in a frequently cited paper called "Hidden Technical Debt in Machine Learning Systems," which was published by Google in 2015 (http://mng.bz/Dg7n).

An effective infrastructure helps to expose and manage inherent complexity, which is the natural state of the world we live in, while making a conscious effort to avoid introducing incidental complexity. Doing this well is hard and requires constant judgment. Fortunately, we have one time-tested heuristic for keeping incidental complexity in check, namely, *simplicity*. "Everything should be made as simple as possible, but no simpler" is a core design principle that applies to all parts of the effective data science infrastructure.

1.3.2   Leveraging existing platforms

Our job, as described in the previous sections, is to build effective, generalized infrastructure for data science based on the eight-layer stack. We want to do this in a manner that makes real-world complexity manageable while minimizing extra complexity caused by the infrastructure itself. This may sound like a daunting task.

Very few companies can afford dedicating large teams of engineers for building and maintaining infrastructure for data science. Smaller companies may have one or two engineers dedicated to the task, whereas larger companies may have a small team. Ultimately, companies want to produce business value with data science applications. Infrastructure is a means to this end, not a goal in itself, so it is rational to determine the size of the infrastructure investment accordingly. All in all, we can spend only a limited amount of time and effort in building and maintaining infrastructure.

Luckily, as noted in the very beginning of this chapter, everything presented in this book has been possible to implement technically for decades, so we don't have to start from scratch. Instead of inventing new hardware, operating systems, or data warehouses, our job is to leverage the best-of-the-breed platforms available and integrate them to make it easy to prototype and productionize data science applications.

Engineers often underestimate the gap between "possible" and "easy," as illustrated in figure 1.6. It is easy to keep reimplementing things in various ways on the "possible" side of the chasm, without truly answering the question how to make things fundamentally easier. However, it is only the "easy" side of the chasm that enables us to maximize the four Vs—volume, velocity, variety, and validity of data science applications—so we shouldn't spend too much time on the left bank.

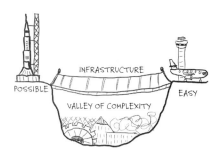

Figure 1.6   Infrastructure makes possible things easy.

This book helps you to build the bridge first, which is a nontrivial undertaking by itself, leveraging existing components whenever possible. Thanks to our stack with distinct layers, we can let other teams and companies worry about individual components. Over time, if some of them turn out to be inadequate, we can replace them with better alternatives without disrupting users.

HEAD IN THE CLOUDS

Cloud computing is a prime example of a solution that makes many things technically possible, albeit not always easy. Public clouds, such as Amazon Web Services, Google Compute Platform, and Microsoft Azure, have massively changed the infrastructure landscape by allowing anyone to access foundational layers that were previously available only to the largest companies. These services are not only technically available but also drastically cost-effective when used thoughtfully.

Besides democratizing the lower layers of infrastructure, the cloud has qualitatively changed the way we should architect infrastructure. Previously, many challenges in architecting systems for high-performance computing revolved around resource management: how to guard and ration access to limited compute and storage resources, and, correspondingly, how to make resource usage as efficient as possible.

The cloud allows us to change our mindset. All the clouds provide a data layer, like Amazon S3, which provides a virtually unlimited amount of storage with close to a perfect level of durability and high availability. Similarly, they provide nearly infinite, elastically scaling compute resources like Amazon Elastic Compute Cloud (Amazon EC2) and the abstractions built on top of it. We can architect our systems with the assumption that we have an abundant amount of compute resources and storage available and focus on cost-effectiveness and productivity instead.

This book operates with the assumption that you have access to cloudlike foundational infrastructure. By far the easiest way to fulfill the requirement is to create an account with one of the cloud providers. You can build and test the stack for a few hundred dollars, or possibly for free by relying on the free tiers that many clouds offer. Alternatively, you can build or use an existing private cloud environment. How to build a private cloud is outside the scope of this book, however.

All the clouds also provide higher-level products for data science, such as Azure Machine Learning (ML) Studio and Amazon SageMaker. You can typically use these products as end-to-end platforms, requiring minimal customization, or, alternatively, you can integrate parts of them in your own systems. This book takes the latter approach: you will learn how to build your own stack, leveraging various services provided by the cloud as well as using open source frameworks. Although this approach requires more work, it affords you greater flexibility, the result is likely to be easier to use, and the custom stack is likely to be more cost-efficient as well. You will learn why this is the case throughout the coming chapters.

To summarize, you can leverage the clouds to take care of low-level, undifferentiated technical heavy lifting. This allows you to focus your limited development budget on unique, differentiating business needs and, most important, on optimizing data scientist productivity in your organization. We can use the clouds to increasingly shift our focus from technical matters to human matters, as we will describe in the next section.

1.4   *Human-centric infrastructure*

The infrastructure aims at maximizing the productivity of the organization on multiple fronts. It supports more projects, delivered faster, with more reliable results, covering more business domains. To better understand how infrastructure can make this happen, consider the following typical bottlenecks that occur when effective infrastructure is not available:

- *Volume*—We can't support more data science applications simply because we don't have enough data scientists to work on them. All our existing data scientists are busy improving and supporting existing applications.
- *Velocity*—We can't deliver results faster because developing a production-ready version of model X would be a major engineering effort.
- *Validity*—A prototype of the model was working fine in a notebook, but we didn't consider that it might receive data like Y, which broke it in production.
- *Variety*—We would love to support a new use case Z, but our data scientists only know Python, and the systems around Z only support Java.

A common element in all these cases is that *humans are the bottleneck*. Besides some highly specialized applications, it rarely happens that projects can't be delivered because of fundamental limitations in hardware or software. A typical bottleneck is caused by the fact that humans can't deliver software (or hardware, if operating outside the cloud) fast enough. Even if they were capable of hacking code fast enough, they may be busy maintaining existing systems, which is another critically human activity.

This observation helps us to realize that although "infrastructure" sounds very technical, we are not building infrastructure for the machines. We are building infrastructure to make humans more productive. This realization has fundamental ramifications to how we should think about and design infrastructure for data scientists— for fellow human beings, instead of for machines.

For instance, if we assume that human-time is more expensive than computer-time, which is certainly true for most data scientists, it makes sense to use a highly expressive, productivity-boosting language like Python instead of a low-level language like C++, even if it makes workloads more inefficient to process. We will dig deeper into this question in chapter 5.

In the previous section, we noted how we want to leverage existing platforms to their fullest extent and integrate them to form our infrastructure stack. Our goal should be to do this in a manner that provides a cohesive user experience, minimizing the cognitive overhead that the user would have to experience if they had to understand and operate each layer independently. Our hypothesis is that by reducing the cognitive overhead related to the infrastructure, we can boost productivity of data scientists in the area where it matters the most, namely, data science itself.

1.4.1 Freedom and responsibility

Netflix, the streaming video company, is well-known for its unique culture, which is described in detail in a recent book, *No Rules Rules: Netflix and the Culture of Reinvention* (Penguin Press, 2020) by Erin Meyer and Reed Hastings, a cofounder and long-time CEO of Netflix. One of Netflix's core values is "freedom and responsibility," which empowers all employees with a great degree of freedom to determine how they do their job. The other side of the coin is that the employees are always expected to consider what is in the best interest of the company and act responsibly. Metaflow, a framework for human-centric data science infrastructure, which we will introduce in chapter 3, was born at Netflix where it was heavily influenced by the company's culture.

We can apply the concept of freedom and responsibility to the work of data scientists and to the data science infrastructure in general. We expect that data scientists are experts in their own domain, such as in matters related to feature engineering and model development. We don't expect that they are experts in systems engineering or other topics related to infrastructure. However, we expect that they are responsible enough to choose to leverage data science infrastructure, if it is made available. We can map this idea to our infrastructure stack as shown in figure 1.7.

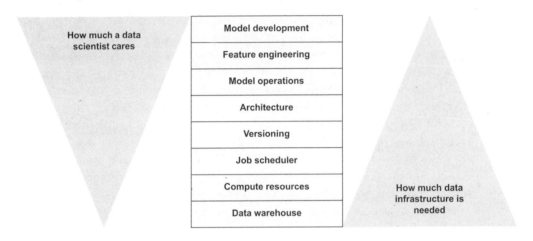

Figure 1.7   Infrastructure complements the interests of a data scientist.

The triangle on the left side depicts the areas of expertise and interest of data scientists. It is the widest at the top of the stack, which is most specific to data science. The infrastructure should grant them the most freedom at these layers, allowing them to freely choose the best modeling approaches, libraries, and features based on their expertise. We expect data scientists to be autonomous—more about that later—so they should care about model operations, versioning, and architecture a bit, which is a part of their responsibility.

The triangle on the right side depicts the freedom and responsibility of the infrastructure team. The infrastructure team should have the greatest degree of freedom to choose and optimize the lowest layers of the stack, which are critical in the technical point of view. They can do it without limiting the freedom of data scientists too much. However, their responsibility lessens toward the top of the stack. The infrastructure team can't be responsible for the models themselves, because often they don't have the expertise and definitely not the scale to support all use cases.

The purpose of this arrangement is twofold: on the one hand, we can maximize the productivity and happiness of an individual data scientist by letting them focus on things they like and know how to execute well with a great degree of freedom. On the other hand, we can realize the four Vs, which are in the interest of the company, by asking data scientists to use the stack responsibly, including the parts in the middle which they may feel less passionate about. The result is a healthy balance between the needs of the company and the happiness of the data scientist.

1.4.2 Data scientist autonomy

Thus far, we have casually talked about "the infrastructure team" and "data scientists." However, the actual cast of characters in a data science project can be more colorful, as shown next:

- *A data scientist* or *machine learning researcher* develops and prototypes machine learning or other data science models.
- *A machine learning engineer* implements the model in a scalable, production-ready way.
- A *data engineer* sets up data pipelines for input and output data, including data transformations.
- A *DevOps engineer* deploys applications in production and makes sure that all the systems stay up and running flawlessly.
- An *application engineer* integrates the model with other business components, such as web applications, which are the consumers of the model.
- An *infrastructure or platform engineer* provides general pieces of infrastructure, such as data warehouses or compute platforms, for many applications to use.

In addition to this technical team, the data science project may have involvement from *business owners*, who understand the business context of the application; *product managers*, who map the business context to technical requirements; and *project/program managers* who help to coordinate cross-functional collaboration.

Anyone who has been involved in a project that involves many stakeholders knows how much communication and coordination is required to keep the project moving forward. Besides the coordination overhead, it can be challenging to increase the number of concurrent data science projects for the simple reason that there are not enough people to fill all the roles in all the projects. For these and many other reasons, many companies find it desirable to reduce the number of people involved in projects, as long as the execution of projects doesn't suffer.

The goal of our infrastructure stack is to make it possible to merge the first four technical roles so that the data scientist is empowered to take care of all these functions autonomously within a project. These roles may still exist in the company, but instead of every project requiring these roles to be present, the roles can be assigned to a few key projects, or they can support more horizontal, cross-project efforts.

To summarize, the data scientist, who is not expected to suddenly become an expert in DevOps or data engineering, should be able to implement models in a scalable manner, to set up data pipelines, and to deploy and monitor models in production independently. They should be able to do this with minimal additional overhead, allowing them to maintain focus on data science. This is the key value proposition of our human-centric data science infrastructure, which we will start building in the next chapters from the ground up.

Summary

- Although it is possible to develop and deliver data science projects without dedicated infrastructure, effective infrastructure makes it possible to develop a greater volume and variety of projects, delivered with a higher velocity, without compromising the validity of results.
- A full infrastructure stack of systems is needed to support data scientists, from foundational layers like data and compute to higher-level concerns like feature engineering and model development. This book will go through all the layers systematically.
- There isn't a one-size-fits-all approach to data science. It is beneficial to be able to customize layers of the infrastructure stack to address your specific needs, which this book will help you do.
- A modern data science application is a sophisticated, complex machine, involving many moving pieces. Managing this inherent complexity well, as well as avoiding introducing any unnecessary complexity while doing it, is a key challenge of data science infrastructure.
- Leveraging existing, battle-hardened systems, such as public clouds, is a good way to keep complexity in check. The coming chapters will help you to choose suitable systems at each layer of the stack.
- Ultimately, humans tend to be the bottleneck in data science projects. Our key focus should be to improve the usability of the whole stack and, hence, improve the productivity of data scientists.

The toolchain
of data science

This chapter covers

- The key activities that the data scientist engages in on a daily basis
- The essential toolchain that makes the data scientist productive
- The role of workflows in the infrastructure stack

Every profession has its tools of the trade. If you are a carpenter, you need saws, rulers, and chisels. If you are a dentist, you need mirrors, drills, and syringes. If you are a data scientist, what are the essential tools that you need in your daily job?

Obviously, you need a computer. But what's the purpose of the computer? Should it be used to run heavy computation, train models, and such, or should it be just a relatively dumb terminal for typing code and analyzing results? Because production applications execute outside personal laptops, maybe prototyping should happen as close to the real production environment as possible, too. Answering questions like this can be surprisingly nontrivial, and the answers can have deep implications for the whole infrastructure stack.

As we highlighted in chapter 1, ultimately these tools exist to boost the productivity of the data scientist. We must carefully think through the actions that form the body of the data scientist's daily work: exploring and analyzing data, writing code, evaluating it, and inspecting results. How can we make these actions as frictionless as possible, knowing that they may be repeated hundreds of times every day? There isn't a single right answer. This chapter will give you food for thought and technical guidance for setting up a toolchain that works for your company and technical environment.

Think of the full stack of data science as a jet fighter—a complex feat of engineering consisting of a myriad of interconnected components. This chapter deals with the cockpit and the dashboard that the pilot uses to operate the machine. In the engineering point of view, the cockpit might feel a bit secondary, essentially just a control stick and a bunch of buttons (or in the case of data science, just an editor and a notebook) compared to 30,000 pounds of heavy engineering underneath, but often it is the component that determines the success or failure of a mission.

FOLLOWING THE JOURNEY OF A DATA SCIENTIST

To make the discussion more concrete and grounded to the needs of real-world businesses, we will follow the journey of a hypothetical data scientist, Alex, throughout the book. Alex's journey features typical challenges that a data scientist faces in a modern business environment. Alex helps to keep our focus on human-centric infrastructure and to demonstrate how infrastructure can grow incrementally together with the company. Each section begins with a motivating scenario related to Alex's life at work, which we will analyze and address in the section in detail.

Besides Alex the data scientist, the cast of characters includes Harper, who is the founder of the startup where Alex works. We will also meet Bowie, who is an infrastructure engineer whose duties include providing support for data scientists. This book is targeted at all the Alexes and Bowies out there, but the broader context might be interesting for Harpers, too.

Alex has a PhD in marine biology. After realizing that people with skills in statistical analysis, basic machine learning, and rudimentary knowledge of Python are highly valued as data scientists, Alex decides to move from academia to industry.

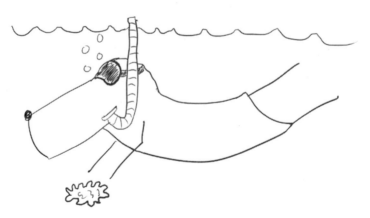

2.1 Setting up a development environment

Alex joins Harper's startup, Caveman Cupcakes, which manufactures and delivers soon-to-be-personalized paleo cupcakes, as its first data scientist. Bowie, who is an infrastructure engineer at Caveman, helps Alex get started. Alex asks Bowie if data scientists at Caveman can use Jupyter notebooks to get their job done. It would be great if they did, because Alex became very familiar with notebooks in academia. Hearing this makes Bowie realize that data scientists have special tooling needs. What tools should they install, and how should they be configured to make Alex most productive?

If you have time to set up only one piece of infrastructure well, make it the development environment for data scientists. Although this may sound obvious, you would be surprised to know how many companies have a well-tuned, scalable production infrastructure, but the question of how the code is developed, debugged, and tested in the first place is solved in an ad hoc manner. Instead of treating personal workstations merely as an IT problem, we should consider the development environment as an integral part of the effective infrastructure. After all, arguably the most important success factor of any data science project is the people involved and their productivity.

A dictionary defines *ergonomics* as "the study of people's efficiency in their working environment," which nicely summarizes the focus of this chapter. The development environment for data science needs to optimize the ergonomics of the following two human activities:

1 *Prototyping*—The iterative process that translates human knowledge and expertise into functional code and models

2 *Interaction with production deployments*—The act of connecting the code and models to surrounding systems and operating these production deployments so that they can produce sustainable business value

Figure 2.1 Prototyping loop

The prototyping loop, which is depicted in the figure 2.1, is familiar from software engineering where it is called the *REPL,* the read-evaluate-print loop. You develop code in an editor, evaluate it with an interactive interpreter or a terminal, and analyze the results. Based on the results, you fix and improve the code and restart the loop. The loop works similarly for data science: you develop a model or code that processes data, evaluate it, and analyze the results.

To boost the productivity of data scientists, we want to make each iteration of this loop as quick and effortless as possible. This involves optimizing each step as well as the transitions between the steps: how long does it take to write a snippet of code and evaluate it? How easily can you fetch the results and start analyzing them? Is it easy to explore, analyze, and understand the outcomes and change the code accordingly? Ultimately, we need cooperation between all layers of the infrastructure stack to answer these questions, but we will start laying the groundwork in the following subsections.

After countless iterations of the prototyping loop, the data scientist has a piece of code that produces a promising model or other desired output. Although this is a big milestone for the data scientist, many open questions remain: will the model produce expected results when connected to real-world data? Will the model scale to all data it needs to handle? Is the model robust against changes that will happen over time? Will there be any other operational surprises?

Trying to answer these questions in a prototyping environment is hard. Instead, we should make it easy to deploy the model to a production environment as an experiment, so we can observe how the model performs in practice. It is expected that the first versions of the model won't work flawlessly, but production failures provide invaluable information that we can use to improve the model.

Conducting controlled empirical experiments like this is the core of the scientific method. The scientist formulates a hypothesis, performs an experiment, and analyzes the results. Compare this to how SpaceX developed a new reusable rocket, Falcon 9, iteratively through 20 test launches before the first successful booster landing, as depicted in figure 2.2.

Figure 2.2   SpaceX
iterating on Falcon 9

This cycle of deploying to production, observing issues, and fixing them using the prototyping loop forms a higher-order loop, which we call *interaction with production deployments*.

As shown in figure 2.3, a production deployment is not a one-way waterfall but an iterative loop, working in conjunction with the prototyping loop. We want to make it easy for the data scientist to understand how and why the model fails in production and help them reproduce any issues locally, so they can improve the model using their familiar prototyping loop. Notably, in successful projects, these loops become infinite loops: a successful model is subject to never-ending improvement and debugging.

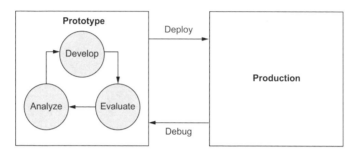

Figure 2.3   Interaction with production deployments

In the world of software engineering, the concept is called *continuous delivery* (CD). Although CD systems, like GitHub Actions (github.com/features/actions), can be used to facilitate data science deployments, some crucial differences exist between data science applications and traditional software. Consider the following:

- *Correctness*—It is relatively easy to confirm through automated tests that traditional software works correctly *before* it is deployed to production. This is typically not the case with data science. The goal of deploying, such as performing an A/B experiment, is to validate the correctness *after* the deployment.
- *Stability*—Again, it is relatively easy to confirm through automated tests that traditional software works as expected in its well-defined environment. In contrast, data science applications are subject to constantly changing data, which exposes them to surprises that happen after deployment.
- *Variety*—It is possible to develop a traditional software component that does the job it is intended to do more or less perfectly. In contrast, it is hard to reach such a level of perfection with models because we always have new ideas and data that we can test. Correspondingly, it is desirable to be able to deploy many versions of the model in parallel and iterate quickly.
- *Culture*—The world of DevOps and infrastructure engineering has a deep culture and jargon of its own, which is not covered by most data science curricula. Following our human-centric ethos, it is not reasonable to expect that data scientists, who are experts in their own domain, will suddenly become experts in another domain.

We can learn from and partially leverage existing CD systems as we build effective infrastructure tailored for the needs of data science. The two loops introduced earlier are conceptual sequences of actions that the scientist repeats to develop, deploy, and debug data science applications. The remainder of this chapter will make them more concrete. We will cover the actual tools that the data scientist should use and discuss how to best set them up. Though it is impossible to prescribe a single correct way of configuring your data science environment—details depend on your surrounding business infrastructure—we will provide enough technical background and evaluation rubrics so you will be able to make informed decisions based on your exact needs. Figure 2.4 gives you an idea of what to expect.

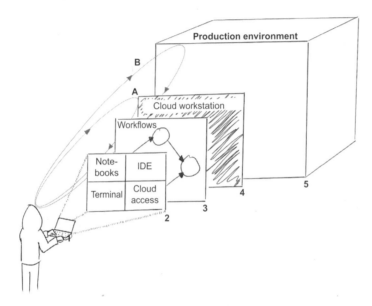

Figure 2.4   The elements of the data science toolchain

1 Our focal point is the data scientist, who will use the toolchain to power the two core activities: prototyping loop (A) and interaction with production deployments (B).

2 In the following subsections, we will cover the key productivity tools that we should provide for the scientist.

3 In section 2.2, we will highlight why it is useful to structure data science applications as workflows.

4 We will also make the case for running the prototyping loop in an environment that resembles the production environment as closely as possible—in practice, backing the prototyping loop with a cloud instance.

5 This chapter introduces a user interface, a cockpit that the scientist uses to command and control the production environment, which will be covered in detail in subsequent chapters.

2.1.1 Cloud account

The infrastructure we will build in this book assumes that you have an account with a public cloud provider such as Amazon Web Services (AWS), Google Cloud Platform (GCP), or Microsoft Azure. We will use AWS in all the examples because it is the most widely used cloud platform today. You should be able to adapt examples and concepts to other cloud environments, including private clouds, relatively easily.

AWS provides a free tier that allows you to set up the bare-bones infrastructure introduced in this book for minimal or no cost. Hence, it is highly encouraged that you create an AWS account, unless you have one already. Creating one is easy—just follow the instructions at aws.amazon.com/free.

Many companies have existing cloud accounts. You should be able to use them for the purposes of this book. We won't cover how to configure user accounts and perform authentication and authorization, such as IAM users and policies for AWS. These concerns are not specific to data science, and you should be able to use the same policies that you have used before.

2.1.2 Data science workstation

The data scientist needs a workstation to drive the prototyping loop, that is, develop, test, and deploy code and models. These days, the physical workstation is typically a personal laptop. However, the production code and models should never run on a laptop, due to the need for high availability and scalability. Instead, we deploy the production models in a cloud environment. In addition to differences in development and production hardware, the operating system is often different. It is common to use either OS X or Windows on laptops and Linux on servers.

A technical gap often occurs between the development workstation and the production environment, which can cause friction when interacting with production deployments. The gap is not unique to data science. For instance, web application developers often operate in a similar environment. However, the gap is especially problematic for data science for a few reasons. The modern modeling libraries tend to be highly optimized to specific GPU and CPU architectures, in contrast to, say, JavaScript libraries. Also, large-scale data processing tends to push both hardware and software much harder than typical non–data science applications, amplifying any differences in behavior between the environments.

As many software developers have experienced the hard way, it can be frustrating to debug your code when the production environment differs significantly from the development environment. We can address the gap by unbundling the prototyping loop. Instead of running every step—development, evaluation, and analysis—on laptops, we can run any or all of these steps in the cloud. In practice, this means that we need a semipersistent Linux instance or a container in the cloud that the data scientist can connect to.

Setting up a system that can launch and terminate such instances on demand requires upfront configuration as well as training for data scientists. When deciding whether you want to provide a fully local (laptop-based), a fully remote (cloud-based), or a hybrid solution, consider the list of pros and cons presented in table 2.1.

Table 2.1   **Laptops vs. a cloud instance as a development environment**

	Laptop	Cloud instance
Ease of setup	Instantly familiar.	Has a learning curve.
Ease of use	Easy initially, harder for complex cases, such as deployments.	Harder initially; benefits clearer in more complex cases.
Speed of prototyping loop	Rapid transitions between steps, but the evaluation speed may be slower because of limited hardware.	Potentially slower transitions between steps, but higher evaluation speed.
Ease of support	Harder to monitor; harder to provide interactive support remotely.	Easy—a support person can use standard monitoring tools to observe the instance and/or log in to the instance remotely.
Scalability	Not scalable—the hardware is fixed.	Scalable—the instance size can be chosen based on the use case.
Interaction with production deployments	Potential cross-platform issues (OS X vs. Linux).	Minimal difference between prototyping and production environments.
Security	Many issues because the same laptop is used for many purposes besides data science; the laptop may get lost physically.	Easier to secure and monitor—similar to any other cloud instance. It is possible to use standard cloud-based authentication and authorization systems like AWS IAM.
Homogeneity	Every data scientist is likely to have a slightly different environment, which makes issues harder to debug.	Easier to ensure that the environments are highly uniform.

To summarize table 2.1, a cloud-based workstation requires more up-front work on the infrastructure side, but it can pay big dividends when it comes to security, operational concerns, scalability, and interaction with production deployments. This will become more clear as you go through the later chapters in the book. However, you can certainly get started quickly with a laptop-based approach and revisit the decision later as your needs grow.

How to provide a cloud-based workstation depends on your business environment: what cloud providers you use, how the rest of your infrastructure is set up, and what kind of security policies data scientists need to comply with. To give you an idea of available options, we list a few prototypical examples next. It is likely that new solutions will become available over the coming years, so this list is far from comprehensive.

A GENERAL-PURPOSE CLOUD IDE: AWS CLOUD9

AWS Cloud9 is a general-purpose, cloud-based integrated development environment (IDE)—a code editor—that works in the browser backed by servers provided by

AWS—EC2 instances—running Linux. Using AWS Cloud9 feels pretty similar to using your laptop in the following ways:

- The editor feels like a local editor, and it comes with a built-in debugger. The command-line session feels like a local terminal.

- It manages a standard EC2 instance attached to an editor session, which you can use to back the prototyping loop and to interact with production deployments. Alternatively, you can configure it to connect to an existing EC2 instance for more control.

- There is no extra cost besides the usual EC2 fees, and unused instances are stopped automatically, so it can be a very cost-effective solution.

A downside is that AWS Cloud9 doesn't have any built-in support notebooks (more about notebooks in the next section), although with some custom work, it is possible to use the underlying EC2 to back notebook kernels, too.

A DATA SCIENCE-SPECIFIC ENVIRONMENT: AMAZON SAGEMAKER STUDIO
Amazon SageMaker Studio is a hosted version of the JupyterLab data science environment, which is tightly integrated with the AWS data science services. Although you can use it as a general-purpose code editor, similar to AWS Cloud9, it is more centered around notebooks in the following ways:

- SageMaker Studio manages instances backing notebooks and terminals for you, similar to AWS Cloud9, but instead of using normal EC2 instances, it uses more expensive ML-specific instance types.

- Existing users of Jupyter and JupyterLab will feel right at home.

- Integration to the AWS data science services is handy if you use them.

Other cloud providers have similar offerings as a part of their platform, such as Azure Machine Learning Studio by Microsoft. A complete data science environment is most useful if you want to leverage the provider's other services that are integrated with it. Otherwise, a simpler editor might be easier to use and operate.

A LOCAL EDITOR BACKED BY A CLOUD INSTANCE: VISUAL STUDIO CODE
Both AWS Cloud9 and SageMaker Studio are fully cloud-based, including a browser-based editor. Although this approach has many benefits—it is easy operationally and can be very secure—some people find browser-based editors more cumbersome to use than local editors. A happy medium can be to use a local editor, like PyCharm or Visual Studio Code (VS Code), backed by a cloud instance.

In particular, VS Code is a popular, very capable editor, which comes with well-integrated support for remote code execution, called Visual Studio Code Remote—SSH. Using this feature, you can evaluate any code using an arbitrary cloud instance of your choosing. Also, VS Code comes with built-in support for notebooks, which it can run on the same remote instance, providing a frictionless user experience for data scientists.

The main downside of the hybrid approach is that you have to deploy a mechanism to manage the cloud instances used by the local editor. This can be accomplished with a project like Gitpod (https://www.gitpod.io). For instance, a relatively simple approach could be to launch a container for each user and configure their editors to connect to their personal container automatically.

2.1.3 Notebooks

The previous section covered the very basics of the prototyping loop: develop code in an editor, evaluate it in a terminal, and analyze results printed out on the terminal. This has been the classic way of developing software for decades.

Many data scientists are familiar with another way of software development: writing and evaluating code in a single document called a notebook. A defining feature of the notebook approach is that code can be authored incrementally as small snippets, or cells, which can be evaluated on the fly so that their results are shown and stored next to the code. Notebooks support rich output types, so instead of just outputting plain text, as in a terminal, the output can include arbitrary visualizations. This method is convenient when prototyping new data science applications or analyzing existing data or models.

Many independent notebook environments are available, most of them targeting specific programming languages. Well-known environments include RMarkdown notebooks for R, Zeppelin and Polynote for Scala, Mathematica for Wolfram Language, and Jupyter for Python (and other languages), which is the most popular notebook environment today.

Given the ubiquity and usefulness of notebooks in data science, it would be hard to imagine an infrastructure for data science that didn't support notebooks. Some infrastructures take the approach to the extreme and suggest that all data science code should be authored in notebooks, as notebooks. Although notebooks are undoubtedly useful for exploratory programming, analysis, teaching, and quick prototypes, it is less clear if they are the best approach for general software development, which is a big part of real-world data science projects. To better understand the role of notebooks in the data science stack, let's start by looking at their unique benefits, which follow:

- The prototyping loop is extremely fast. You write a snippet of code in a cell, and with a click of a button, you can evaluate it and see the results next to the code. No need to switch between windows or tabs.
- Results can be plots, graphs, or arbitrary visualizations. Data frames, that is, tables of data, are automatically visualized in a tabular format.
- The notebook format encourages creation of linear narratives, which can be easy for humans to read and understand. The result can look like an executable research paper.
- Most notebook GUIs work in the browser with a simple backend process that can be run locally, so you can get started with minimal setup.

- In particular, different platforms widely use, teach, and support Jupyter notebooks. Correspondingly, tons of materials and examples are available online.
- Many modern data science libraries are designed to be used in notebooks. They come with built-in visualizations and APIs that make notebook use convenient.

All the benefits of notebooks relate to the user experience. They can make data scientists, not computers, more effective and efficient. On the flip side, notebooks require a stack of infrastructure of their own, resulting in extra complexity, which can lead to brittleness. Because computers don't care about notebooks, we can execute code without them when humans are not in the loop, which is the case in production deployments.

Another question relates to the linear, narrative nature of notebooks. Whereas humans are good at reading and understanding linearly progressing stories, like the one you are reading right now, computer programs tend to be nonlinear in nature. It is considered a good software engineering practice to structure a program as independent but interacting modules, each of which has a clear logical role. The modules call each other arbitrarily, forming a call graph rather than a linear narrative.

You can also reuse and share these modules across many projects, complicating the dependency graph further. To manage a large software project, a version control system like Git is a must. Technically it is possible to write arbitrary code in notebooks, version-control them, and maybe even create composable notebooks, but this is pushing the limits of the paradigm, requiring layers of nonstandard tooling.

Whereas notebooks with their mixed-media outputs are great for exploration and analysis, traditional IDEs and code editors are optimized for structured programming. They make it easy to manage and author even large codebases that are divided across multiple files. Some modern IDEs like PyCharm, VS Code, or JupyterLab support both modalities in a single interface, trying to combine the best of both worlds.

This book advocates for a pragmatic approach: we can use notebooks for the use cases where they shine and stick with traditional software engineering tools elsewhere. Figure 2.5 extends the earlier figure 2.3 by overlaying the suggested tools in the prototyping and production loops.

Imagine starting to work on a new data science project. Even before you start creating the first prototype, that is, entering the prototyping loop, you might want to spend

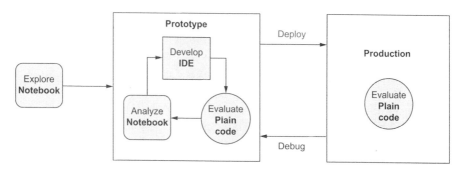

Figure 2.5   Suggested tools for the prototyping and production loops

some time just understanding the data and the problem domain. Notebooks are a good tool for such open-ended exploration, which doesn't aim at producing any persistent software artifacts.

After the initial exploration phase, you start prototyping a solution. The solution, a data science application, is fundamentally a piece of software, often consisting of multiple modules, so we can use a tool optimized for this purpose: an IDE or a code editor. The result is an application, a script, which we can evaluate as plain code both locally and in production without any added complexity. When code fails or you want to improve the model, you can go back to notebooks again for analysis and exploration. We will see in later chapters what this might look like in practice. As noted earlier, modern IDEs can make switching between the notebook and the editor modes seamless, so transitioning between the steps of the loop can happen with minimal friction.

SETTING UP A JUPYTER NOTEBOOK ENVIRONMENT

What does setting up a notebook environment mean in practice? First, let's consider the high-level architecture of Jupyter (many other notebook environments have a similar architecture), as presented in figure 2.6.

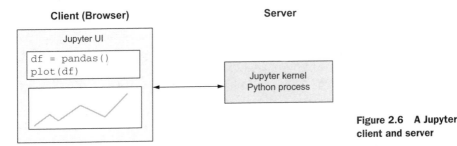

Figure 2.6   A Jupyter client and server

Notebooks consist of two major parts: a web-based UI that runs in the browser and a backend process, a kernel, which manages all state and computation requested by the UI. Each notebook session is backed by a unique kernel, so it is common to have multiple kernels running in parallel when multiple notebooks are open in separate browser tabs.

In the point of view of infrastructure, the key question is where to run the kernel. It is a Python process that needs to be executed on a server of some kind. The simplest option is to run the kernel on the user's laptop as a local process, which is the leftmost option 1 presented in figure 2.7.

In option 1, all computation initiated by the notebook happens on the user's laptop, similar to any Python script. This approach has all the pros and cons of local code evaluation, which we covered in table 2.1. In particular, the environment is unscalable and hard to control in a uniform manner. The main upside of this approach is simplicity—you can get going by executing the following commands on your laptop:

```
# pip install jupyter
# jupyter-notebook
```

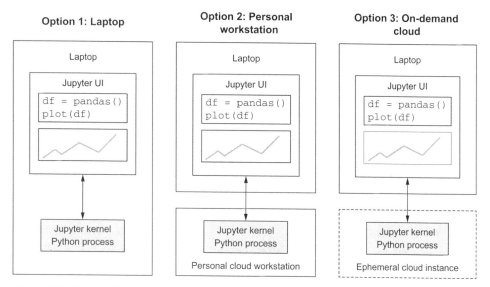

Figure 2.7 Three options for running the Jupyter kernel

Option 2 works around the limitations of the local approach by running the kernel on a cloud instance—the same cloud workstation that we discussed in the previous section. The cloud workstation can be scaled based on the needs of the user and use case, and it can provide a uniform environment for all data scientists. A downside is that an infrastructure team needs to set up the workstation, including a secure network connection, such as a virtual private network (VPN), between the cloud workstation and local laptop. However, after the initial configuration cost, this setup can be highly productive for data science.

Option 3 is a "serverless" approach to notebooks. Whereas option 2 provides an illusion of a persistent, stateful laptop-in-the-cloud—like a personal workstation—option 3 eliminates the notion that any server is required to run the kernel in the first place. After all, all the user sees is the browser-based Jupyter UI, so they shouldn't have to care about the backend.

In practice, option 3 requires a portal that allows one to open a notebook. When a notebook is opened, an ephemeral instance is provisioned for the notebook on the fly. Examples of this approach include Google Colab and an open source MyBinder.org.

The main downside of this approach, besides operational complexity, is that notebooks are stateless. There is no persistent local filesystem or dependencies that automatically persist across notebook kernels. This makes the experience quite different from a local laptop that maintains state until you explicitly erase it. Also, this approach doesn't allow interaction with local editors, like VS Code, which is possible with option 2. Option 3 can be great for quick scratchpad environments or for users who don't need a full-fledged persistent workstation.

2.1.4   *Putting everything together*

Let's summarize what we have covered in the previous sections:

1 To boost the productivity of data scientists, we should optimize the ergonomics of two key activities: the prototyping loop and interaction with production deployments.

2 There are many good reasons to enable data scientists to work seamlessly with the cloud from the get-go. In particular, it will make interaction with production deployments easier.

3 Modern editors make it possible to push code evaluation to the cloud. This can make the evaluation environments more scalable, easier to manage, and closer to the production deployments than evaluating code on the laptop. However, they require some up-front configuration effort by the infrastructure team.

4 Notebooks are an indispensable tool for some data science activities, complementing traditional software development tools. You can run notebooks on the same cloud workstation that supports other code evaluation.

Figure 2.8 illustrates the architecture of a cloud workstation for data science. You have many ways to implement the setup in practice. You can pick an editor or an IDE that works for your needs. You can use notebooks either in a standalone fashion in the browser or embedded in the editor, such as using Visual Studio Code or PyCharm. Or you can pick a notebook environment that includes a full-fledged code editor, like JupyterLab. The workstation instance can be a container running on a cloud-based container platform, for example, AWS Elastic Container Service (ECS).

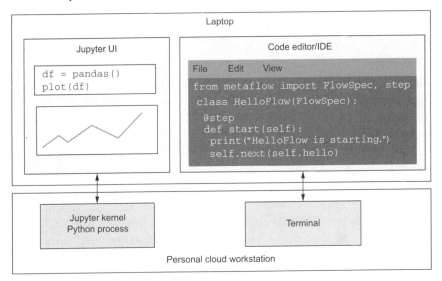

Figure 2.8   Cloud workstation for data science

Figure 2.9 shows a Visual Studio Code session with an embedded editor, terminal, and notebook. With a single click, the scientist can execute the code in the editor on the

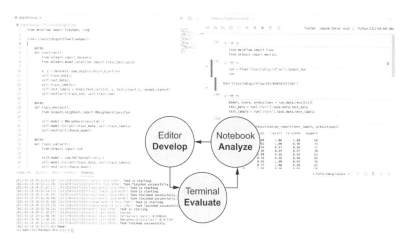

Figure 2.9   A Visual Studio Code setup that covers the complete prototyping loop

terminal. With another click, they can update the notebook view that visualizes the results. The terminal and the notebook kernel can either execute locally or on a cloud workstation.

With a setup like this, the scientist can quickly iterate through the steps of the prototyping loop, as overlaid in the figure.

2.2   *Introducing workflows*

On the second day at Caveman, Alex joins an onboarding session led by Harper. Harper explains how the company sources their organic ingredients from multiple vendors, how they produce a wide variety of cupcakes using artisanal methods, and how they handle nationwide logistics. Alex is puzzled by the intricate value chain that it takes to produce paleo cupcakes. How are data scientists at the company supposed to process all relevant data, keep models up-to-date, and send updated predictions to various business systems? The level of complexity seems to be beyond what Alex had had to deal with previously in academia using notebooks.

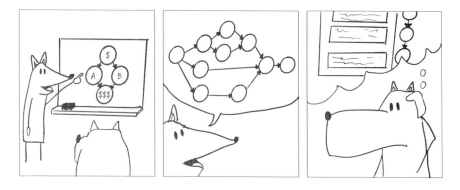

The development environment we introduced in the previous section was the very first stop in our journey in producing robust, production-ready data science applications. It provides the means to write code, evaluate it, and analyze the results. Now, what code should we write and how?

When terms like *machine learning, artificial intelligence,* or *data science* are mentioned, they often evoke the idea of a *model.* By a model, we mean any kind of computational abstraction of the world that takes some input, performs some computation, and produces an output, as concisely depicted in figure 2.10. In the realm of data science, these models are often expressed as artificial neural networks or using statistical methods like logistic regression.

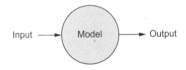

Figure 2.10   A model

Building accurate models for real-world phenomena is not easy. Historically, it has been done by scientists who have gone through extensive theoretical training and who have a deep understanding of their problem domain. Depending on the company, there may be an expectation that data scientists mainly focus on building models. However, building practically useful models in a business context is quite a different experience from publishing model designs in a research paper.

Consider a common business context like that of Caveman Cupcakes introduced earlier. Alex the data scientist faces the following three challenges:

1 It is probably not feasible to model the whole business of Caveman Cupcakes as a single model. Instead, the data scientist is expected to focus on modeling some specific business problems, for example, to build a computer vision model to detect faulty cupcakes on the production line automatically, or to use mixed-integer programming to optimize logistics. As a result, over time data scientists at the company will produce a set of models, each with its own requirements and characteristics.

2 In a business context, the model can't be just an abstract mathematical construct. It needs to perform the computation in practice, which means that it needs to be implemented in a programming language, and it needs to execute reliably. This can be a highly nontrivial exercise in software engineering, in particular because we can't wait for the results infinitely. We may need to run some operations in parallel and some on specialized hardware like GPUs.

3 Besides the big circle in figure 2.10, the model, we must not forget the two arrows: the input and the output. Our model needs to receive accurate, often constantly updating data, which is not a small feat. Finally, the results of a model need to end up somewhere where they can benefit the business, such as a database, a planning spreadsheet, or another software component.

To summarize, the data scientist needs to understand the business problem that needs to be solved, design a model, implement it as software, make sure it gets the correct data, and figure out where to send the results. To make this happen, the data scientist spends a good amount of time in the prototyping loop we introduced in the previous section.

Once we solve this particular business problem adequately, we repeat the same process for another business problem. This cycle is repeated infinitely. The models are never perfect, and rarely does a company run out of business problems to optimize.

Furthermore, all these systems must be kept running reliably, preferably 24/7. This requires a lot of interaction with production deployments, because models are constantly exposed to real-world entropy and data, which erodes them, similar to any real-world machine that is exposed to the elements. This is the second loop we discussed in the previous section.

As a result, we get a jungle of data pipelines and models—a big humming factory as depicted in figure 2.11—which requires constant maintenance. To keep the factory understandable and operable, we need to impose some structure on how these models are built. This is the main motivation for making the modeling and data pipelines, or workflows, as first-class entities in our infrastructure.

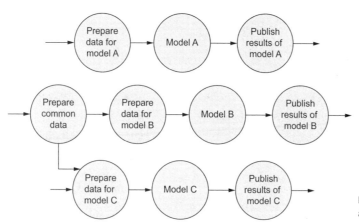

Figure 2.11 Many models and data pipelines

2.2.1 The basics of workflows

In this context, a workflow is a *directed graph*, that is, a set of nodes or steps (depicted as circles in figure 2.12) connected by directional edges (arrows). This representation captures the before-and-after relationship between steps. For instance, in figure 2.12, we know unambiguously that A must happen before B.

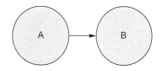

Figure 2.12 A workflow where A happens before B

The order of steps isn't always fully unambiguous. In figure 2.13, we know that A must execute before B and C that execute before D, but the mutual order between B and C is left undefined.

We can use workflows like this to indicate that we don't care whether B executes before C, as long as both of them are executed before D. This feature is useful because it allows us to execute B and C in parallel.

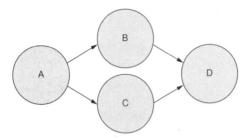

Figure 2.13   A workflow where B and C may be executed in any order

Figure 2.14 depicts a directed graph that has a cycle: after C, we go back to A again. Naturally, this results in an infinite loop unless we define some kind of conditional that defines a stopping condition. Alternatively, we can just disallow graphs with cycles and decide that only such graphs, directed acyclic graphs or DAGs, are valid workflows. In fact, just supporting DAGs is a common choice made by workflow engines.

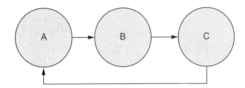

Figure 2.14   A workflow with a cycle, i.e., a cyclic graph

Why should Alex or any other data scientist care about DAGs? Consider the following three reasons:

1. They introduce a common vocabulary—steps and transitions between them—which make it easier to write and understand nontrivial applications that are structured as DAGs.
2. They allow us to be explicit about the order of operations. This is useful especially when the order is anything more complex than a simple linear order, like what you see in a notebook. By making the order of operations clear and explicit, our jungle of data pipelines and models becomes more manageable.
3. They allow us to indicate when the order of operations doesn't matter, like in figure 2.13. We can parallelize these operations automatically, which is the key to high performance. Plenty of opportunities for parallelization arise in a typical data science application, but in most cases, computers can't figure them out automatically if they are not made explicit.

To summarize, at the high level, you can view DAGs as a language, not so much as a programming language but rather as a formal construct for human-to-human communication. They allow us to speak about even complex sequences of operations in a concise and understandable manner.

2.2.2   Executing workflows

If DAGs are just an abstract way to talk about the structure of data science applications, how does the rubber meet the road—that is, how are workflows executed in practice?

Ultimately, executing a workflow is a job of a *workflow orchestrator*, aka a *job scheduler*, which we will discuss next. Before we dive deeper into various orchestrators—and there are hundreds of them—it is useful to take a deeper look at the concerns required to turn an abstract DAG into executing code.

Concrete workflows involve three separate concerns: what code should be executed (what's inside a step), where the code should be executed concretely (a computer somewhere needs to execute the code), and how the steps should be orchestrated. The three concerns map to the different layers of the infrastructure stack we introduced in chapter 1, as depicted in figure 2.15.

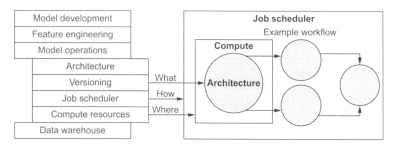

Figure 2.15   The three concerns of workflow execution

The architecture layer defines what code the data scientist is supposed to write in a step. It is *the user interface layer* to workflows. Different workflow frameworks provide different kinds of abstractions, optimized for different use cases. Some of them are graphical (you can define a workflow by dragging and dropping circles), some are configuration-based, and some are defined as code.

In the data scientist's point of view, the architecture layer is the most visible part of workflows. The layers toward the top of the stack are closer to the data scientist's interests. The architecture layer pretty much defines what kind of data science applications are natural to express in the system, which makes it perhaps the most important consideration when choosing a workflow framework.

The *compute resources* layer determines where the user's code is executed concretely. Imagine a workflow with 600 parallel steps. Each step executes for 30 seconds on a 16-core CPU. If the compute layer includes only one 16-core instance (maybe the compute layer is a laptop!), executing the steps takes five hours. In contrast, if the compute layer is a cluster of 100 instances, the steps execute in three minutes. As you can see, the compute layer makes a big difference for the *scalability* of workflows, which we will discuss in detail in chapters 4 and 5.

Finally, we need a system that walks through the DAG, sending each step to the compute layer and waiting for their completion before continuing. We call this system a job scheduler. The scheduler layer doesn't need to care about what code is being executed and where computers that execute the code reside exactly. Its sole responsibility is to schedule the steps in the right order as defined by the DAG, making sure that a step finishes successfully before its successors in the graph are executed (the technical term for this is *topological order*).

Although this process may sound deceptively simple, the job scheduler layer is the guarantor of the *robustness and operability* of workflows. It needs to monitor whether the compute layer completes steps successfully, and if it doesn't, it needs to retry them. It may need to do this for hundreds of thousands of concurrently executing steps across tens of thousands of workflows. In the user's point of view, it is desirable that the job scheduler has a way to observe executions, maybe a GUI, and a way to alert owners if their workflow fails.

Besides operational concerns, we can distinguish between two major types of job schedulers based on how they want the DAG to be specified. Schedulers that require the DAG to be fully specified before an execution starts are called to schedule *static DAGs*. The other type of schedulers allow the DAG to be constructed incrementally during execution, which is called a *dynamic DAG*. Both approaches have their pros and cons.

Every workflow framework needs to address all three concerns. Each concern is a deep topic in itself, requiring nontrivial efforts in engineering. On top of this, the concerns interact in various ways. Different frameworks end up making different technical choices that affect scalability and robustness, and these choices affect the user experience, depending on what use cases they target and what kind of tradeoffs they are ready to make. As a result, hundreds of workflow frameworks all look seemingly similar on the surface—all of them claim to execute DAGs—but significant differences exist under the hood.

2.2.3 *The world of workflow frameworks*

The Wikipedia article for *scientific workflow systems* lists 20 notable workflow frameworks that target scientific applications. Another article for *workflow management systems* lists many more such systems for business-oriented use cases. Both lists miss many popular open source frameworks and well-funded startups. The landscape is also changing quickly, so by the time you are reading this book, any attempt to list all frameworks would be woefully outdated.

Instead of trying to rank all frameworks out there, we provide the following rubric for evaluating frameworks. The rubric is based on the three concerns we touched in the previous section:

1 *Architecture*—What the actual code looks like and how the system looks and feels to the data scientist. Do the abstractions provided by the system make data scientists more productive and allow them to ship end-to-end data science applications faster?

2 *Job scheduler*—How workflows are triggered, executed, and monitored, and how failures are handled. How easy it is to manage a whole jungle of workflows without downtime?

3 *Compute resources*—Where the code executes in practice. Can the system handle steps with different resource requirements, such as GPUs, and how many steps can the system execute in parallel?

Your particular use cases and business environment should determine how you weigh these three dimensions. For a small startup with a handful of small use cases, compute resources might not be a big concern. For a company that has one large-scale use case, compute resources may be more important than anything else. A desirable architecture looks very different for a tightly knit team of Haskell experts versus a large, distributed organization of data scientists from diverse backgrounds.

Table 2.2 provides an example rubric for comparing workflow frameworks. We chose five popular frameworks for illustration. Because this book is about infrastructure for data science, we focused the comparison to the following concerns that matter to data science applications:

- Is the architecture specifically designed to support data science applications, or is it generic in nature?
- Is the scheduler highly available (HA) by design, that is, is the scheduler itself a single point of failure? This is important, because none of the workflows can be more reliable than the scheduler that orchestrates them. Optimally, we would like to be able to keep any number of workflows running without having to worry about the scheduler ever failing.
- How flexible is the support for compute resources? Data science applications tend to be compute-heavy and sometimes finicky about their hardware requirements (e.g., particular models of GPUs), so this is a useful feature.

Table 2.2   An example rubric for evaluating workflow frameworks

	Architecture	**Scheduler**	**Compute**
Apache Airflow	Arbitrary Python code, not specific to data science	Nice GUI; scheduler not HA	Many backends supported through *executors*.
Luigi	Arbitrary Python code, not specific to data science	Bare-bones; not HA	By default, the scheduler executes Python classes, *Tasks*, locally. They can push work to other systems.
Kubeflow Pipelines	Python, targeting data science use cases	Nice GUI; uses a project called Argo under the hood; some HA provided by Kubernetes	Steps are run on a Kubernetes cluster.
AWS Step Functions	JSON-based configuration called Amazon States Language	HA by design; managed by AWS	Integrations with some AWS services.
Metaflow	Python, targeting data science use cases	Local scheduler for prototyping; supports HA schedulers like Step Functions for production	Supports local *tasks* as well as external compute platforms.

Here's a quick overview of the covered frameworks:

- *Apache Airflow* is a popular open source workflow management system that was released by Airbnb in 2015. It is implemented in Python and uses Python to define workflows. Multiple commercial vendors, including AWS and GCP, provide managed Airflow as a service.
- *Luigi* is another well-known Python-based framework that was open sourced by Spotify in 2012. It is based on the idea of dynamic DAGs, defined through data dependencies.
- *Kubeflow Pipelines* is a workflow system embedded in the open source Kubeflow framework for data science applications running on Kubernetes. The framework was published by Google in 2018. Under the hood, the workflows are scheduled by an open source scheduler called Argo that is popular in the Kubernetes ecosystem.
- *AWS Step Functions* is a managed, not open source, service that AWS released in 2016. DAGs are defined in the JSON format using Amazon States Language. A unique feature of Step Functions is that workflows can run for a very long time, up to a year, relying on the guarantees of high availability provided by AWS.
- *Metaflow* is a full-stack framework for data science applications, originally started by the author of this book and open sourced by Netflix in 2019. Metaflow focuses on boosting the productivity of data scientists holistically, treating workflows as a first-class construct. To achieve scalability and high availability, Metaflow integrates with schedulers like AWS Step Functions.

Besides the frameworks listed here, many other promising frameworks exist, some of which target data science applications specifically. Instead of focusing on any particular framework, which are well documented online, the purpose of this book is to introduce the full stack of data science infrastructure, which workflows are a part of, so that you can choose the best technical approach for each layer.

When choosing a workflow framework specifically for data science use cases, keep the following factors in mind:

1 In most business environments, productivity of data scientists should be a top priority. Choose a framework with an architecture that works well for data science use cases specifically. Building data science applications takes much more than just workflows, so consider the full data science stack (figure 1.3) when making the choice, not just the scheduler layer.

2 In the long term, operational concerns such as robustness, scalability, and high availability of the system tend to dominate other technical concerns. These features are both an emergent characteristic of the design of the system as well as a result of years of battle-hardening with actual use cases, so fixing them overnight is not easy. Hence, it makes sense to choose a system with an established track record of operability and scalability. We will cover this topic in detail in chapter 4.

3 Not being constrained by compute resources can be a huge productivity boost, so choose a framework that integrates seamlessly with your compute layer. More about this in chapter 3.

In the following chapters we will use Metaflow, which hits the three marks listed previously, as an example framework. The principles and examples are generic enough so that it shouldn't be hard to adapt the examples to other frameworks if needed.

If setting up everything we covered in this chapter feels like a large investment, don't worry—you can scale the capabilities of the toolchain in stages as the needs of your business grow. Table 2.3 provides the recommended configurations for organizations of different sizes, based on the number of data scientists served by the infrastructure. The options in parentheses refer to figure 2.7.

Table 2.3   How much to invest in a development environment

	Small (1–3 users)	Medium (3–20 users)	Large (20+ users)
Cloud account	Recommended	Must	Must
Data science workstation	A laptop will suffice. Specify a common setup for all data scientists.	Consider an off-the-shelf cloud offering or a simple manually launched cloud workstation with an integrated IDE.	Invest in a self-service, automatically provisioned workstation with an integrated IDE.
Notebooks	Run notebook kernels locally on laptops (option 1).	A simple approach is to support notebook kernels on the cloud workstation (option 2). If notebooks are leveraged actively, consider providing ephemeral notebooks as well (option 3).	
Workflows	Highly recommended— you can run workflows on a single instance using a simple scheduler.	Choose a workflow scheduler that maximizes productivity and speed of iteration.	Choose a scheduler that provides high-availability, observability, and scalability, in addition to productivity.

Summary

- Data scientists need a development environment that provides excellent ergonomics for the following two key activities:
  - Prototyping loop: writing, evaluating, and analyzing application code
  - Interaction with production deployments: deploying, monitoring, and debugging production applications
- A cloud-backed data science workstation is an effective way to handle the two activities. You can develop code locally but evaluate it in an environment that resembles production.
- Notebooks are a necessary but not sufficient part of the data science toolchain. Notebooks excel at scratchpad-style prototyping and at analyzing results. You can integrate them to work in tandem with an IDE and a terminal on the workstation.

- Workflows are a useful abstraction for structuring data science applications. Workflows provide a number of benefits: they are easy to understand and explain, they help in managing complexity as the number of data science applications grows, and they can make execution more scalable and performant.
- Tens of different workflow frameworks exist. Pick one that provides excellent ergonomics for building data science applications specifically.
- A job scheduler is responsible for executing workflows. Pick a scheduler that integrates well with your compute infrastructure and is sufficiently scalable and highly available.

Introducing Metaflow

This chapter covers

- Defining a workflow in Metaflow that accepts input data and produces useful outputs
- Optimizing the performance of workflows with parallel computation on a single instance
- Analyzing the results of workflows in notebooks
- Developing a simple end-to-end application in Metaflow

You are probably anxious to roll up your sleeves and start hacking actual code, now that we have a development environment set up. In this chapter, you will learn the basics of developing data science applications using Metaflow, a framework that shows how different layers of the infrastructure stack can work together seamlessly.

The development environment, which we discussed in the previous chapter, determines *how* the data scientist develops applications: by writing code in an editor, evaluating it in a terminal, and analyzing results in a notebook. On top of this toolchain, the data scientist uses Metaflow to determine *what* code gets written and *why*, which is the topic of this chapter. The next chapters will then cover the infrastructure that determines *where* and *when* the workflows are executed.

We will introduce Metaflow from the ground up. You will first learn the syntax and the basic concepts that allow you to define basic workflows in Metaflow. After this, we will introduce branches in workflows. Branches are a straightforward way to embed concurrency in workflows, which often leads to higher performance through parallel computation.

Finally, we put all these concepts into action by building a realistic classifier application. By going through an end-to-end project, you will learn how Metaflow powers the prototyping loop by providing tools for local code evaluation, debugging, and result inspection in notebooks.

After reading this chapter, you, or the data scientists you support, will be able to develop fully functional data science applications by combining Metaflow with other off-the-shelf libraries. The subsequent chapters will build on this foundation and show how you can make applications more scalable, highly available, and amenable to collaboration by utilizing the full infrastructure stack. You can find all code listings for this chapter at http://mng.bz/xnB6.

3.1   The basics of Metaflow

Alex realizes that the job of a data scientist entails much more than just building models. As the first data scientist at Caveman Cupcakes, Alex has a great opportunity to help the company by building complete data science solutions independently. Alex finds the situation both exhilarating and terrifying. Alex is a marine biologist by training, not a software engineer—hopefully, building the necessary software around models won't be too daunting. Bowie recommends that they take a look at Metaflow, a framework that is supposed to make building end-to-end data science applications easy.

Metaflow was started at Netflix in 2017 to help data scientists build, deliver, and operate complete data science applications independently. The framework was designed to address a practical business need: a large company like Netflix has tens if not hundreds of potential use cases for data science, similar to those of Caveman Cupcakes. The company wants to test new ideas quickly in a realistic setup, preferably without having to allocate a large team to work on an experimental idea, and then promote the most promising experiments to production without too much overhead.

The ideas introduced in chapter 1 serve as a motivation for Metaflow: we need to account for the full stack of data science, we want to cover the whole life cycle of projects from prototype to production, and we want to do this by focusing on data scientist productivity. We can use the four Vs introduced in chapter 1 to answer the question, "Why Metaflow?" as follows:

- *Volume*—Metaflow helps to deliver more data science applications with fewer human resources involved. It reduces accidental complexity in the humming factory of data science applications by providing a uniform way to build them, leveraging the common language of workflows.
- *Variety*—Metaflow is not optimized for any particular type of data science problems. It helps deliver a diverse set of applications by being more opinionated at the lower layers of the stack and less opinionated about the top, domain-specific layers.
- *Velocity*—Metaflow speeds up the prototyping loop, as well as interaction with production deployments. It does this by prioritizing human productivity in all parts of the framework, for example, by allowing data scientists to use idiomatic Python.
- *Validity*—Metaflow makes applications more robust by enforcing best practices that make building and operating production-grade applications feasible, even by data scientists without a DevOps background.

In the data scientist's point of view, Metaflow is all about making the prototyping loop and interaction with production deployments, which we introduced in section 2.1, as smooth as possible. Doing this well requires that all layers of the infrastructure stack are integrated seamlessly. Whereas some frameworks tackle only workflows, compute resources, or model operations, Metaflow aims to address the full stack of data science, as depicted in figure 3.1.

In the engineering point of view, Metaflow acts as a substrate for integrations rather than as an attempt to reinvent individual layers of the stack. Companies have built or bought great solutions for data warehousing, data engineering, compute platforms, and job scheduling, not to mention the vibrant ecosystem of open

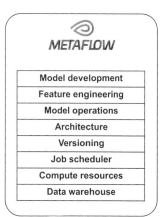

Figure 3.1 Metaflow binds together the layers of the data science stack.

source machine learning libraries. It would be unnecessary and unproductive to try to replace the existing established systems to accommodate the needs of data scientists. We should want to integrate data science applications into the surrounding business systems, not isolate them on an island.

Metaflow is based on a plugin architecture that allows different backends to be used for different layers of the stack, as long as the layers can support a set of basic operations. In particular, Metaflow is designed to be a cloud-native framework, relying on basic compute and storage abstractions provided by all major cloud providers.

Metaflow has a gentle adoption curve. You can get started with the "single-player mode" on a laptop and gradually scale the infrastructure out to the cloud as your needs grow. In the remaining sections of this chapter, we will introduce the basics of Metaflow. In the chapters to follow, we will expand its footprint and show how to address increasingly complex data science applications, spanning all the layers of the stack, and enhance collaboration among multiple data scientists.

If you want to build your infrastructure using other frameworks instead of Metaflow, you can read the next sections for inspiration—the concepts are applicable to many other frameworks, too—or you can jump straight in to chapter 4, which focuses on a foundational layer of the stack: compute resources.

3.1.1   *Installing Metaflow*

Metaflow greatly benefits from a cloud-based development environment, introduced in section 2.1, notebooks included. However, you can get started with just a laptop. As of the writing of this book, Metaflow supports OS X and Linux but not Windows. If you want to test Metaflow on Windows, you can use either the Windows Subsystem for Linux, a local Linux-based Docker container, or a cloud-based editor as discussed in the previous chapter.

Metaflow supports any Python version later than Python 3.5. After installing a Python interpreter, you can install Metaflow as any other Python package using `pip` as follows:

```
# pip install metaflow
```

In this book, lines prefixed with #, like the previous one, are meant to be executed in a terminal window without the hash mark.

> **NOTE** In all examples, we assume that the `pip` and `python` commands refer to the latest version of Python, which should be later than Python 3.5. In some systems, the correct commands are called `pip3` and `python3`. In this case, substitute the commands in examples accordingly.

You can confirm that Metaflow works simply by executing the following code:

```
# metaflow
```

If Metaflow was installed correctly, this should print a top-level help with a header like so:

```
Metaflow (2.2.5): More data science, less engineering
```

You can follow the examples in this chapter without a cloud (AWS) account, but if you want to try out all examples in the coming chapters, you will need one. You can sign up for a free account at https://aws.amazon.com/free.

3.1.2 Writing a basic workflow

As described in the previous chapter, the concept of a workflow helps to structure a data science application. It is considerably easier to think of your application in terms of steps of a workflow rather than as a set of arbitrary Python modules, especially if you are not a software engineer by training.

Imagine Alex, our protagonist, writing a Metaflow workflow. Alex is already familiar with notebooks, so the concept of writing small snippets of Python as steps sounds doable. Steps are like notebook cells on steroids. It would require much more cognitive effort to piece together an application using arbitrary Python classes, functions, and modules.

Let's start with a classic Hello World example. Everything in Metaflow is centered on the concept of a workflow, or simply a flow, which is a directed acyclic graph (DAG), as discussed in section 2.2. Our `HelloWorldFlow`, defined in listing 3.1, corresponds to the DAG depicted in figure 3.2.

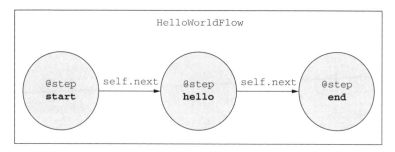

Figure 3.2 `HelloWorldFlow`

To define a workflow in Metaflow, you must follow these six simple rules:

1   *A flow* is defined as a Python class that is derived from the `FlowSpec` class. You can name your flows freely. In this book, by convention the flow class names end with a `Flow` suffix, as in `HelloWorldFlow`. You can include any methods (functions) in this class, but methods annotated with `@step` are treated specially.

2   *A step* (node) of the flow is a method of the class, annotated with the `@step` decorator. You can write arbitrary Python in the method body, but the last line is special, as described next. You can include an optional docstring in the method, explaining the purpose of the step. After the first example, we will omit docstrings to keep listings concise in the book, but it is advisable to use them in real-life code.

3   Metaflow executes the method bodies as an atomic unit of computation called *a task*. In a simple flow like this, there is a one-to-one correspondence between a step and a task, but that's not always the case, as we will see later in section 3.2.3.

4   The first step must be called `start`, so the flow has an unambiguous starting point.

5   The edges (arrows) between steps are defined by calling `self.next (step_name)` on the last line of the method, where `step_name` is the name of the next step to be executed.

6   The last step must be called `end`. Because the `end` step finishes the flow, it doesn't need a `self.next` transition on the last line.

7   One Python file (module) must contain only a single flow. You should instantiate the flow class at the bottom of the file inside an `if __name__ == '__main__'` conditional, which causes the class to be evaluated only if the file is called as a script.

The corresponding source code is listed in the next code listing.

Listing 3.1   Hello World

```
from metaflow import FlowSpec, step

class HelloWorldFlow(FlowSpec):        ◁──────  A workflow is defined by
                                                subclassing from FlowSpec.

    @step                         ────  The first step must be called start.
    def start(self):          ◁──────
        """Starting point"""
        print("This is start step")
        self.next(self.hello)      ◁──────  A call to self.next() denotes
    @step                                   an edge in the workflow.
    def hello(self):
        """Just saying hi"""
        print("Hello World!")
        self.next(self.end)

    @step
    def end(self):       ◁────  The last step must be called end.
        """Finish line"""
        print("This is end step")

if __name__ == '__main__':       ────  Instantiating the workflow
    HelloWorldFlow()         ◁──────   allows it to be executed.
```

The @step decorator denotes a step in the workflow.

Here's how to read and comprehend code that corresponds to a Metaflow flow:

1   First, find the `start` method. You know that this is where the execution starts. You can read the method to understand what it is doing.

2   See what the next step is by looking at the last line of `start`. In this case, it is `self.hello`, that is, the `hello` method.

3 Read the code for the next step, and identify the step after that. Keep doing this until you reach the end step.

Doing this is simpler than trying to understand an arbitrary set of Python functions and modules that don't even have a clear beginning and end. Save the code in a file, helloworld.py. You can execute the Python as any Python script. First, try running the following:

```
# python helloworld.py
```

This will validate the flow structure without executing any steps. Metaflow has a number of rules for what is considered a valid DAG. For instance, all steps must be connected to each other, and there must not be any cycles in the graph. If Metaflow detects any issues with your DAG, a helpful error message is shown.

Metaflow also runs a basic code check, a *linter*, every time you execute the script, which can detect typos, missing functions, and other such syntactic errors. If any issues are found, an error is shown and nothing else is run. This can be a huge time-saver, because issues can be detected before any time is spent on running the code. However, sometimes the linter can produce false positives. In this case, you can disable it by specifying the following:

```
# python helloworld.py --no-pylint
```

Now try running the next code:

```
# python helloworld.py show
```

This should print out a textual representation of the DAG, which for HelloWorldFlow corresponds to figure 3.2. You can see that docstrings are included in the output, so you can use the show command to get a quick idea of what an unfamiliar flow does.

Now, the moment of truth: let's execute the flow, as shown next! We call an execution of a flow *a run*:

```
# python helloworld.py run
```

This command executes the start, hello, and end methods in order. If all goes well, you should see a bunch of lines printed out that look like this:

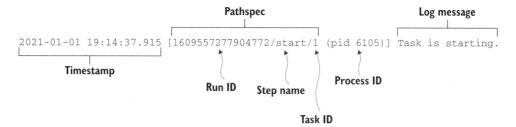

Every line printed from your flow to the standard output (aka *stdout*) or the standard error (aka *stderr*) streams will get a header like shown previously. Let's parse the header as follows:

- *Timestamp* denotes when the line was output. You can take a look at consecutive timestamps to get a rough idea of how long different segments of the code take to execute. A short delay may occur between a line being output and the minting of a timestamp, so don't rely on the timestamps for anything that requires accurate timekeeping.
- The following information inside the square brackets identifies a task:
  - Every Metaflow run gets a unique ID, a *run ID*.
  - A run executes the steps in order. The step that is currently being executed is denoted by *step name*.
  - A step may spawn multiple tasks using the `foreach` construct (see section 3.2.3), which are identified by a *task ID*.
  - The combination of a flow name, run ID, step name, and a task ID uniquely identifies a task in your Metaflow environment, among all runs of any flow. Here, the flow name is omitted because it is the same for all lines. We call this globally unique identifier a *pathspec*.
  - Each task is executed by a separate process in your operating system, identified by a *process ID*, aka *pid*. You can use any operating system–level monitoring tools, such as *top*, to monitor resource consumption of a task based on its process ID.
- After the square bracket comes a *log message*, which may be a message output by Metaflow itself, like "Task is starting" in this example, or a line output by your code.

What's the big deal about the IDs? Running a countless number of quick experiments is a core activity in data science—remember the prototyping loop we discussed earlier. Imagine hacking many different variations of the code, running them, and seeing slightly different results every time. After a while, it is easy to lose track of results: was it the third version that produced promising results or the sixth one?

In the old days, a diligent scientist might have recorded all their experiments and their results in a lab notebook. A decade ago, a spreadsheet might have served the same role, but keeping track of experiments was still a manual, error-prone process. Today, a modern data science infrastructure keeps track of experiments automatically through *an experiment tracking system*.

An effective experiment tracking system allows a data science team to inspect what has been run, identify each run or experiment unambiguously, access any past results, visualize them, and compare experiments against each other. Moreover, it is desirable to be able to rerun a past experiment and reproduce their results. Doing this accurately is much harder than it sounds, so we have dedicated many pages for the topic of *reproducibility* in chapter 6.

Standalone experiment tracking products can work with any piece of code, as long as the code is instrumented appropriately to send metadata to the tracking system. If you use Metaflow to build data science applications, you get experiment tracking for free—Metaflow tracks all executions automatically. The IDs shown earlier are a part of this system. They allow you to identify and access results immediately after a task has completed.

We will talk more about accessing past results in section 3.3.2, but you can get a taste by using the `logs` command, which allows you to inspect the output of any past run. Use the `logs` command with a pathspec corresponding to the task you want to inspect. For instance, you can copy and paste a pathspec from the output your run produces and execute the next command:

```
# python helloworld.py logs 1609557277904772/start/1
```

You should see a line of output that corresponds to the `print` statement in the step you inspected. The `logs` subcommand has a few options, which you can see by executing `logs --help`.

Finally, notice how Metaflow turns a single Python file into a command-line application without any boilerplate code. You don't have to worry about parsing command-line arguments or capturing logs manually. Every step is executed as a separate operating system–level subprocess, so they can be monitored independently. This is also a key feature enabling fault tolerance and scalability, as we will learn in chapter 4.

3.1.3 Managing data flow in workflows

Data science applications are all about processing data. A prototypical application ingests raw data from a data warehouse, transforms it in various ways, turns it into features, and maybe trains a model or does inference with an existing model. A trained model or predictions are then the output data of the workflow. To be able to build a workflow like this, you need to answer the following three questions:

1. How should the workflow access the input data?
2. How should the workflow move transformed data, that is, the workflow's internal state, across steps?
3. How should the workflow make its outputs accessible by outside systems?

By answering the three questions, you determine the *data flow* of the application, that is, the mechanisms for transporting data through the workflow. Figure 3.3 depicts data flow in the context of a workflow that consists of three steps, A, B, and C.

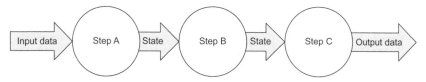

Figure 3.3   Data flow from input to output

In the workflow depicted in figure 3.3, step A comes before step B. Because steps are executed in order, any data processed by step A could be made available to step B, but not vice versa. This way, the workflow order determines how data can flow through the graph. Using Metaflow terminology, data flows from the start step toward the end step, like water flowing in a river from upstream to downstream but never the reverse.

To illustrate why being explicit about the data flow and state is useful, consider the example shown in figure 3.4 that shows a simple Jupyter notebook.

Figure 3.4 Hidden state and undefined data flow in a notebook

The output may seem surprising. Why is the value of x printed out as 2, even though it was just assigned to be 1 in the previous cell? In this case, the user first evaluated all cells from the top to the bottom and then decided to reevaluate the middle cell. Evaluating cells out of order is a common practice in notebooks. It is a part of their appeal as an unconstrained scratchpad.

The Jupyter kernel maintains the state of all variables under the hood. It lets the user evaluate the cells in whichever order, based on its hidden state. Like in this case, the results can be very surprising and practically impossible to reproduce. In contrast, workflows solve the problem by making the evaluation order and the corresponding data flow explicit.

Instead of using a notebook, the three cells could be organized as a workflow like the one depicted in figure 3.3, which would make it impossible to produce inconsistent results. Notebooks have an important role in the data science stack—they are convenient for quick explorations and analysis. However, as exemplified earlier, it is better to structure any serious application or modeling code as a workflow with an unambiguous data flow.

TRANSFERRING AND PERSISTING STATE IN A WORKFLOW

What does the data flow look like in practice? If all steps were executed within a single process on a single computer, we could keep the state in memory, which is the ordinary way of building software. A challenge for data science workflows is that we may want to execute steps on different computers in parallel or to access special hardware like GPUs. Hence, we need to be able to *transfer state* between steps, which may execute on physically separate computers.

We can do this by *persisting state*, that is, by storing all data that is relevant for subsequent steps, after a step completes. Then, when a new step starts, even on another computer, we can load the state back and continue execution. Figure 3.5 illustrates this idea.

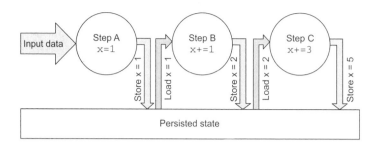

Figure 3.5
Transferring state
between steps through
a common datastore

In figure 3.5, the state consists of a single variable, x. The variable is first initialized in step A and then incremented by steps B and C. When a step finishes, the value of x is persisted. Before a step starts, its value is loaded back. Naturally, the process needs to be repeated for every piece of state, for every variable, that needs to be accessed across steps.

You can implement the idea of a persisted state in many different ways. Many workflow frameworks are not particularly opinionated about it. It is up to the user to decide how to load and store the state, maybe using a database as the persistence layer. The resulting workflow code can resemble that shown in figure 3.6. Each step includes code for loading and storing data. Although this approach is flexible, it adds quite a bit of boilerplate code. Worse, it adds cognitive overhead to the data scientist, because they have to decide explicitly what data to persist and how.

Figure 3.6 Persisting state manually

In our experience, data scientists can be quite conservative when storing data that may feel superfluous, in particular the workflow's internal state, if they need to make an explicit choice about it, like in figure 3.6. If the workflow framework makes it tedious to move state between steps, the user may be tempted to pack many unrelated operations in a single step, to avoid having to add boilerplate code for loading and storing data. Or, they may choose to persist only the outputs that are absolutely required by downstream consumers.

Although technically such a parsimonious approach can work, being too frugal with data is not great for the long-term health of the application. First, the workflow structure should primarily optimize for the logical structure of the application, so other human readers can easily understand it. For instance, it makes sense to have separate steps for data preprocessing and model training—you shouldn't merge the steps just to avoid having to transfer state. Second, imagine the workflow failing in production. You want the maximum, not minimal, amount of information to understand what went wrong.

To summarize, it is beneficial to have a mechanism for state transfer that makes it nearly transparent to the user. We don't want the user to have to worry about the technical detail that the steps may execute on physically distinct computers. Also, we don't want them to compromise the readability of the workflow to avoid having to use boilerplate code.

Most important, we want to encourage the user to persist data liberally, even if persisting it is not strictly necessary to make the workflow functional. The more data is persisted for every run, the more *observable* the workflow becomes, complementing metadata stored by the experiment tracking system. If enough data is persisted after each step, we can get a comprehensive idea of the workflow's status during and after execution, as illustrated by figure 3.7.

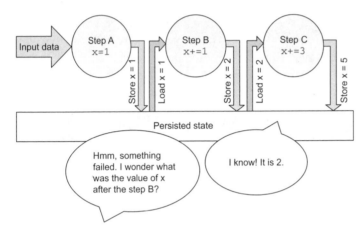

Figure 3.7   Persisted state allows you to observe workflow execution.

This approach pays great dividends in the long term. You will be able to monitor and debug workflows more effectively and reproduce, reuse, and share their results without extra work. On the flip side, storing data costs money, but thanks to the cloud, storage costs are becoming quite insignificant compared to the data scientist's time. Besides, we are not advocating for storing copies of the *input data* over and over again—more about this in chapter 7.

METAFLOW ARTIFACTS

To give an example of how you can make the data flow nearly transparent to the user, let's consider how Metaflow does it. Metaflow automatically persists all *instance variables,* that is, anything assigned to `self` in the step code. We call these persisted instance variables *artifacts.* Artifacts can be any data: scalar variables, models, data frames, or any other Python object that can be serialized using Python's `pickle` library. Artifacts are stored in a common data repository called a *datastore,* which is a layer of persisted state managed by Metaflow. You can learn more about the datastore later in this chapter in the sidebar box, "How Metaflow's datastore works."

Each step may produce any number of artifacts. After a step has completed, its artifacts are persisted as immutable units of data in the datastore. Those artifacts are permanently bound to the step, identified by the pathspec that produced them. This is crucial for experiment tracking: we want to produce an accurate and unmodifiable audit trail of what was produced during a run. However, subsequent steps may read the artifact and produce their own version of it.

To make this concept more concrete, let's start with a simple example that adds state and a counter variable, `count`, in a slightly modified version of `HelloWorldFlow`, which we introduced in listing 3.1. For clarity, let's rename the flow to `CounterFlow`.

As illustrated in figure 3.8, we initialize a counter variable, `count`, to zero in the `start` step. We do this simply by creating an instance variable in Python as usual, `self.count = 0`. In the following `add` step we increment `count` by one: `self.count += 1`. We increment `count` once more in the `end` step before printing out the final value, which is 2.

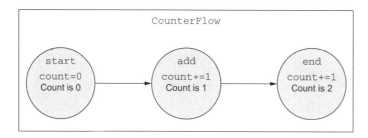

Figure 3.8
`CounterFlow`

The next listing shows the corresponding code.

Listing 3.2   A simple flow that maintains state

```python
from metaflow import FlowSpec, step

class CounterFlow(FlowSpec):

    @step
    def start(self):
        self.count = 0        ◁─── Initializes the count to zero
        self.next(self.add)

    @step
    def add(self):
        print("The count is", self.count, "before incrementing")
        self.count += 1       ◁─┐
        self.next(self.end)     │
                                │  Increments the
    @step                       │  count by one
    def end(self):              │
        self.count += 1       ◁─┘
        print("The final count is", self.count)    ◁─── Shows the final count

if __name__ == '__main__':
    CounterFlow()
```

Save the flow code to a file called counter.py and execute it as before, like so:

```
# python counter.py run
```

In addition to the usual messages output by Metaflow, you should see a line saying, "the count is 0 before incrementing," and "The final count is 2." Assuming you are already familiar with the basics of Python, you will notice that the flow behaves like any Python object when `self.start()`, `self.add()`, and `self.end()` are called in a sequence. For a refresher of how instance variables (data attributes) work in Python, take a look at the Python tutorial section about instance variables at http://mng .bz/AyDQ.

By design, the syntax of managing state in Metaflow looks like idiomatic, straight-forward Python: just create instance variables with `self` as usual. It is equally easy to exclude temporary values that are not worth saving: just create ordinary, noninstance variables that will be cleaned up after the step function exits.

> **RULE OF THUMB** Use instance variables, such as `self`, to store any data and objects that may have value outside the step. Use local variables only for inter-mediary, temporary data. When in doubt, use instance variables because they make debugging easier.

By design, the state management looks almost trivially simple in Metaflow but a lot is happening under the hood. Metaflow must address the following two key challenges related to data flow:

1 Each task is executed as a separate process, possibly on a separate physical com-puter. We must concretely move state across processes and instances.
2 Runs may fail. We want to understand why they failed, which requires under-standing of the state of the flow prior to the failure. Also, we may want to restart failed steps without having to restart the whole flow from the beginning. All these features require us to persist state.

To address these challenges, Metaflow snapshots and stores the state of the workflow, as stored in `self`, after every task. Snapshotting is one of the key features of Metaflow that enable many other features, such as resuming workflows and executing tasks on disparate compute environments and, in particular, easy observability of workflows.

You can observe instance variables as soon as a task completes, even when a run is still executing. You can do this in multiple ways of doing, but an easy way is to use the `dump` command, which works similar to the `logs` command that we used earlier. Just copy and paste a pathspec of a task that you want to observe, such as the following example:

```
# python counter.py dump 1609651059708222/end/3
```

If you used a pathspec corresponding to the end task, like in the previous example, you should see a line printed out that says `count` has a value of 2. Expectedly, the value will be lower for earlier steps. Besides the dump command, you can access artifacts programmatically, for example, in a notebook using the Metaflow Client API, which we will cover in section 3.3.2.

This discussion touched on only the basics of artifacts. The next section about *parameters* shows how artifacts can be passed into a run from outside the flow. The next chapter will go into detail about how to deal with large datasets, which sometimes require special treatment. Later, in chapter 6, we will discuss how to handle complex objects, such as machine learning models, as artifacts.

How Metaflow's datastore works

You don't need these technical details to use or operate Metaflow successfully, but in case you're curious, here is how Metaflow's datastore works under the hood. After Metaflow finishes evaluating a task, it inspects what instance variables have been created by the user code. All variables are serialized, that is, converted to bytes, and stored in a *datastore* managed by Metaflow. These serialized objects, called artifacts, are a key concept in the Metaflow universe.

The following figure illustrates how data is moved and persisted in the datastore in the case of CounterFlow. After the start step finishes, Metaflow detects the count variable. Its value of 0 is serialized to bytes, currently using the Python's built-in pickle library, but this is considered an internal implementation detail that is subject to change. Let's assume the byte sequence corresponding to 0 is ab0ef2. These bytes are stored in the datastore (unless they exist there already) as an immutable blob, an artifact. After this, internal metadata is updated so that the count variable refers to the artifact ab0ef21 at the start step.

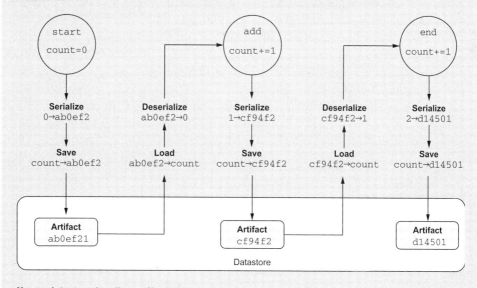

How a datastore handles artifacts internally

(continued)

When the add step accesses count for the first time, Metaflow fetches it from the datastore based on metadata. We know that add gets its values from start because of the flow order. The add step increments the value of count, which causes a new artifact to be created. It is important to note that we don't change the previously stored value of count, because its historical value at start hasn't changed. Each step has its own set of artifacts. The process is repeated for the end step.

Metaflow's datastore is organized as a *content-addressed storage*, bearing conceptual similarity to the Git version-control system. Internally, artifacts are named using the hash of their contents, and hence, only one copy of its unique value needs to be stored. In other words, the datastore de-duplicates artifacts automatically. This means that disk space is used efficiently, and in most cases, you don't have to worry about creating too many artifacts to conserve space.

WHAT SHOULD BE A STEP?

When you are developing a new flow, you may wonder what operations should belong to the same step and when it makes sense to split a large step into multiple separate steps. Although there isn't a single right answer, it may be helpful to think of steps as *checkpoints*. As discussed previously, artifacts are persisted when a step—a task launched by the step, to be precise—finishes. After artifacts have been persisted successfully, they become available for inspection, as described in section 3.3.2. Also, you will be available to resume execution at an arbitrary step, as described in section 3.3.3. Therefore, it makes sense to keep steps reasonably small in terms of execution time, so if failures happen, you won't lose too much work. Or, if you want to monitor the state of a run in near real time, you will need small steps, too.

On the other hand, persisting artifacts and launching tasks creates some overhead. If your steps are way too small, the overhead starts dominating the total execution time. This overhead is quite easy to notice, though: you can always merge tiny steps back together if it becomes an issue.

Another consideration is the readability of the code. If you execute

```
# python counter.py show
```

do you find the graph meaningful? It is likely that steps that are too large hurt comprehensibility more than steps that are too small.

> **RULE OF THUMB**   Structure your workflow in logical steps that are easily explainable and understandable. When in doubt, err on the side of small steps. They tend to be more easily understandable and debuggable than large steps.

3.1.4   Parameters

In the previous section, we learned how we can pass data downstream in a flow using artifacts, that is, by assigning variables to self. But what if you want to pass in data to start, that is, set parameters for the flow?

For instance, imagine that you are experimenting with a new model, and you train it with various parameterizations. When you analyze the results of your experiments afterward, you should know what parameters were used to train a particular version of the model. As a solution, Metaflow provides a special artifact called `Parameter`, which you can use to pass data into a run. `Parameter` artifacts are tracked like any other artifacts, so you can check the parameters assigned to any past run.

Parameters are a flow-level, that is, a class-level, construct. They are not bound to any particular step and are automatically made available to all steps, including `start`. To define a `Parameter`, you have to specify the following four elements:

1. Create a `Parameter` instance at the class level.
2. Assign the parameter to an artifact, for example, `animal` and `count` in listing 3.3.
3. Specify the name of the parameter that is shown to the user, for example, `creature` and `count`, as shown next. The artifact name and the parameter name can be the same, but they don't have to be, as illustrated in listing 3.3.
4. Decide on the type of the parameter. By default, parameters are strings. You can change the type either by specifying a `default` value for the parameter, like for `count` as shown in the next code listing, or by explicitly setting the type to one of the basic scalar types of Python—`str`, `float`, `int`, or `bool`—as for `ratio` in listing 3.3.

Besides these required elements, `Parameter` supports a set of optional arguments. Typical options include `help`, which specifies a user-visible help text, and `required=True`, which indicates that the user must supply a value for the parameter. By default, all parameters are optional. They receive a value of `None` if no `default` is specified and the user didn't provide a value. The following listing shows an example.

Listing 3.3   A flow with parameters

```
from metaflow import FlowSpec, Parameter, step

class ParameterFlow(FlowSpec):

    animal = Parameter('creature',              ⬅┐
                   help="Specify an animal",      │
                   required=True)                 │
                                                  │  Parameters are
    count = Parameter('count',              ⬅────┤  defined at the class
                   help="Number of animals",      │  level, outside steps.
                   default=1)                      │
                                                  │
    ratio = Parameter('ratio',              ⬅────┘
                   help="Ratio between 0.0 and 1.0",
                   type=float)

    @step
    def start(self):
```

```
        print(self.animal, "is a string of", len(self.animal), "characters")
        print("Count is an integer: %s+1=%s" % (self.count, self.count + 1))
        print("Ratio is a", type(self.ratio), "whose value is", self.ratio)
        self.next(self.end)

    @step
    def end(self):
        print('done!')

if __name__ == '__main__':
    ParameterFlow()
```

Save the code to a file called parameters.py and try to run it as usual:

```
# python parameters.py run
```

This fails with the error, Missing option '--creature', because the creature parameter has required=True. If this was a real flow, this error would be a good reason to check the help for the flow, as follows:

```
# python parameters.py run --help
```

A bunch of options are listed. The user-defined parameters are at the top of the option list with their help texts shown. Try setting a value for –creature as follows:

```
# python parameters.py run --creature seal
```

The flow should run, and you see an output corresponding to the assigned parameter values. Note that ratio doesn't have a default, so it is set to None. Let's try specifying all the values, as shown here:

```
# python parameters.py run --creature seal --count 10 --ratio 0.3
```

Notice how count and ratio are converted to the correct Python types automatically.

> **NOTE** Parameters are constant, immutable values. You can't change them in your code. If you want to mutate a parameter, create a copy of the parameter value, and assign it to another artifact.

SPECIFYING PARAMETERS AS ENVIRONMENT VARIABLES

If you execute the same run command line frequently, maybe with slight modifications, it may get frustrating to specify the same parameters over and over again. For convenience, you can specify any options as environment variables, too.

To do this, set an environment variable whose name matches the option name, prefixed with METAFLOW_RUN_. For instance, we can fix the value of creature for parameters.py as follows:

```
# export METAFLOW_RUN_CREATURE=dinosaur
```

Now you can run `ParameterFlow` without specifying –creature, because its value is specified via an environment variable, as shown next:

```
# python parameters.py run --ratio 0.25
```

If both an environment variable and a command-line option are set, the latter takes precedence, as you can see by executing the following:

```
# python parameters.py run --creature otter --count 10 --ratio 0.3
```

The `creature` should be set to `otter`, not `dinosaur`.

COMPLEX PARAMETERS

The previous mechanism works for basic scalar parameters that are strings, integers, floating-point numbers, or Boolean values. Most basic flows need nothing besides these basic types as parameters.

But sometimes, you might need a parameter that is a list or a mapping of some sort, or a complex combination of these. A challenge is that because parameters are typically defined on the command line as a string, we need a way to define nonscalar values as strings so they can be passed in as a `Parameter`. This is where JSON-encoded parameters come in handy.

The next listing shows a simple example that accepts a dictionary as a parameter.

> **Listing 3.4   A flow with a JSON-typed parameter**

```python
from metaflow import FlowSpec, Parameter, step, JSONType

class JSONParameterFlow(FlowSpec):

    mapping = Parameter('mapping',
                        help="Specify a mapping",
                        default='{"some": "default"}',
                        type=JSONType)

    @step
    def start(self):
        for key, value in self.mapping.items():
            print('key', key, 'value', value)
        self.next(self.end)

    @step
    def end(self):
        print('done!')

if __name__ == '__main__':
    JSONParameterFlow()
```

Defines a JSON-typed parameter, imports JSONType, and specifies it as the parameter type

Save the snippet to a file called json_parameter.py. You can pass in a mapping, a dictionary, on the command line as follows:

```
# python json_parameter.py run --mapping '{"mykey": "myvalue"}'
```

Note that the dictionary is enclosed in single quotes to avoid the special characters from confusing the shell.

It is not convenient to specify a large JSON object inline on the command line. For large JSON objects, a better approach is to read the value from a file using a standard shell expression. If you don't have a large JSON file for testing handy, you can create one—let's call it myconfig.json—as follows:

```
# echo '{"largekey": "largevalue"}' > myconfig.json
```

Now you can provide this file as a parameter like so:

```
# python json_parameter.py run --mapping "$(cat myconfig.json)"
```

The shell expression, `$(cat myconfig.json)`, substitutes the value on the command line with the contents of a file, myconfig.json. In this case, we must enclose the shell expression in double quotes.

FILES AS PARAMETERS

The mechanisms shown previously allow you to parameterize a run with small values, or maybe configuration files, passed on the command line. They are not intended to be a mechanism for passing in large amounts of input data.

In real-life data science applications, however, it is not always easy to draw the line between parameters and input data. Large configuration files may be larger than the smallest datasets. Or you may have a medium-size auxiliary dataset that feels like a parameter, although the actual input data is provided through a separate channel.

Metaflow provides a special parameter called `IncludeFile`, which you can use to include small or medium-size datasets in a run as an artifact. A typical example would be a CSV (comma-separated value) file. There isn't an exact limit for the size of files that can be handled by `IncludeFile`, but its performance isn't optimized for big data—say, files larger than a gigabyte. Consider it a supersized `Parameter`, as illustrated in figure 3.9, rather than a mechanism for large-scale data processing, which will be covered in chapter 7.

Let's take a look at an example in listing 3.5. It accepts a CSV file as a parameter and parses it. The example uses Python's built-in CSV parser from the `csv` module, so it can handle quoted values and configurable field delimiters. You can change the default delimiter, a comma, by specifying the `--delimiter` option.

To test the flow, you can create a simple CSV file, test.csv, which contains any comma-separated values, like here:

```
first,second,third
a,b,c
```

The `csv.reader` function will take the CSV data as a file object, so we wrap our string-valued `self.data` artifact in a `StringIO`, which makes it an in-memory file object.

Figure 3.9 Parameters are meant only for small and medium-size datasets.

IncludeFile, is_text=True indicates that the corresponding artifact should be returned as a Unicode string instead of a bytes object.

Listing 3.5 A flow that includes a CSV file as a parameter

```
from metaflow import FlowSpec, Parameter, step, IncludeFile

from io import StringIO
import csv

class CSVFileFlow(FlowSpec):

    data = IncludeFile('csv',
                       help="CSV file to be parsed",
                       is_text=True)

    delimiter = Parameter('delimiter',
                          help="delimiter",
                          default=',')

    @step
    def start(self):
        fileobj = StringIO(self.data)
        for i, row in enumerate(csv.reader(fileobj,
     delimiter=self.delimiter)):
            print("row %d: %s" % (i, row))
        self.next(self.end)

    @step
    def end(self):
        print('done!')

if __name__ == '__main__':
    CSVFileFlow()
```

Save the code to csv_file.py. You can run it as follows:

```
# python csv_file.py run --csv test.csv
```

You should see parsed fields of the CSV file printed out. You might wonder how this simple example is different from just opening the CSV file directly in the code, for example, by using `csv.reader(open('test.csv'))`. The key difference is that `IncludeFile` reads the file and persists it as an immutable Metaflow artifact, attached to the run. Consequently, the input file is snapshotted and versioned together with the run, so you can access the original data, even if `test.csv` is changed or lost. This can be very useful for reproducibility, as we will learn in chapter 6.

Now you know how to define sequential workflows that may receive data from the outside world through parameters and process it in multiple steps that share state via artifacts. In the next section, we will learn how to run many such sequences of steps concurrently.

3.2   Branching and merging

Alex is positively surprised by the fact that defining basic workflows in Metaflow isn't much harder than writing code in notebooks. But is there any benefit to writing code this way? At this point, purported benefits of workflows seem quite abstract. Alex chats with Bowie over coffee, reminiscing about a project that took nine minutes to execute in a notebook. Bowie points out that workflows make it easy to execute operations in parallel, which can make processing much faster. The idea of getting stuff done faster resonates with Alex—maybe this is a killer feature of workflows!

Workflows provide an abstraction of concurrency—branching—that allow efficient use of parallel compute resources, such as multicore CPUs and distributed compute clusters. Although several other paradigms enable parallel computing, many of them are notoriously hard to get right, multithreaded programming being a well-known example. Workflows are uniquely powerful because they make parallelism accessible to nonexpert software developers, including data scientists.

When should one use branches? Let's start by considering a linear workflow that doesn't have branches. Designing a linear workflow isn't too hard, typically. It is often quite evident that we must do A before B and only after B can C happen. The A→B→C order is imposed by the data flow: C needs some data from B that needs data from A.

Correspondingly, you should use branches whenever the data flow allows it. If A produces data that can be used by both B and C, and there's no other data being shared between B and C, then B and C should branch off from A, so they can be run concurrently. Figure 3.10 depicts a concrete example of this. To train any models, we need to fetch a dataset that is performed by step A. We want to train two separate versions of the model using the data produced by step A. There's nothing that step B requires from step C or vice versa, so we should specify them as independent branches. After steps B and C complete, we want to choose the best model in step D, which obviously requires input from both steps B and C.

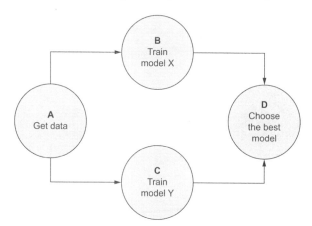

Figure 3.10   A basic workflow with two branches

We could express the DAG of figure 3.10 as a linear DAG, A→B→C→D or A→C→B→D, and get exactly the same results. These DAGs would be slower to execute because Metaflow wouldn't be able to run steps B and C in parallel. Besides performance benefits, branches can make workflows more readable by highlighting the actual data flow and interdependencies between steps. Hence, we recommend the following best practice.

> **RULE OF THUMB**   Whenever you have two or more steps that can be executed independently, make them parallel branches. It will make your workflow easier to understand, because the reader can see what steps don't share data just by looking at the workflow structure. It will make your workflow faster, too.

You may wonder whether the system could figure out an optimal DAG structure automatically. *Automatic parallelization* has been an active research topic in computer science for decades, but, alas, it is practically impossible to do this using arbitrary, idiomatic Python code. The main obstacle is that often the flow code itself does not contain enough information about what can be parallelized, because the steps interact with other third-party libraries and services. We have found that letting the user stay in control is less confusing than relying on a half-baked, error-prone automation. Also, ultimately, workflows are a medium of human communication. No automated system can decide the most understandable way to describe a business problem to a human being.

3.2.1   Valid DAG structures

We call a step that fans out branches, like step A in figure 3.10, a *split step*. Correspondingly, we call a step that fans in branches, like step D in figure 3.10, a *join step*. To keep the data flow easy to understand, Metaflow requires that every split step have a corresponding join step. You can think of split as the left parenthesis, (, and join as the right one,). A properly parenthesized expression (like this one) needs parentheses on both sides. You can nest splits and joins as deeply as needed.

Figure 3.11 shows an example of a valid DAG with nested branches. The graph has three split steps, shaded light gray. Each split step is matched by a join step, shaded dark gray.

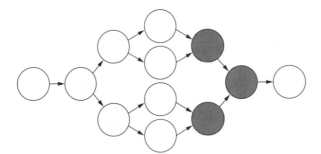

Figure 3.11   A valid DAG with two levels of nested branches

Note that just having the same number of splits and joins isn't sufficient—there's another rule to follow.

> **RULE**   A join step can join only steps that have a common split parent.

Figure 3.12 shows a DAG with two invalid splits, shown in dark and light gray. The dark gray split should have a corresponding dark gray join, but here the dark gray join tries to join a light gray step, which is not allowed—a join step can join only steps from a common split parent. When you plot a valid Metaflow DAG, edges (arrows) never have to cross.

The reason for these rules goes back to the data flow: we need to keep track of the lineage of artifacts, which could get very confusing in a graph with crossing edges.

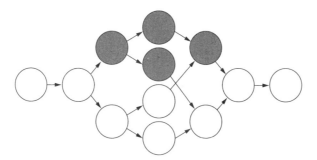

Figure 3.12   An invalid DAG, where splits and joins don't match

3.2.2   *Static branches*

Earlier, in chapter 2, we introduced the concept of *a static DAG*, that is, a DAG whose structure is fully known before execution begins. All examples depicted earlier, for instance, the one in figure 3.10, have been static DAGs with static branches. In this section, we will show how static branches are defined in Metaflow.

Before we get to the syntax of splits and joins, we need to cover the following important topic: in branches, the data flow, that is, the artifacts, will diverge by design. When we reach a join step, we must decide what to do with divergent values. In other words, we must *merge* artifacts. The question of merging often trips up new users of Metaflow, so let's start with a simple example.

Let's expand our original `CounterFlow` example from listing 3.2 by adding another branch, as depicted in figure 3.13. Here, `start` is our split step. We have one branch, `add_one`, which increments `count` by one, and another branch, `add_two`, which increments it by two. Now, going in the `join` step, we have two possible values for `count`, 1 and 2. We must decide which one is the right value going forward.

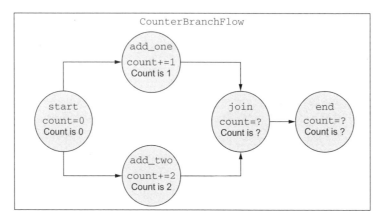

Figure 3.13   `CounterBranchFlow`

In this example, similar to real-life flows, there isn't an unambiguous right or wrong answer for what value count should get in the join step. The right choice depends on the application: maybe it should be the maximum of the two, like in listing 3.6; maybe it should be the average; or maybe it should be the sum. It is up to the user to define how the values should be merged. For instance, considering the "choose the best model" step in figure 3.10, the step would iterate through models X and Y and choose the one with the highest score.

Although it is easy to see that the question of count needs to be resolved in figure 3.13, there's an additional challenge: Metaflow can't detect reliably which artifacts have been modified, so a join step needs to *decide what to do with all artifacts coming upstream.* If you don't do anything in a join step, downstream steps won't have access to any data prior to the join, except the parameters that are constant and, hence, guaranteed to be always available.

> **RULE**   join steps act as barriers in the data flow. You must explicitly merge all artifacts except parameters to let data flow through downstream.

In listing 3.6, which corresponds to figure 3.13, we added another artifact, creature, to demonstrate this. If the join step doesn't do anything with creature, it won't be available in the end step, although the branches didn't modify it at all.

The syntax for defining a split for a static branch is simple: just list all branches as arguments to self.next. join steps take an extra argument that is by convention called inputs, which gives you access to artifacts from each inbound branch. A join step doesn't have to be called join—it is recognized as a join step solely based on the extra argument.

The inputs object allows you to access the branches in the following three ways:

1 You can iterate over inputs. It is common to merge artifacts using Python's built-in functions, like min, max, or sum, with a generator expression that loops over the inputs. This is how we pick the maximum of counts in the next listing.

2 With static branches, you can refer to branches by their names, like in the print statements in the next listing.

3 You can refer to branches by index. It is common to use the first branch, inputs[0], to reassign artifacts that are known to be constant across all branches. This is how we reassign the creature artifact in the following listing.

Listing 3.6   A flow with static branches

```
from metaflow import FlowSpec, step

class CounterBranchFlow(FlowSpec):

    @step
    def start(self):
        self.creature = "dog"
```

```
        self.count = 0
        self.next(self.add_one, self.add_two)
```

A static branch is defined by giving all outbound steps as arguments to self.next.

```
    @step
    def add_one(self):
        self.count += 1
        self.next(self.join)

    @step
    def add_two(self):
        self.count += 2
        self.next(self.join)

    @step
    def join(self, inputs):
```

A join step is defined by an extra inputs argument to step.

```
        self.count = max(inp.count for inp in inputs)
        print("count from add_one", inputs.add_one.count)
        print("count from add_two", inputs.add_two.count)
```

We can also print values from specific named branches.

We take the maximum of two counts by iterating over inputs.

```
        self.creature = inputs[0].creature
        self.next(self.end)
```

To reassign unmodified artifacts, we can just refer to the first branch by index.

```
    @step
    def end(self):
        print("The creature is", self.creature)
        print("The final count is", self.count)

if __name__ == '__main__':
    CounterBranchFlow()
```

Save the code to counter_branch.py. You can run it as follows:

```
# python counter_branch.py run
```

The final count printed should be 2, that is, the maximum of the two branches. You can try commenting out the self.creature line in the join step to see what happens when not all artifacts required by the downstream steps—end in this case—are handled by join. It will crash because self.creature is not found.

In the logs, notice how the *pid*, the process identifier, is different for add_one and add_two. Metaflow executes the two branches as separate processes. If your computer has multiple CPU cores, which is almost certain on any modern system, the operating system is likely to execute the processes on separate CPU cores, so the computation is physically happening in parallel. This means that you can get results up to twice as fast compared to running them sequentially.

MERGE HELPER

You may wonder what happens if you have many artifacts. Is it really necessary to reassign all of them explicitly? All of them do need to be reassigned, but to avoid boilerplate code, Metaflow provides a helper function, merge_artifacts, which does most

of the grunt work for you. To see it in action, you can replace the line that reassigns
the constant artifact:

```
self.creature = inputs[0].creature
```

with the following line:

```
self.merge_artifacts(inputs)
```

If you run the flow again, you see that it works equally well with merge_artifacts.

As you can imagine, merge_artifacts can't do all the merging for you. It doesn't
know that you want to use the maximum of counts, for instance. It relies on you first
merging all diverged artifacts explicitly, like we did with count in listing 3.6. When you
call merge_artifacts after all diverged artifacts have been reassigned, it will reassign
all the remaining, nondivergent artifacts—that is, artifacts that have the same value in
all branches—for you automatically. It will fail loudly if any divergent artifacts remain.

Sometimes you may have artifacts that don't have to be visible downstream, so you
don't want to merge them, but they would confuse merge_artifacts. Listing 3.7
demonstrates such a case. We define an artifact, increment, in the two branches with
two different values. We consider it as an internal detail to the step, so we don't want
to merge it. However, we want to save it in an artifact in case we need to debug code
later. We can use the exclude option in merge_artifacts to list all artifacts that can
be safely ignored.

Listing 3.7   Merging branching using the merge helper

```
from metaflow import FlowSpec, step

class CounterBranchHelperFlow(FlowSpec):

    @step
    def start(self):
        self.creature = "dog"
        self.count = 0
        self.next(self.add_one, self.add_two)

    @step
    def add_one(self):
        self.increment = 1              ◁──────┐
        self.count += self.increment            │  The value of increment
        self.next(self.join)                    │  diverges between the
                                                │  two branches.
    @step                                       │
    def add_two(self):                          │
        self.increment = 2              ◁──────┘
        self.count += self.increment
        self.next(self.join)

    @step
```

```
    def join(self, inputs):
        self.count = max(inp.count for inp in inputs)
        print("count from add_one", inputs.add_one.count)
        print("count from add_two", inputs.add_two.count)
        self.merge_artifacts(inputs, exclude=['increment'])  ⊲
        self.next(self.end)

    @step
    def end(self):
        print("The creature is", self.creature)
        print("The final count", self.count)

if __name__ == '__main__':
    CounterBranchHelperFlow()
```

We must explicitly ignore the diverged artifact, because we are not handling it explicitly.

Save the code to counter_branch_helper.py. You can run it as follows:

```
# python counter_branch_helper.py run
```

The output is the same as in listing 3.6. You can remove the `exclude` option to see the error that `merge_artifacts` raises when it faces artifacts with diverged values. Besides `exclude`, `merge_artifacts` has a few more convenient options that you can peruse in the online documentation of Metaflow.

3.2.3 *Dynamic branches*

In the previous section, we showed how you can fan out to a predefined list of named steps, each performing a different operation. Concurrent operations like this are sometimes called *task parallelism*. In contrast, what if you want to perform essentially the same operation but with different input data? *Data parallelism* like this is extremely common in data science applications. An article written by Intel director James Reinders about task parallelism on ZDNet (http://mng.bz/j2Dz) describes the two types of parallelism as follows:

> *Data parallelism involves running the same task on different components of data, whereas task parallelism is distinguished by running many different tasks at the same time on the same data.*

In the context of data science, data parallelism occurs in many contexts, for instance, when you train or score models in parallel, process shards of data in parallel, or do hyperparameter searches in parallel. In Metaflow, data parallelism is expressed via the `foreach` construct. We call `foreach` branches *dynamic branches*, because the width, or the cardinality, of the branch is determined dynamically at the runtime based on data, not in the code as with static branches.

> **NOTE** Whereas static branches are suitable for expressing concurrency in code, that is, operations that are always concurrent no matter what data is being processed, dynamic branches are suitable for expressing concurrency in data.

In figure 3.10, we sketched how a static DAG could be used to build two models, X and Y, in parallel. The structure makes sense if training X and Y require substantially different code—maybe X is a decision tree and Y is a deep neural network. However, this approach wouldn't make sense if the code in various branches is equal but only the data is different. For instance, consider training a decision tree model for each country in the world, as depicted in figure 3.14.

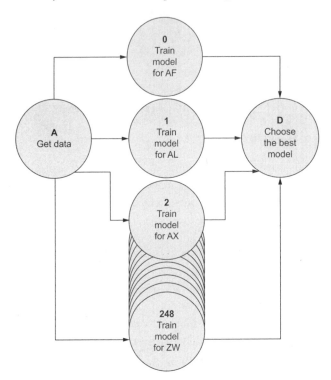

Figure 3.14   **A workflow with dynamic, data-driven branches**

A construct called `foreach` in Metaflow allows you to run a copy of a step for each value of a given list, hence the name *for-each*. Many programming languages, including Python, provide a similar function called `map`. Like `map`, `foreach` takes a user-defined function (a step in Metaflow) and applies it to each item of the given list, saving and returning the result (artifacts in Metaflow).

The logistics of splitting and joining work exactly the same way as for static branches, except for a slightly different syntax used in the split step. In particular, you need to merge artifacts for `foreach` similarly as with static branches. This next listing demonstrates the syntax for `foreach`.

Listing 3.8   A flow with a `foreach` branch

```
from metaflow import FlowSpec, step

class ForeachFlow(FlowSpec):
```

```
    @step
    def start(self):
        self.creatures = ['bird', 'mouse', 'dog']
        self.next(self.analyze_creatures, foreach='creatures')
```
**A foreach branch is defined
with the foreach keyword
that refers to a list.**

```
    @step
    def analyze_creatures(self):
        print("Analyzing", self.input)
        self.creature = self.input
        self.score = len(self.creature)
        self.next(self.join)
```
**self.input points to an
item of the foreach list.**

```
    @step
    def join(self, inputs):
        self.best = max(inputs, key=lambda x: x.score).creature
        self.next(self.end)

    @step
    def end(self):
        print(self.best, 'won!')

if __name__ == '__main__':
    ForeachFlow()
```

A foreach split is defined by calling self.next with a reference to a step as usual and a keyword argument foreach, which takes an artifact name, a string, as its value. The artifact referred to by foreach should be a Python list. In this example, the foreach artifact is called creatures.

The analyze_creatures step will be called for each item of the list, in this case, three times. In the foreach step, you have access to a special attribute called self .input, which contains an item from the foreach list that is assigned for the currently executing branch. Note that self.input is not available outside foreach, so if you want to keep the value, you should assign it to another artifact, like we did with self.creature later.

This example also demonstrates a common pattern of picking a branch that maximizes some artifact value, in this case, score. Python's built-in max function accepts an optional key argument, which defines a function that produces a sort key that is used to define the maximum. In effect, this is an implementation of *arg max* in Python, which is a very common operation in data science, especially in the context of foreaches.

Save the code to foreach.py, and run it as follows:

```
# python foreach.py run
```

You can see that three instances of analyze_creatures were running concurrently, each getting a different value from the creatures list. Each creature was scored based on the length of their name and mouse won.

This is the first example that shows how a single step spawns multiple tasks. In the logs, you can see each task having a unique ID, like `analyze_creatures/2` and `analyze _creatures/3`, which are used to uniquely identify branches of the `foreach`.

Numerical computing loves dynamic branching

The pattern of executing a piece of code for different parts of data in parallel and then collecting the results is universal in numerical computing. In the literature, the pattern goes by names such as the following:

- Bulk synchronous parallel (a concept first introduced in the 1980s)
- MapReduce (popularized by an open source data processing framework, Hadoop)
- Fork-Join model (e.g., `java.util.concurrent.ForkJoinPool` in Java)
- Parallel map (e.g., in Python's `multiprocessing` module)

If you are curious, you can use Google to find more details about these concepts. They are all similar to the `foreach` construct in Metaflow.

In a typical data science application, parallelism takes place at many levels. For instance, at the application level, you can use Metaflow's `foreach` to define a workflow that trains a separate model for each country, like in figure 3.14. Then at the low level, close to the metal, models are trained using an ML library like TensorFlow that parallelizes matrix calculations over multiple CPU cores using a similar pattern internally.

The philosophy of Metaflow is to focus on the high-level, human-centric concerns regarding the overall structure of the application and let off-the-shelf ML libraries handle machine-centric optimizations.

3.2.4 *Controlling concurrency*

A single `foreach` can be used to fan out even tens of thousands of tasks. In fact, `foreach` is a key element of the scalability story of Metaflow, as described in chapter 4. As a side effect, a `foreach` branch can accidentally launch so many concurrent tasks on your laptop that it starts glowing red hot. To make life easier for your laptop (or data center), Metaflow provides a mechanism for controlling the number of concurrent tasks.

The concurrency limit doesn't change the workflow structure in any way—the code stays intact. By default, the limit is enforced during execution by Metaflow's built-in *local scheduler*, which takes care of executing the workflow when you type run. As discussed in chapter 6, Metaflow supports other schedulers for use cases that require higher availability and scalability.

To see how the concurrency limit works in practice, let's use the code in listing 3.9 as an example. It shows a flow that includes a `foreach` over a list with a thousand items.

Listing 3.9 A flow with a 1000-way foreach

```
from metaflow import FlowSpec, step

class WideForeachFlow(FlowSpec):

    @step
    def start(self):
        self.ints = list(range(1000))
        self.next(self.multiply, foreach='ints')

    @step
    def multiply(self):
        self.result = self.input * 1000
        self.next(self.join)

    @step
    def join(self, inputs):
        self.total = sum(inp.result for inp in inputs)
        self.next(self.end)

    @step
    def end(self):
        print('Total sum is', self.total)

if __name__ == '__main__':
    WideForeachFlow()
```

Save the code to wide_foreach.py. Try running it as follows:

```
# python wide_foreach.py run
```

This should fail with an error message about `start` spawning too many child tasks. Because defining `foreaches` is so easy in Metaflow, you can inadvertently use a very large list in `foreach`, possibly including millions of items. Running a flow like this would take a good while to execute.

To prevent silly and possibly expensive mistakes from happening, Metaflow has a safeguard for the maximum size of a `foreach`, by default 100. You can raise the limit with the `--max-num-splits` option, like here:

```
# python wide_foreach.py run --max-num-splits 10000
```

If you run wide `foreaches` all the time, it might be easier to set an environment variable, like so:

```
# export METAFLOW_RUN_MAX_NUM_SPLITS=100000
```

Theoretically, all 1,000 tasks of the `foreach` in listing 3.9 could be run concurrently. However, remember that each task becomes a process of its own, so it is likely that your operating system wouldn't be too happy managing a thousand active processes running concurrently. Besides, it wouldn't make things any faster because your computer doesn't have 1,000 CPU cores, so most of the time tasks would just idle in the operating system's execution queue.

To power the prototyping loop, the run command in particular, Metaflow includes a built-in workflow scheduler, similar to those listed in section 2.2.3. Metaflow refers to this scheduler as *the local scheduler,* distinguishing it from other schedulers that can orchestrate Metaflow flows, as we will learn in chapter 6. The local scheduler behaves like a proper workflow scheduler: it processes steps in the flow order, translating steps to tasks and executing tasks as processes. Importantly, it can control how many tasks are executed concurrently.

You can use the --max-workers option to control the maximum number of concurrent processes launched by the scheduler. By default, the maximum is 16. For local runs, like the ones we have been executing thus far, there isn't much benefit in setting the value higher than the number of CPU cores in your development environment. Sometimes you may want to lower the value to conserve resources on your computer. For instance, if a task requires 4 GB of memory, you can't run 16 of them concurrently unless your computer has at least 16*4=64 GB of memory available.

You can experiment with different values of max-workers. For instance, compare the execution times

```
# time python wide_foreach.py run --max-num-splits 1000 --max-workers 8
```

versus

```
# time python wide_foreach.py run --max-num-splits 1000 --max-workers 64
```

We will learn more about the effects of max-workers in chapter 5. Figure 3.15 summarizes the two options.

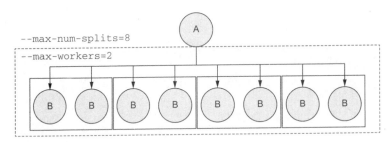

Figure 3.15   The effect of max-num-splits and max-workers

The step A is a foreach split that spawns eight tasks of step B. In this case, if you specified any value lower than 8 for --max-num-splits, the run would crash, because the option controls the maximum width of the foreach branch. All eight tasks will be run regardless of the value of --max-workers, because it controls only concurrency. Here, setting `--max-workers=2` informs the local scheduler to run at most two tasks concurrently, so the eight tasks will be executed as four mini-batches.

Congratulations! You are now able to define arbitrary workflows in Metaflow, manage data flow through branches, and execute even large-scale test cases on your laptop without melting it! With this foundation, we can proceed to building our first real-life data science application.

3.3 Metaflow in Action

As the first actual data science project, Harper suggests that Alex could build an application that predicts the type of a promotional cupcake that a new customer is most likely to enjoy, given a set of known attributes about the customer. Luckily, thus far customers have manually picked their favorites, so their past choices can be used as labels in the training set. Alex recognizes that this is a simple classification task, which shouldn't be too hard to implement using an off-the-shelf machine learning library. Alex starts developing a prototype using Metaflow.

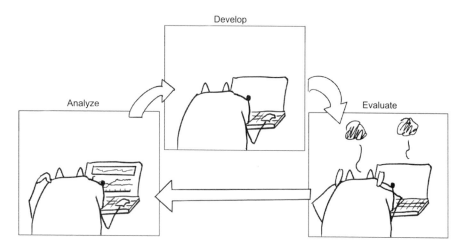

Now that we have covered the basics of Metaflow, we can build a simple but functional data science application. The application creates a dataset for training and testing, trains two different classifier models, and chooses the best performing one. The workflow resembles the one shown in figure 3.10.

Don't worry if you are not an expert in machine learning. The application, like all the other examples in this book, demonstrates the development experience and infrastructure for data science, not modeling techniques. If you are curious about the modeling side of things, you can learn more in the tutorial for *Scikit-Learn* (https://scikit-learn.org/stable/tutorial/), which this example is based on.

We will build the example incrementally through multiple iterations, as we would if we were prototyping a real-life application. This is a good opportunity to put the workstation set up with an IDE, notebooks, and a cloud instance outlined in chapter 2 into action, too.

3.3.1 *Starting a new project*

Starting a new project from scratch can feel overwhelming: You are staring at a blank file in the editor, not knowing how and where to begin. Thinking about the project in terms of a workflow can help. We might have only a faint idea of what needs to be done, but at least we know that the workflow will have a start step in the beginning and an end step in the end.

We know that the workflow will need to get some input data, and it will need to write the results somewhere. We know that some processing will need to happen between start and end, which we can figure out iteratively. Figure 3.16 depicts the approach as a spiral.

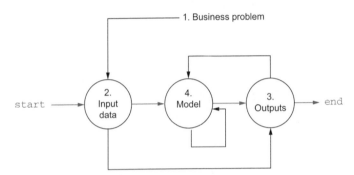

Figure 3.16   **The spiral recipe for starting a new project**

Follow the path indicated by the black arrows when starting a new project:

1 What is the business problem we are trying to solve?
2 What input data can we use? How and where can we read it?
3 What should be the output data? How and where should we write it?
4 What techniques can we use to produce a better output based on the input?

The arrows show the workflow order. You can see that we build the workflow from the outside in. This spiral approach is useful for the following reasons, which have been proven true over many data science projects:

1 It is easy to overlook details of the actual problem we are trying to solve, especially when dealing with a new and exciting model. The problem should dictate the solution, not the other way around.
2 Discovering, verifying, cleaning, and transforming suitable input data is often harder than expected. Better to start the process as early as possible.
3 Integrating the results to the surrounding business systems can also be harder than expected—better to start early. Also, there may be surprising requirements for the outputs, which may inform the modeling approach.

4 Start with the simplest possible modeling approach and get an end-to-end work-flow working with it. After a basic application works, we can measure results in the real business context using real data, which makes it possible to start improving the model rigorously. If the project is successful, this step never ends—there are always ways to improve the model.

Infrastructure should make it easy to follow the spiral recipe. It should support iterative development out of the box. Let's see how the recipe works in practice with Metaflow.

PROJECT SKELETON

Our toy business problem is to classify wine—not exactly cupcakes, but close enough. Conveniently, a suitable dataset is packaged with Scikit-Learn. The example will contain nothing specific to this dataset, so you can use the same template to test other datasets, too.

We start by installing the Scikit-Learn package as follows:

```
# pip install sklearn
```

We will learn more sophisticated ways of handling dependencies in chapter 6, but installing the package system-wide works for now. Following the spiral, we start with a simple skeleton version of the flow that loads only the input data. We will add more functionality in this flow later, as depicted in figure 3.17. The corresponding code is shown in listing 3.10.

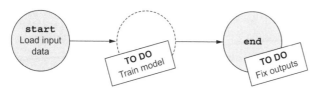

Figure 3.17 The first iteration of `ClassifierTrainFlow`

Listing 3.10   First iteration of `ClassifierTrainFlow`

```
from metaflow import FlowSpec, step

class ClassifierTrainFlow(FlowSpec):

    @step                                          ⫤ Does imports inside
    def start(self):                                 the step code, not at
        from sklearn import datasets                 the top of the file
        from sklearn.model_selection import train_test_split

        X, y = datasets.load_wine(return_X_y=True)  ◁── Loads the dataset
        self.train_data,\
        self.test_data,\
        self.train_labels,\
        self.test_labels = train_test_split(X, y, test_size=0.2, random_state=0)
        print("Data loaded successfully")
        self.next(self.end)
```

Splits the dataset into a test set containing 20% of the rows and a training set with the rest

```
    @step
    def end(self):
        self.model = 'nothingburger'     ◁─────  Dummy placeholder
        print('done')                            for the actual model

if __name__ == '__main__':
    ClassifierTrainFlow()
```

We use functions from Scikit-Learn to load the dataset (load_wine) and split it into a train and test sets (train_test_split). You can look up the functions online for more information, but it is not essential for this example.

> **NOTE**   It is considered a good practice in Metaflow to have import statements inside the steps that use the modules and not at the top of the file. This way imports are executed only when needed.

Save the code to classifier_train_v1.py and run it, as shown here:

```
# python classifier_train_v1.py run
```

The code should execute successfully. To confirm that some data has been loaded, you can execute a command like the following:

```
# python classifier_train_v1.py dump 1611541088765447/start/1
```

Replace the pathspec with a real one that you can copy and paste from the output of the previous command. The command should show that some artifacts have been created, but they are too large to be shown. This is promising—some data was fetched—but it would be nice to actually see the data. We will learn how to do this next.

3.3.2   *Accessing results with the Client API*

In section 3.1.2, we learned that Metaflow persists all instance variables, such as train_data and test_data in listing 3.10, as artifacts in its own datastore. After artifacts have been stored, you can read them programmatically using the Metaflow Client, or the Client API. The Client API is the key mechanism that allows you to inspect results and use them across flows.

> **NOTE**   You can use the Client API to read artifacts. Artifacts can't be mutated after they have been created by a run.

The Client API exposes a hierarchy of containers, which can be used to refer to different parts of a run, that is, an execution of a flow. Besides a single run, the containers allow you to navigate the whole Metaflow universe, including all the runs by you and your colleagues, assuming you use a shared metadata server (more about this in chapter 6). The container hierarchy is depicted in figure 3.18.

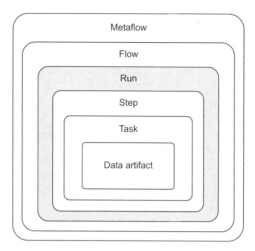

**Figure 3.18   The container
hierarchy of the Client API**

What you can find inside each container follows:

- *Metaflow*—Contains all flows. You can use it to discover flows created by you and your colleagues.
- *Flow*—Contains all runs that have been executed with a `FlowSpec` class.
- *Run*—Contains all steps of a flow whose execution was started during this run. Run is the core concept of the hierarchy, because all other objects are produced through runs.
- *Step*—Contains all tasks that were started by this step. Only `foreach` steps contain more than one task.
- *Task*—Contains all data artifacts produced by this task.
- *Data artifact*—Contains a piece of data produced by task.

Besides acting as containers, the objects contain other metadata, such as the time of creation and tags. Notably, you can also access logs through the `Task` object.

You can instantiate a Client API object in the following three ways:

1 You can instantiate any object directly with a pathspec that uniquely identifies the object in the hierarchy. For instance, you can access the data of a particular run with `Run(pathspec)`, for example, `Run("ClassifierTrainFlow/1611541088765447")`.

2 You can access a child object with the bracket notation. For example, `Run ("ClassifierTrainFlow/1611541088765447")['start']` returns the `start` step.

3 You can iterate over any container to access its children. For instance, `list (Run("ClassifierTrainFlow/1611541088765447"))` returns a list of all `Step` objects that correspond to the given `Run`.

In addition, the Client API contains a number of handy shortcuts for navigating the hierarchy, which we will cover in the coming examples.

INSPECTING RESULTS IN A NOTEBOOK

You can use the Client API anywhere Python is supported: in a script, with an interactive Python interpreter (just execute `python` to open one), or in a notebook. Notebooks are a particularly handy environment for inspecting results because they support rich visualizations.

Let's inspect the results of `ClassifierTrainFlow` from listing 3.10 in a notebook. First, open a notebook either in your editor or by executing `jupyter-notebook` on the command line in the same working directory where you executed your Metaflow runs.

We can use the notebook to inspect the data we loaded earlier. Specifically, we want to inspect an artifact called `train_data` that was created at the `start` step. To do this, copy the lines from the next listing in a notebook cell.

Listing 3.11   Inspecting data in a notebook

```
from metaflow import Flow
run = Flow('ClassifierTrainFlow').latest_run
run['start'].task.data.train_data
```

Using the Client API is all about navigating the object hierarchy shown in figure 3.18. `Flow.latest_run` is a shortcut that gives the latest Run of the given Flow. We use `['start']` to access the desired Step, then the `.task` shortcut to get the corresponding Task object, and `.data` to take a peek at the given artifact. The result should look something like figure 3.19.

```
In [11]:  from metaflow import Flow

 In [9]:  run = Flow('DigitsTrainFlow').latest_run
          run

Out[9]:  Run('DigitsTrainFlow/1611556523340289')

In [10]:  run['start'].task.data.train_data

Out[10]:  array([[ 0.,  0.,  0., ...,  5.,  0.,  0.],
                 [ 0.,  3., 10., ...,  2.,  0.,  0.],
                 [ 0.,  0.,  6., ...,  8.,  0.,  0.],
                 ...,
                 [ 0.,  0.,  5., ...,  0.,  0.,  0.],
                 [ 0.,  0.,  4., ...,  0.,  0.,  0.],
                 [ 0.,  0.,  6., ..., 11.,  0.,  0.]])
```

Figure 3.19   Using the Client API in a notebook

The Client API is meant for easy exploration of data. Here are some exercises you can try by yourself:

- Try inspecting other artifacts created by the run, for example, `train_labels` or `model`.
- Run the flow again. Note how `.latest_run` returns a different Run ID. Now try to inspect a previous run.
- Try exploring other attributes of the objects, for example, `.created_at`. Hint: You can use `help()` to see documentation—try `help(run)`.

ACCESSING DATA ACROSS FLOWS

Figure 3.20 shows how our project has progressed through the first two steps, from the business problem definition to setting up the input data in `ClassifierTrainFlow`. Now that we have confirmed that the input data has been loaded correctly, we can proceed to the next step in our spiral, namely, outputs of the project. We would like to use a model, to be trained by `ClassifierTrainFlow`, to classify unseen data points, in this case, wines.

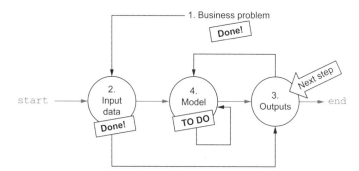

Figure 3.20 Focusing on the outputs of the project next

It is common to split a predictive application like this into two flows: a flow that trains a model and another one that uses the model to provide predictions for unseen data. The split is useful because the prediction or inference flow is often run independently and more frequently than the training flow. For instance, we may train a new model once a day but predict new data once an hour.

Let's prototype a prediction flow, `ClassifierPredictFlow`, to accompany our training flow `ClassifierTrainFlow`. The key idea is to access a previously trained model, which we can do using the Client API. For this example, we accept a data point to be classified as a numerical vector specified as a JSON-typed `Parameter` (see listing 3.4 for a reminder of how it works). As an exercise, you can replace this with a CSV file of data points (see listing 3.5 for an example), which would be a more realistic approach. The first iteration of the flow is shown in the following code listing.

Listing 3.12   First iteration of `ClassifierPredictFlow`

```
from metaflow import FlowSpec, step, Flow, Parameter, JSONType

class ClassifierPredictFlow(FlowSpec):
```

```
         vector = Parameter('vector', type=JSONType, required=True)

         @step
         def start(self):                                      Finds the latest training
             run = Flow('ClassifierTrainFlow').latest_run   ◁── run using the Client API
             self.train_run_id = run.pathspec
             self.model = run['end'].task.data.model       ◁──┐ Obtains the actual
             print("Input vector", self.vector)               │ model object
             self.next(self.end)

         @step
         def end(self):
             print('Model', self.model)

     if __name__ == '__main__':
         ClassifierPredictFlow()
```

Saves the pathspec of the training run for lineage tracking

Save the code to classifier_predict_v1.py, and run it as follows:

```
# python classifier_predict_v1.py run --vector '[1,2]'
```

The run should report the model as "nothingburger" as specified in our project skeleton in listing 3.10. This is the spiral approach in action: we establish and verify connections between all parts of the end-to-end application before worrying about the actual model.

Note how we persist an artifact, `train_run_id`, that includes the pathspec of the training run. We can use this artifact to keep track of *model lineage*: if predictions contain surprises, we can track down the exact training run that produced the model that produced the results.

3.3.3   *Debugging failures*

Now that we have a skeleton flow both for the input and the output of the project, we get to the fun part: defining a machine learning model. As it commonly happens in real-world projects, the first version of the model won't work. We will get to practice how to debug failures with Metaflow.

Another common characteristic of a data science project is that initially we are not sure what kind of model would work best for the given data. Maybe we should train two different types of models and choose the one that performs the best, as we discussed in the context of figure 3.10.

Inspired by the Scikit-Learn tutorial, we train a K-nearest neighbor (KNN) classifier and a support vector machine (SVM). Don't worry if these techniques are not familiar to you—knowing them is not essential for this example. You can refer to the Scikit-Learn tutorial for more information about the models.

Training a model is often the most time-consuming part of a flow, so it makes sense to train models in parallel steps to speed up execution. The next listing expands the earlier `ClassifierTrainFlow` skeleton from listing 3.10 by adding three new steps in the middle: `train_knn` and `train_svm`, which are parallel branches, and `choose_model`, which chooses the best performing model of the two.

Listing 3.13   Almost working `ClassifierTrainFlow`

```
from metaflow import FlowSpec, step

class ClassifierTrainFlow(FlowSpec):

    @step
    def start(self):                          ←——  No changes in the start step
        from sklearn import datasets                besides updated self.next().
        from sklearn.model_selection import train_test_split

        X, y = datasets.load_wine(return_X_y=True)
        self.train_data,\
        self.test_data,\
        self.train_labels,\
        self.test_labels = train_test_split(X, y, test_size=0.2, random_state=0)
        self.next(self.train_knn, self.train_svm)

    @step
    def train_knn(self):                                        ←——
        from sklearn.neighbors import KNeighborsClassifier

        self.model = KNeighborsClassifier()
        self.model.fit(self.train_data, self.train_labels)
        self.next(self.choose_model)

    @step
    def train_svm(self):                                        ←——
        from sklearn import svm

        self.model = svm.SVC(kernel='polynomial')
        self.model.fit(self.train_data, self.train_labels)
        self.next(self.choose_model)

    @step
    def choose_model(self, inputs):                             ←——
        def score(inp):
            return inp.model,\
                   inp.model.score(inp.test_data, inp.test_labels)

        self.results = sorted(map(score, inputs), key=lambda x: -x[1])
        self.model = self.results[0][0]
        self.next(self.end)

    @step
    def end(self):            ←——  The end step is modified to print
        print('Scores:')            out information about the models.
        print('\n'.join('%s %f' % res for res in self.results))

if __name__ == '__main__':
    ClassifierTrainFlow()
```

This line will cause an error: the argument should be 'poly'.

New training steps are added in the middle of the flow.

The two `train_` steps fit a model using training data from the artifacts `train_data` and `train_labels` that we initialized in the `start` step. This straightforward approach works well for small and medium-size datasets. Training larger models using larger amounts of data sometimes requires different techniques, which we will discuss in chapter 7.

The `choose_model` step uses Scikit-Learn's `score` method to score each model using test data. The models are sorted in the descending order (thanks to `-x[1]`, which negates the score in the `sort key`) by their score. We store the best model in the `model` artifact, which will be used later by `ClassifierPredictFlow`. Note that all models and their scores are stored in the `results` artifact, allowing us to inspect the results later in a notebook.

Save the code again to classifier_train.py, and run it as shown here:

```
# python classifier_train.py run
```

Ouch! The code in listing 3.13 fails with an error like `ValueError: 'polynomial' is not in list`.

Errors such as this are an expected part of the prototyping loop. In fact, many features of Metaflow and other similar frameworks are specifically designed to make debugging failures easier. Whenever something fails, you can triage and fix the issue by following the steps suggested in figure 3.21.

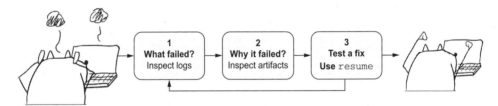

Figure 3.21   The debugging loop

Let's go through the steps one by one.

1. FINDING ERROR MESSAGES IN LOGS

The first step is to try to understand what failed exactly, in particular, which step failed and with what error message. If you are running flows manually, you should see a stack trace on the terminal, prefixed with the step name (`train_svm` in the case of `ClassifierTrainFlow` from earlier).

Especially with wide `foreaches`, it is possible that so many error messages appear on the terminal that reading them becomes hard. In this situation, the `logs` command (see section 3.1.1), which can be used to show the output of an individual task, can come in handy. However, the command is useful only if you know what step or task might have failed. It is not helpful for finding a failed needle in a haystack.

Alternatively, you can use the Client API, for example, in a notebook to comb through all tasks automatically. You can copy and paste the next snippet in a notebook.

Listing 3.14 Accessing logs with the Client API

```
from metaflow import Flow
for step in Flow("ClassifierTrainFlow").latest_run:
    for task in step:
        if not task.successful:
            print("Task %s failed:" % task.pathspec)
            print("-- Stdout --")
            print(task.stdout)
            print("-- Stderr --")
            print(task.stderr)
```

You can replace `Flow().latest_run` with a `Run` object referring to a specific run, such as `Run("ClassifierTrainFlow/1611603034239532")`, to analyze the logs of any past run. A benefit of using the Client API is that you can use the full power of Python to find what you need. For instance, you can see only logs containing a specific term by adding a conditional like

```
if 'svm' in task.stderr:
```

in the code.

2. UNDERSTANDING WHY THE CODE FAILED

Once you have figured out what failed, you can start analyzing why it failed. Often, this step involves double-checking the documentation (and googling!) of the API that failed. Metaflow supports debugging as usual with a few extra tools.

Use the Client API to inspect artifacts that represent the state of the execution before the failure. A major motivation for storing as much information as possible as artifacts is to help reconstruct the state of the flow before a failure. You can load artifacts in a notebook, inspect them, and use them to test hypotheses related to the failure. Learn to love the artifacts!

Metaflow is compatible with debuggers, like the ones embedded in Visual Studio Code and PyCharm. Because Metaflow executes tasks as separate processes, debuggers need a bit of extra configuration to work correctly. You can find instructions for configuring debuggers in popular editors in the online documentation of Metaflow. Once you have a debugger configured, you can use it to inspect the live code as usual.

Commonly, computationally-intensive code involving large amounts of data fails because of resource exhaustion, such as running out of memory. We will learn more about how to deal with these issues in chapter 4.

3. TESTING FIXES

Finally, you can attempt to fix the code. A hugely beneficial feature of Metaflow is that you don't have to restart the whole run from the beginning to test the fix. Imagine having a flow that first spends 30 minutes processing input data, then three hours training a model, and then fails at the end step due to a misspelled name. You can fix the typo in a minute, but it would be frustrating to have to wait for 3.5 hours to confirm that the fix works.

Instead, you can use the resume command. Let's use it to fix the error in listing 3.13. Instead of "polynomial" as an argument to the model in the train_svm step, the argument should be 'poly'. Replace the incorrect line with this:

```
svm.SVC(kernel='poly')
```

You could run the code again with the run command, but instead of doing that, try:

```
# python classifier_train.py resume
```

This command will find the previous run, clone the results of all of the steps that succeeded, and resume execution from the step that failed. In other words, it won't spend time re-executing already successful steps, which in the previous example would have saved 3.5 hours of execution time!

If your attempt to fix the code wasn't successful, you can try another idea and resume again. You can keep iterating on fixes for as long as needed, as depicted by the back arrow in figure 3.21.

In the previous example, resume reuses the results of the train_knn step that succeeded. However, in some cases, fixing one step might necessitate changes in successful steps, too, which then you may want to resume as well. You can do this by instructing resume to resume execution from any step that precedes the failed step, such as:

```
# python classifier_train.py resume train_knn
```

This will force resume to rerun both the train_knn and train_svm steps, as well as any subsequent steps. Failed steps and steps that follow them are always rerun.

By default, resume finds the latest run ID that was executed in the current working directory and uses it as the *origin run*, that is, the run whose results are cloned for the resumed run. You can change the origin run to any other run of the same flow using the --origin-run-id option as follows:

```
# python classifier_train.py resume --origin-run-id 1611609148294496 train_knn
```

This will resume the execution of a past run 1611609148294496 starting from the train_knn step using the latest version of the code in classifier_train.py. The origin run doesn't have to be a failed run, nor does it have to be a run executed by you! In chapter 5, we will use this feature to resume failed production runs locally.

Resumed runs are registered as normal runs. They will get their own unique Run ID, so you can access their results using the Client API. However, you won't be able to change the parameters of the run that was resumed, because changing them might affect the results of tasks to be cloned, which could lead to inconsistent results overall.

3.3.4   *Finishing touches*

After fixing `ClassifierTrainFlow`, it should complete successfully and produce a valid model. To complete `ClassifierPredictFlow` (listing 3.12), add the following line to its end step:

```
print("Predicted class", self.model.predict([self.vector])[0])
```

To test predictions, you have to supply a vector on the command line. The wine dataset contains 13 attributes for each wine. You can find their definitions in the Scikit-Learn's dataset page (http://mng.bz/ZAw9). For instance, here's an example that uses a vector from the training set:

```
# python classifier_predict.py run --vector
➥ '[14.3,1.92,2.72,20.0,120.0,2.8,3.14,0.33,1.97,6.2,1.07,2.65,1280.0]'
```

The predicted class should be 0. Congratulations—we have a working classifier!

What if the classifier produces incorrect results? You can use the combination of Scikit-Learn's model insight tools and the Client API to inspect the models as shown in figure 3.22.

```
In [1]:   from metaflow import Flow
          from sklearn import metrics

In [3]:   run = Flow('ClassifierTrainFlow').latest_run
          run

Out[3]:   Run('ClassifierTrainFlow/1611617953113492')

In [5]:   model, score = run.data.results[0]
          test_data = run['start'].task.data.test_data
          test_labels = run['start'].task.data.test_labels

In [6]:   metrics.plot_confusion_matrix(model, test_data, test_labels)

Out[6]:   <sklearn.metrics._plot.confusion_matrix.ConfusionMatrixDisplay at 0x7f8fe3512610>
```

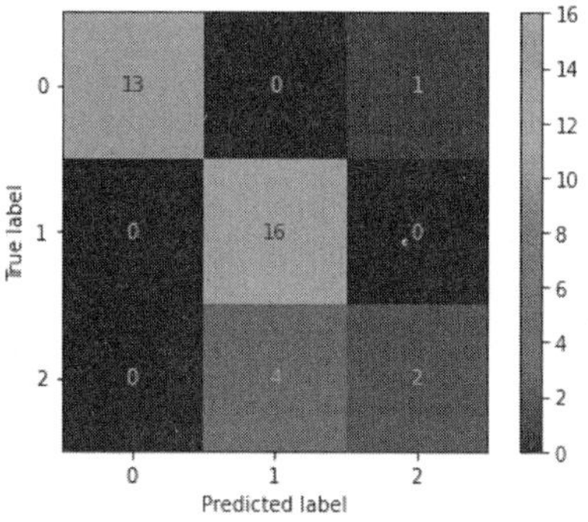

Figure 3.22   A notebook for inspecting a classifier model

Now that the application seems to work end-to-end, let's summarize what we built. The application demonstrates many key concepts of Metaflow and data science applications in general. Figure 3.23 illustrates the overall architecture of our final application.

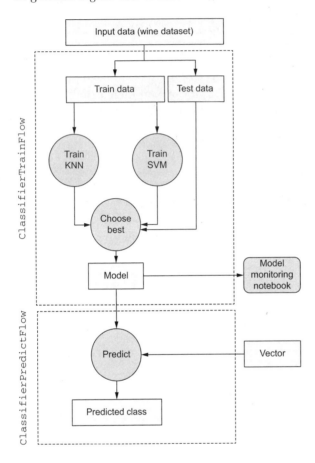

Figure 3.23   The architecture of classifier application

Reading the figure from the top down:

1 We obtained input data and split it into a train and test sets, which were stored as artifacts.
2 We trained two alternative models as parallel branches . . .
3 . . . and chose the best performing one based on the accuracy with test data.
4 The chosen model was stored as an artifact, which we can inspect together with other artifacts in a notebook using the Client API.
5 A separate prediction flow can be called as often as needed to classify new vectors using the trained model.

Although this section featured a minimal toy example (can you imagine that we implemented the application depicted in figure 3.23 in less than 100 lines of code!), the architecture is perfectly valid for production-grade applications. You can replace the input data with your own dataset, improve the modeling steps according to your actual needs, add more details in the notebook to make it more informative, and replace the single `--vector` input for predictions, such as with a CSV file.

The rest of this book answers the following questions (as well as many others) that you are likely to face when you adapt this application, and other data science applications of similar nature, to real-world use cases:

- What if I have to handle a terabyte of input data?
- What if I want to train 2,000 models instead of two and training each model takes an hour?
- After adding the actual modeling and data processing code in the flow, the file is getting quite long. Can we split the code into multiple files?
- Am I supposed to keep running flows manually in production? Can we schedule them to run automatically?
- When I call `Flow().latest_run`, I want to be sure that the latest run refers to my latest run, not to my colleague's latest run. Can we isolate our runs somehow?
- Our production flows run with an older version of Scikit-Learn, but I want to prototype a new model using the latest experimental version of Scikit-Learn—any ideas?

Fear not—the rest of the infrastructure will build seamlessly on the foundation that we laid out in this chapter. If you made it this far, you have a good grasp of the essentials, and you can skip any sections in subsequent chapters that are not relevant for your use cases.

Summary

- How to define workflows with Metaflow:
  - You can define basic workflows in Metaflow and test them on your laptop or a cloud workstation.
  - Metaflow tracks all executions automatically, giving them unique IDs, so your project stays organized throughout iterations without extra effort. Unique IDs allow you to find logs and data related to any task easily.
  - Use artifacts to store and move data within workflows.
  - Parameterize workflows using special artifacts called `Parameter`.
  - Use notebooks with the Client API to analyze, visualize, and compare metadata and artifacts from any past runs.
- How to do parallel computation with Metaflow:
  - Use branches to make your application more understandable by making data dependencies explicit as well as to achieve higher performance.
  - You can run either one operation on multiple pieces of data using dynamic branches, or you can run many distinct operations in parallel using static branches.

- How to develop a simple end-to-end application:
  - It is best to develop applications iteratively.
  - Use `resume` to continue execution quickly after failures.
  - Metaflow is designed to be used with off-the-shelf data science libraries like Scikit-Learn.

Scaling with the compute layer 4

This chapter covers

- Designing scalable infrastructure that allows data scientists to handle computationally demanding projects
- Choosing a cloud-based compute layer that matches your needs
- Configuring and using compute layers in Metaflow
- Developing robust workflows that handle failures gracefully

What are the most fundamental building blocks of all data science projects? First, by definition, *data* science projects use *data*. At least small amounts of data are needed by all machine learning and data science projects. Second, the *science* part of data science implies that we don't merely collect data but we use it for something, that is, we *compute* something using data. Correspondingly, *data* and *compute* are the two most foundational layers of our data science infrastructure stack, depicted in figure 4.1.

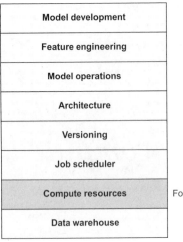

Model development
Feature engineering
Model operations
Architecture
Versioning
Job scheduler
Compute resources
Data warehouse

Focus of this chapter

Figure 4.1   Data science infrastructure stack with the compute layer highlighted

Managing and accessing data is such a deep and broad topic that we postpone an in-depth discussion about it until chapter 7. In this chapter, we focus on the *compute* layer of the stack, which answers a seemingly simple question: After a data scientist has defined a piece of code, such as a step in a workflow, where should we execute it?

A straightforward answer, which we touched in chapter 2, is to execute the task on a laptop or on a cloud workstation. But what if the task is too demanding for the laptop—say it requires 64 GB of memory? Or, what if the workflow includes a `foreach` construct that launches 100 tasks? A single workstation doesn't have enough CPU cores to run them in parallel, and running them sequentially may be inconveniently slow. This chapter proposes a solution: we can execute tasks outside a personal workstation on a cloud-based compute layer.

You have many ways to implement a compute layer. The exact choice depends on your specific requirements and use cases. We will walk through a number of common choices and discuss how you can choose one that fits your needs. We will introduce an easy option, a managed cloud service called *AWS Batch*, to demonstrate the compute layer in action using Metaflow. Building on the foundation laid out in this chapter, the next chapter will provide more hands-on examples.

Fundamentally, we care about the compute layer because it allows projects to handle more computation and more data. In other words, the compute layer allows projects to be more *scalable*. Before we dive deep into the technical details of the compute layer, we start by exploring what scalability, and its sibling concept *performance*, mean, and why and when they matter for data science projects. As you will learn, the topic of scalability is a surprisingly nuanced one. Understanding it better will help you make the right technical choices for your projects.

From the infrastructure point of view, our aspirational goal is to allow data scientists to work on any business problem effectively and efficiently without being constrained by the size of the problem. Many data scientists feel that being able to harness large amounts of data and compute resources gives them superpowers. The feeling is justified: using the techniques introduced in this chapter, a data scientist can harness computing power that would have required a supercomputer a few decades ago with just tens of lines of Python.

A downside of any compute layer is that tasks can fail in surprising ways compared to the tight confines of a laptop. To boost the productivity of data scientists, we want to handle as many errors automatically as possible. When unrecoverable errors happen, we want to make the debugging experience as painless as possible. We will discuss this toward the end of the chapter. You can find all code listings for this chapter at http://mng.bz/d2lN.

4.1   What is scalability?

Alex feels a great sense of pride for having built the first application that trains a model and produces predictions. But Bowie is concerned: as their cupcake business grows, hopefully exponentially, can Alex's Python scripts handle the scale of data that they might be facing in the future? Alex is no scalability expert. Although Bowie's concerns are understandable, Alex feels that they might be a bit premature. Their business is nowhere near such scale yet. In any case, if Alex could choose, the easiest solution would be to get a big enough laptop that can run the existing scripts with bigger data. Instead of spending time reengineering the existing scripts, Alex would rather focus on perfecting the models and understanding the data better.

In this scenario, whose concerns are more valid? Bowie has a valid concern from the engineering point of view: the Python scripts running on Alex's laptop won't be able to handle data of arbitrary size. Alex's concern is valid, too: the scripts may be adequate for their situation today and possibly for the near future. In the business point of view, it might make more sense to focus on the quality of results rather than the scale.

Also, although Alex's dream of handling scalability just by getting a bigger laptop may sound silly and unrealistic from a technical point of view, it is a reasonable idea from a productivity point of view. Theoretically, an infinitely large laptop would make it possible to use existing code without changes, allowing Alex to focus on data science instead of the intricacies of distributed computing.

If you were Harper, a business leader, would you side with Bowie and suggest that Alex reengineer the code to make it scalable, diverting Alex's attention from models, or let Alex focus on improving the models, which may lead to failures in the future? It is not an easy call. Many people would say "it depends." A wise leader might prefer a balanced approach that makes the code just scalable enough so that it won't collapse under realistic loads in the near future and let Alex spend the remaining time on ensuring the quality of the results.

Finding such a balanced approach is the main theme of this section. We want to optimize the productivity of data scientists, business needs, and engineering concerns simultaneously, emphasizing the dimensions that are pertinent for each use case. We want to provide generalized infrastructure that allows each application to be pragmatic, not dogmatic about scalability, striking a balance that fits their specific needs.

4.1.1   *Scalability across the stack*

If you have worked on a data science project that involves demanding training or data processing steps, it is likely that you have heard or thought questions like "Does it scale?" or "Is it fast enough?" In casual discussions, the terms *scalability* and *performance* are used interchangeably, but they are in fact independent concerns. Let's start with the definition of *scalability*:

> *Scalability is the property of a system to handle a growing amount of work by adding resources to the system.*

Let's unpack the definition as follows:

1 Scalability is about *growth*. It doesn't make sense to talk about the scalability of a static system with static inputs. However, you can talk about the *performance* of such a system—more about that soon.

2 Scalability implies that the system has to perform *more work*, for example, handle more data or train a larger number of models. Scalability is not about optimizing the performance for a fixed amount of work.

3 Scalable systems leverage *additional resources* added to the system efficiently. If the system is able to handle more work by adding some resources, such as more computers or more memory, the system is scalable.

Whereas scalability is about growth, *performance* is about the system's capabilities, independent of growth. For instance, we can measure your performance in making an omelet: how quickly can you make one, what's the quality of the result, or how much waste is produced as a side effect? There isn't a single measure of performance or scalability; you have to define the dimension you are interested in.

If you are building a single application, you can focus on making that particular application scalable. When building infrastructure, you need to consider not only how individual applications can be made scalable, but also how the whole infrastructure scales when the number of distinct applications grows. Also, the infrastructure needs to support a growing number of engineers and data scientists who build the applications.

Hence, when building effective infrastructure, we are not only concerned about the scalability of a particular algorithm or a workflow. Rather, we want to optimize scalability across all layers of the infrastructure stack. Remember the following four Vs we introduced in chapter 1:

1 *Volume*—We want to support *a large number* of data science applications.
2 *Velocity*—We want to make it easy and *quick* to prototype and productionize data science applications.
3 *Validity*—We want to make sure that the results are valid and consistent.
4 *Variety*—We want to support *many different kinds* of data science models and applications.

Almost all the Vs are related to scalability or performance. *Volume* is concerned with a growing number of applications, which is the motivation for having generalized infrastructure in the first place. *Velocity* is concerned about speed—speed of code, projects, and people, that is, *performance*. Contrasting *validity* against scalability is such an important topic that it deserves a discussion of its own in the next chapter. Finally, *variety* refers to our ability to work on an increasingly diverse set of use cases, using a diverse set of tools. We shouldn't assume there's a silver bullet solution to scalability, despite what ads may try to tell you. All in all, scalability in its different forms is a fundamental thread that runs throughout this book. Figure 4.2 shows how scalability touches all layers of the data science infrastructure stack.

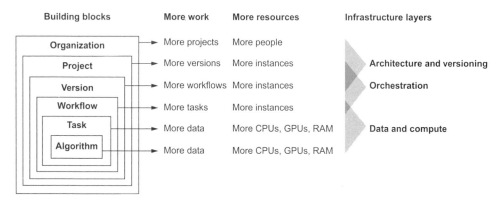

Figure 4.2   Types of scalability across the infrastructure stack

Let's unpack the figure. On the leftmost column, we have the building blocks of a data science application. They form a hierarchy: an algorithm is contained by a task, which is contained by a workflow, and so on. This hierarchy expands the one we covered in the context of Metaflow in figure 3.18.

Each of these building blocks can scale independently. Following our definition, scalability involves two factors: more work and more resources. The More work column shows the type of work that the corresponding building block needs to handle, that is, its major dimension of scalability. The More resources column shows resources we can add to the building block to make it scale. The Infrastructure layers column shows the piece of infrastructure that manages the resources. By design, the layers cooperate, so there's some overlap between their responsibilities. Let's go through the blocks one by one as follows:

- At the core of an application, there's typically *an algorithm* that performs numerical optimization, trains a model, and so forth. Often, the algorithm is provided by an off-the-shelf library like TensorFlow or Scikit-Learn. Usually, the algorithm needs to scale when it must handle a larger amount of data, but other dimensions of scalability exist as well, such as the complexity of the model. Modern algorithms can use all available resources, CPU cores, GPUs, and RAM on the compute instance effectively, so you can scale them by increasing the capacity of the instance.

- The algorithm doesn't run itself. It needs to be called by the user code, such as a Metaflow task. The task is an operating system–level process. To make it scale, you can use various tools and techniques (more about them in section 4.2) to employ all available CPU cores and RAM on the instance. Often, when using highly optimized algorithms, you can outsource all scalability concerns to the algorithm, and the task can stay relatively simple, like we did with Scikit-Learn in section 3.3.

- A data science application or workflow consists of multiple tasks. In fact, a workflow can spawn an arbitrary number of tasks when leveraging data parallelism, such as dynamic branches, which we covered in section 3.2.3. To handle a large number of concurrent tasks, the workflow can fan out the work to multiple compute instances. We will practice these topics later in this chapter and in the next chapter.

- To encourage experimentation, we should allow data scientists to test multiple different *versions* of their workflows, maybe with slightly different variations in data or the model architecture. To save time, it is convenient to be able to test the versions in parallel. To handle multiple parallel workflow executions, we need a scalable workflow orchestrator (see chapter 6) as well as many compute instances.

- It is common for a data science organization to work on a wide variety of data science *projects* concurrently. Each project has its own business goals, represented by bespoke workflows and versions. It is important that we minimize interference among projects. For each project, we should be able to choose the architecture, algorithms, and scalability requirements independently. Chapter 6 will shed more light on the questions of versioning, namespaces, and dependency management.

- It is desirable for the *organization* to be able to scale the number of concurrent projects by hiring more people. Importantly, a well-designed infrastructure can help with this scalability challenge as well, as discussed later.

To summarize, data science projects operate on two resources: people and compute. It is the job of the data science infrastructure to match the two effectively. Scalability is not only about making individual workflows finish faster through more compute resources, but also about enabling more people to work on more versions and more projects, that is, enabling the culture of experimentation and innovation. Because this important aspect is often ignored in technical discussions, we spend a few pages on this topic before diving into technical details.

4.1.2 Culture of experimentation

A modern, effective data science organization encourages data scientists to innovate and experiment with new approaches and alternative implementations relatively freely, without being constrained by the technical limitations of the compute layer. This sounds good on paper, but why isn't it a reality at most organizations today?

The price of compute cycles has gone down drastically over time, partly thanks to the cloud, whereas the price of talented people has gone up. An effective infrastructure can arbitrage this imbalance: we can provide expensive people with easy access to cheap compute resources to maximize their productivity. We want to enable access in a manner that allows the organization itself to scale.

A fundamental reason scaling organizations is hard is the communication overhead. For a group of N people to communicate with one another, they need N^2 lines of communication. In other words, the communication overhead grows quadratically with the number of people. A classic solution is a hierarchical organization, which restricts the information flow to avoid quadratic growth. However, many modern, innovative data science organizations would rather avoid a strict hierarchy and information bottlenecks.

Why do people need to communicate in the first place? Coordination and knowledge sharing are common reasons. Historically, in many environments, accessing shared resources, like computers, has required quite a bit of both. This situation is illustrated in figure 4.3.

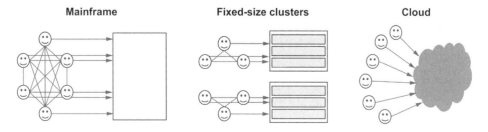

Figure 4.3 Coordinating access to shared compute resources

Imagine you worked at a college computer lab in the 1960s. The lab might have a single computer, a large *mainframe*. Because the compute power and storage was extremely limited, you probably needed to coordinate with all your colleagues who got to use the computer. The communication overhead would be quadratic relative to the number of colleagues. In an environment like this, to maintain your sanity, you would actively try to limit the number of people who could access the computer.

Let's say you worked at a midsize company in the early 2000s. The company has its own datacenter, where it can provision compute resources like *fixed-size clusters* to different teams based on business requirements and guidance from the capacity-planning team. This model is clearly more scalable than the mainframe model, because each individual team can coordinate access to their dedicated resources among themselves. A downside is that the model is quite rigid—provisioning more resources as a team's needs grow could take weeks, if not months.

Today, the *cloud* provides a semblance of unlimited compute capacity. The compute resources are not scarce anymore. Because the paradigm shift has happened quite quickly, it is understandable that many organizations still treat the cloud as if it was a fixed-size cluster or a mainframe. However, the cloud allows us to change that mindset and get rid of the coordination overhead altogether.

Instead of humans carefully coordinating access to a shared, scarce resource among themselves, we can rely on the infrastructure to facilitate relatively open access to the cornucopia of compute resources. A cloud-based compute layer, which we discuss in the next section, makes it easy to execute nearly arbitrary amounts of compute in a cost-effective manner. It allows data scientists to experiment freely and handle large datasets without having to constantly worry about resource overconsumption or interfering with their colleagues work, which is a huge boon for productivity.

As a result, organizations can handle more projects, teams can experiment more effectively, and individual scientists can work on much larger-scale problems. Besides the quantitative change of more scale, the cloud enables a qualitative change as well—we can double-down on the idea of *data scientist autonomy*, as described in section 1.3. Instead of having to coordinate work with machine learning engineers, data engineers, and DevOps engineers, an individual data scientist can drive the prototyping loop and interaction with production deployments all by themselves.

MINIMIZE INTERFERENCE TO MAXIMIZE SCALABILITY

Why has it been so critical to control and coordinate access to compute resources previously? One reason is scarcity. If there are more tasks, workflows, versions, or projects than what the system has capacity to handle, some control is needed. Today, in most scenarios, the cloud provides enough capacity that this argument becomes moot.

Another argument is *fragility*. If an inattentive user can break the system, having a layer of supervision seems like a good idea. Or maybe the system is designed in a way that workloads can easily interfere with each other. This is a valid argument for many systems that are still actively used today. For instance, a single bad query can impact all users of a shared database.

If we want to maximize the scalability of organizations, we want to minimize the communication and coordination overhead between people. Optimally, we want to remove the need for coordination—particularly if coordination is required to avoid breakage. As an infrastructure provider, our goal, at least aspirationally, is to make sure that no workload can break the system or cause adverse side effects for its neighbors.

Because data science workloads tend to be experimental in nature, we can't expect that the workloads themselves are particularly well behaving. Instead, we must make sure that they are properly *isolated*, so even if they fail hard, they have a limited *blast radius*, that is, they cause a minimal amount of collateral damage by interfering with other workloads.

> **SCALABILITY TIP**   Minimizing interference among workloads through isolation is an excellent way to reduce the need for coordination. The less coordination is needed, the more scalable the system becomes.

Luckily, modern cloud infrastructure, container management systems in particular, help us achieve this relatively easily as we will learn in the next section. Other key elements of isolation are versioning, namespaces, and dependency management, which we will cover in more detail in chapter 6.

4.2   *The compute layer*

Instead of a giant laptop, it would be desirable to have a setup that allows Alex to throw any number of tasks, large and small, to a cloud-based compute environment that would automatically scale to handle the tasks. Alex wouldn't have to change the code or care about any other details besides collecting the results. Optimally, the environment would be such that Bowie would have to spend only little time maintaining it.

Let's start with the big picture. Figure 4.4 shows how the layers of the infrastructure stack participate in workflow execution. We use workflows as the user interface to define tasks that need to be executed, but the compute layer doesn't have to care about the workflow per se—it cares only about individual tasks. We will use a workflow

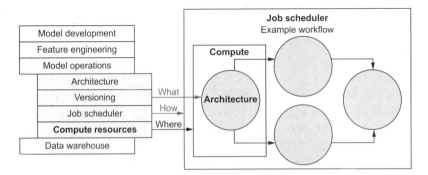

Figure 4.4   The role of the computer layer: Where tasks are executed

orchestrator, the job scheduler layer in our stack, to determine *how* to schedule individual tasks and *when* the workflow should be executed. More about this in chapter 6.

Also, the compute layer doesn't need to care *what* is being computed and *why*—the data scientist answers these questions as they architect the application. This corresponds to the architecture layer in our infrastructure stack. The compute layer needs to decide only *where* to execute a task, in other words, *finding a big enough computer that can execute a task.*

To do its job, the compute layers needs to provide a simple interface: it accepts a task together with resource requirements (how many CPUs or how much RAM the task requires), executes it (maybe after a delay), and allows the requester to query the status of the work performed. Although doing this may seem straightforward, building a robust compute layer is a highly nontrivial engineering challenge. Consider the following requirements:

- The system needs to handle a large number of concurrent tasks, potentially hundreds of thousands or millions of them.
- The system needs to manage a pool of physical computers that are used to execute tasks. Preferably, physical computers can be added and removed from the pool on the fly without causing any downtime.
- Tasks have different resource requirements. The system needs to match each task to a computer that has at least the required amount of resources available. Doing the matching, or *packing*, efficiently at scale is a notoriously hard problem. If you are a theory geek, you can search the phrases *Bin Packing problem* and *Knapsack problem* to learn more about the computational complexity of task placement.
- The system must anticipate that any computer can fail, data centers can catch fire, any task may behave badly or even maliciously, and software has bugs. Regardless, the system shouldn't go down under any circumstances.

For many decades, building large-scale systems that fulfill these requirements was the realm of *high-performance computing* (HPC). The industry was dominated by specialized vendors delivering expensive systems to governments, research institutions, and large companies. Smaller companies and institutions relied on various home-grown solutions that were often brittle and expensive to maintain, at least in terms of person hours.

The advent of public clouds like AWS has changed the landscape drastically. Today, with a few clicks, you can provision a compute layer that operates robustly at the scale of relatively recent supercomputers. Of course, most of us don't need a supercomputer-scale compute layer. The cloud allows us to start small—starting from the capacity of a small laptop—and keep scaling resources elastically as the needs grow. The best part is that you pay only for what you use, which means that a small compute layer used occasionally can be more affordable than a physical laptop of the same size.

The public cloud mostly frees us from having to deal with the previous requirements by ourselves. However, the level of abstraction they provide—answering the question of *where* to execute tasks and executing them for us—is still pretty low-level. To make the compute layer usable and useful for data science workloads, one needs to make a number of architectural choices on top of the interfaces provided by the cloud.

Different systems make different engineering tradeoffs. Some optimize for latency—that is, how fast tasks start—some for the types of computers available, some for the maximum scale, some for high availability, and some for cost. As a result, it is not feasible to think that there is or will be a single universal compute layer.

Also, different workflows and applications have different compute requirements, so it is beneficial for the data science infrastructure to support a selection of compute layers, ranging from local laptops and cloud workstations to special-purpose clusters of GPUs or other hardware accelerators for ML and AI. Fortunately, we can abstract a good amount of this inevitable diversity away. The different flavors of compute layers can adhere to a common interface and architecture, as discussed in the next section.

4.2.1 Batch processing with containers

A system that processes tasks that start, take input data, perform some processing, produce output, and terminate is said to perform *batch processing*. Fundamentally, the compute layer we describe here is a batch-processing system. In our workflow paradigm, illustrated in figure 4.5, a step in the workflow defines one or more tasks that are executed as batch jobs.

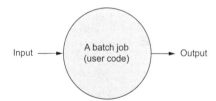

Figure 4.5 A batch job, for instance, a task in a workflow

> ### Batch processing vs. stream processing
> An alternative to batch processing, which deals with discrete units of computation, is *stream processing*, which deals with a continuous stream of data. Historically, the vast majority of ML systems and applications requiring high-performance computing have been based on batch processing: data goes in, some processing is done, and results come out.

(continued)

During the past decade, increased sophistication of applications has driven demand for stream processing, because it allows results to update with a much lower delay, say, in a matter of seconds or minutes, in contrast to batch jobs, which are typically run at most once an hour. Today, popular frameworks for stream processing include Kafka, Apache Flink, or Apache Beam. In addition, all major public cloud providers offer stream-processing-as-a-service, such as Amazon Kinesis or Google Dataflow.

Fortunately, the choice is not either/or. You can have an application use the two paradigms side by side. Many large-scale ML systems today, such as the recommendation system at Netflix, are mostly based on batch processing with some stream processing included for components that need to update frequently.

A major benefit of batch jobs is that they are easier to develop, easier to reason about, and easier to scale than their streaming counterparts. Hence, unless your application really requires stream processing, it is reasonable to start with a workflow of batch jobs as discussed in this chapter. We will discuss more advanced use cases that require real-time predictions and/or stream processing in chapter 8.

A batch job consists of arbitrary code defined by the user. In the case of Metaflow, each task, defined by a step method, becomes a single batch job. For instance, the `train_svm` step in the next code sample, copied from listing 3.13, would be a batch job.

Listing 4.1   An example batch job

```
@step
def train_svm(self):
    from sklearn import svm          ⤛——— An external dependency
    self.model = svm.SVC(kernel='poly')
    self.model.fit(self.train_data, self.train_labels)
    self.next(self.choose_model)
```

A job scheduler takes this snippet, which we call *user code*, sends it to the compute layer for execution, and waits for the execution to complete before continuing to the next steps in the workflow. Easy enough!

One more important detail: in this example, the user code refers to an external dependency, the `sklearn` library. If we tried to execute the user code in a pristine environment that doesn't have the library installed, the code would fail to execute. To execute successfully, the batch job needs to package both the user code as well as any dependencies that the code requires.

Today, it is common to package user code and its dependencies as a *container image*. A *container* is a way to provide an isolated execution environment inside of a physical computer. Providing such "virtual computers" inside a physical computer is called *virtualization*. Virtualization is beneficial, because it allows us to pack multiple tasks inside a single physical computer while letting each task operate as if they occupied a whole computer by themselves. As discussed in section 4.1.1, providing strong isolation like this allows each user to focus on their work, boosting productivity, because they don't have to worry about interfering with anyone else's work.

WHY DO CONTAINERS MATTER?

A container allows us to package, ship, and isolate the execution of batch jobs. To give a real-world analogue, consider that a container is a physical container, like an animal crate. First, you can visit an animal shelter (*a container registry*) and find a prepackaged feral cat in a crate (*a container image*). The container contains both a cat (*user code*) as well as its dependencies, for example, food (*libraries*). Next, you can deploy the container (or several) in your house (*a physical computer*). As each cat is *containerized*, they can't cause damage to your house or to each other. Without containerization, the house would likely turn into a battleground.

From the point of view of a compute layer, the user code submitted to the system resembles feral cats. We shouldn't assume that any code behaves well. Although we don't assume that data scientists are malevolent per se, it gives users great freedom to experiment and overall peace of mind if they know that, in the worst case, they can break only their own code. The system guarantees that no matter what, the user can never interfere with production systems or tasks of their colleagues. Containers help to provide such a guarantee. Figure 4.6 summarizes the discussion.

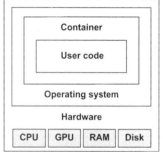

Figure 4.6   Container on a compute instance

> **PRODUCTIVITY TIP**   Containers boost productivity by granting users the freedom to experiment without having to fear that they can break something by accident or interfere with their colleagues' work. Without containers, a rogue process can hog an arbitrary amount of CPU or memory or fill the disk, which can cause failures in neighboring but unrelated processes on the same instance. Compute- and data-intense machine learning processes are particularly prone to these issues.

The outer box represents a single computer. The computer provides certain fixed hardware, such as CPU cores, possibly GPUs, RAM (memory), and disk. The computer runs an operating system, such as Linux. The operating system provides mechanisms to execute one or more isolated containers. Inside the container, which provides all the necessary dependencies, the user code is executed.

A number of different container formats exist, but today, *Docker* is the most popular one. Creating and executing Docker containers isn't particularly hard (if you are curious, see https://docs.docker.com), but we shouldn't assume that data scientists package their own code as containers manually. Packaging every iteration of the code as a separate container image would just slow down their prototyping loop and thus hurt their productivity.

Instead, we can containerize their code and dependencies automatically, as exemplified by Metaflow in section 4.3. Under the hood, the data science infrastructure can leverage containers to their fullest potential without ever having to surface containers, a technical detail, directly to the user. The data scientist can merely declare the code they want to execute (steps in workflow) and dependencies they require. We will cover dependency management in detail in chapter 7.

FROM A CONTAINER TO A SCALABLE COMPUTE LAYER

Now we have learned that we can define a batch job as a container that contains the user code and its dependencies. However, when it comes to scalability and performance, containerization doesn't benefit anything by itself. Executing a piece of code inside a Docker container on your laptop isn't any faster or more scalable than executing it as a normal process.

Scalability is what makes a compute layer interesting. Remember the definition of scalability: a scalable system is able to handle a growing amount of work by adding resources to the system. Correspondingly, a compute layer is scalable if it can handle more tasks by adding more computers, or instances, to the system. This is the exact feature that makes cloud-based compute layers so appealing. They are able to increase or decrease the number of physical computers handling tasks automatically based on demand. Figure 4.7 illustrates how a scalable compute layer works in the context of workflow orchestration.

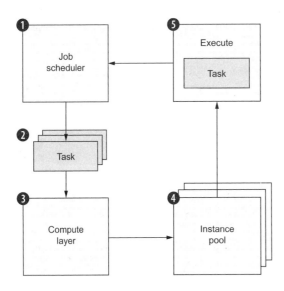

Figure 4.7   Task-scheduling cycle

Let's go through the figure step by step:

1   A job scheduler, like Metaflow's internal scheduler invoked with the run command, begins executing a workflow. It walks through the steps of the workflow in order. Each step yields one or more tasks, as we learned in chapter 3.

2 The scheduler submits each task to the compute layer as an independent batch job. In the case of a `foreach` branch, a large number of tasks may be submitted to the compute layer simultaneously.

3 The compute layer manages a pool of instances as well as a queue of tasks. It tries to match tasks to computers that have suitable resources to execute the task.

4 If the compute layer notices way more tasks exist than available resources, it can decide to increase the number of instances in the instance pool. In other words, it provisions more computers to handle the load.

5 Eventually, a suitable instance is found where a task can be executed. The task is executed in a container. Once the task has finished, the scheduler is notified, so it can proceed to the next step in the workflow graph and the cycle restarts.

Note that the compute layer can handle incoming tasks from any number of workflows concurrently. As illustrated here, the compute layer gets a constant stream of task submissions. It executes them without caring *what* the task does internally, *why* it needs to be executed, or *when* it was scheduled. Simply, it finds an instance *where* to execute the task.

To make the steps 3–5 happen, the compute layer needs several components internally. Figure 4.8 shows the high-level architecture of a typical compute layer.

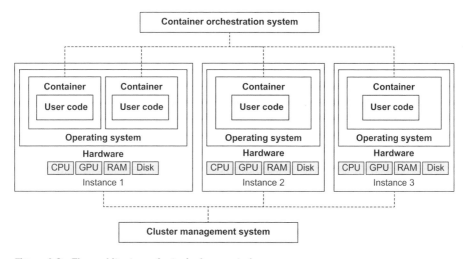

Figure 4.8   The architecture of a typical compute layer

- In the middle, we have a pool of instances. Each instance is a computer like the one depicted in figure 4.6. They are machines that execute one or more concurrent containers, which in turn are used to execute the user code.

- At the bottom, a component called the *cluster management system* is depicted. This system is responsible for managing the pool of instances. In this case, we have a pool of three instances. The cluster management system adds and removes instances from the pool as the demand—the number of pending tasks—increases or decreases, or as instances are detected to be unhealthy. Note that the instances don't need to have uniform hardware. Some instances may have more CPUs, some more GPUs, and some more RAM.

- At the top, we have a *container orchestration system*. It is responsible for maintaining a queue of pending tasks and placing and executing them in containers on the underlying instances. It is the job of this system to match tasks, based on their resource requirements, to the underlying instances. For instance, if a task requires a GPU, the system needs to find an instance with a GPU in the underlying pool and wait until the instance is not busy executing previous tasks before placing the task on the instance.

Fortunately, we don't need to implement container orchestration systems or cluster management systems from scratch—they are notoriously complex pieces of software. Instead, we can leverage existing battle-hardened compute layers provided either as open source or as managed services by the cloud providers. We list a selection of such systems in the next section. As you evaluate these systems by yourself, it is good to keep these figures in mind, because they can help you understand how the systems work under the hood and motivate various tradeoffs that the systems have needed to make.

4.2.2 Examples of compute layers

Let's go through some compute layers that you can start using today. Now that you have a basic understanding of how these systems work under the hood, you can appreciate that each system optimizes for slightly different characteristics—no system is perfect at everything. Luckily, we are not limited to a single choice. Our infrastructure stack can provide different compute layers for different use cases.

Figure 4.9 illustrates why supporting multiple compute layers can come in handy. Don't worry if you don't recognize the names of the compute layers in the figure—Spark, AWS Batch, SageMaker, and AWS Lambda. We will cover them in more detail soon.

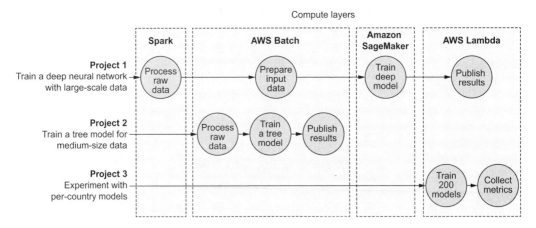

Figure 4.9   Examples of workflows that use multiple compute layers

The figure depicts the following three projects, each with a workflow of their own:

- Project 1 is a large, advanced project. It needs to process a large amount of data, say a text corpus of 100 GB, and train a massive deep neural network model based on it. First, large-scale data processing is performed with Spark, which is optimized for the job. Additional data preparation is performed on a large instance managed by AWS Batch. Training a large-scale neural network requires a compute layer optimized for the job. We can use Amazon SageMaker to train the model on a cluster of GPU instances. Finally, we can send a notification that the model is ready using a lightweight task launched on AWS Lambda.

- Project 2 trains a decision tree using a medium-scale, say, 50 GB, dataset. We can process data of this scale, train a model, and publish results, on standard CPU instances with, say, 128 GB of RAM. A general-purpose compute layer like AWS Batch can handle the job easily.

- Project 3 represents an experiment conducted by a data scientist. The project involves training a small model for each country in the world. Instead of training 200 models sequentially on their laptop, they can parallelize model training using AWS Lambda, speeding up their prototyping loop.

As figure 4.9 illustrates, the choice of compute layers depends on the type of projects you will need to support. It is a good idea to start with a single, general-purpose system like AWS Batch and add more options as the *variety* of use cases increases.

Crucially, although the infrastructure stack may support multiple compute layers, we can limit the amount of complexity exposed to the user. All we have to do is to write workflows in Python, maybe using specific libraries in the case of specialized compute layers. Also keep in mind the ergonomics of the two loops, prototyping and production deployments, which we discussed in section 2.1. Typically, prototyping requires quick iterations with smaller amounts of data, whereas production deployments emphasize scalability.

How should one evaluate the strengths and weaknesses of different compute layers? You can pay attention to the following features:

- *Workload support*—Some systems are specialized for certain types of workloads, for example, big data processing or managing multiple GPUs, whereas others are general purpose, working with any types of tasks.

- *Latency*—Some systems try to guarantee that tasks start with a minimal delay. This is convenient during prototyping, when it might be frustrating to wait for minutes for a task to start. On the other hand, startup latency doesn't make any difference to scheduled nightly runs.

- *Workload management*—How does the system behave when it receives more tasks than what it can deploy to the instance pool immediately? Some systems start declining tasks, some add them to a queue, and some may start killing, or *pre-empting*, already executing tasks so that higher priority tasks can execute in their place.

- *Cost-efficiency*—As described earlier, a key lever to cost optimization is utilization. Some systems are much more aggressive at driving up utilization whereas others take a laxer approach. Also, the granularity of billing in cloud systems varies: some bill by the hour, some by the second, and some even by the millisecond.
- *Operational complexity*—Some systems are rather easy to deploy, debug, and maintain, whereas others may require constant monitoring and upkeep.

Next, we list a few popular choices for compute layers. The list is not exhaustive by any means, but it gives you an idea how to compare relative benefits of various options.

KUBERNETES

Kubernetes (often abbreviated as K8S) is the most popular open source container orchestration system today. It originates from Google, which had been operating a similar compute layer internally for years. You can deploy K8S in a private data center, even on your laptop (search for *Minikube* for instructions), but it is commonly used as a managed cloud service, such as Elastic Kubernetes Service (EKS) by AWS.

Kubernetes is an extremely flexible system. Consider it a toolkit for building your own compute layer or a microservice platform. With flexibility comes a great deal of complexity. Kubernetes and services around it evolve quickly, so it takes expertise and effort to stay up-to-date with its ecosystem. However, if you need an infinitely extensible foundation for a custom compute layer, Kubernetes is a great starting point. See table 4.1 for characteristics of Kubernetes.

Table 4.1   Characteristics of Kubernetes

Workload support	General-purpose.
Latency	K8S is primarily a container orchestration system. You can configure it to work with various cluster management systems that handle scalability. The choice has a major effect on startup latency of tasks.
Workload management	Although K8S provides only minimal workload management out of the box, you can make K8S work with any work queue.
Cost efficiency	Configurable; depends mainly on the underlying cluster management system.
Operational complexity	High; K8S has a steep learning curve. Managed cloud solutions like EKS make this a bit easier.

AWS BATCH

AWS provides a number of container orchestration systems: ECS (Elastic Container Service), which runs containers on top of EC2 instances that you can manage; Fargate, which is a serverless orchestrator (i.e., no EC2 instances to be managed); and EKS, which manages containers with Kubernetes. AWS Batch is a layer on top of these systems, providing batch-compute capabilities for the underlying orchestrators, in particular, a task queue.

AWS Batch is one the simplest solutions for operating a cloud-based compute layer. You define the types of instances you want to have in your instance pool, called the *compute environment*, and one or more *job queues*, which store pending tasks. After this, you can start submitting tasks to the queue. AWS Batch takes care of provisioning instances, deploying containers, and waiting until they have executed successfully. A downside of this simplicity is that AWS Batch provides only a limited amount of extensibility and configurability for more advanced use cases. You can read more about AWS Batch in section 4.3. See table 4.2 for characteristics of AWS Batch.

Table 4.2   Characteristics of AWS Batch

Workload support	General purpose.
Latency	Relatively high; as the name implies, AWS Batch is designed for batch processing with the assumption that startup latencies are not a major issue. A task may take anywhere between seconds to a few minutes to start.
Workload management	Includes a built-in work queue.
Cost efficiency	Configurable; you can use AWS Batch with any instance types without extra cost. It also supports *spot instances*, which are considerably cheaper than normal, on-demand EC2 instances. Spot instances may be terminated abruptly, but this is usually not an issue for batch jobs that can be retried automatically.
Operational complexity	Low; relatively simple to set up and almost maintenance-free.

AWS LAMBDA

AWS Lambda is often characterized as a *function-as-a-service*. Instead of defining servers or even containers, you simply define a snippet of code, a task in our parlance, which AWS Lambda executes when a triggering event occurs without any user-visible instances. Since December 2020, AWS Lambda allows tasks to be defined as container images, which makes AWS Lambda a valid option for a compute layer.

Compared to AWS Batch, the biggest difference is that Lambda doesn't expose the instance pool (aka compute environment) at all. Although tasks can request additional CPU cores and memory, options for resource requirements are much more limited. This makes AWS Lambda most suitable for lightweight tasks with modest requirements. For instance, you can use Lambda to process small to medium amounts of data rapidly during prototyping. See table 4.3 for characteristics of AWS Lambda.

Table 4.3   Characteristics of AWS Lambda

Workload support	Limited to lightweight tasks with a relatively short runtime.
Latency	Low; AWS Lambda is optimized for tasks that start in a second or less.
Workload management	In the *Asynchronous Invocation* mode, Lambda includes a work queue. The queue is more opaque than the job queue of AWS Batch, for instance.
Cost efficiency	Great; tasks are billed by millisecond, so you truly pay only for what you use.
Operational complexity	Very low; simple to set up and practically maintenance-free.

APACHE SPARK

Apache Spark is a popular open source engine for large-scale data processing. It differs from the previously listed services by relying on a specific programming paradigm and data structures to achieve scalability. It is not suitable for executing arbitrary containers. However, Spark allows code to be written in JVM-based languages, Python, or SQL, so it can be used to execute arbitrary code as long as the code adheres with the Spark paradigm. You can deploy a Spark cluster on your own instances, or you can use it as a managed cloud service, for example, through AWS Elastic MapReduce (EMR). See table 4.4 for characteristics of Apache Spark.

Table 4.4   Characteristics of Apache Spark

Workload support	Limited to code written with Spark constructs.
Latency	Depends on the underlying cluster management policy.
Workload management	Includes a built-in work queue.
Cost efficiency	Configurable, depending on the cluster setup.
Operational complexity	Relatively high; Spark is a sophisticated engine that requires specialized knowledge to operate and maintain.

DISTRIBUTED TRAINING PLATFORMS

Although you can use a general-purpose compute layer like Kubernetes or AWS Batch to train sizable models, especially when powered by GPU instances, a specialized compute layer is needed to train the largest deep neural network models, such as for massive-scale compute vision. It is possible to build such a system using open source components, such as using a project called *Horovod*, which originated from Uber, or *TensorFlow distributed training*, but many companies may find it easier to use a managed cloud service such as distributed training by SageMaker or Google's Cloud TPU.

These systems are optimized for very specific workloads. They employ large clusters of GPUs, and sometimes custom hardware, to speed up tensor or matrix computations required by modern neural networks. If your use cases require the training of massive-scale neural networks, having such a system as a part of your infrastructure may be necessary. See table 4.5 for characteristics of distributed training platforms.

Table 4.5   Characteristics of distributed training platforms

Workload support	Very limited; optimized for training massive-scale models.
Latency	High; optimized for batch processing.
Workload management	Task-specific, opaque workload management.
Cost efficiency	Typically very expensive.
Operational complexity	Relatively high, although cloud services are considerably easier to operate and maintain compared to on-premise solutions.

LOCAL PROCESSES

Historically, most data science workloads have been executed on personal computers, such as on laptops. A modern take on this is a cloud workstation, as described in section 2.1.2. Although a workstation is not a compute layer in the sense of what is shown in figure 4.8, it can be used to execute processes and containers, and for most companies, it is the first compute layer supported in the absence of other systems.

When viewed from the point of view of compute, a personal workstation has one major upside and one major downside. The upside is that the workstation provides a very low latency and, hence, a quick prototyping loop. The downside is that it doesn't scale. Therefore, workstations are best used for prototyping, while all heavy lifting is offloaded to other systems. See table 4.6 for characteristics of local processes.

Table 4.6 Characteristics of local processes

Workload support	General purpose.
Latency	Very low; processes start instantly.
Workload management	Configurable, nothing by default.
Cost efficiency	Cheap, but the amount of compute is limited.
Operational complexity	Moderate; workstations need maintenance and debugging. Providing and maintaining a uniform environment for all users can be hard.

COMPARISON

As the variety of use cases supported by the infrastructure increases, so does the need to provide compute layers optimized for particular workloads. As the provider of the data science infrastructure, you need to evaluate what systems should be included in your stack, when, how, and why.

To help you with the task, table 4.7 provides a rough summary of the main strengths and weaknesses of the systems we covered. One star indicates that the system doesn't excel at a particular area, two stars indicates acceptable behavior, and three stars indicate that the system shines at the task.

Table 4.7 Comparison of a selection of common compute layers

	Local	Kubernetes	Batch	Lambda	Spark	Distributed training
Excels at general-purpose compute	☆ ☆	☆ ☆ ☆	☆ ☆ ☆	☆ ☆	☆ ☆	☆
Excels at data processing	☆ ☆	☆ ☆	☆ ☆	☆	☆ ☆ ☆	☆ ☆
Excels at model training	☆ ☆	☆ ☆	☆ ☆	☆	☆ ☆	☆ ☆ ☆
Tasks start quickly	☆ ☆ ☆	☆ ☆	☆ ☆	☆ ☆ ☆	☆ ☆	☆

Table 4.7   Comparison of a selection of common compute layers *(continued)*

	Local	Kubernetes	Batch	Lambda	Spark	Distributed training
Can queue a large number of pending tasks	☆	☆ ☆	☆ ☆ ☆	☆ ☆ ☆	☆ ☆ ☆	☆ ☆
Inexpensive	☆ ☆ ☆	☆ ☆	☆ ☆	☆ ☆ ☆	☆ ☆	☆
Easy to deploy and operate	☆ ☆	☆	☆ ☆	☆ ☆ ☆	☆	☆
Extensibility	☆ ☆ ☆	☆ ☆ ☆	☆ ☆	☆	☆ ☆	☆ ☆

Don't get too concerned about individual assessments—they can be challenged. The main take-home message is that there isn't a single system that can handle all workloads optimally. Also, if you compare columns, you can see that some systems overlap in functionality (e.g., Kubernetes and Batch) versus others that are more complementary (e.g., Lambda and Spark).

As an exercise, you can create your own version of table 4.7. Include features that matter to you as rows and systems that you may consider using as columns. The outcome of the exercise should be a complementary set of systems that match the needs of data science projects you need to support. If you are unsure, a good starting point follows.

> **RULE OF THUMB**   Provide one general-purpose compute layer like Kubernetes or AWS Batch for heavy lifting and a low-latency system like local processes for prototyping. Use more specialized systems as required by your use cases.

No matter what systems you end up choosing, make sure they can be integrated seamlessly into a cohesive user experience for the data scientist. From the user's point of view, it is a nuisance that multiple systems need to exist in the first place. However, pretending that this is not the reality often leads to even more friction and frustration.

In section 4.3, we get to roll up our sleeves and start practicing compute layers and scalability for real using Metaflow. Also, the section will serve as an example of how multiple compute layers can happily coexist behind a single cohesive user interface.

Considering cost

Many companies are concerned about the cost of using a cloud-based compute layer. When it comes to cost optimization, a key observation is that an idling instance costs the same amount of money as an instance that performs work. Hence, a key lever to minimize cost is to maximize *utilization*, that is, the share of time spent on useful work. We define utilization as the percentage of the total uptime that is used to execute tasks, as shown here:

$$utilization = \frac{time\ used\ to\ excecute\ tasks}{total\ instance\ uptime}$$

Now, assuming that we can't affect the time that it takes for tasks to execute, we achieve the minimal cost when the time used to execute tasks equals the total instance uptime, that is, we attain 100% utilization. In practice, utilization of a typical compute layer is far from 100%. In particular, old-school data centers might have utilization of 10% or less. You can drive up utilization in the following two ways:

- You can minimize the *total instance uptime* by shutting down instances as soon as tasks finish.
- You can maximize *time used to execute tasks*, for example, by sharing the instances with as many projects and workflows as possible, so the instances don't run out of work while they are up.

You can use the compute layer described in this section to achieve both goals. First, it is easy to shut down cloud-based instances when they run out of work automatically, so you pay only for the exact set of tasks that you need to execute. Second, thanks to strong isolation guarantees provided by virtualization and containerization, you can safely share the same instances with multiple teams. This increases the number of tasks submitted to the compute layer, which drives up utilization.

It is good to keep in mind that in most cases, the hourly cost of a data scientist is much higher than that of an instance. Any opportunity to save data scientist hours by using more instance hours is usually worth it. For instance, it might be more cost effective to run experiments using naive, inefficient code, knowing that it requires more instance hours, rather than spend many days or weeks optimizing the code by hand.

4.3 The compute layer in Metaflow

Alex's laptop sounds like a jet engine every time it executes a model-training step. Instead of buying noise-canceling headphones, it seems like a smart idea to leverage the cloud for demanding compute tasks. Bowie helps Alex to configure Metaflow to use AWS Batch as a compute layer, which enables Alex to prototype workflows locally and execute them in the cloud with a click of a button. For Alex, this feels like a silent superpower!

Metaflow supports pluggable compute layers. For instance, you can execute lightweight tasks locally but offload heavy data processing and model training to a cloudbased compute layer. Or, if your company has an existing container management system like Kubernetes, you can use it as a centralized compute layer instead of having to operate a separate system for data science.

By default, Metaflow uses local processes running on your personal workstation as the compute layer. This is convenient for quick prototyping. To demonstrate how local processes work in practice, take a look at the next listing.

Listing 4.2 Local processes as a compute layer

```
from metaflow import FlowSpec, step
import os

global_value = 5      ◁——— Initializes a global variable

class ProcessDemoFlow(FlowSpec):

    @step
    def start(self):                      Modifies the value of
        global global_value               the global variable
        global_value = 9
        print('process ID is', os.getpid())
        print('global_value is', global_value)
        self.next(self.end)

    @step
    def end(self):
        print('process ID is', os.getpid())
        print('global_value is', global_value)

if __name__ == '__main__':
    ProcessDemoFlow()
```

Save the code to process_demo.py. Here, `global_value` is initialized as a module-level global variable. Its value is changed from 5 to 9 in the `start` step. The value is printed again in the `end` step. Can you guess whether the value printed at the `end` step will be 5 or 9? Execute the following code to test it:

```
# python process_demo.py run
```

The value is 9 at the `start` step as expected. The value at the `end` step is 5. If `start` and `end` were ordinary Python functions executed sequentially, the value would stay as 9. However, Metaflow executes each task as a separate local process, so the value of `global_value` is reset back to 5 at the beginning of each task. If you want to persist the change across tasks, you should store `global_value` as a data artifact in `self`, instead of relying on a module-level variable. You can also see that the process ID is distinct for the two tasks, which wouldn't be the case if the tasks were executed by the same

Python process. Executing Metaflow tasks as independent units of computation matters for the compute layer.

> **NOTE**   Metaflow tasks are isolated units of computation that can be executed on various compute layers. A single workflow can farm out tasks to many different compute layers, using the most suitable system for each task.

Metaflow's approach to computation is based on the following three assumptions on the nature of generalized infrastructure for data science:

- *Infrastructure needs to support a wide variety of projects that have varying needs for computation.* Some need lots of memory on a single instance, some need many small instances, and some require specialized hardware like GPUs. There is no one-size-fits-all approach for all compute needs.
- *A single project or a workflow has varying needs for computation.* Data processing steps may be IO-intensive, possibly requiring lots of memory. Model training may require specialized hardware. Small coordination steps should execute quickly. Although technically, one could run the whole workflow on the largest possible instances, in many cases, it would be cost prohibitive. It is better to give the user an option to *adjust the resource requirements for each step individually.*
- *The needs of a project vary over its lifetime.* It is convenient to prototype the first version quickly using local processes. After this, you should be able to test the workflow at scale using more compute resources. Finally, the production version should be both robust and scalable. You are ready to make different kinds of tradeoffs when it comes to latency, scalability, and reliability at different points in the project's life cycle.

Next, we show how you can set up infrastructure that works this way using local processes and AWS Batch.

4.3.1   Configuring AWS Batch for Metaflow

AWS Batch provides a convenient abstraction for use cases that need to execute units of computation—jobs—to completion without any user intervention. Under the hood, AWS Batch is a relatively simple job queue that offloads the management of compute resources to other AWS services.

You can find step-by-step installation instructions for AWS Batch in Metaflow's online documentation (see the Administrator's Guide to Metaflow at metaflow.org). You can use either the provided *CloudFormation* template that sets up everything for you with a click of a button, or you can follow the manual installation instructions if you want to set it up by yourself, possibly customizing the setup as you go.

After you have configured AWS Batch for Metaflow, data scientists can use it in a straightforward manner, as described in the next section, without having to worry about implementation details. However, it is beneficial for the operators of the system to understand the high-level architecture, which is depicted in figure 4.10.

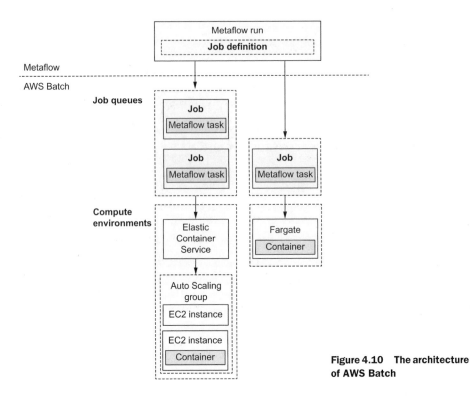

Figure 4.10   The architecture of AWS Batch

Let's start with the following four concepts, boldfaced in figure 4.10, which you see mentioned often in the documentation of AWS Batch:

- *Job definition*—Configures the execution environment for a job: CPU, memory, environment variables, and so on. Metaflow takes care of creating a suitable job definition for each step automatically, so you don't have to worry about it.

- *Job*—A single unit of computation. Each job is executed as an independent container. Metaflow maps each Metaflow task to a single Batch job automatically. Hence, in the context of AWS Batch, we can talk about tasks and jobs interchangeably.

- *Job queue*—Jobs are sent to a job queue to wait for execution. A queue may have any number of tasks pending. You can set up multiple queues, for example, to distinguish between low-priority and high-priority jobs. The figure illustrates two queues: one with two jobs and another with one job.

- *Compute environment*—A pool of compute resources where jobs get executed. AWS Batch can manage the compute environment for you, adding more compute resources to the environment when the queue gets longer, or you can manage the compute environment by yourself. Thanks to autoscaling compute environments, AWS Batch can be used as an elastically scaling compute layer. The figure illustrates two compute environments: one using EC2 instances and another one using Fargate. A detailed discussion follows later.

When you start a Metaflow run that uses AWS Batch, the execution proceeds as follows:

1   Prior to starting any tasks, Metaflow makes sure that the correct job definitions are created on Batch.

2   Metaflow creates *a job package* that includes all Python code corresponding to the flow. The package is uploaded to the datastore in AWS S3 (more about job packages in chapter 7).

3   Metaflow walks through the DAG. When it encounters a task that should be executed on Batch, it submits a job request to a job queue that has been configured in advance.

4   If there aren't enough compute resources in the compute environment and it hasn't reached its maximum limit, Batch scales up the environment.

5   Once resources are available, Batch schedules a job for execution.

6   The Metaflow task encapsulated in a Batch job is executed in a container.

7   Metaflow polls the status of the task. Once Batch reports that the task has completed successfully, Metaflow continues executing subsequent tasks, going back to step 3, until the end step has completed.

CHOOSING THE COMPUTE ENVIRONMENT

If you let AWS Batch manage the compute environment for you, it will use a container management service provided by AWS like *Elastic Container Service* (ECS) to execute containers. Behind the scenes, ECS launches EC2 compute instances using a managed Auto Scaling group, which is a set of instances that can grow and shrink automatically on demand basis. These instances will show up in the EC2 console like any other instances in your account.

A benefit of using ECS is that you can use any EC2 instance types in your compute environment. You can choose a selection of instances with a high amount of memory, many CPU cores, or even multiple GPUs. ECS schedules the job on the most suitable instance that can accommodate its resource requirements.

Alternatively, you can choose to use *AWS Fargate* as a compute environment. Fargate doesn't use EC2 instances directly, so you won't see any instances on your EC2 dashboard. Also, you can't choose the instance types directly. Fargate finds a suitable instance for each job automatically based on its resource requirements. However, the range of supported resource requirements is more limited compared to ECS. The biggest benefit of Fargate over ECS is that jobs start quicker.

As a yet another alternative, you can manage your *own pool of EC2 instances* behind ECS. Though this route is more tedious, it allows the maximum degree of customizability. You can set up the instances however you want. This approach may be useful if you have special security or compliance requirements.

From the point of view of a Metaflow task, the compute environment doesn't make any difference. Once a suitable instance is found for the task, it is executed in a container using the same container image, regardless of the environment. As mentioned earlier in this chapter, the compute layer determines only *where* the task is executed.

Finally, here is the good news for cost-conscious companies: you don't pay any premium for using the instances with AWS Batch. You pay only the per-second price of the EC2 instances of your choosing, which makes AWS Batch one of the most cost-effective compute layers. You can reduce costs even further by using *Spot Instances*, which are the same EC2 instances but come with a caveat that they may be interrupted at any point in time. This isn't as bad as it sounds—Metaflow can retry interrupted jobs automatically using the @retry decorator (see section 4.4). The main cost is an extra delay in execution time when interruptions occur.

CONFIGURING THE CONTAINER

Whereas the compute environment determines how hardware like CPUs and memory are made available for jobs, the container settings determine the software environment for Metaflow tasks. Pay attention to the two settings described next.

First, you must configure the security profile, aka *an IAM role*, that determines what AWS resources Metaflow tasks are allowed to access. At the minimum, they need to be able to access an S3 bucket, which is used as the Metaflow datastore. If you use AWS Step Functions for job scheduling as described in chapter 6, you must allow access to a DynamoDB table as well. If you use the provided CloudFormation template, a suitable IAM role is created for you automatically.

Second, optionally, you can configure *the default container image* that is used to execute tasks. The image determines what libraries are available for the task by default. For instance, if you have set up cloud-based workstations as described in chapter 2, you can use the same image for workstations and task execution (you'll learn more about dependency management in chapter 6). If you don't specify any image, Metaflow chooses a generic Python image.

THE FIRST RUN WITH AWS BATCH

To use AWS Batch with Metaflow, you need to complete the following steps. The steps are executed automatically by the provided CloudFormation template, but it is not hard to complete them manually. See Metaflow's online documentation for detailed instructions.

First, start by installing and configuring awscli, a command-line tool for interacting with AWS, as follows:

```
# pip install awscli
# aws configure
```

If you don't use the CloudFormation template but you want to configure AWS Batch manually, execute the following steps:

1. Initialize an S3 bucket for the Metaflow datastore.
2. Set up a VPC network for the compute environment.
3. Set up a Batch job queue.
4. Set up a Batch compute environment.
5. Set up an IAM role for containers.

After you have either executed the CloudFormation template or the previous manual steps, run `metaflow configure aws` to configure the services for Metaflow. That's it!

After you have completed these steps, let's test that the integration works. Execute the following command, which runs process_demo.py from listing 4.2 using AWS Batch:

```
# python process_demo.py run --with batch
```

The command should produce output that looks like this:

```
[5c8009d0-4b48-40b1-b4f6-79f6940a6b9c] Task is starting (status SUBMITTED)...
[5c8009d0-4b48-40b1-b4f6-79f6940a6b9c] Task is starting (status RUNNABLE)...
[5c8009d0-4b48-40b1-b4f6-79f6940a6b9c] Task is starting (status STARTING)...
[5c8009d0-4b48-40b1-b4f6-79f6940a6b9c] Task is starting (status RUNNING)...
[5c8009d0-4b48-40b1-b4f6-79f6940a6b9c] Setting up task environment.
```

The example omits Metaflow's standard prefix on each line to save space. The long ID in square brackets is the AWS Batch job ID corresponding to the Metaflow task. You can use it to cross-reference Metaflow tasks and AWS Batch jobs visible in the AWS Console UI.

The first four "Task is starting" lines indicate the state of the task in the Batch queue as follows:

- *SUBMITTED*—The task is entering the queue.
- *RUNNABLE*—The task is pending in the queue, waiting for a suitable instance to become available.
- *STARTING*—A suitable instance was found, and the task is starting on it.
- *RUNNING*—The task is running on the instance.

It is typical for tasks to stay in the RUNNABLE state for up to a few minutes as AWS Batch scales up the compute environment. If the compute environment has reached its maximum size, the task needs to wait for previous tasks to finish, which might take even longer.

The run should complete successfully after a few minutes. Its output should be similar to that of the local run. Although this first run doesn't seem like much—the run using AWS Batch completes *slower* than the local run due to the overhead of launching tasks in the cloud—you now have a virtually unlimited amount of processing power at your disposal! We will put this capability into action in the next section and even more in the next chapter.

> **Troubleshooting RUNNABLE tasks**
>
> A common symptom of AWS Batch not working correctly is a task that seems to be stuck in the RUNNABLE state forever. A number of things may cause this, all related to the compute environment (CE).

(continued)

If you are using an EC2-backed compute environment (not Fargate), you can check what instances have been created in the CE by logging on to the EC2 console and searching for the tag `aws:autoscaling:groupName:` followed by the CE name. Based on the returned list of instances, you can troubleshoot the issue as follows:

- *No instances*—If no instances were returned, it is possible that your CE is unable to launch instances of the desired type. For instance, your AWS account may have reached its limit of EC2 instances. You may be able to see why there are no instances by checking the status of the Auto Scaling group named after the CTE.
- *Some instances but no other tasks running*—It is possible that your task requests resources, for example, memory or GPUs using the `@resources` decorator discussed later, can't be fulfilled by the CE. In this case, the task will stay in the queue forever. You can kill the task (job) in the AWS Batch console.
- *Some instances and other running tasks*—Your cluster may be busy processing the other tasks. Wait for the other tasks to finish first.

If the problem persists, you can contact the online support of Metaflow.

4.3.2 *@batch and @resources decorators*

Now that you have configured AWS Batch, you can choose to execute any run in the cloud just by using `run --with batch`. All features of Metaflow, such as artifacts, experiment tracking, parameters, and the Client API, work in exactly the same way as before when using AWS Batch as the compute layer.

As discussed at the beginning of this chapter, the main motivation for having a cloud-based compute layer is scalability: you can handle more demanding compute, more data, than what you can handle at a local workstation. Let's test scalability in practice. The next code listing presents a flow that tries to allocate 8 GB of memory by creating a string of eight billion characters.

> **Listing 4.3   A flow that uses a lot of memory**

```
from metaflow import FlowSpec, step

LENGTH = 8_000_000_000          ◁——————   Sets the length to eight billion
                                           characters. The underscores are
class LongStringFlow(FlowSpec):            added to aid readability.

    @step
    def start(self):
        long_string = b'x' * LENGTH    ◁——   Tries to allocate
        print("lots of memory consumed!")    8 GB of memory
        self.next(self.end)

    @step
    def end(self):
```

```
        print('done!')

if __name__ == '__main__':
    LongStringFlow()
```

Save the code in long_string.py. If you have at least 8 GB of memory available on your workstation, you can start by running the flow locally like so:

```
# python long_string.py run
```

The run may fail with a `MemoryError` if not enough memory is available. Next, let's execute the flow on Batch as follows:

```
# python long_string.py run --with batch
```

Metaflow executes the task on Batch with its default memory settings, which provide less than 8 GB of memory for the task. The task is likely to fail with a message like the following:

```
AWS Batch error:
OutOfMemoryError: Container killed due to memory usage This could be a
    transient error. Use @retry to retry.
```

Although you can't easily increase the amount of memory on your workstation like on a laptop, we can request more memory from our compute layer. Rerun the flow as follows:

```
# python long_string.py run --with batch:memory=10000
```

The `memory=10000` attribute instructs Metaflow to request 10 GB of memory for every step of the flow. The unit for `memory` is megabytes, so 10,000 MB equals 10 GB. Note that if your compute environment doesn't provide instances with at least 10 GB of memory, the run will get stuck in the RUNNABLE state. Assuming suitable instances can be found, the run should complete successfully.

This is vertical scaling in action! We are able to request instances with specific hardware requirements simply on the command line. Besides memory, you can request a minimum number of CPU cores with the `cpu` attribute or even GPUs with the `gpu` attribute. For instance, the next command-line code provides every task with 8 CPU cores and 8 GB of memory:

```
# python long_string.py run --with batch:memory=8000,cpu=8
```

Because data science workloads tend to be resource hungry, it is very convenient to be able to test code and scale workloads this easily. You can request any amount of memory that is supported by EC2 instances in your compute environment. As of the writing of this book, the largest instance has 768 GB of memory, so with a suitable compute environment, you can request up to --with batch:memory=760000, leaving 8 GB for the operating system on the instance.

You can handle quite sizable datasets with this much memory. If you are worried about cost, consider that the function executes for less than a minute. Even if you executed the task on the largest and the most expensive instance, it would cost only about 10 cents, thanks to per-second billing. You could push the cost down even further by using spot instances in your compute environment as discussed earlier.

SPECIFYING RESOURCE REQUIREMENTS IN THE CODE

Let's say you share long_string.py with a colleague. Following the previous approach, they would need to know the specific command-line code, run --with batch: memory=10000, to run the flow successfully. We know that the amount of memory is a strict requirement—the flow won't succeed without at least 8 GB of memory—so we can annotate the requirement directly in the code by adding

```
@batch(memory=10000)
```

above @step for the start step. Remember to add from metaflow import batch at the top of the file, too.

Now, your colleagues can run the flow with the run command without any extra options. As an additional benefit, only the start step annotated with the @batch decorator is executed on AWS Batch, and the end step, which doesn't have any resource requirements, executes locally. This illustrates how you can use multiple compute layers rather seamlessly in a single workflow.

> **NOTE** The --with option is shorthand for assigning a decorator, like batch, to every step on the fly. Hence run --with batch is equivalent to adding the @batch decorator manually to every step of the flow and executing run. Correspondingly, any attributes added after a colon, like batch:memory=10000, map directory to the arguments given to the decorator, like @batch(memory=10000).

Now imagine that you share a version of long_string.py that is annotated with @batch publicly. A stranger wants to execute the code, but their compute layer is Kubernetes, not AWS Batch. Technically, they should be able to execute the flow successfully on a 10 GB instance provided by Kubernetes. For situations like this, Metaflow provides another decorator, @resources, which lets you specify the resource requirements in a compute layer–agnostic manner. You could replace the @batch decorator with the following:

```
@resources(memory=1000)
```

However, in contrast to @batch, the @resources decorator doesn't determine which compute layer is used. If you run the flow without options, it executes locally, and @resources has no effect. To run the flow with AWS Batch, you can use run --with batch without any attributes. The @batch decorator knows to pick the resource requirements from @resources. Correspondingly, the stranger could run the flow on their Kubernetes cluster using something akin to run --with kubernetes.

It is considered a best practice to annotate steps that have high resource requirements with @resources. If the step code can't succeed without a certain amount of
memory or, say, a model training step won't execute quickly enough without a certain
number of CPU or GPU cores, you should make the requirement explicit in the code.
In general, it is preferable to use @resources rather than @batch or other compute-
layer-specific decorators when possible, so anyone running the flow can choose a suitable compute layer on the fly.

We will go through many more examples of scalability using @resources and AWS
Batch in the next chapter. Before getting there, though, we will cover an inevitable
fact of life: surprises happen, and things don't always work as expected.

4.4   Handling failures

*One day, the cloud-based compute environment at Caveman Cupcakes started behaving
erratically. Alex's tasks that had been running flawlessly for weeks started failing without a
clear reason. Bowie noticed that the cloud provider's status dashboard reported "increased
error rates." Alex and Bowie couldn't do anything about the situation besides wait for the
cloud to fix itself and trying to limit the impact to their production workflows.*

Alex's and Bowie's scenario is hardly hypothetical. Although the cloud provides a
rather practical illusion of infinite scalability, it doesn't always work flawlessly. Errors in
the cloud tend to be stochastic in nature, so the higher the number of concurrent
jobs, the more likely you will hit a random transient error. Because these errors are an
inevitable fact of life, we should be prepared to handle them proactively. It is useful to
distinguish between two types of failures, shown here:

1 *Failures in the user code*—The user-written code in steps may contain bugs, or it
   may call other services that behave erroneously.
2 *Platform errors*—The compute layer that executes the step code may fail for a
   number of reasons, such as hardware failures, networking failures, or inadver-
   tent changes in configuration.

Failures that happen in the user code, such as failed database connections, can be typically handled inside the user code itself, which distinguishes the first category from the second. There's nothing you can do in your Python code to recover from, say, the underlying container management system failing. Consider the example shown in the next code listing.

Listing 4.4 Failing due to division by zero

```
from metaflow import FlowSpec, step

class DivideByZeroFlow(FlowSpec):

    @step
    def start(self):
        self.divisors = [0, 1, 2]
        self.next(self.divide, foreach='divisors')

    @step
    def divide(self):
        self.res = 10 / self.input        ◁──┐ This will fail with
        self.next(self.join)                   ZeroDivisionError.

    @step
    def join(self, inputs):
        self.results = [inp.res for inp in inputs]
        print('results', self.results)
        self.next(self.end)

    @step
    def end(self):
        print('done!')

if __name__ == '__main__':
    DivideByZeroFlow()
```

Save the flow in zerodiv.py and run it as follows:

```
# python zerodiv.py run
```

The run will fail and throw an exception, `ZeroDivisionError: division by zero`. This is clearly a logical error in the user code—accidental division-by-zero errors are quite common in numerical algorithms. If we suspect that a block of code may fail, we can use Python's standard exception-handling mechanisms to handle it. Fix the divide step as follows:

```
    @step
    def divide(self):
        try:
            self.res = 10 / self.input
        except:
            self.res = None
        self.next(self.join)
```

After the fix, the flow will run successfully. Following this pattern, it is advisable to try to handle as many exceptions in the step code as possible for the following reasons:

1   If you consider possible error paths while writing the code, you can also implement the paths for error recovery, for example, what exactly should happen when Zero-DivisionError is raised. You can implement a "plan B" as a part of your logic, because only you know the right course of action in your particular application.

2   It is faster to recover from errors in the user code. For instance, if you are calling an external service, such as a database, in your step, you can implement a retry logic (or rely on the database client's built-in logic) that retries a failed connection without having to retry the whole Metaflow task, which incurs a much higher overhead.

Even if you follow this advice, tasks may still fail. They may fail because you didn't consider some unforeseen error scenario, or they may fail due to a platform error, say, a data center may catch fire. Metaflow provides an additional layer of error handling that can help in these scenarios.

4.4.1   Recovering from transient errors with @retry

The flow presented in listing 4.4 fails predictably every time it is executed. Most platform errors and some errors in the user code behave more randomly—for instance, AWS Batch may schedule a task to be executed on an instance with failing hardware. The compute environment will eventually detect the hardware failure and decommission the instance, but this may take a few minutes. The best course of action is to retry the task automatically. There's a good chance that it won't hit the same transient error again. The following listing simulates an unlucky transient error: it fails every other second.

Listing 4.5   Retry decorator

```python
from metaflow import FlowSpec, step, retry

class RetryFlow(FlowSpec):

    @retry
    @step
    def start(self):
        import time
        if int(time.time()) % 2 == 0:       # The conditional is true,
            raise Exception("Bad luck!")     # depending on the second
        else:                                # when the line is executed.
            print("Lucky you!")
        self.next(self.end)

    @step
    def end(self):
        print("Phew!")

if __name__ == '__main__':
    RetryFlow()
```

Save the flow in retryflow.py and run it as follows:

```
# python retryflow.py run
```

You should see a bunch of exceptions printed out when the execution hits the "Bad luck" branch. Thanks to the @retry flag, any failure in the start step causes it to be retried automatically. It is likely that the execution will eventually succeed. You can rerun the flow a few times to see the effect.

A key feature of @retry is that it also handles platform errors. For instance, if a container fails on AWS Batch for any reason, including the data center catching fire, the @retry decorator will cause the task to be retried. Thanks to the sophistication of the cloud, there's a good chance that a retried task will be rerouted to a nonburning data center and will succeed eventually.

Note that when you start a run on your workstation, the run will succeed only if the workstation stays alive for the whole duration of the execution. The retrying mechanism of the @retry decorator is implemented by the DAG scheduler, which in the case of local runs is the built-in scheduler of Metaflow. If the scheduler itself dies, it will take all executions down with it, which is not desirable for business-critical production runs. Addressing this shortcoming is a key topic of chapter 6, which focuses on production deployments. We will learn how we can make the scheduling itself tolerant against platform errors.

Escaping a burning data center

How can a task succeed even if a data center is on fire? AWS has the concept of Availability Zones (AZ), which are physically-distanced data centers, limiting the impact radius of any real-world disaster. In the case of AWS Batch, a compute environment may launch instances on multiple AZs transparently, so when instances become unavailable in one AZ, instances in another AZ can take over.

AVOIDING RETRIES SELECTIVELY

You may wonder why the user has to worry about the @retry decorator—couldn't Metaflow retry all tasks automatically? A challenge is that steps may have side effects. Imagine a step that increments a value in a database, for instance, the balance of a bank account. If the step crashes after the increment operation and was retried automatically, the bank account would get credited twice.

If you have a step like this that shouldn't be retried, you can annotate it with a decorator @retry(times=0). Now, anyone can run the flow simply by executing

```
# python retryflow.py run --with retry
```

which will add a @retry decorator to every step, but the step with @retry(times=0) will be retried zero times. You can also use the times attribute to adjust the number of retries to be higher than the default. In addition, you can specify another attribute, `minutes_between_retries`, which tells the scheduler to wait for the given number of minutes between retries.

> **RECOMMENDATION** Whenever you run a flow in the cloud, such as when using AWS Batch, it is a good idea to run it `--with retry`, which takes care of transient errors automatically. If your code shouldn't be retried, annotate it with `@retry(times=0)`.

4.4.2 Killing zombies with @timeout

Not all errors manifest themselves as exceptions or crashes. A particularly annoying class of errors causes tasks to get stuck, blocking the execution of a workflow. In machine learning, this situation can happen with numerical optimization algorithms that converge very slowly with a particular dataset. Or, you may call an external service that never returns a proper response, causing the function call to block forever.

You can use the `@timeout` decorator to limit the total execution time of a task. The next listing simulates a task that takes too long to complete occasionally. When that happens, the task is interrupted and retried.

Listing 4.6 Timeout decorator

```python
from metaflow import FlowSpec, timeout, step, retry
import time

class TimeoutFlow(FlowSpec):

    @retry
    @timeout(seconds=5)          ◁─┐ The task will time
    @step                             │ out after 5 seconds.
    def start(self):
        for i in range(int(time.time() % 10)):   ◁─┐ This block of code
            print(i)      #B                           │ takes from 0–9
            time.sleep(1)      #B                       │ seconds to execute.
        self.next(self.end)

    @step
    def end(self):
        print('success!')

if __name__ == '__main__':
    TimeoutFlow()
```

Save the flow in timeoutflow.py and run it as follows:

```
# python timeoutflow.py run
```

If you get lucky, the run may succeed on the first try. You can try again to see `@timeout` and `@retry` in action. The `start` task is interrupted after 5 seconds. When this happens, `@retry` takes care of retrying the step. Without `@retry`, the run would crash when a timeout occurs. Besides `seconds`, you can set the timeout value as `minutes` or `hours` or a combination of thereof.

4.4.3   *The decorator of last resort: @catch*

Machine learning workflows can power business-critical systems and products used by millions of people. In critical production settings like this, the infrastructure should ensure that workflows degrade gracefully in the presence of errors. In other words, even when errors happen, they shouldn't cause the whole workflow to fail.

Let's say you have a step in a workflow that connects to a database to retrieve fresh data used to update a model. One day, the database is down, and the connection fails. Hopefully, your step has the `@retry` decorator, so the task is retried a few times. What if the database outage persists over all retries? When the maximum number of retries has been reached, the workflow crashes. Not great.

Or consider another real-life scenario: a workflow trains a separate model for each country of the world using a 200-way `foreach`. The input dataset contains a daily batch of events by country. One day, the model training step fails for Andorra, because there were no new events produced for the small country. Naturally, the data scientist should have included quality checks for data before it is fed into the model, but this issue never occurred during testing, so it is an understandable human error. Also in this case, the whole workflow failed, leading to a few hours of frantic troubleshooting.

Metaflow provides a decorator of last resort, `@catch`, which is executed after all retries have been exhausted. The `@catch` decorator swallows all errors produced by the task, allowing execution to continue, even if the task failed to produce anything useful. Crucially, `@catch` allows the creation of an indicator artifact, so subsequent steps can handle failed tasks gracefully.

Let's apply the `@catch` decorator to our previous example, `DivideByZeroFlow` from listing 4.4. Let's call the new version, shown here, `CatchDivideByZeroFlow`. Structurally, this example is similar to the Andorra example: it has a `foreach` with a faulty task that shouldn't cause the whole workflow to fail.

Listing 4.7   Demonstrating the @catch decorator

```
from metaflow import FlowSpec, step, retry, catch

class CatchDivideByZeroFlow(FlowSpec):

    @step
    def start(self):
        self.divisors = [0, 1, 2]
        self.next(self.divide, foreach='divisors')

    @catch(var='divide_failed')
    @retry(times=2)
    @step
    def divide(self):
        self.res = 10 / self.input
```

Retrying is futile in this case. → `@retry(times=2)`

Creates an indicator artifact, divide_failed, which is set to True if the task fails → `@catch(var='divide_failed')`

```
        self.next(self.join)

    @step
    def join(self, inputs):
        self.results = [inp.res for inp in inputs if not inp.divide_failed]
        print('results', self.results)
        self.next(self.end)

    @step
    def end(self):
        print('done!')

if __name__ == '__main__':
    CatchDivideByZeroFlow()
```

Save the flow in catchflow.py and run it as follows:

```
# python catchflow.py run
```

Notice that one of the `divide` tasks fails and is retried, and finally `@catch` takes over and prints an error message about `ZeroDivisionError`. Crucially, `@catch` allows the execution to continue. It creates an artifact, `divide_failed=True`, for the task that failed—you can name the artifact freely. The subsequent `join` step uses this artifact to include results only from tasks that succeeded. If you are curious, you can run the flow with AWS Batch as follows:

```
# python catchflow.py run --with batch
```

You can see that the decorators will work the same way, regardless of the compute layer.

Use `@catch` to annotate complex steps, such as model training or database access, which may fail in unforeseeable ways but whose failure shouldn't crash the whole workflow. Just make sure that you handle missing results gracefully in the subsequent steps.

SUMMARY: HARDENING A WORKFLOW GRADUALLY

This section introduced four mechanisms for dealing with failures proactively: Python's standard `try-except` construct, `@retry`, `@timeout`, and `@catch`. These decorators are optional, acknowledging the fact that handling failures isn't the first priority when prototyping a new project. However, as the project matures, you can use the decorators to harden your workflow and make it more production-ready. You can gradually harden your workflows in this order:

1 Use `try-except` blocks in your code to handle obvious exceptions. For instance, you can wrap any data processing in `try-except` because the data may evolve in surprising ways. Also, it is a good idea to wrap any calls to external services like databases and possibly include use case–specific retrying logic.

2 Use @retry to handle any transient platform errors, that is, any random issues happening in the cloud. In particular, using @retry is crucial with workflows that launch many tasks, such as using foreach. You can execute any flow robustly in the cloud simply by using run --with batch --with retry. For extra safety, you can make @retry more patient—for example, @retry(times=4, minutes_between_retries=20) gives the task over one hour to succeed.

3 Use @timeout to annotate steps that may get stuck or that may execute for an arbitrarily long time.

4 Use @catch to prevent complex steps, for example, model training or data processing, from crashing the whole workflow. Remember to check the indicator artifact created by @catch in subsequent steps to account for missing results.

Summary

- Effective infrastructure helps data science scale at many levels. It allows you to handle more people, more projects, more workflows, more compute, and more data.

- Versioning and isolation helps to scale people and the number of projects, because less coordination is required. A cloud-based compute layer allows data scientists to scale the compute resources, allowing them to handle more demanding models and more data.

- Use a cloud-based compute layer to handle more tasks (horizontal scalability) and larger tasks (vertical scalability) than what a single workstation can handle.

- Leverage existing container management systems to execute isolated units of batch computation in the cloud.

- The infrastructure can support a selection of compute layers, each optimized for a specific set of workloads.

- An easy way to get started with cloud-based compute is to use AWS Batch with Metaflow.

- Use the @resources decorator to annotate the resource requirements for each step.

- Metaflow provides three decorators that allow you to gradually harden your workflows against failures: @retry, @catch, and @timeout.

Practicing scalability
and performance

This chapter covers

- Developing a realistic, performant data science project iteratively
- Using the compute layer to power demanding operations, such as parallelized model training
- Optimizing the performance of numerical Python code
- Using various techniques to make your workflows more scalable and performant

In the previous chapter, we discussed how scalability is not only about being able to handle more demanding algorithms or handle more data. At the organizational level, the infrastructure should scale to a large number of projects developed by a large number of people. We recognized that scalability and performance are separate concerns—you can have one without the other. In fact, the different dimensions of scalability and performance can be at odds with each other.

Imagine having an experienced engineer implementing a highly optimized, high-performance solution in the C++ language. Although the solution scales at the technical level, it is not very scalable organizationally if no one else in the team knows the C++ language. Conversely, you can imagine a very high-level ML solution that builds models with a click of a button. Everyone knows how to click the button, but the solution is too inflexible to scale to a wide variety of projects and is unable to handle large amounts of data. This chapter advocates for a pragmatic approach to scalability and performance that features the following points:

1   Effective infrastructure needs to handle a wide variety of projects, so instead of a one-size-fits-all solution, it can provide an easy-to-use toolbox of robust ways to achieve *good enough* scalability and performance.

2   To address organizational scalability—we want to make projects understandable by the widest number of people—our main tool is *simplicity*. People have a limited cognitive bandwidth, so overengineering and overoptimizing incur a real human cost.

We can summarize these two points in a simple mnemonic, presented in figure 5.1.

Here, *simple* refers to the idea that anyone new to the project can view the source code and quickly comprehend how it works. *Complex* is the opposite: it takes a lot of effort to understand how the code works. *Slow* means that the solution may hit scalability limits, and it makes people wait for results longer than what would be optimal, but, nonetheless, *it works*. *Fast* means that the solution is perfectly adequate for the problem at hand: it scales well enough and provides results quickly enough.

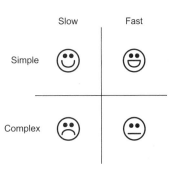

Figure 5.1   A pragmatic approach to scalability

By optimizing for simplicity, we also optimize for the *validity* of results. As Tony Hoare, a famous computer scientist, has said, "There are two ways to write code: write code so simple there are obviously no bugs in it, or write code so complex that there are no obvious bugs in it." Because data science applications tend to be statistical by nature—bugs and biases can lurk in models without producing clear error messages—you should prefer simple code over non-obvious bugs. Only when it is absolutely clear that the application requires higher scalability or performance should you increase its complexity proportionally.

In this chapter, we will develop a realistic ML application that has nontrivial requirements for scalability and performance. We practice developing a data science application incrementally, always striving for the simplest possible approach that is correct and delivers the desired results. In other words, we want to stay on the first row of figure 5.1. We will demonstrate a number of approaches that help in achieving good enough scalability and performance.

We will use the tools introduced in the previous chapter: vertical and horizontal scalability using the compute layer. Although it is possible to run the examples on a laptop, they are more fun and realistic if you have a cloud-based compute layer like AWS Batch set up as instructed earlier. As before, we will use Metaflow to demonstrate the concepts and get hands-on practice, but you can adapt the examples to other frameworks because the general principles are framework-agnostic. You can find all code listings for this chapter at http://mng.bz/yvRE.

5.1 Starting simple: Vertical scalability

We will start building a realistic ML application that uses natural language processing (NLP) to model and analyze Yelp reviews. We will follow the spiral approach, introduced in chapter 3 and depicted in figure 5.2, to develop the application.

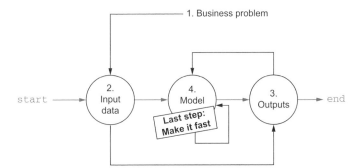

Figure 5.2 The spiral approach with optimizations as the last step

Although the topic of this chapter is *practicing scalability*, the following steps precede any scalability concerns, as shown in figure 5.2:

1 Understand the business problem thoroughly. Maybe the business context allows us to go with a simpler, less scalable, but more obviously correct solution.
2 Get access to relevant input data, and make sure that the data is correct and will stay correct. Also, estimate the scale and the growth rate of the data.
3 Make sure that the results of your application can be consumed properly and that they produce the desired action.
4 Develop a small-scale but functional prototype that allows you to test the application with real data to ensure its correctness end-to-end.

To implement these steps, we can choose the simplest scalability approach that allows us to build a functional prototype. The first version doesn't have to be particularly scalable. We can fix it later, after we have confirmed that everything else works. To quote Kent Beck, an accomplished software architect, our order of priorities should be: "Make it work, make it right, make it fast."

5.1.1   *Example: Clustering Yelp reviews*

Let's start with a hypothetical business problem: a startup wants to build a better version of Yelp, the review site. To understand the strengths and weaknesses of Yelp's product, they want to analyze the different types of reviews that people have contributed to Yelp.

We don't have any existing taxonomy of reviews, so instead of classifying reviews to known buckets, we will rely on *unsupervised learning*, which, in this case, groups Yelp reviews to sets of similar-looking reviews. You can read more about unsupervised learning and document clustering in the documentation for Scikit-Learn at http://mng.bz/M5Mm.

To accomplish the task, we can access a publicly available corpus of 650,000 Yelp reviews. The dataset is publicly available by Fast.AI (https://course.fast.ai/datasets) and is conveniently hosted in AWS S3 by the Registry of Open Data on AWS at https://registry.opendata.aws/fast-ai-nlp/. The dataset is about 500 MB uncompressed, so it is large enough to practice scalability but small enough to be handled on any medium-size cloud instance or a workstation. A good starting point is to see what the data looks like. A Jupyter notebook works well for this purpose, as depicted in figure 5.3.

```
In [1]: import tarfile
        from metaflow import S3

In [2]: with S3() as s3:
            res = s3.get('s3://fast-ai-nlp/yelp_review_full_csv.tgz')
            with tarfile.open(res.path) as tar:
                datafile = tar.extractfile('yelp_review_full_csv/train.csv')
                reviews = [line.decode('utf-8') for line in datafile]

In [3]: print('\n'.join(reviews[:2]))

        "5","dr. goldberg offers everything i look for in a general practitioner.  he's nice and easy
        to talk to without being patronizing; he's always on time in seeing his patients; he's affili
        ated with a top-notch hospital (nyu) which my parents have explained to me is very important
        in case something happens and you need surgery; and you can get referrals to see specialists
        without having to see him first.  really, what more do you need?  i'm sitting here trying to
        think of any complaints i have about him, but i'm really drawing a blank."

        "2","Unfortunately, the frustration of being Dr. Goldberg's patient is a repeat of the experi
        ence I've had with so many other doctors in NYC -- good doctor, terrible staff.  It seems tha
        t his staff simply never answers the phone.  It usually takes 2 hours of repeated calling to
        get an answer.  Who has time for that or wants to deal with it?  I have run into this problem
        with many other doctors and I just don't get it.  You have office workers, you have patients
        with medical needs, why isn't anyone answering the phone?  It's incomprehensible and not work
        the aggravation.  It's with regret that I feel that I have to give Dr. Goldberg 2 stars."
```

Figure 5.3   Inspecting the Yelp dataset in a notebook

The next listing shows the code used in figure 5.3.

Listing 5.1   Inspecting the Yelp review dataset

```
import tarfile
from metaflow import S3
```

```
with S3() as s3:    #A
    res = s3.get('s3://fast-ai-nlp/yelp_review_full_csv.tgz')
    with tarfile.open(res.path) as tar:
        datafile = tar.extractfile('yelp_review_full_csv/train.csv')
        reviews = [line.decode('utf-8') for line in datafile]
print('\n'.join(reviews[:2]))
```

Extracts a data file from the tar package

Uses Metaflow's built-in S3 client to load the publicly available Yelp dataset

Loads all reviews, one review per line, in a list

Prints the first two reviews as a sample

Here, we use Metaflow's built-in S3 client to load data from Amazon S3—you will learn more about it in chapter 7. The dataset is stored in a compressed tar archive, which we uncompress to extract reviews. There's one review per line, prefixed by a star rating. Our application doesn't need to care about the rating column.

> **RECOMMENDATION**   The dataset used in this chapter, yelp_review_full_csv.tgz, is about 200 MB. Downloading it over a slow internet connection might take a few minutes. If the examples feel too slow on a laptop, consider using a cloud workstation, such as AWS Cloud9 IDE, to execute all examples in this chapter.

You can see a few samples of the review data in figure 5.3. As expected, reviews are arbitrary paragraphs of written English. Before we can perform any clustering on the data, we must convert the strings to a numerical representation. Such a vectorization step is a common preprocessing step in machine learning tasks that involve natural language. Don't worry if you haven't done any NLP before: we will cover everything you need to know in the next subsection.

ONE-MINUTE PRIMER TO NATURAL LANGUAGE PROCESSING

A classic way to encode natural language in a numerical form is called the *bag-of-words* representation. Using the bag-of-words model, we can represent a collection of documents as a matrix where each row is a document and columns correspond to all unique words across all documents. The order of the columns and rows is arbitrary. The values of the matrix indicate the number of times each word occurs in a document. Figure 5.4 illustrates the concept.

Original documents   **Bag-of-words matrix**

	are	fun	cats	dogs	eat	fish
cats are fun →	1	1	1	0	0	0
dogs are fun →	1	1	0	1	0	0
cats eat fish →	0	0	1	0	1	1

Figure 5.4   Bag-of-words matrix

Note how most values in the matrix in figure 5.4 are zero. This is expected, because practically all documents contain only a small subset of all possible words. Hence, it is common to encode the matrix as a *sparse matrix*, meaning that we use a data structure that allows us to store only the nonzero elements of the matrix. In the following examples, we will use Scikit-Learn's `scipy.sparse` module to store documents as bag-of-words sparse matrices. We will dive deeper into how these matrices are implemented internally in section 5.3.1.

You can get surprisingly good results in many NLP tasks, like classification and clustering, using a simple bag-of-words representation, despite the fact that it loses the order of words. In a few of the examples that follow, we will perform document clustering. We want to group documents in K non-overlapping groups or clusters so that documents assigned to the same cluster are maximally *similar* to each other. Crucially, you have to choose the number of clusters K beforehand—there isn't a universally agreed-upon method within the data science community of choosing it automatically.

In this example, *document similarity* refers to the number of common words among documents. For instance, the first two documents in figure 5.4 have two words in common (*are, fun*) versus the third document, which has at most one word in common with them. Hence, it makes sense to assign the first two documents in one cluster and the third document in a separate cluster.

To perform clustering, we will use the most well-known clustering technique, the K-means clustering algorithm, as implemented in Scikit-Learn. If you are curious, you can read more about K-means at http://mng.bz/aJlY. The details of the algorithm don't matter here, besides the fact that it is a somewhat demanding algorithm computationally—the execution time grows quadratically in terms of the matrix size. This makes it a fun and realistic test case for scalability and performance.

5.1.2   *Practicing vertical scalability*

We encountered the idea of vertical scalability in the previous chapter when we introduced the `@batch` and `@resources` decorators. This is by far the easiest form of scaling: vertical scalability refers to the idea of handling more compute and larger datasets just by using larger instances. Naturally, you can't rely on vertical scaling on your laptop because you can't add more CPU cores or memory to it programmatically. In contrast, it is easy to achieve vertical scaling with a cloud-based compute layer like AWS Batch, which can deliver any instances available in the cloud.

Let's start by loading the Yelp reviews dataset and constructing a corresponding bag-of-words representation of it. We will use the same dataset in many flows, so we will develop utility functions to handle data to avoid duplicating the same code across flows. As usual in Python, we store the function in a separate file, a *module*, which the flows can import.

Our module contains two utility functions: `load_yelp_reviews`, which downloads the dataset and extracts a list of documents from it, and `make_matrix`, which converts a list of documents to a bag-of-words matrix. The `load_yelp_reviews` function looks very similar to the code we used to inspect data in a notebook (listing 5.1). In fact, a benefit of creating a separate module is that we can use the same module in our Meta-flow flow and in a notebook.

> **RECOMMENDATION** It is considered a good practice to place related functions in logically organized modules. You can share the modules across many flows and use them in notebooks as well. Furthermore, you can test modules independently.

Create a file named scale_data.py, and store the code from the next listing in it.

Listing 5.2 Functions to process the Yelp review dataset

```
import tarfile
from itertools import islice
from metaflow import S3

def load_yelp_reviews(num_docs):
    with S3() as s3:      #B
        res = s3.get('s3://fast-ai-nlp/yelp_review_full_csv.tgz')
        with tarfile.open(res.path) as tar:
            datafile = tar.extractfile('yelp_review_full_csv/train.csv')
            return list(islice(datafile, num_docs))

def make_matrix(docs, binary=False):
    from sklearn.feature_extraction.text import CountVectorizer
    vec = CountVectorizer(min_df=10, max_df=0.1, binary=binary)
    mtx = vec.fit_transform(docs)
    cols = [None] * len(vec.vocabulary_)
    for word, idx in vec.vocabulary_.items():
        cols[idx] = word
    return mtx, cols
```

- Loads the dataset and extracts a list of documents from it
- Uses Metaflow's built-in S3 client to load the publicly available Yelp dataset
- Converts a list of documents to a bag-of-words matrix
- Extracts a data file from the tar package
- Returns the first num_docs lines from the file
- Creates a list of column labels
- CountVectorizer creates the matrix.

As in our notebook example, the function loads the publicly available Yelp dataset from S3 using Metaflow's built-in S3 client, which we will cover in more detail in chapter 7. The load_yelp_reviews function takes a single argument, num_docs, which indicates how many documents (reviews, one per line) to read from the dataset. We will use num_docs to control the dataset size.

The make_matrix function takes a list of documents in docs and uses Scikit-Learn's CountVectorizer to create a matrix from documents. We give it the following parameters:

- min_df specifies that included words need to occur in at least 10 documents. This gets rid of many typos and other spurious words.
- max_df specifies that all words that occur in more than 10% of all documents are excluded. They are typically common English words that are rather uninformative for our use case.
- binary can be used to indicate that only the occurrence of a word in a document matters. The result is 0 or 1, regardless of how many times the word occurs in the document. Finally, we create a list of column labels so we know which word corresponds to which column.

Composing your workflows from modular components like `scale_data.py` offers many benefits: you can test them independently, use them in a notebook during prototyping, and package and share them across multiple projects. Metaflow packages all modules in the current working directory together with the flow, so they are available automatically inside containers executed by the compute layer. We will discuss this and other topics related to management of software libraries in chapter 6.

> **RECOMMENDATION**   Implement complex business logic, like modeling code, as separate modules that can be called by the workflow. This makes the logic easier to test in notebooks and by automated test suites. It also makes the modules shareable across multiple workflows.

Next, let's compose a simple flow that we can use to test the function. We follow the spiral approach: we start with a simple flow that does almost nothing and keep adding functionality to it iteratively. In the same directory where you stored scale_data.py, create a new file, kmeans_flow_v1.py with the following code.

Listing 5.3   The first iteration of `KMeansFlow`

```
from metaflow import FlowSpec, step, Parameter

class KmeansFlow(FlowSpec):
    num_docs = Parameter('num-docs', help='Number of documents', default=1000)

    @step
    def start(self):                                        Imports the module we
        import scale_data                                   created earlier and uses
        scale_data.load_yelp_reviews(self.num_docs)         it to load the dataset
        self.next(self.end)

    @step
    def end(self):
        pass

if __name__ == '__main__':
    KmeansFlow()
```

The `start` step imports the module we created in listing 5.2 and uses it to load the dataset. Use the parameter `num_docs` to control the dataset size. The default is to load only the first 1,000 documents. The uncompressed dataset is about 500 MB, so executing this example requires more than half a gigabyte of memory. The directory structure needs to look like the following to ensure that Metaflow packages all modules properly:

```
my_dir/
my_dir/scale_data.py
my_dir/kmeans_flow_v1.py
```

You can choose the name for the directory my_dir freely. Make sure your working directory is my_dir and execute the flow as usual:

```
# python kmeans_flow_v1.py run
```

Especially on a local laptop, this might take a few minutes to execute. If all goes well, it should complete without any errors. This is a good sanity check before we start adding more functionality to the flow.

DEFINING DEPENDENCIES WITH @CONDA

Next, let's expand KmeansFlow to perform clustering using the K-means algorithm. We can use an off-the-shelf implementation of K-means provided by Scikit-Learn. In chapter 3, we installed Scikit-Learn simply by running pip install on the local workstation. However, the locally installed library isn't automatically available in all containers that are executed by the compute layer.

We could choose a container image that has all the libraries we need preinstalled, but managing multiple images that match the needs of every project can get cumbersome. As an alternative, Metaflow provides a more flexible approach, the @conda decorator, which doesn't require you to create or find suitable images manually.

In general, dependency management is a nontrivial topic that we will cover in detail in the next chapter. For the purposes of this section, you will just need to make sure that you have the Conda package manager installed—see the appendix for instructions. After this, all you need to do is to include the @conda_base line in your code as shown in listing 5.4:

```
@conda_base(python='3.8.3', libraries={'scikit-learn': '0.24.1'})
```

This line instructs Metaflow to install the Python version 3.8.3 with Scikit-Learn version 0.24.1 in all compute layers where the code is executed, including local runs.

> **NOTE** When you run a flow with @conda for the first time, Metaflow resolves all dependencies that are needed and uploads them to S3. This might take a few minutes, particularly if you are executing the code on your laptop. Be patient—this happens only during the first execution!

The next code snippet expands the first version of KMeansFlow from listing 5.3. It uses our scale_data module to create a bag-of-words matrix from the Yelp dataset. The matrix is clustered in a new step, train_kmeans.

Listing 5.4   The final version of KMeansFlow

```
from metaflow import FlowSpec, step, Parameter, resources, conda_base, profile

@conda_base(python='3.8.3', libraries={'scikit-learn': '0.24.1'})  ⊲─┐   Declares the
class KmeansFlow(FlowSpec):                                             libraries we will
                                                                       need in tasks
    num_docs = Parameter('num-docs', help='Number of documents', default=1000000)
```

```
@resources(memory=4000)            ◁────  Requires 4 GB of memory
@step                                      to preprocess data
def start(self):
    import scale_data                                   Imports the module we
    docs = scale_data.load_yelp_reviews(self.num_docs)  created earlier and uses
    self.mtx, self.cols = scale_data.make_matrix(docs)  it to load the dataset
    print("matrix size: %dx%d" % self.mtx.shape)
    self.next(self.train_kmeans)
                                            Requires 4 GB of memory and
@resources(cpu=16, memory=4000)   ◁────     16 CPU cores to run K-means
@step
def train_kmeans(self):
    from sklearn.cluster import KMeans       Uses a profile to measure and prints
    with profile('k-means'):         ◁───── the time it takes to run K-means
        kmeans = KMeans(n_clusters=10,
                        verbose=1,
                        n_init=1)        Runs K-Means and stores
        kmeans.fit(self.mtx)             the results in clusters
        self.clusters = kmeans.labels_
        self.next(self.end)

@step
def end(self):
    pass

if __name__ == '__main__':
    KmeansFlow()
```

Save the code to kmeans_flow_v2.py. You can see that we used the @resources decorator to declare that the start and train_kmeans steps require 4 GB of memory. The extra gigabytes are needed to keep the bag-of-words matrix in memory and account for all the related overhead. The train_kmeans step uses a small utility function provided by Metaflow, profile, which measures and prints the time needed to execute a block of code. Its single argument is a prefix included in the output, so you know which block of code the measurement relates to.

> **TIP**   Use the profile context manager in Metaflow to quickly figure out how long certain operations inside a step take.

The KMeans object is used to run the algorithm. It takes the number of clusters (the K in K-means), here called n_clusters, as an argument, which we set to a somewhat arbitrary number, 10. In the next section, we will explore other values for K. The next argument, verbose, provides some information about the progress of the algorithm, and n_init=1 implies that we need to run the algorithm only once. A higher number might lead to better results. The result of the algorithm is an array, stored in self.clusters, which assigns each document to a cluster. We will take a deeper look at the results in the next section.

Run the flow with AWS Batch as follows:

```
# python kmeans_flow_v2.py --environment=conda run --with batch
```

The `--environment=conda` flag is required to indicate that we want to handle dependencies using Conda. If you want to run the code locally or your compute environment doesn't have instances with 4 GB of memory and 16 CPU cores available, you can process fewer documents by specifying a smaller value for the `num-docs` parameter, such as `run --num-docs 10000`. Hopefully, the run completes successfully—that's all we have to accomplish for now. We will dig deeper in the results in the next section.

Here's what's interesting about this flow: the dataset contains 650,000 documents, and the corresponding matrix contains about 48,000 unique words. Hence, the matrix size is 650,000 * 48,000, which would take more than 100 GB of memory if it was stored as a dense matrix. Because it is stored as a sparse matrix, it will fit in less than 4 GB. Running K-means for a matrix of this size is computationally expensive. Luckily, the implementation in Scikit-Learn can parallelize the algorithm automatically over multiple CPU cores that we requested with `@resources(cpu=16)`. As a result, you can make K-means complete faster just by increasing the number of CPU cores, as illustrated in figure 5.5.

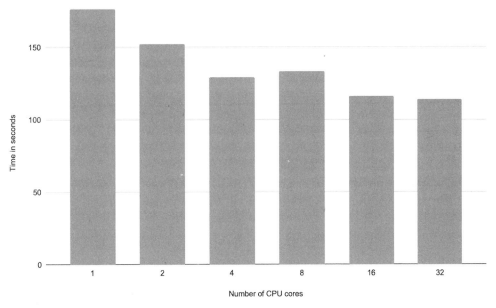

Figure 5.5   Execution time vs. the number of CPU cores used

For this dataset, you can get up to 40% performance improvement by using multiple CPU cores. As an exercise, you can try another, faster version of K-means called `Mini-BatchKMeans`. The sweet spot for `@resources` depends on the dataset size, the algorithm, and its implementation. In this case, going beyond four cores doesn't seem to offer much of a benefit. Beyond this number, the amount of work executed by an additional core isn't enough to justify the communication and coordination overhead. In general, this behavior is typical for most modern ML algorithm implementations: the more CPU cores or GPUs you run them on, the faster they will run, up to a limit.

> **NOTE**   In contrast to the memory limit, the CPU limit is a *soft limit* on AWS Batch. The task can use all available CPU cores on the instance if there are no other tasks executing on it simultaneously. The limit applies when multiple tasks need to share the instance. In most cases, this behavior is desirable, but it makes benchmarking tricky, because a task with, for example, four CPUs, may end up using more CPU cores opportunistically.

The most appealing feature of vertical scaling is its effortlessness—the data scientist just needs to modify one line of code, @resources, to handle larger datasets faster, as shown earlier. Although this approach doesn't provide infinite scalability, oftentimes, it is just enough for the task at hand, as discussed in the next subsection.

5.1.3   *Why vertical scalability?*

From an engineering point of view, it is easy to have a knee-jerk reaction to vertical scalability: it is not "real" scalability—it hits a hard ceiling at the largest available instance size. As of writing of this book, the largest commonly available EC2 instances on AWS provide 48 CPU cores and 768 GB of memory. Clearly, if you need more cores or more memory, vertical scalability won't help you.

Instead of relying on potentially misleading intuitions, it is a good idea to carefully evaluate whether vertical scalability could be sufficient and for how long. Thanks to the simplicity of vertical scalability, you can build the first version of an application quickly and verify its correctness and value before complicating the implementation. Surprisingly often, vertical scalability is just good enough.

SIMPLICITY BOOSTS PERFORMANCE AND PRODUCTIVITY

It is hard to beat vertical scalability when it comes to simplicity. You can write the most idiomatic, readable, and straightforward Python code and just adjust the numbers in @resources to match the requirements of the code. It has no new paradigms to learn. If and when things fail, no hidden layers of abstraction cause surprises or convoluted error messages. This is hugely important for the productivity and autonomy of data scientists—they can focus on modeling without having to worry about scalability or performance too much.

When it comes to implementing machine learning and data science workloads in Python, the simplicity of the user-facing APIs is deceiving. Under the hood, the best libraries are highly optimized using low-level languages like C++ so they can leverage the available resources on a single instance very efficiently.

Consider the example of modeling frameworks. In the early 2010s, much effort was put into providing scalable implementation of traditional ML algorithms on top of scalable frameworks like Hadoop and Spark. These frameworks are good examples of inherently scalable systems that have a limited single-computer performance.

In the latter half of the 2010s, it started becoming obvious that single-computer, vertically-scaled training algorithms, like the ones provided by XGBoost or Tensorflow, could easily outperform their nominally more scalable counterparts, particularly when accelerated with GPUs. Not only were these implementations much faster, they were also considerably easier to operate and develop with because they lacked the inherent complexity of scalable, distributed systems.

This highlights the difference of scalability and performance: a system consisting of multiple low-performance but parallel units can scale well, but such a distributed system tends to incur inherent communication and coordination overhead, which can make it *slower* than its nondistributed counterparts for small- and medium-sized workloads. Notably, sometimes unscalable approaches can outperform their scalable counterparts, even with unexpectedly large workloads.

> **SCALABILITY TIP**   Don't overestimate the performance of nominally scalable systems, and don't underestimate the performance of a single instance solution. When in doubt, benchmark. Even if a distributed solution might scale better, carefully consider its operational cost and the cost to the data scientist's productivity. For concrete examples of this effect, see a paper titled "Scalability! But at What COST?" published in 2015 by Frank McSherry and others (http://mng.bz/OogO).

CONSIDER THE NATURE OF YOUR PROBLEM

When thinking about the nature of your problem, consider the following two factors, which are often underappreciated. First, real-life scalability always has an upper bound. In the physical world, nothing is truly infinite. In the examples presented in this chapter, we use a static dataset of 650,000 Yelp reviews. With a static dataset like this, it is easy to see that scalability isn't likely to be a concern.

Even if the dataset wasn't static, its size may be naturally capped. For instance, consider a dataset providing statistics for each US ZIP code. There are about 40,000 ZIP codes in the US, and the number is pretty much guaranteed to stay stable. If you can get your workflow to handle about 40,000 ZIP codes without trouble, you shouldn't have any scalability concerns.

Second, a single modern computer can have a surprising amount of resources. Anything in the order of billions might feel like a lot to a human being, but keep in mind that a single modern computer can do about two billion arithmetic operations *per second* and can keep about 27 billion English words *in memory at the same time*. Computers just operate at a different order of magnitude than our limited cognition.

The effect is even more pronounced with specialized hardware like GPUs that are widely used to train deep neural networks and other modern model architectures. As of the writing of this book, AWS provides instances with eight high-performance GPUs. You can use a machine like this to train huge models. Because the communication overhead between GPU and CPU cores is minimal within a machine, a single instance can outperform a cluster of instances that is supposed to have more computing power, looking at the raw numbers.

Last, computers haven't stopped growing. Although the single-core performance hasn't grown much over the past 10 years, the number of cores in a single instance has, as well as the amount of memory and the speed of local storage. As an example, consider storing data about every Netflix subscriber in an in-memory data frame on a single instance. It might feel like a bad idea because the number of Netflix subscribers quickly grows every year!

Instead of relying on a gut reaction, it is a good idea to check the math. In 2011, Netflix had 26 million subscribers, and the largest AWS instance provided 60 GB of memory, meaning you could have stored about 2.3 KB of data per subscriber. In 2021, Netflix had 207 million subscribers, and the largest AWS instance provides 768 GB of memory, so, surprisingly, today you have more headroom for per-subscriber data—3.7 KB. In other words, if your use case fits within these bounds, you could have handled scalability simply by updating the number in @resources for over 10 years and counting!

> **SCALABILITY TIP**   Estimate the upper bound of your growth before worrying about scalability. If the upper bound is low enough compared to the available compute resources over time, you might not need to worry about scalability at all.

5.2 *Practicing horizontal scalability*

As suggested by the previous section, it is always advisable to start a project by thinking through the problem as well as the scale and the growth rate of the data and compute involved. If nothing suggests otherwise, vertical scalability is a good starting point. What would suggest otherwise? In other words, in what scenarios should you consider using multiple parallel instances instead of a single one?

5.2.1 *Why horizontal scalability?*

As a rule of thumb, you should consider horizontal scalability, that is, using multiple instances, if you answer "yes" to any of the following three questions:

- Are there significant chunks of compute in your workflow that are *embarrassingly parallel*, meaning they can perform an operation without sharing any data besides inputs?
- Is the dataset size too large to be conveniently handled on the largest available instance type?
- Are there compute-intensive algorithms, such as model training, that are too demanding to be executed on a single instance?

The items are listed in the order of descending frequency: the first two scenarios are way more typical than the last one. Let's unpack the scenarios one by one.

EMBARRASSINGLY PARALLEL TASKS

In distributed computing, a problem is called *embarrassingly parallel* if "little or no effort is needed to separate the problem into a number of parallel tasks." In the context of Metaflow-style workflows, the definition coincides with dynamic `foreach` tasks that don't need to share any data with each other, besides sharing common input data.

Cases like this are common in data science applications: training a number of independent models, fetching multiple datasets, benchmarking a number of algorithms against a dataset, to name a few. You might be able to handle all these cases using vertical scalability, possibly utilizing multiple cores on a single instance, but typically there's little gain in doing so.

Remember that the key motivations for vertical scalability are simplicity and performance. The implementation of a typical embarrassingly parallel task looks practically the same, regardless of whether it is executed on a single instance or multiple—it is just a function or a Metaflow step. Because tasks are fully independent, there's no performance penalty in executing them on separate instances. Hence, in cases like these, you can unlock massive scalability by using `foreach` in Metaflow without sacrificing simplicity or performance. We will practice one common case of embarrassing parallelism in the next section, hyperparameter search, which involves building many independent models.

LARGE DATASETS

As of the writing of this book, the largest commonly available EC2 instance has 768 GB of memory. This means that just by relying on vertical scalability, you can load maybe 100 GB of data in a pandas DataFrame that has quite a bit of memory overhead. If you need to handle more data, which is not uncommon these days, it is not feasible to solely rely on vertical scalability.

In many cases, the easiest approach to handling large datasets is to use a compute layer, like Apache Spark, that is specifically optimized for such use cases. Another approach is to divide data to smaller individual chunks or shards so that each shard can be handled on a large instance. We will discuss these approaches in chapter 7.

DISTRIBUTED ALGORITHMS

Besides input data, it is possible that the algorithm to be executed, say, model training, is too demanding for a single instance. For instance, this could be the case with a massive-scale computer vision model. Although it is common to have a dataset that is larger than a single instance, having a model of this scale is much less so. A single P4-type AWS instance with eight GPUs and over a terabyte of memory can fit a huge model.

Operating distributed model training and other distributed algorithms can be nontrivial. Networking must be optimized for low-latency communication, instances must be placed accordingly to minimize latency, and a pool of tightly coupled instances must be carefully coordinated and synchronized, all while keeping in mind that instances may fail at any time.

Fortunately, many modern machine learning libraries like PyTorch Lightning provide abstractions that make distributed training a bit easier. In addition, specialized compute layers like Amazon Sagemaker and Google's Cloud TPUs can manage the complexity for you.

Many real-world data science applications employ a mixture of many of these approaches: data is preprocessed using Spark and loaded as shards in parallel to produce a matrix or a tensor that is trained on a single vertically scaled instance. The beauty of organizing applications as workflows is that you can choose the most appropriate way to scale each step of the workflow, instead of trying to fit all tasks into a single paradigm. The next section demonstrates a straightforward but common case of embarrassing parallelism: building multiple K-means models in parallel to find the best-performing model.

5.2.2   *Example: Hyperparameter search*

In this section, we expand our earlier K-means example by showing how to address a common task in machine learning projects: *hyperparameter search and optimization,* using horizontal scalability. In the previous section, we simply fixed the number of clusters, the *K* parameter in K-means, to 10 clusters without any justification. The number of clusters is a *hyperparameter* for the K-means algorithm—a parameter that we need to define before the algorithm runs.

Typically, there isn't an unambiguously right choice for the hyperparameter values. Because we can't define the right values in advance, it is often desirable to run the algorithm with a number of different hyperparameter values and choose the one that performs the best. Sophisticated hyperparameter optimizers can generate new values on the fly and stop when results don't seem to improve. A simpler approach, demonstrated here, is just to define a list of hyperparameters to try in advance and evaluate the results in the end. A benefit of this simple approach is that the algorithm can be evaluated for each parametrization independently—a perfect use case for horizontal scalability.

How to define "the best result" for a clustering algorithm is a nontrivial question in itself. You can group documents in many equally good ways. In this example, the choice is yours. You can characterize each cluster by listing the most frequent words in the cluster. As we will show next, you can look at the clusters and decide which hyperparameter values produce the most entertaining results. Listing 5.5 shows a function, top_words, which computes the most frequent words for each cluster. Save it to a separate module, analyze_kmeans.py.

Listing 5.5   Computing the top words for each cluster

**Chooses rows from the bag-of-words matrix
that correspond to the current cluster**

```
from itertools import islice

def top_words(num_clusters, clusters, mtx, columns):
    import numpy as np
    top = []
    for i in range(num_clusters):
        rows_in_cluster = np.where(clusters == i)[0]
        word_freqs = mtx[rows_in_cluster].sum(axis=0).A[0]
```

**Processes each of
the K clusters**

**Computes
columnwise
sums, that is,
the frequencies
of each word for
the cluster**

```
        ordered_freqs = np.argsort(word_freqs)
        top_words = [(columns[idx], int(word_freqs[idx]))
                     for idx in islice(reversed(ordered_freqs), 20)]
        top.append(top_words)
    return top
```

**Sorts the columns by their frequencies
and produces a list of top-20 words**

This function uses a number of tricks from the NumPy package: it chooses a subset of rows from a matrix using `where`, it produces columnwise sums with `sum(axis=0)`, and produces column indices in the sorted order using `argsort`. If you are curious, you can take a look at the NumPy documentation to learn more about these functions. Knowing NumPy is not critical for this example.

We will use Metaflow's `foreach` construct, introduced in section 3.2.3, to run a number of K-means algorithms in parallel, leveraging AWS Batch as an autoscaling compute layer. The corresponding flow is visualized in figure 5.6.

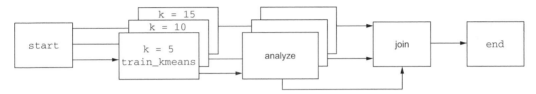

Figure 5.6 The DAG corresponding to `ManyKmeansFlow`

This demonstrates horizontal scalability in action. The flow trains a number of K-means clusterings concurrently, for various values of the parameter K (the number of clusters), and produces a summary of the results for analysis. The following listing shows the code for the flow, `ManyKmeansFlow`, which is based on our earlier `KMeansFlow`.

Listing 5.6 Searching hyperparameters for K-means

```
from metaflow import FlowSpec, step, Parameter, resources, conda_base, profile

@conda_base(python='3.8.3', libraries={'scikit-learn': '0.24.1'})
class ManyKmeansFlow(FlowSpec):

    num_docs = Parameter('num-docs', help='Number of documents', default=1000000)

    @resources(memory=4000)
    @step
    def start(self):
        import scale_data
        docs = scale_data.load_yelp_reviews(self.num_docs)
        self.mtx, self.cols = scale_data.make_matrix(docs)
        self.k_params = list(range(5, 55, 5))
        self.next(self.train_kmeans, foreach='k_params')

    @resources(cpu=4, memory=4000)
    @step
    def train_kmeans(self):
```

Produces a bag-of-words matrix using the scale_data module

Defines a list of hyperparameters for foreach

Trains a K-means clustering inside foreach

```
        from sklearn.cluster import KMeans
        self.k = self.input
        with profile('k-means'):
            kmeans = KMeans(n_clusters=self.k, verbose=1, n_init=1)
            kmeans.fit(self.mtx)
        self.clusters = kmeans.labels_
        self.next(self.analyze)

    @step
    def analyze(self):                                  Produces a list of top
        from analyze_kmeans import top_words    ◁──┘   words for each cluster
        self.top = top_words(self.k, self.clusters, self.mtx, self.cols)
        self.next(self.join)

    @step
    def join(self, inputs):                             Groups all top lists by the
        self.top = {inp.k: inp.top for inp in inputs} ◁──┘ hyperparameter value
        self.next(self.end)

    @step
    def end(self):
        pass

if __name__ == '__main__':
    ManyKmeansFlow()
```

The highlight of this flow is the list of hyperparameters defined in k_params. We produce 10 separate clusterings, that is, 10 separate train_kmeans tasks, varying the number of clusters between 5 and 50. Depending on the configuration of your compute environment, all the 10 tasks may run in parallel. The system scales nearly perfectly: If producing one clustering takes about two minutes, you can produce 10 clusterings in parallel in about two minutes as well! You can run the flow with the following code:

```
# python many_kmeans_flow.py --environment=conda run --with batch --with retry
```

By default, Metaflow will run at most 16 tasks in parallel, and, hence, it will submit at most 16 (in this case, 10) tasks to AWS Batch simultaneously. Depending on your compute environment, AWS Batch may decide to run multiple containers concurrently on a single instance, or it may decide to launch more instances to handle the queued tasks. You can control the level of parallelism with the --max-workers option, as described in section 3.2.4.

This example illustrates the benefits of a cloud-based compute layer, like AWS Batch. Not only can you launch larger instances, as we covered in the previous section, but you can *launch any number of them in parallel*. Without a scalable compute layer, you would have to execute the K-means algorithms sequentially, which would take about 20 minutes, in contrast to getting results in two minutes, thanks to horizontal scalability. As instructed in the previous chapter, we use --with retry to handle any transient failures, which are bound to happen occasionally when running hundreds of Batch jobs in parallel.

Currently, Metaflow can handle thousands of concurrent tasks without issues. Considering that each task can request high @resources, you can employ tens of thousands of CPU cores and nearly a petabyte of RAM in a single workflow!

INSPECTING RESULTS

When the run completes, you will have 10 different clusterings available for inspection. You can inspect the results using the Metaflow Client API on an interactive Python shell or using a notebook, as described in section 3.3.2. Here's how to do it easily. First, access the results of the latest run as follows:

```
>>> from metaflow import Flow
>>> run = Flow('ManyKmeansFlow').latest_run
```

Thanks to the fact that Metaflow persists results of all runs, you can inspect and compare results between runs, too.

We produced an artifact top in the join step, which contains a conveniently aggregated set of top words for each cluster, keyed by the hyperparameter value, that is, the number of clusters. Here, we take a peek at the results of the K-means with 40 clusters as follows:

```
>>> k40 = run.data.top[40]
```

40 clusters are available for inspection. Let's spot-check a few of them, looking at the top 5 words and their frequencies in the cluster like so:

```
>>> k40[3][:5]
[('pizza', 696), ('cheese', 134), ('crust', 102), ('sauce', 91), ('slice', 52)]
```

which seems to be about pizza reviews. The next one seems to be about hotels:

```
>>> k40[4][:5]
[('her', 227), ('room', 164), ('hotel', 56), ('told', 45), ('manager', 41)]
```

And this one seems to be about car rentals:

```
>>> k40[30][:5]
[('car', 20), ('hertz', 19), ('gold', 14), ('says', 8), ('explain', 7)]
```

By default, K-means doesn't guarantee that results will always be the same. For instance, random initialization causes results to be slightly different in every run, so don't expect to see exactly the same results as shown here. As an exercise, you can come up with a creative way to tabulate and visualize the clusterings in a notebook.

5.3   *Practicing performance optimization*

Thus far we have learned about the two main dimensions of scalability: vertical scalability (using a bigger instance) and horizontal scalability (using more instances). Notably, both of these techniques allow us to handle larger datasets and more demanding algorithms with minimal changes in the code. Scalability like this is appealing from a productivity point of view: the cloud allows us to solve problems by throwing more hardware at them so we can spare human resources for more interesting tasks.

In what situations should we consider spending a data scientist's time on optimizing code by hand? Consider that you have a computationally expensive algorithm, say, model training, implemented as a Python function. Executing the function takes five hours. Depending on how the algorithm is implemented, vertical scalability might not help much if the algorithm can't take advantage of multiple CPU cores, more memory, or GPUs efficiently. Horizontal scalability doesn't help, either. You could execute the function in 100 parallel tasks, but each one of them would still take five hours, so the total execution time is still five hours.

A critical question is whether it matters that the execution takes five hours. Maybe the workflow is scheduled to run nightly, so it doesn't make a huge difference whether it runs for five or two hours—the results are ready by morning in any case. However, if the function needs to be run hourly, we have a problem. It is simply impossible to produce hourly results with a function that takes five hours to execute.

In a situation like this, a data scientist needs to spend time rethinking the algorithm to make it more performant. A key lesson of the next section is that even performance optimization is a spectrum. The data scientist doesn't have to throw away the Python implementation and rewrite the algorithm, say, in C++. They can use number of tools and techniques to gradually optimize the algorithm to the point that it is *good enough*.

The next section will walk through a realistic example that shows how a numerically intensive algorithm that is initially implemented in straightforward Python can be gradually optimized to the point where its performance becomes comparable to a sophisticated multicore C++ implementation. As you will see, a simple optimization that is easy to implement yields 80% of benefits. Squeezing out the last 20% of performance takes 80% of the time.

> **PERFORMANCE TIP**   Premature optimization is the root of all evil. Don't worry about performance until you have exhausted all other easier options. If you must optimize performance, know when to stop.

5.3.1   *Example: Computing a co-occurrence matrix*

The previous sections used a bag-of-words matrix that records the relationship between documents and words. From this matrix, we can derive another interesting matrix: a *word-word co-occurrence matrix*. The co-occurrence matrix records how frequently a word occurs in the same document with any other word. It can be useful for understanding semantic similarity between words, and having the matrix makes it possible to compute various word-level metrics quickly. Figure 5.7 expands our earlier bag-of-words example to show the corresponding co-occurrence matrix.

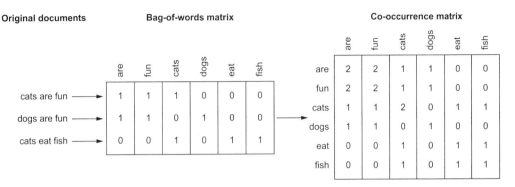

Figure 5.7 **From original documents to a word-word co-occurrence matrix**

If the dimensions of a bag-of-word matrix are N*M, where N is the number of documents and M is the number of unique words, the corresponding co-occurrence matrix has the dimensions of M*M. Crucially, the bag-of-words-matrix contains all the information we need to construct the corresponding co-occurrence matrix. A simple way to construct a co-occurrence matrix is to iterate through all rows of the bag-of-matrix matrix and, for each row, produce all pairs of words and increase their count in the co-occurrence matrix.

We can take advantage of the fact that the bag-of-words matrix is a sparse matrix, that is, it doesn't store any zero entries, which wouldn't affect the co-occurrence matrix anyway. To be able to design an efficient algorithm to process the data, let's take a peek under the hood of scipy.sparse.csr_matrix, which implements the sparse matrix. The *compressed sparse row* (CSR) matrix in SciPy is composed of three dense arrays, as illustrated in figure 5.8:

1 indptr indicates where each row begins and ends in the indices array. This array is needed, because each document can contain a different number of unique words. The indptr array contains an extra element in the end, to indicate the length of the last document.
2 indices indicates which columns (words) have nonzero values on this row.
3 data contains the frequency of each word in each document. It is aligned with the indices array.

To construct the co-occurrence matrix, we don't care how many times a word occurs in a document. Hence, our bag-of-words matrix can be a binary matrix, and, correspondingly, the data array is redundant because it is all ones.

Equipped with this problem definition and knowledge of the data structure behind the sparse matrix, we can implement the first variant of an algorithm that computes a co-occurrence matrix for the Yelp dataset.

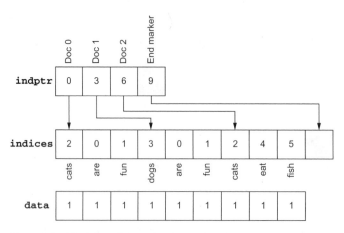

Figure 5.8   The internal data structures of `scipy.sparse.csr_matrix`

VARIANT 1: A PLAIN PYTHON IMPLEMENTATION

Imagine that a data scientist needs to compute a co-occurrence matrix as a preprocessing step for another algorithm. Maybe the simplest approach would be to compute co-occurrences directly on the text data, iterating documents string by string, but this would be a very slow approach. Let's assume that the data scientist has already produced a bag-of-words matrix using our `scale_data` module. The data scientist writes an algorithm that iterates through the sparse matrix to construct a co-occurrence matrix. Their solution could look like the one shown next.

Listing 5.7   First variant: Co-occurrences in pure Python

```
def simple_cooc(indptr, indices, cooc):
    for row_idx in range(len(indptr) - 1):              ◁── Iterates over all rows of
        row = indices[indptr[row_idx]:indptr[row_idx+1]]     the bag-of-words matrix
        row_len = len(row)
        for i in range(row_len):          ◁── Increments the diagonal of
            x = row[i]                         the matrix, which indicates
            cooc[x][x] += 1   ◁──              the word frequency
            for j in range(i + 1, row_len):
                y = row[j]
                cooc[x][y] += 1   ◁── Increments the word-word pair
                cooc[y][x] += 1       count—the matrix is symmetric
```

Iterates over all nonzero columns (words) in a row

```
def new_cooc(mtx):                        ◁── A utility function to create a
    import numpy as np                        new co-occurrence matrix
    num_words = mtx.shape[1]
    return np.zeros((num_words, num_words), dtype=np.int32)

def compute_cooc(mtx, num_cpu):           ◁── An interface function that
    cooc = new_cooc(mtx)                      creates and populates a new
    simple_cooc(mtx.indptr, mtx.indices, cooc)   co-occurrence matrix
    return cooc
```

Save the code in listing 5.7 in a separate module named cooc_plain.py. This time, the exact filename matters, as we will see soon. The implementation is straightforward: we iterate over all pairs of words over all rows and increment word-word counts in the target matrix as we go. Besides the core algorithm, simple_cooc, we include a helper function to allocate a new co-occurrence matrix of the right shape, new_cooc, and a function to create and populate the matrix, compute_cooc, which we will use as an entry point to the module. These functions will come in handy soon.

Let's create a flow to test the algorithm. The next listing shows a flow that supports pluggable algorithms. We can use it to test other variants besides cooc_plain.py, too. Save the flow to cooc_flow.py.

Listing 5.8 A flow that produces a co-occurrence matrix

```
from metaflow import FlowSpec, conda_base, step, profile, resources, Parameter
from importlib import import_module

@conda_base(python='3.8.3',                          We will need Numba later, so we
            libraries={'scikit-learn': '0.24.1',     will include it as a dependency.
                       'numba': '0.53.1'})    ◁
class CoocFlow(FlowSpec):
                                                          Specifies which algorithm
                                                                variant to use
    algo = Parameter('algo', help='Co-oc Algorithm', default='plain')    ◁
    num_cpu = Parameter('num-cpu', help='Number of CPU cores', default=32)
    num_docs = Parameter('num-docs', help='Number of documents', default=1000)

    @resources(memory=4000)       The start step uses               Note binary=True,
    @step                         scale_data similar to             which indicates that
    def start(self):   ◁          our previous examples.            we need only a
        import scale_data                                           binary matrix.
        docs = scale_data.load_yelp_reviews(self.num_docs)
        self.mtx, self.cols = scale_data.make_matrix(docs, binary=True)   ◁
        print("matrix size: %dx%d" % self.mtx.shape)
        self.next(self.compute_cooc)
                                            Producing the result can
    @resources(cpu=32, memory=64000)   ◁    take quite a bit of memory.
    @step
    def compute_cooc(self):
        module = import_module('cooc_%s' % self.algo)
        with profile('Computing co-occurrences with the %s
            algorithm' % self.algo):
            self.cooc = module.compute_cooc(self.mtx, self.num_cpu)   ◁
        self.next(self.end)
                                                          Computes the
    @step                                             co-occurrence matrix
    def end(self):
        pass

if __name__ == '__main__':
    CoocFlow()
```

Loads a pluggable variant defined by the algo parameter

Here, the `start` step is familiar from our previous examples. The only difference is that we specify `binary=True` because for co-occurrences, we don't care about the frequency of words in a document. The `compute_cooc` supports pluggable algorithms. instead of hardcoding an `import` statement, we choose which variant to import based on a parameter, `algo`. We use Python's built-in `importlib.import_module` to import a module from a file prefixed with the string `cooc_`.

> **TIP** Dynamic loading of modules using `importlib.import_module` is a great way to implement plugins for flows. Often, the overall structure of DAG doesn't change between plugins, so you can keep the DAG static but choose the desired functionality on the fly.

Let's start by testing the flow locally with a small subset of data, 1,000 documents, as follows:

```
# python cooc_flow.py --environment=conda run --num-docs 1000
```

This will use the `cooc_plain` module that we defined previously. It seems executing the algorithm with 1,000 rows (documents) and 1,148 columns (words) takes about five seconds, which, on first glance, doesn't seem too bad.

Try increasing `--num-docs` to 10,000. Now, the algorithm takes 74 seconds! If you dare, you can try executing it with the full dataset. It takes ages to finish. You can try executing it `--with batch` varying `@resources`, but the timings won't nudge—this algorithm is not performant nor scalable. If the task is to produce a co-occurrence matrix for the full dataset of 650,000 documents, clearly this algorithm is not going to work.

VARIANT 2: LEVERAGING A HIGH-PERFORMANCE LIBRARY

Whenever a basic Python implementation turns out to be too slow, it is advisable to try to find an off-the-shelf library that contains an optimized implementation of the same algorithm. Given the vastness of the Python data science ecosystem, you often learn that someone has implemented a suitable solution already. Or, even if a perfectly matching solution doesn't exist, someone might have implemented an efficient building block that we can use to optimize our solution.

Unfortunately, in the case of our example, it seems that Scikit-Learn doesn't provide a function for computing a co-occurrence matrix. For the purposes of our example, we ignore the fact that a suitable implementation might exist elsewhere.

The data scientist turns to a colleague who has experience in high-performance numerical computing. The colleague points out that the algorithm implemented by `cooc_plain` is effectively an algorithm for matrix multiplication. It turns out that computing a co-occurrence matrix *C* based on a binary bag-of-words matrix *B* corresponds exactly to the following matrix equation:

$$C = B^T B$$

where B^T denotes the transpose (rotation) of the matrix of B. If you multiply an M*N matrix with an N*M matrix, the result is an M*M matrix, which, in this case, is exactly our co-occurrence matrix. Implementing this variant of the algorithm is embarrassingly simple, as shown in the following code listing.

Listing 5.9   Second variant: Leveraging linear algebra

```
def compute_cooc(mtx, num_cpu):
    return (mtx.T * mtx).todense()
```

Save the code in listing 5.9 in cooc_linalg.py, for a variant based on linear algebra. Thanks to pluggable algorithm support in CoocFlow, we can test this variant simply by running the following code:

```
# python cooc_flow.py --environment=conda run --num-docs 10000 --algo linalg
```

This variant finishes in 1.5 seconds instead of 74 seconds—a 50× speedup! The code is simpler and faster than the original Python version, which is perfect.

Because the code performs so well, you can go ahead and try it with the full dataset by specifying --num-docs 1000000. Alas, the run will likely fail due to an out-of-memory exception. You can resort to vertical scaling and try it --with batch, but even with 64 GB, the run keeps failing.

A problem with this variant is that taking the transpose of the original matrix, mtx.T, makes a copy of the full dataset, doubling the memory requirement in addition to having to store the co-occurrence matrix in memory. Although the cooc_plain variant doesn't perform well, at least it was more space efficient, avoiding unnecessary copies.

In this case, you can keep increasing memory requirements until the algorithm completes successfully. Given the elegant simplicity of this algorithm, relying on vertical scalability would be an appealing solution. However, for the sake of discussion, let's say the data scientist can't rely on the highest-memory instances, so they must keep seeking a more optimal variant.

VARIANT 3: COMPILING PYTHON WITH NUMBA

Colleagues of our data scientist point out that the main problem with variant 1 is that it is written in Python. Had it been written in C++, it would likely perform much better while not wasting space unnecessarily like variant 2. This is a valid argument from a technical point of view, but including a piece of custom C++ in a Python project feels like a hassle, not to mention that our data scientist isn't familiar with C++.

Fortunately, a few libraries can help make numerical Python code faster by compiling it to machine code, similar to what a C++ compiler would do. The most well-known compilers for Python are Cython (cython.org) and Numba (numba .pydata.org).

These compilers can't magically make any piece of Python as fast as C++, but they shine at optimizing functions that perform numerical computation, typically using

NumPy arrays. In other words, a function like `simple_cooc` that performs loops over a few NumPy arrays should be squarely in the domain of these compilers.

The next code snippet shows how to compile the `simple_cooc` function on the fly using Numba. Save this variant to cooc_numba.py.

Listing 5.10   Third variant: Co-occurrences with Numba

```
def compute_cooc(mtx, num_cpu):
    from cooc_plain import simple_cooc, new_cooc
    cooc = new_cooc(mtx)
    from numba import jit
    fast_cooc = jit(nopython=True)(simple_cooc)     ◁── Compiles the simple_cooc
    fast_cooc(mtx.indptr, mtx.indices, cooc)            function on the fly using Numba
    return cooc
```

The hard thing about using Numba is writing a function that avoids using any idiomatic Python constructs like objects and dictionaries and avoids allocating memory. You must focus on simple arithmetic on arrays, like `simple_cooc` does. Once you have managed to do this, using Numba is easy. Like listing 5.10 shows, all you have to do is call the `jit` function and pass the function to be called as an argument.

The result is a version of the given function, here `fast_cooc`, that is typically significantly faster than the original version. This magic is made possible by the fact that Numba compiles the function to machine code, which is virtually indistinguishable from a version written in C++. The `nopython=True` flag indicates that the function doesn't use any Python constructs, so a slow compatibility layer with Python can be avoided.

Test this variant as follows:

```
# python cooc_flow.py --environment=conda run --num-docs 10000 --algo numba
```

This version of the algorithm takes 2.7 seconds, so it is slightly slower than `cooc_linalg`, which ran for 1.5 seconds. The difference is understandable because the Numba timing includes compilation time as well. Notably, this version doesn't take any extra space. This variant is able to handle the full dataset in 50 seconds—not too shabby!

VARIANT 4: PARALLELIZING THE ALGORITHM OVER MULTIPLE CPU CORES

Although variant 3 is able to handle the full dataset quite quickly, it is a fundamentally unscalable algorithm: adding more memory or CPU resources doesn't make it any faster or capable of having larger matrices. Presumably, one could get results even faster if the algorithm was able to leverage multiple CPU cores that we can easily request with `@resources`.

Note that this optimization comes with a cost: the implementation is more complex than variants 2 and 3. One needs to be much more careful in confirming that it works correctly. As it often happens with performance optimizations, the first 20% of the effort can bring 80% of the benefits. Spending time to squeeze the last bits of performance is not worth it for most use cases. Consider this variant through this cautionary lens.

Looking at the algorithm in `simple_cooc`, we can see that the outer loop iterates over the rows of the input matrix. Could we split the input matrix so that each CPU core handles only a subset, a shard, of the rows? A challenge is a row may update any location of the result matrix that would need to be shared across all CPU cores. Sharing writable data across multiple worker processes or threads is a hard problem that we would rather avoid.

A simple insight comes to the rescue: we can let each thread write to a private copy of the co-occurrence matrix, which we can simply sum together in the end. A downside is that the memory consumption increases again, but in contrast to variant 2, we need copies of co-occurrence matrices that are smaller than the full dataset. Save the variant in the next listing in cooc_multicore.py.

> **Listing 5.11 Fourth variant: Using Numba with multiple CPU cores**

```python
from concurrent import futures
import math

def compute_cooc_multicore(row_indices, columns, cooc, num_cpu, fast_cooc):
    num_rows = len(row_indices) - 1
    batch_size = math.ceil(num_rows / num_cpu)
    batches = [(cooc.copy(),
                row_indices[i * batch_size:(i+1) * batch_size + 1])
               for i in range(num_cpu)]

    with futures.ThreadPoolExecutor(max_workers=num_cpu) as exe:
        threads = [exe.submit(fast_cooc, row_batch, columns, tmp_cooc)
                   for tmp_cooc, row_batch in batches]
        futures.wait(threads)

    for tmp_cooc, row_batch in batches:
        cooc += tmp_cooc

def compute_cooc(mtx, num_cpu):
    from numba import jit
    from cooc_plain import simple_cooc, new_cooc
    cooc = new_cooc(mtx)
    fast_cooc = jit(nopython=True, nogil=True)(simple_cooc)
    fast_cooc(mtx.indptr, mtx.indices, cooc)
    compute_cooc_multicore(mtx.indptr, mtx.indices, cooc, num_cpu, fast_cooc)
    return cooc
```

Annotations:
- **Shards the input matrix to num_cpu equal-size shards or batches, each with a private output matrix**
- **Waits for the threads to complete**
- **Uses a thread pool to process the batches over num_cpu threads on multiple CPU cores in parallel**
- **Aggregates the private output matrices to a single output matrix**
- **Notes the nogil=True flag, which allow Python to execute the threads in a truly parallel fashion**

The algorithm works by splitting the rows of the input matrix into `num_cpu` equal-size shards or batches. Each batch gets its own private output matrix, created with `cooc.copy()`, so the threads don't need locking or another way to coordinate updates. The batches are submitted to a thread pool that has `num_cpu` worker threads. After the threads have completed populating their private subsets of the co-occurrence matrix, the results are merged in the final output matrix. You can benchmark this version against earlier variants with the following code:

```
# python cooc_flow.py --environment=conda run --num-docs 10000 --algo multicore
```

If you have come across multithreading in Python before, you may have heard of the *Global Interpreter Lock* (GIL) in Python (if you are curious, you can learn more about GIL at https://wiki.python.org/moin/GlobalInterpreterLock). In short, the GIL prevents multiple threads executing Python code from running in parallel effectively. However, the GIL limitation doesn't apply to this algorithm, because we use Numba to compile the Python code to machine code, similar to variant 3. Therefore, in the Python interpreter's point of view, we are executing not Python code but rather native code, which is free from the limitations of GIL. We just need to remember to add `nogil=True` to the `jit` call to remind Numba about this detail.

This variant is a great example of how going multicore is not a panacea. Although reading the rows of the matrix is an embarrassingly parallel problem, requiring no coordination between threads, writing the output isn't. In this case, the cost we pay is duplication of the output matrix. Another approach would be to apply locking to the output matrix. In any case, each new thread increases the cost a bit. As a result, adding cores helps, but only to a limit, similar to what we experienced with the parallelization of K-means in section 4.3.1. Figure 5.9 illustrates the effect.

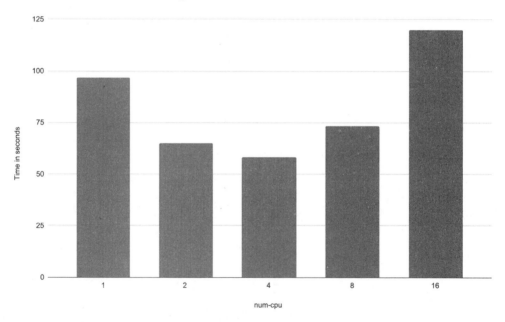

Figure 5.9   Execution time vs. the number CPU cores in the multithreaded case

Figure 5.9 shows that running the algorithm with num_cpu=1 takes about 100 seconds for a version of the full matrix. For this dataset, the sweet spot seems to be at num_cpu=4, which improves performance by about 40%. Beyond this, the overhead of creating and aggregating per-thread output matrices overtakes the benefits of handling increasingly small input shards in each thread.

SUMMARIZING THE VARIANTS

This section illustrated a realistic journey of optimizing performance of a numerically intensive algorithm as follows:

1. First, we started with a simple version of the algorithm.

2. It turned out that the algorithm really isn't performant enough, given the requirements of the use case, so we evaluated whether there's an easy way out by resorting to vertical or horizontal scalability. It turned out that neither of these approaches speeded up execution adequately with the simple algorithm.

3. We evaluated whether an off-the-shelf optimization implementation was available. We figured out an elegant and performant solution based on simple linear algebra. However, the solution had the side effect of increased memory consumption, which we could solve by vertical scalability. Had this been a real use case, variant 2, with vertical scalability (high-memory instances), seems like a good choice based on effort, performance, and maintainability.

4. To illustrate a more advanced optimization, we introduced Numba, which worked well for this use case. However, the default implementation doesn't take advantage of multiple CPU cores.

5. Finally, we implemented a compiled, multicore variant, the performance of which should compare favorably against a well-optimized, parallelized C++ algorithm. Yet, we managed to do it all in fewer than 100 lines of Python.

Figure 5.10 shows a performance benchmark of the four variants.

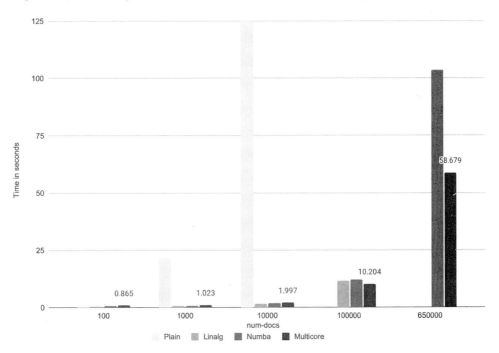

Figure 5.10 Performance of the four variants vs. the number of documents

When the dataset is small enough—100 documents here—the implementation doesn't make any difference. With 1,000 documents, the plain Python implementation starts being clearly slower, although in absolute terms, the execution time may be tolerable. At 10,000 documents and beyond, the plain version becomes practically unusable, so it is excluded from the large-scale benchmarks. The three performant variants are nearly equally performant, except the linalg variant runs out of memory with 64 GB at the highest scale. The complexity of the multicore variant starts paying off only with the full dataset. Figure 5.10 condenses the key learnings of this section as follows:

- The original plain implementation was impractically inefficient. Something needed to be done.
- A simple observation of how to leverage an existing high-performance library to implement the linalg solution produced massive speedups with minimal effort.
- It was possible to implement a custom solution, multicore, that performed even better than linalg, but the implementation is significantly more complex.
- We were able to implement all solutions in Python without having to switch to a high-performance but low-level language like C++.

These learnings are readily applicable to many other numerically intensive Python tasks. The modern Python data science ecosystem provides a hugely powerful and versatile toolkit for implementing high-performance algorithms.

5.3.2   *Recipe for fast-enough workflows*

Now that we have practiced scalability and performance in a number of scenarios, we can summarize the learnings of this chapter in a simple recipe that you can apply to your own use cases as follows:

1. Start with the simplest possible approach. A simple, obviously correct solution provides a robust foundation for gradual optimization.
2. If you are concerned that the approach is not scalable, think when and how you will hit the limits in practice. If the answer is never, or at least not any time soon, you can increase complexity only when it becomes necessary.
3. Use vertical scalability to make the simple version work with realistic input data.
4. If the initial implementation can't take the advantage of hardware resources provided by vertical scalability, consider using an off-the-shelf optimized library that can.
5. If the workflow contains embarrassingly parallel parts and/or data can be easily sharded, leverage horizontal scalability for parallelism.
6. If the workflow is still too slow, carefully analyze where the bottlenecks lie. Consider whether simple performance optimizations could remove the bottleneck, maybe using one of the tools from the Python data science toolkit.
7. If the workflow is still too slow, which is rare, consider using specialized compute layers that can leverage distributed algorithms and specialized hardware.

Summary

- It is advisable to start with a simple approach, initially optimizing for correctness rather than performance or scalability.
- Vertical scalability contributes to the productivity of data scientists: they can make workflows handle more data and more demanding computation using simple and understandable Python code, just by requesting more hardware resources from the cloud.
- Horizontal scalability is useful in handling three scenarios: embarrassingly parallel tasks, large datasets, and distributed algorithms.
- It is advisable to postpone performance optimizations until they become absolutely necessary. When optimizing performance, look for simple optimizations that can yield big benefits by analyzing bottlenecks carefully.
- The Python data science ecosystem includes a huge number of tools that can help optimize performance gradually. In particular, many problems can be solved by using foundational packages like Scikit-Learn, NumPy, and Numba.
- You can easily combine horizontal and vertical scalability and high-performance code in a single workflow to address the scalability needs of your task at hand.

Going to production

Thus far we have been starting all workflows on a personal workstation, maybe a laptop. However, it is not a good idea to run business-critical applications in a prototyping environment. The reasons are many: laptops get lost, they are hard to control and manage centrally, and, more fundamentally, the needs of rapid, human-in-the-loop prototyping are very different from the needs of *production deployments*.

What does "deploying to production" mean exactly? The word *production* is used frequently but is seldom defined precisely. Although particular use cases may have their own definitions, we recognize the following two characteristics that are common in most production deployments:

- *Automation*—Production workflows should run without any human involvement.
- *High availability*—Production workflows should not fail.

The main characteristic of production workflows is that they should run without a human operator: they should start, execute, and output results *automatically*. Note that automation doesn't imply that they work in isolation. They can start as a result of some external event, such as new data becoming available.

They should not fail, at least not frequently, because failures make it harder for other systems to depend on the application, and fixing failures requires slow and tedious human intervention. In technical terms, not failing and being dependable mean that the application is *highly available*.

Automation and high availability are almost always necessary requirements for production deployments, but they are not always sufficient. Your particular use cases may have additional requirements, for instance, around low latency predictions, ability to handle massive datasets, or integration with specific production systems. This chapter discusses how to satisfy both the common and bespoke requirements of production deployments.

As we discussed in chapter 2, prototyping and interacting with production deployments are separate but intertwined activities. The act of prototyping can't be automated, prototypes are certainly not highly available, and their defining characteristic is human involvement. Production deployments are the opposite.

We should make it easy to move between the two modalities, because data science projects aren't waterfalls that lead from a prototype to a final deployment in a linear process. Instead, data science applications should be iterated constantly. Deploying to production should be a simple, frequent, unremarkable event—a concept that software engineers call *continuous deployment*. Making all projects continuously deployable is a worthy goal, which we start exploring in this chapter and continue in chapter 8. To counter common misconceptions, it is useful to recognize that "production" does *not* imply the following:

- Not all production applications handle large amounts of compute or data. You can certainly have small-scale but business-critical applications that must not fail. Also, not all production applications need to exhibit high performance.
- There isn't necessarily only one production deployment of an application. Especially in the context of data science, it is common to have multiple production deployments side by side, such as for the purpose of A/B testing.
- Production doesn't imply any particular technical approach: production applications can be workflows running nightly, microservices serving real-time requests, workflows updating Excel sheets, or any other approach required by the use case.
- Going to production doesn't have to be a tedious and anxiety-inducing process. In fact, effective data science infrastructure should make it easy to deploy early versions to production so their behavior can be observed in a realistic setting.

However, production should always imply a level of *stability*. In this chapter, we introduce a number of time-tested defensive techniques to protect production deployments. These techniques build upon the ones introduced in earlier chapters. A robust, scalable compute layer is a critical element of production readiness.

Starting with the fundamentals, section 6.1 covers executing workflows in a stable manner outside of a personal workstation, without any human intervention. This is the main concern of the *job scheduler* layer in our infrastructure stack, depicted in figure 6.1.

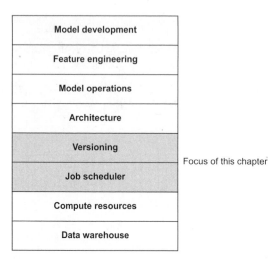

Focus of this chapter

Figure 6.1   The stack of effective data science infrastructure

After this, we focus on keeping the workflow's execution environment as stable as possible, which is the role of the *versioning* layer in the stack. Many production failures happen not because the application itself fails but because something in its environment changes. Whereas techniques like `@retry`, introduced in chapter 4, handle failures originating from the user code, section 6.2 shows how to guard against failures caused by changes in the software environment *surrounding* the user code, such as new releases of rapidly evolving libraries like TensorFlow or pandas.

Section 6.3 focuses on preventing human errors and accidents. We need to execute production workflows in isolated and versioned environments so that data scientists can keep experimenting with new versions, without having to fear they will interfere with production deployments. Optimally, you should be able to ask a fresh intern to create a version of a production application and deploy it in parallel to the main version, knowing that they can't do anything to break the existing version, not even by accident.

You don't need to apply all techniques presented in this chapter to every project. Defensive features that make an application more robust can slow down prototyping, and they can make it harder to deploy and test new production versions, hurting overall productivity. Fortunately, production-readiness is a spectrum, not a binary label.

You can prototype a project quickly on a local workstation, deploy an early version to production as described in section 6.1, and apply techniques from sections 6.2 and 6.3 later as the stakes become higher. In other words, you can *harden projects gradually* against failures as the project matures.

Inevitable tradeoffs exist between the needs of prototyping and production. A central goal of effective data science infrastructure is finding good compromises between the two modalities. Figure 6.2 illustrates the typical tradeoffs on the project's maturation path.

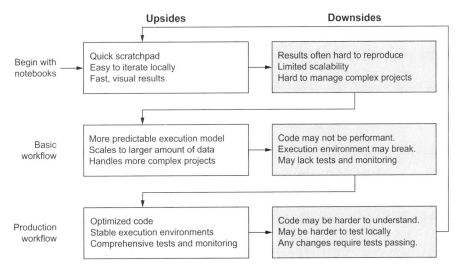

Figure 6.2 The maturation path of a typical data science project

At each stage on the project's maturation path, you need to address a new set of deficiencies. Over time, as the project becomes more robust, some flexibility is lost. New versions of the project can start the cycle from the beginning, incrementally improving the production version.

The earlier chapters of this book have led you to the "basic workflow" stage. This chapter teaches you the next level of production-readiness. By the end of the chapter, you will reach a level that has been proven sufficient to power some of the most business-critical ML applications at Netflix and other large companies. You can find all code listings for this chapter at http://mng.bz/06oW.

6.1 Stable workflow scheduling

Harper takes Alex to tour the company's new cupcake production facility. Encouraged by Alex's promising prototypes, Harper wants to start using machine learning to optimize operations at the facility. Harper reminds Alex that any unplanned interruptions in the cupcake pipeline affect the company's revenue directly, so, hopefully, Alex's models will work flawlessly. Hearing this, Bowie suggests that they should start scheduling training and optimization workflows in a much more robust environment than Alex's laptop.

This section answers a simple question: How can I execute my workflows reliably without human intervention? Thus far, we have been executing workflows on the command line by executing a command like

```
# python kmeans_flow.py run
```

Typing the command requires human intervention, so this is not a good approach for production deployments that should run automatically. Moreover, if you close your terminal while the command is executing, the workflow crashes—the workflow is not highly available. Note that for prototyping use cases, the run command is perfect, because it affords very quick iterations.

In chapter 2, we discussed production-grade workflow schedulers or orchestrators, which are the right tool for the job. Figure 6.3 reminds us of the role of the job scheduling layer: the job scheduler only needs to walk through the steps of the workflow, that is, decide *how* to orchestrate the DAG and send each task to the compute layer, which decides *where* to execute them. Crucially, neither the job scheduler nor the compute layer need to care *what* gets executed exactly—more about that later.

Although walking through a DAG doesn't sound hard, remember that we are talking about production use cases: the orchestrator may need handle large workflows

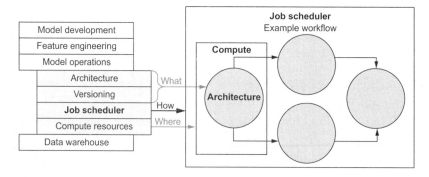

Figure 6.3   The role of the scheduling layer: How to orchestrate the DAG

with tens of thousands of tasks, there may be thousands of such workflows executing concurrently, and the orchestrator should be able to handle a plethora of failure scenarios gracefully, including the data center where the orchestrator itself executes. Moreover, the orchestrator must be able to trigger workflow executions on various conditions, such as when new data arrives, and it should provide ergonomic UIs for monitoring and alerting. All in all, building such a system is a highly nontrivial engineering challenge, so it is wise to rely on the best available off-the-shelf systems and services for the job. We listed a few suitable candidates in chapter 2.

This is the approach taken by Metaflow as well. Metaflow includes a local scheduler that is good enough for prototyping—the one that powers the run command. For production use cases, you can deploy your Metaflow workflow to a few different production schedulers without changing anything in the code. We will use one such scheduler, AWS Step Functions, to demonstrate the idea in this section. Note that, in general, the discussion of this section is not specific to AWS Step Functions. You can apply the pattern to other job schedulers as well.

However, before we get to production scheduling, we must take care of one other detail: we need a centralized service to track execution metadata across all runs, because we can't rely on locally stored metadata when orchestrating workflows in the cloud.

6.1.1 Centralized metadata

In chapter 3, we talked about *experiment tracking*—the concept of keeping track of executions and their results. The term is a bit misleading. We are interested in keeping track of not only *experiments* but also production executions. Hence, we prefer to use a generic term *metadata* to refer to all bookkeeping activities. Figure 6.4 shows the role of metadata tracking in the context of task execution.

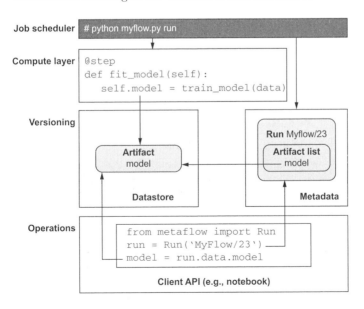

Figure 6.4 The role of the Metaflow metadata service

At the top, we have a job scheduler that walks through the DAG. The figure shows Metaflow's local scheduler as an example, but the job scheduler could be a production scheduler as well, such as AWS Step Functions. The scheduler sends tasks to the compute layer, which executes the user code. The user code produces results, or artifacts, such as `self.model` in the figure, which are stored in a datastore as discussed in chapter 3.

On the side, the metadata service keeps track of all runs and tasks that are started. Also, when an artifact is written to the datastore, the metadata service records the location of the artifact in the datastore. Crucially, metadata doesn't record the data itself because it is already in the datastore. This allows us to keep the metadata service relatively lightweight—it is responsible only for bookkeeping, not large-scale data or compute.

After data and metadata have been stored, they can be queried from outside systems. For instance, as we have seen in previous chapters, we can use the Metaflow Client API to query runs and their results in a notebook. The Client API talks to the metadata service to figure out what runs are available and to the datastore to access their results.

Most modern frameworks for data science and ML infrastructure provide a service for centralized metadata tracking. For instance, MLflow (https://mlflow.org) provides a Tracking Server, and Kubeflow (https://kubeflow.org) comes with a built-in centralized dashboard that stores and shows all executions that have been executed.

By default, Metaflow tracks metadata in local files. This is sufficient for small-scale, personal prototyping, but for more serious use cases, you should set up a cloud-based centralized metadata service. Centralized metadata tracking provides the following benefits:

- You need a metadata service to be able to use a production scheduler because a cloud-based scheduler doesn't have a concept of "local files."
- You can execute runs anywhere, both in prototyping and production, and rest assured that metadata is always tracked consistently in a single place.
- Centralized metadata enables collaboration because all users can discover and access the results of past runs, regardless of who initiated them. More about this in section 6.3.
- A cloud-based service is more stable: all metadata can be stored in a database that can be replicated and regularly backed up.

SETTING UP A CENTRALIZED METADATA SERVICE FOR METAFLOW

As of the writing of this book, the metadata service provided by Metaflow is a typical containerized microservice that uses Amazon Relational Database Service (RDS) to store the metadata. It is possible to deploy the service on AWS Elastic Container Service (ECS) or on Elastic Kubernetes Service (EKS), for example.

The easiest way to deploy the service is to use the CloudFormation template provided by Metaflow, as instructed by Metaflow's installation instructions (https://docs.metaflow.org). Another benefit of using the CloudFormation template is that it can also set up AWS Step Functions, which we will use in the next section.

After you have set up and configured the Metaflow metadata service, you can use the Client API to access results as before—nothing changes in the user-facing API. You can ensure that Metaflow is using a metadata service instead of local files by running

```
# metaflow status
```

If the service is properly configured, you should see an output like the following:

```
# Using Metadata provider at:
   https://x3kbc0qyc2.execute-api.us-east-1.amazonaws.com/api/
```

You can test that the service works correctly by executing any flow with the `run` command. You should notice that the run and task IDs are much shorter (e.g., `HelloFlow/2` versus `HelloFlow/1624840556112887`) when using the service. The local mode uses timestamps as IDs, whereas the service produces globally unique short IDs.

If you are unsure what metadata service the Client API uses, you can find it using the `get_metadata` function. You can execute a cell like this in a notebook:

```
from metaflow import get_metadata
print(get_metadata())
```

If a service is used correctly, you should see an output like the following:

```
service@https://x3kbc0qyc2.execute-api.us-east-1.amazonaws.com/api/
```

Metaflow stores its configuration at ~/.metaflowconfig/ in the user's home directory. If you have many data scientists in your organization, it is beneficial to share the same set of configuration files with all of them, so they can benefit from a consistent infrastructure and collaborate through a shared metadata service and datastore. On the other hand, if you need to maintain boundaries between organizations, for example, for data governance reasons, you can set up multiple independent metadata services. You can also define hard security boundaries between different datastores by using separate S3 buckets.

After you have configured Metaflow to use an S3-based datastore and centralized metadata, there may be times when you want to test something with a local datastore and metadata, for instance, for troubleshooting purposes. You can do this as follows:

```
# python myflow.py --datastore=local --metadata=local run
```

These options instruct Metaflow to fall back to a local datastore and metadata, regardless of the default configuration.

6.1.2 Using AWS Step Functions with Metaflow

AWS Step Functions (SFN) is a highly available and scalable workflow orchestrator (job scheduler) provided as a cloud service by AWS. Although many other off-the-shelf workflow orchestrators are available, SFN has a number of appealing features compared to alternatives, as described next:

- Similar to AWS Batch, it is a fully managed service. In the operator's point of view, the service is practically maintenance-free.
- AWS has an excellent track record of making services highly available and scalable. Though many alternatives claim to have these characteristics, not all of them work as advertised.
- The total cost of operation can be very competitive compared to the full cost of operating a similar service in-house, particularly considering that keeping the system running requires no staff.
- SFN integrates with other AWS services seamlessly.

When it comes to the downsides of SFN, as of the writing this book, it is hard to define workflows for SFN manually without a library like Metaflow using their native JSON-based syntax, and the GUI is a bit clunky. Also, SFN has some limits that constrain the maximum size of a workflow, which may affect workflows with very wide `foreaches`.

Let's see how it works in practice. First, make sure you have deployed the Step Functions integration to Metaflow as instructed in the Metaflow's documentation. The easiest way is to use the provided CloudFormation template, which sets it up for you, together with a metadata service. Next, let's define a simple flow, shown in the next listing, that we use to test SFN.

Listing 6.1   A simple flow to test Step Functions

```python
from metaflow import FlowSpec, Parameter, step

class SFNTestFlow(FlowSpec):

    num = Parameter('num',
                    help="Give a number",
                    default=1)

    @step
    def start(self):
        print("The number defined as a parameter is", self.num)
        self.next(self.end)

    @step
    def end(self):
        print('done!')

if __name__ == '__main__':
    SFNTestFlow()
```

Save the code to sfntest.py and make sure it works locally:

```
# python sfntest.py run
```

Next, let's deploy the workflow to production! All you have to do is to execute the next command:

```
# python sfntest.py step-functions create
```

If all goes well, you should see output like this:

```
Deploying SFNTestFlow to AWS Step Functions…
It seems this is the first time you are deploying SFNTestFlow to AWS Step
    Functions.

A new production token generated.
The namespace of this production flow is
    production:sfntestflow-0-xjke

To analyze results of this production flow add this line in your notebooks:
    namespace("production:sfntestflow-0-xjke")

If you want to authorize other people to deploy new versions of this flow to
    AWS Step Functions, they need to call
    step-functions create --authorize sfntestflow-0-xjke
when deploying this flow to AWS Step Functions for the first time.
See "Organizing Results" at https://docs.metaflow.org/ for more information
    about production tokens.

Workflow SFNTestFlow pushed to AWS Step Functions successfully.
What will trigger execution of the workflow:
    No triggers defined. You need to launch this workflow manually.
```

We don't have to worry about most of this output for now. We will dive deeper into *production tokens* in section 6.3. It is worth paying attention to the last line, though: as it says, in its current form, the workflow doesn't start automatically. We will need to start or trigger it manually.

What exactly happened when you ran `step-function create`? Metaflow did a bunch of work behind the scenes, which is illustrated in figure 6.5.

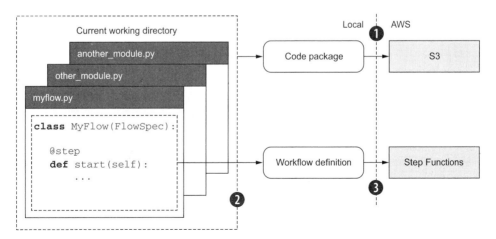

Figure 6.5   How Metaflow deploys to AWS Step Functions

The following sequence of operations was executed:

1. Metaflow packaged all Python code in the current working directory and uploaded it to the datastore (S3) so it can be executed remotely. More about this in the next section.

2. Metaflow parsed the workflow DAG and translated it to a syntax that SFN understands. In other words, it converted your local Metaflow workflow to a bona fide SFN workflow.

3. Metaflow made a number of calls to AWS APIs to deploy the translated workflow to the cloud.

Notably, the user didn't have to change anything in their code to make it deployable to the cloud. This is an important feature of Metaflow: you can test the code locally and with a compute layer of your choice, like AWS Batch, before deploying it to production. It is exactly the same code running in production, so you can be confident that if the code worked during local testing, it will also work in production. Even more important, if the workflow fails in production, you can reproduce and fix the issue locally and deploy a fixed version to production just by running `step-functions create` again—more about this in section 6.3.

> **PRODUCTIVITY TIP** When it comes to interaction with production deployments, which we discussed in chapter 2, it is crucial that the workflows you prototype locally can work in production with minimal changes, and vice versa. This makes it easy to test the code locally before deploying it production and, when tasks fail in production, reproduce those issues locally.

Before we run the workflow, let's log in to the AWS console to see how the workflow looks on the SFN side. Navigate to the Step Functions UI on the AWS Console. You should see a list of workflows, like what is shown in figure 6.6.

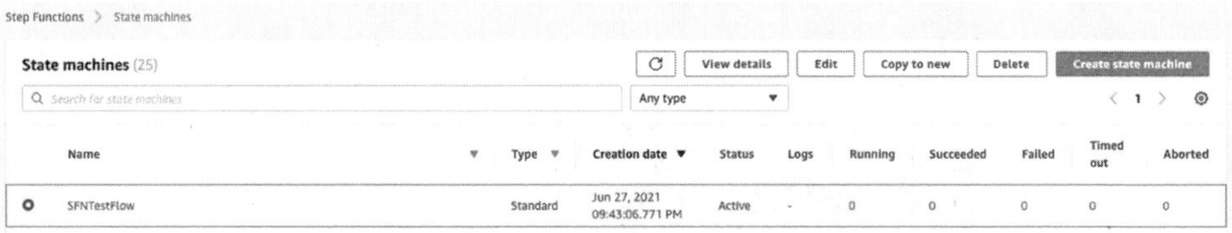

Figure 6.6   List of workflows (state machines) on the AWS Step Functions console

The view shown in figure 6.6 gives you a quick overview of currently executing, succeeded, and failed runs. When you click the name of the run, you will get to the view shown in figure 6.7.

There is not much to see here yet, because there are no executions. Although the "Start execution" button sounds enticing, there is actually a better way to start a run. If you click the button, SFN will ask you to specify a JSON that should include parameters

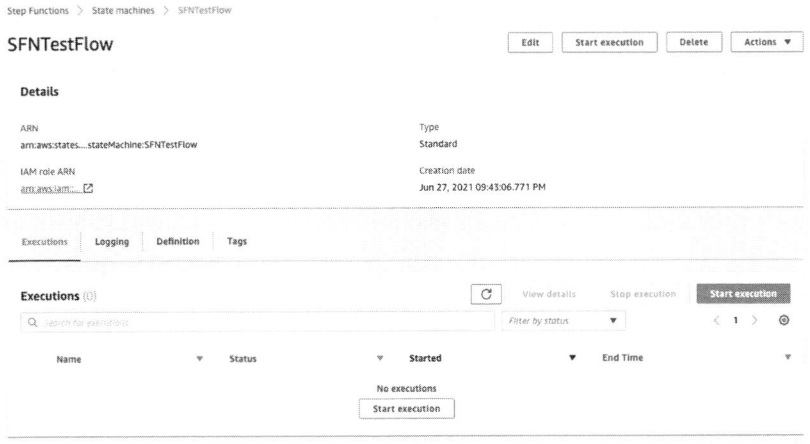

Figure 6.7 A workflow on the AWS Step Functions console

for the flow, which is a bit tedious to do manually. Instead, we can trigger an execution on the command line like so:

```
python sfntest.py step-functions trigger
```

You should see an output like the following:

```
Workflow SFNTestFlow triggered on AWS Step Functions
    (run-id sfn-344c543e-e4d2-4d06-9d93-c673d6d9e167
```

When executing flows on SFN, the Metaflow run IDs correspond to the SFN run IDs, other than the `sfn` prefix added by Metaflow, so it is easy to know what Metaflow runs map to which SFN executions.

The `trigger` command is similar to the `run` command in the sense that they both execute a workflow. However, instead of executing it locally, `trigger` makes the workflow execute on SFN. Crucially, you could shut down your laptop, and the run would keep running on SFN, in contrast to local runs. In fact, SFN supports workflows that execute for as long as a year! It would be quite inconvenient to keep your laptop running without interruptions for that long.

Now if you refresh the workflow listing, you should see a new execution. If you click it, you get to the run view shown in figure 6.8.

Note how the ID in the upper-left corner matches the ID that was output by `trigger`. Conveniently, the run view visualizes the DAG of our workflow. It updates in real time, showing what steps are being executed. If you click a step in the DAG, on the right panel you see a Resource link that takes you to the AWS Batch console that shows an AWS Batch job corresponding to the executing task. On the AWS Batch console, you can click the Log Stream link to see the task's output in real time. You can

Figure 6.8   A run on the AWS Step Functions console

see logs even more easily by using the familiar `logs` command (replace the ID with your ID output by `trigger`):

```
python sfntest.py logs sfn-344c543e-e4d2-4d06-9d93-c673d6d9e167/start
```

All Metaflow commands and the Client API work equally with local runs and runs execution on SFN—only the format of their IDs differ.

As shown next, we can trigger another execution with a custom parameter value

```
python sfntest.py step-functions trigger --num 2021
```

which produces a new run ID like

```
Workflow SFNTestFlow triggered on AWS Step Functions
    (run-id sfn-838650b2-4182-4802-9b1e-420bb726f7bd)
```

You can confirm that the parameter change took effect by inspecting artifacts of the triggered run with the command

```
python sfntest.py dump sfn-838650b2-4182-4802-9b1e-420bb726f7bd/start
```

or by checking the logs of the `start` step. Note that you can list SFN runs on the command line by executing the following:

```
python sfntest.py step-functions list-runs
```

Hence, it is possible to trigger and discover runs as well as examine logs and artifacts without logging in to the SFN console.

Let's take a deep breath and summarize what we just learned:

1 We defined a normal Metaflow workflow that we were able to test locally as before.

2 We used a command, `step-functions create`, to deploy the workflow to a highly available, scalable production scheduler in the cloud, AWS Step Functions.

3 We triggered a production run with `step-functions trigger`, optionally using custom parameters. The workflow would keep running even if you shut down your laptop.

4 We monitored workflow executions in real time on a GUI provided by SFN.

5 We inspected the logs and results of a production run using familiar CLI commands.

The simplicity of the whole process may make it seem deceptively trivial. However, being able to deploy workflows to a production scheduler this easily is truly a super-power for data scientists! Using this approach results in highly available workflows, thanks to SFN. However, we launched the workflow manually with `trigger`, so the setup is not yet fully automated. In the next section, we will address this shortcoming.

6.1.3 *Scheduling runs with @schedule*

Production flows should execute without any human intervention. If you have a complex environment with many interdependent workflows, it is advisable to trigger workflows programmatically based on events, for instance, retrain a model whenever the input data updates. This section focuses on a simpler, more common approach: deploying workflows to run on a predetermined schedule.

Metaflow provides a flow-level decorator, `@schedule`, which allows you to define an execution schedule for the workflow. See an example in the following code listing.

Listing 6.2 A flow with `@schedule`

```
from metaflow import FlowSpec, Parameter, step, schedule

@schedule(daily=True)              ◁──┐  Makes the workflow trigger
class DailySFNTestFlow(FlowSpec):     │  automatically every midnight

    num = Parameter('num',
                    help="Give a number",
                    default=1)

    @step
    def start(self):
        print("The number defined as a parameter is", self.num)
        self.next(self.end)

    @step
```

```
    def end(self):
        print('done!')

if __name__ == '__main__':
    DailySFNTestFlow()
```

Save the code in dailysfntest.py. Here, we define a simple daily schedule by annotating the flow with @schedule(daily=True). This will make the flow start every midnight in the UTC time zone. The @schedule doesn't have any effect when running the flow locally. It will take effect when you execute the following:

```
python dailysfntest.py step-functions create
```

That's it! The workflow will now run automatically once a day. You can observe run IDs of past executions on the SFN UI or with step-functions list-runs as described earlier.

Note that you can't change parameter values for scheduled runs—all parameters are assigned their default values. If you need to parametrize the workflow dynamically, you can do so using arbitrary Python code, for example, in the start step.

Besides running the workflow daily, the following shorthand decorators are available:

- @schedule(weekly=True)—Runs the workflow on Sundays at midnight
- @schedule(hourly=True)—Runs the workflows hourly

Alternatively, you can define a custom schedule with the cron attribute. For instance, this expression runs a workflow daily at 10 a.m.: @schedule(cron='0 10 * * ? *'). You can find more examples of cron schedules and a description of the syntax at http://mng.bz/KxvE.

Now we have learned how to schedule flows for execution without human supervision, which covers the *automation* requirement of production deployments. Next, we will shift our attention to *high availability*, that is, how to keep the deployments stable in the midst of a constantly changing environment.

6.2 *Stable execution environments*

Alex is proud of the modern infrastructure stack that they set up with Bowie. It allows all data scientists at the company to develop workflows locally and deploy them easily to a robust production scheduler in the cloud. Alex heads to a well-deserved vacation. During the vacation, Alex receives a notification alerting that one of the production workflows that had been running flawlessly for weeks had mysteriously crashed last night. As Alex investigates the matter, it turns out that the workflow always installs the latest version of Tensor-Flow. Just yesterday, TensorFlow released a new version that is incompatible with the production workflow. Why do these things always seem to happen during vacation?

Practically all data science and machine learning workflows use third-party libraries. In fact, it is almost certain that the vast majority of all lines of code in your workflows reside in these libraries. During development, you can test the behavior of the library with different datasets and parameterizations to gain confidence that a particular version of the library works correctly, but what happens when a new version is released? Most modern machine learning and data science libraries evolve rapidly.

This problem is not specific to data science. Software engineers have been grappling with *dependency management* for decades. Many established best practices for developing and releasing software libraries exist. For instance, most well-behaving libraries are careful in changing their public APIs, which would break applications that use the library.

The public API of a library is supposed to provide a clear contract. Imagine you have a library that provides a function, `requests.get(url)`, which fetches the given URL over HTTP and returns the content as a byte string. Just reading a short description of the function makes it clear how the function is supposed to behave. Contrast this with a machine learning library that provides the following API for K-means clustering: `KMeans(k).fit(data)`. The contract is much looser: the library may change how the clusters are initialized, which optimization algorithm is used, how the data is handled, and how the implementation is distributed over multiple CPU or GPU cores, without changing the API. All these changes may subtly change the behavior of the library and cause unintentional side effects.

Loose API contracts and the statistical nature of data science in general make dependency management for data science workflows a trickier problem than what software engineers have faced. For instance, imagine that a machine learning library includes a method called `train()`. The method may use a technique like *stochastic gradient descent* internally, which can be implemented in many different ways, each with its own pros and cons. If the implementation changes across library versions, it may have major effects on the resulting model, although, technically, the `train()` API stays intact. Failures in software engineering are often pretty clear—maybe the return type has changed, or the function raises a new exception, causing the program to crash with a verbose error message. In data science, however, you may simply get a slightly skewed distribution of results without any failures, making it hard to even notice that something has changed.

When you are prototyping a new application, it is certainly convenient to have the flexibility to use the latest versions of any libraries. During prototyping, no one relies on the outputs of your workflow, so rapid changes are acceptable and expected. However, when you deploy the workflow in production, being more careful with dependencies starts to matter. You don't want to be notified during vacation about unexpected failures in a production pipeline (like poor Alex) or face hard-to-debug questions about why the results seem subtly different than before. To avoid any surprises, you want production deployments to execute in an environment that is as stable as possible, so that nothing changes without your explicit action and approval.

EXECUTION ENVIRONMENT

What do we mean by the *execution environment*? Consider the Metaflow workflows that we have executed earlier, such as KMeansFlow, which we developed in the previous chapter. When you run a workflow by executing, say, python kmeans_flow.py run, the entry point to execution is kmeans_flow.py, but a number of other modules and libraries need to be present for the flow to execute successfully, which together make the execution environment for kmeans_flow.py. Figure 6.9 illustrates the idea.

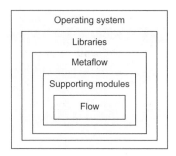

Figure 6.9   Layers of the execution environment of a flow

At the center we have the flow itself, kmeans_flow.py. The flow may use user-defined supporting modules, like scale_data.py, which contain functions for loading data. To execute the flow, you need Metaflow, which is a library in itself. On top of this, you have all other third-party libraries like Scikit-Learn, which we used in the K-means example. Finally, the whole package executes on top of an operating system.

To provide a stable execution environment for production deployments, it is beneficial to freeze an immutable snapshot of all of the layers shown in figure 6.9. Note that this includes all *transitive dependencies*, that is, all libraries that other libraries themselves use. By doing this, you ensure that new library releases can't have unplanned effects on the deployment. You are in control of how and when you want to upgrade libraries.

> **RECOMMENDATION**   To minimize surprises, it is beneficial to freeze all code in the production deployment, including the workflow itself and all of its dependencies.

Technically, we have many ways to implement snapshotting like this. A common way is to package all of the layers shown in figure 6.9 in a container image using a tool like Docker. We discuss this approach in section 6.2.3. Alternatively, Metaflow provides built-in functionality that takes care of snapshotting the layers, which we discuss in the next sections. To make the discussions more fun and concrete, we frame them in the context of a realistic data science application: time-series forecasting.

EXAMPLE: TIME-SERIES FORECASTING

Countless applications exist for time-series forecasting, that is, predicting future data points given historical data. Many techniques for forecasting and many off-the-shelf packages include efficient implementations of these techniques. Packages like these are a typical example of the software libraries we want to include in a data science workflow, so we use a forecasting application to demonstrate the concepts related to dependency management and stable execution environments. In the following examples, we will use a library called Sktime (sktime.org).

Because we just learned how to schedule a workflow to run automatically, let's pick an application that requires frequent updates: weather forecasting. We don't dare to dive deep into meteorology—instead, we simply provide an hourly temperature forecast for the next few days given a series of past temperatures at a given location. Naturally, this is a silly way of forecasting weather, but temperature data is readily available and we can implement the application easily.

We will use a service called OpenWeatherMap (openweathermap.org) to obtain weather data. To use the service, you need to sign up for a free account at the site. After you have signed up, you will receive a private application ID token, which you can input in the following examples. The required token is a string that looks like this: `6e5db45abe65e3110be635abfb9bdac5`.

After you have completed the weather forecasting examples, you can replace the weather dataset with another real-time time series, such as stock prices, as an exercise.

6.2.1 *How Metaflow packages flows*

In chapter 4, we learned how to execute workflows in the cloud simply by executing `run --with batch`. Somehow, Metaflow managed to take the code that you wrote on a local workstation, maybe a laptop, and execute it hundreds or thousands of miles away in a cloud data center. Remarkably, you didn't have to do anything to save or package the code in any particular way to make this happen. This is thanks to the fact that Metaflow packages the user code and its supporting modules automatically in a *code package*.

By default, the code package includes the flow module, any other Python (.py) files in the current working directory and its subdirectories, and the Metaflow library itself. This corresponds to the highlighted layers in figure 6.10.

To see how this works in practice, let's start by creating a supporting module for our weather forecast application. The module, shown in listing 6.3, fetches a time series of temperatures in a given location for the past five days from OpenWeatherMap.

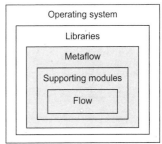

Figure 6.10 What is included in the Metaflow code package

Listing 6.3 A utility module to get temperature time series

An API endpoint that returns
historical weather data

```
from datetime import datetime, timedelta

HISTORY_API = 'https://api.openweathermap.org/data/2.5/onecall/timemachine'

def get_historical_weather_data(appid, lat, lon):        ◁── Returns a time series
    import pandas as pd                                      of temperatures over
    import requests                                          the past five days

    now = datetime.utcnow()
    data = []
    index = []
    for ago in range(5, 0, -1):
        tstamp = int((now - timedelta(days=ago)).timestamp())
        params = {'lat': lat, 'lon': lon, 'dt': tstamp,
                  'appid': appid, 'units': 'imperial'}
        reply = requests.get(HISTORY_API, params=params).json()
        for hour in reply['hourly']:
            data.append(hour['temp'])
            index.append(datetime.utcfromtimestamp(hour['dt']))
    return pd.Series(data=data,
                     index=pd.DatetimeIndex(index, freq='infer'))

def series_to_list(series):                              ◁──
    index = map(lambda x: x.isoformat(), series.index)
    return list(zip(index, series))
```

Does imports inside the function to avoid module-level dependencies

Requests data for the past five days in chronological order

Prepares and sends a request to OpenWeatherMap

Constructs a time series of hourly temperatures

Converts a pandas time series to a list of tuples

Save the code to openweatherdata.py. The module contains two functions: get_historical_weather_data, which returns a time series of temperatures over the past five days, and a utility function, series_to_list, which converts a pandas time series to a list of tuples.

The get_historical_weather_data function takes three arguments: your private appid, which you can obtain by signing up at OpenWeatherMap, and the latitude (lat) and longitude (lon) of the location for which you want the weather data.

The function showcases an important convention: in contrast to the typical Python convention of doing all import statements at the top of the module, we import all third-party modules—that is, modules not in the Python standard library like pandas and Requests—inside the function body. This makes it possible for anyone to import the module, even if they don't have these two libraries installed. They can use some functions of the module without having to install every single dependency.

CONVENTION If you think a supporting module may be used in many different contexts, it is a good idea to import any third-party libraries inside the function body that uses the libraries instead of importing them at the top of the file. This way, the module itself can be imported without having to install the union of all dependencies required by all functions of the module.

The OpenWeatherMap API returns hourly data for a single day in a request, so we need a loop to retrieve data for the past five days. For each day, the service returns a JSON object, which contains an array of hourly temperatures in degrees Fahrenheit. If you prefer Celsius, change units from imperial to metric. We convert the daily arrays to a single pandas time series, which is keyed by a datetime object for each hour. This format makes it easy to plot and use the data for forecasting.

The series_to_list function simply takes a pandas time series like what is produced by get_historical_weather_data and converts it to a Python list of tuples. We will get back to the motivation of this function later.

A benefit of having a separate module is that you can test it easily, independent of any flows. Open a notebook or a Python shell and try the following lines:

```
from openweatherdata import get_historical_weather_data
APPID = 'my-private-token'
LAT = 37.7749
LON = 122.4194
get_historical_weather_data(APPID, LAT, LON)
```

You can replace LAT and LON with a location other than San Francisco. Replace APPID with your private token. If all goes well, you should see a list of temperatures. Note that you need to have pandas installed to be able to do this. If you don't have it installed, don't worry—you will be able to see results soon nonetheless!

Next, we can start developing the actual flow for forecasting. Following our spiral approach to flow development, we don't worry about the forecasting model yet. We just plug in the inputs, which are provided by openweatherdata.py, and some outputs. We'll use @conda to include external libraries as we did in the two previous chapters, and we'll cover this in more detail in the next section. The following listing contains the first iteration of ForecastFlow.

> **Listing 6.4 The first version of `ForecastFlow`**

Loads the input data in the start step using our openweatherdata module

```
from metaflow import FlowSpec, step, Parameter, conda

class ForecastFlow(FlowSpec):

    appid = Parameter('appid', required=True)
    location = Parameter('location', default='36.1699,115.1398')

    @conda(python='3.8.10', libraries={'sktime': '0.6.1'})
    @step
    def start(self):
        from openweatherdata import get_historical_weather_data,
            series_to_list
        lat, lon = map(float, self.location.split(','))
        self.pd_past5days = get_historical_weather_data(self.appid, lat, lon)
        self.past5days = series_to_list(self.pd_past5days)
```

Saves a Python version of the data series in another artifact

Saves the pandas data series in one artifact

```
        self.next(self.plot)

    @conda(python='3.8.10', libraries={'sktime': '0.6.1',
                                       'seaborn': '0.11.1'})
    @step
    def plot(self):
        from sktime.utils.plotting import plot_series
        from io import BytesIO
        buf = BytesIO()
        fig, _ = plot_series(self.pd_past5days, labels=['past5days'])
        fig.savefig(buf)
        self.plot = buf.getvalue()
        self.next(self.end)

    @conda(python='3.8.10')
    @step
    def end(self):
        pass

if __name__ == '__main__':
    ForecastFlow()
```

This is our output step. It plots the time series.

Stores the plot in an artifact

Plots and saves the time series in an in-memory buffer

Save the listing to forecast1.py. To run the listing, you need Conda installed as instructed in the appendix.

The start step is responsible for getting the input data, which it delegates to the supporting module, openweatherdata.py, which we created in listing 6.3. Notably, the start step creates two artifacts: pd_past5days, which contains a pandas time series of temperatures for the past five days, and past5days, which contains the same data converted to a Python list. Note that we didn't have to specify the pandas dependency explicitly because it is a transitive dependency of the Seaborn package.

You may wonder what the point is of storing the same data twice, just in two different formats. The motivation is, again, dependencies: to read pd_past5days using the Client API, for example, in a notebook, you need pandas—a particular version of pandas—to be installed. In contrast, you can read past5days without any dependencies besides Python. We could store only past5days, but other steps of the flow need a pandas version, and they are guaranteed to have the correct version of pandas available, thanks to the @conda decorator.

> **RECOMMENDATION** You should prefer storing artifacts as built-in Python types instead of objects that rely on third-party libraries, because native Python types are universally readable in different contexts without external dependencies. If you need to use a complex object within a flow, consider storing both a shareable Python version as well as an object version as separate artifacts.

Try executing the flow as follows:

```
python forecast1.py  --environment=conda run --appid my-private-token
```

Replace `my-private-token` with your personal `OpenWeatherMap` token. Running the flow for the first time will take a few minutes because the Conda environments need to be initialized. Subsequent runs should be much faster.

After the run has completed, you can open a notebook and instantiate a `Run` object that corresponds to the run that just finished. You can see a temperature plot by executing the following cell:

```
From metaflow import Run
from IPython.display import Image
run = Run('ForecastFlow/16242950734051543')
Image(data=run.data.plot)
```

Replace the run ID with an actual ID from your run. Figure 6.11 shows what the result looks like. It shows a plot of hourly temperatures in Las Vegas, unless you change the `--location`, over five days. In this case, you can see a clear pattern of temperature variation between day and night. Your time series will look different because the weather is not constant.

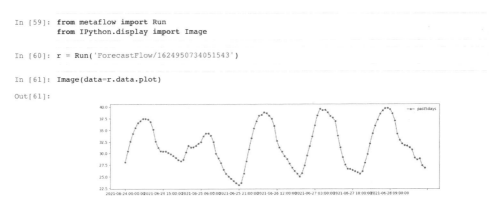

Figure 6.11   A time series of hourly temperatures in Las Vegas

The fact that you can show the plot with a single statement highlights another important detail about dependency management: sometimes it is beneficial to produce images inside Metaflow instead of in a notebook. Although you could call `plot_series` with `pd_past5days` in a notebook as well, it would require that you have the pandas, Sktime, and Seaborn packages installed and available in your notebook kernel. Even if you have them installed, your colleague might not.

How to produce and store images inside Metaflow is demonstrated by the `plot` step. Many visualization libraries like Matplotlib allow a plot to be rendered and saved in an in-memory buffer (`buf`). You can then save bytes from the buffer, that is, an image file, in a Metaflow artifact (here, `self.plot`), so the Client API can easily retrieve it.

RECOMMENDATION   If your flow benefits from plots that should be easily accessible by multiple stakeholders, consider producing and saving them inside Metaflow steps instead of in a notebook. This way stakeholders don't need to install any additional dependencies to be able to see the images.

This pattern of producing plots inside Metaflow is particularly useful for production deployments, after you have determined what plots are useful for monitoring the flow, and it is beneficial to be able to share them widely. In contrast, during prototyping, it is probably easier to design and iterate on visualizations rapidly in a notebook.

METAFLOW CODE PACKAGE

Now that we have a working flow, we can get back to the original question of this section: what is included in a Metaflow code package, and how is it constructed?

You can see the contents of the code package by executing `package list`:

```
python forecast1.py --environment=conda package list
```

Note that you need to specify `--environment=conda` for all commands, including `package list`, that apply to a flow using the `@conda` decorator. You can also set an environment variable, `METAFLOW_ENVIRONMENT=conda`, to avoid having to set the option explicitly.

You should see a long list of files. Notice the following two things about the list:

1   By default, Metaflow includes all files ending with the .py suffix—that is, Python source files—in the current working directory and its subdirectories in the job package. This allows you to use custom modules and Python packages in your projects easily—just include them in the same working directory.

2   Metaflow includes Metaflow itself in the job package, which allows you to use generic container images in the cloud, because they don't need to have Metaflow preinstalled. Also, it guarantees that the results you see locally match the results you get in the cloud.

Sometimes you may want to include files other than Python in the code package. For instance, your data processing step may execute SQL statements stored in separate .sql files or your code may call a custom binary. You can include any files in the job package by using the –package-suffixes option. Consider a hypothetical project with the following directory structure:

```
mylibrary/__init__.py
mylibrary/database.py
mylibrary/preprocess.py
sql/input_data.sql
myflow.py
```

Here, `mylibrary` is a *Python package* (if you are not familiar with Python packages, see http://mng.bz/95g0) that contains two modules, `database` and `preprocess`. Packages allow you to group multiple interrelated modules as a library. You can use the custom package in your step code simply by writing the following:

```
from mylibrary import preprocess
```

This will work even when you execute a hypothetical flow in myflow.py

```
python myflow.py run --batch
```

or deploy it to step functions, because Metaflow packages all Python files recursively in the job package. However, to include input_data.sql in the code package, you need to execute

```
python myflow.py --package-suffixes .sql run --batch
```

which instructs Metaflow to include all .sql files in addition to .py files in the code package. To access the SQL file in your code, you can open the file as usual, like so:

```
open('sql/input_data.sql')
```

Note that you should always use relative paths instead of absolute paths (any path starting with a slash) like /Users/ville/arc/sql/input_data.sql in your Metaflow code because absolute paths won't work outside your personal workstation.

Technically, you could include arbitrary data files in the code package as well. However, as the name implies, code packages should be used only for executable code. It is better to handle data as data artifacts that benefit from deduplication and lazy loading. You can use the IncludeFile construct covered in chapter 3 to bundle arbitrary data files in your runs, which is a good solution for small datasets. The next chapter provides more ideas for managing large datasets.

6.2.2 *Why dependency managements matters*

In the previous section, we learned how Metaflow packages local Python files automatically in a code package that can be shipped to different compute layers, like AWS Batch, for execution. In terms of stable execution environments, we covered the three innermost layers of the onion, as depicted in figure 6.12, but code packages don't address the question of third-party libraries.

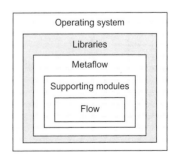

Why can't we include libraries in the code package, too? Most important, modern ML libraries tend to be complex beasts, implemented in large part in compiled languages like C++. They have much more involved requirements than simple Python packages. In particular, practically all libraries depend on many other libraries, so

Figure 6.12 Focusing on the libraries layer of the execution environment

the "libraries" layer includes not only the libraries you import directly, such as TensorFlow, but also all libraries—tens of them—that TensorFlow uses internally.

We call these libraries-used-by-libraries *transitive dependencies*. To determine the full set of libraries that need to be included in the execution environment of a task, we must identify all libraries and their transitive dependencies. Determining this graph of dependencies—the operation is commonly called *dependency resolution*—is a surprisingly nontrivial problem.

You might wonder, isn't this a solved problem already? After all, you can `pip install tensorflow`, and often it just works. Consider the following two problems that you may have faced, too:

1 *Conflicts*—The more libraries you install, the more likely it is that the dependency graph of a library you want to install conflicts with an existing library, and installation fails. For instance, many ML libraries such as Scikit-Learn and TensorFlow require specific versions of the NumPy library, so it is common to have conflicts related to a wrong version of NumPy.

   Issues like this can be hard to debug and solve. A common solution is that someone at the company carefully maintains a mutually compatible set of packages, which is a tedious job. Worse, it limits the speed of iteration. Different projects can't make choices independently because everybody must work with a common blessed set of libraries.

   Another common solution to limit the size of the dependency graph and, hence, minimize the likelihood of conflicts is to use *virtual environments* (see http://mng.bz/j2aV). With virtual environments, you can create and manage isolated sets of libraries. This is a great concept, but managing many virtual environments manually can be tedious as well.

2 *Reproducibility*—`pip install` (or `conda install`) performs dependency resolution from scratch by default. This means that you may get a different set of libraries every time you run, for example, `pip install tensorflow`. Even if you require a specific version of TensorFlow, it is possible that its transitive dependencies have evolved over time. If you want to reproduce the results of a past execution, say, a run that happened a month ago, it might be practically impossible to determine the exact set of libraries used to produce the results.

   Note that virtual environments don't help with this reproducibility problem by default, because `pip install tensorflow` is equally unpredictable inside a virtual environment. To get a stable execution environment, you need to freeze the whole virtual environment in itself.

The first problem hurts prototyping, as you can't experiment with the latest libraries easily. The second problem hurts production, because production deployments may fail due to surprising changes in their libraries. These problems are universal to every infrastructure—they are not specific to Metaflow or any other technical approach.

CONTAINERS FOR DEPENDENCY MANAGEMENT

Today, the most common solution for dependency management is to use a container image. As we briefly discussed in chapter 4, container images can encapsulate all of the layers in figure 6.12, including the operating system, albeit often the operating system *kernel*—the core of the operating system that interacts with hardware—is shared among many containers.

From the dependency management point of view, container images work like virtual environments, with similar pros and cons: they can help partition dependency graphs to avoid conflicts. A downside is that you need a system, such as a *continuous integration and deployment* (CI/CD) setup with a container registry, to create and manage a zoo of images. Most companies manage only a handful of production-ready images to reduce the amount of complexity.

Furthermore, although executing the same code on the same image guarantees a high level of reproducibility, producing reproducible images requires some effort. If you simply use `pip install tensorflow` in your image specification (e.g., Dockerfile), you have simply pushed the reproducibility problem one layer deeper.

Metaflow works well for container-based dependency management. Assuming you have a mechanism to create images, you can create an image that contains all the libraries you need and let Metaflow's code package overlay the user code on top of the base image on the fly. This is a solid solution, especially for production deployments.

For prototyping, a challenge is that creating and using containers locally is not straightforward. To address this shortcoming, Metaflow comes with built-in support for the Conda package manager, which combines an easy prototyping experience with stable production environments.

A PRAGMATIC RECIPE FOR DEPENDENCY MANAGEMENT

You can adopt a layered approach to dependency management, to balance the needs of rapid prototyping and stable production. A pragmatic recipe follows:

- Define the DAG and simple steps inside a flow module. For simple flows and prototyping, this may be all you need. You can rely on whatever libraries you have installed locally.
- Create separate *supporting modules* for logically related sets of functions. A separate module can be shared across flows and can be used outside Metaflow, such as in a notebook. Separate modules are also amenable to testing, for example, using standard unit-testing frameworks like PyTest (pytest.org).
- Use Python *packages to create custom libraries* that consist of multiple modules. As long as the package is in the same directory hierarchy as the main flow module, it will be included in the code package automatically.
- Manage *third-party libraries* using `@conda`.
- If you have complex dependency management needs that `@conda` can't handle and/or your company has a working setup for creating *container images*, use them as an alternative or complement to `@conda`.

These layers work well together: a complex project can consist of many flows, and these flows may share many modules and packages. They can run on a company-specific base image with project-specific dependencies overplayed on top of them using @conda.

6.2.3 *Using the @conda decorator*

Conda (https://conda.io) is an open source package manager that is widely used in the Python data science and machine learning ecosystem. Although Conda doesn't solve all dependency management problems by itself, it is a solid tool that you can use to solve the problems described earlier. Metaflow provides a built-in integration with Conda for the following reasons:

- The Conda ecosystem contains a huge number of ML and data science libraries.
- Conda helps solve the conflict problem by providing built-in virtual environments and a robust dependency resolver. It allows us to solve the reproducibility problem by freezing environments, as we will see soon.
- Conda handles not only Python dependencies but also system libraries. This is an important feature for data science libraries in particular, because they contain many compiled components and non-Python transitive dependencies. As a bonus, Conda handles the Python interpreter itself as a dependency, so you can use different versions of Python.

To see how Metaflow uses Conda to solve the dependency management problems in practice, let's continue our forecasting example. The following code listing contained a skeleton flow that fetched input data—the temperature over the past five days—and plotted it. We will expand the flow in this code by adding a step, forecast, that performs the actual forecasting.

Listing 6.5 `ForecastFlow` with a forecast step

```
from metaflow import FlowSpec, step, Parameter, conda, schedule

@schedule(daily=True)            ◁─┐   Schedules the forecast
class ForecastFlow(FlowSpec):      │   to run daily

    appid = Parameter('appid', default='your-private-token')  ◁─  Replaces the default
    location = Parameter('location', default='36.1699,115.1398')     with your actual
                                                                     OpenWeatherData
                                                                     API token

    @conda(python='3.8.10', libraries={'sktime': '0.6.1'})    ┐  The start step is
    @step                                                     │  exactly the same
    def start(self):                            ◁─────────────┘  as before.
        from openweatherdata import get_historical_weather_data,
        ⮑ series_to_list
        lat, lon = map(float, self.location.split(','))
        self.pd_past5days = get_historical_weather_data(self.appid, lat, lon)
        self.past5days = series_to_list(self.pd_past5days)
        self.next(self.forecast)

    @conda(python='3.8.10', libraries={'sktime': '0.6.1'})
```

Saves the predictions in a plain Python list for easy access

```
@step
def forecast(self):
    from openweatherdata import series_to_list
    from sktime.forecasting.theta import ThetaForecaster
    import numpy
    forecaster = ThetaForecaster(sp=48)
    forecaster.fit(self.pd_past5days)
    self.pd_predictions = forecaster.predict(numpy.arange(1, 48))
    self.predictions = series_to_list(self.pd_predictions)
    self.next(self.plot)
```

Creates a predictor that looks at the past 48 hours to predict the next 48 hours

```
@conda(python='3.8.10', libraries={'sktime': '0.6.1',
                                    'seaborn': '0.11.1'})
@step
def plot(self):
    from sktime.utils.plotting import plot_series
    from io import BytesIO
    buf = BytesIO()
    fig, _ = plot_series(self.pd_past5days,
                         self.pd_predictions,
                         labels=['past5days', 'predictions'])
    fig.savefig(buf)
    self.plot = buf.getvalue()
    self.next(self.end)
```

Plots the historical data and the forecast

```
@step
def end(self):
    pass


if __name__ == '__main__':
    ForecastFlow()
```

Save the code to forecast2.py. Note that we added the `@schedule` decorator so the flow can be run on a production scheduler, Step Functions, automatically. This requires that you include your personal OpenWeatherMap API token as the default value in the `appid` parameter, because no custom parameter values can be specified for scheduled runs.

The `forecast` step is the new and exciting part in this flow. It uses a particular method for time-series prediction called *the Theta method,* implemented in Sktime by the class `ThetaForecaster`. You can learn the method in detail at https://sktime.org. The method is useful for our temperature forecasting application because it accounts for seasonality. Looking at figure 6.13, it is clear that temperatures follow a diurnal cyclical pattern, at least in the desert city of Las Vegas. We use the past 48 hours to forecast the next 48 hours. Note that we store the predictions in an easily accessible pure-Python artifact, `predictions`, in addition to a pandas time-series `pd_predictions`, as discussed earlier in this chapter. We plot the predictions together with historical data in the `plot` step. Now you can run the following:

```
python forecast2.py  --environment=conda run
```

Using a notebook, like we did before, we can plot the results as shown in figure 6.13.

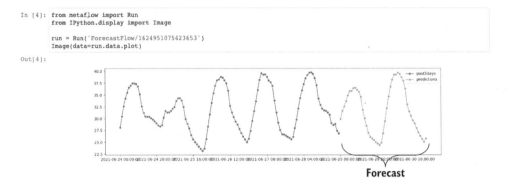

```
In [4]:  from metaflow import Run
         from IPython.display import Image

         run = Run('ForecastFlow/1624951075423653')
         Image(data=run.data.plot)
Out[4]:
```

Forecast

Figure 6.13   Forecasted hourly temperatures for Las Vegas

Just by looking at figure 6.13, the forecast seems believable for this particular time series. As an exercise, you can test different methods and parameterizations for different locations. To make the exercise even more realistic, you can use OpenWeather-Map APIs to obtain real forecasts that are based on real meteorology and compare your forecasts to theirs programmatically. Also, you can back-test forecasts by seeing how well you could have forecasted historical data based on older historical data.

Discovering Conda packages

In all examples so far, we have simply provided a predefined list of `libraries` for every `@conda` decorator. How do you find library versions that are available in the first place?

Conda has the concept of Channels, which correspond to different providers of packages. The original company behind Conda, Anaconda, maintains default channels for Conda. Another common channel is Conda Forge, which is a community-maintained repository of Conda packages. You can set up a custom, private Conda channel, too.

To find packages and available versions, you can either use the `conda search` command on the command line, or you can search packages at https://anaconda.org. (Note that .org is the community site whereas .com refers to the company.)

This book is not about time-series forecasting, but rather about infrastructure, so we will focus on unpacking how the `@conda` decorator works. After you start a run, but before any tasks execute, `@conda` performs the following sequence of actions:

1 It walks through every step of the flow and determines which virtual environments need to be created. Every unique combination of Python version and libraries requires an isolated environment.

2 If an existing environment is found locally that has the right Python version and libraries, it can be used without changes. This is why subsequent executions are faster than the first one.

3 If an existing environment is not found, Conda is used to perform dependency resolution to resolve the full list of libraries, including transitive dependencies, which need to be installed.

4 Installed libraries are uploaded in the datastore, such as S3, to make sure they can be accessed quickly and reliably by all tasks. A fast internet connection or using a cloud-based workstation helps make this step fast.

This sequence ensures that there's a stable execution environment for each step, which includes all libraries requested. Reflecting on the problems of dependency management, note that we did the following here:

- We minimize the likelihood of dependency conflicts by having minimally small environments—a separate virtual environment for each step. Maintaining environments this granular would be quite infeasible to do manually, but Metaflow handles it for us automatically.

- Dependency resolution is performed only once to reduce the likelihood of surprises during development.

- The list of dependencies is declared in the code itself, so the version information is stored in a version control system both by Metaflow and also by Git, if you use Git to store your workflows. This ensures a decent level of reproducibility, because you and your colleagues have an explicit declaration of the dependencies needed to reproduce results.

UNSAFE STEPS

Note that when you use –environment=conda, all steps are executed in an isolated Conda environment, even if they don't specify an explicit @conda decorator. For instance, the end step in listing 6.5 is executed in a bare-bones environment with no extra libraries, because it didn't specify any library requirements. You can't import any libraries (outside Metaflow itself) that are not explicitly listed in @conda. This is a feature, not a bug—it ensures that steps don't accidentally rely on libraries that are not declared in the code, which is a critical feature to ensure *reproducibility*.

However, in some special cases, you may need to mix isolated steps with "unsafe" steps. For instance, your workstation or the underlying container image may contain libraries that you can't install with Conda. You can declare a step unsafe by adding the decorator @conda(disabled=True), which makes the step execute as if no Conda was used. Note that doing this negates many benefits of Conda, especially when it comes to production deployments discussed later.

THE @CONDA DECORATOR IN THE CLOUD

Remarkably, you can run exactly the same code in the cloud as follows:

```
python forecast2.py  --environment=conda run --with batch
```

When running with a cloud-based compute layer like AWS Batch, the execution begins with the same sequence of operations as listed earlier. However, Metaflow needs to perform extra work to recreate the virtual environments in containers on the fly. Here's what happens in the cloud before a task executes:

1   The compute layer launches a preconfigured container image. Notably, the container image doesn't need to include Metaflow, the user code, or its dependencies. Metaflow overlays the execution environment on top of the image.

2   The code package includes the exact list of libraries that need to be installed. Notably, dependency resolution is not run again, so all tasks are guaranteed to have precisely the same environments. Note that this wouldn't be the case if you ran `pip install some_package` inside your step code. It is possible that tasks would end up with slightly different execution environments, leading to hard-to-debug failures.

3   Metaflow pulls the required libraries from its own datastore where they have been cached. This is critical for two reasons. First, imagine running a wide `foreach`, for example, hundreds of instances in parallel. If all of them hit an upstream package repository in parallel, it would amount to a *distributed denial of service attack*—the package repository can refuse to serve the files to so many parallel clients. Second, occasionally the package repositories delete or change files, which could lead to a task failing—again in a hard-to-debug fashion.

These steps guarantee that you can *prototype quickly* and locally with your favorite libraries that can be specific to each project, and you can execute the same code at scale in the cloud without having to worry about the execution environment.

We can piggyback on the same mechanism to achieve robust production deployments. Let's test the idea by deploying the forecasting flow to production, as follows:

```
python forecast2.py  --environment=conda step-functions create
```

Similar to the `run` command, `step-functions create` performs the four steps of dependency resolutions prior to the production deployment. Consequently, the production deployment is guaranteed to be isolated from any changes in the flow code (thanks to the code package), as well as changes in its dependencies (thanks to @conda) and transient errors in package repositories (thanks to package caching in the datastore). All in all, you are guaranteed to have stable execution environments.

Congratulations—you just deployed a real data science application to production! You can use the Step Functions UI to observe daily runs. As an exercise, you can create a notebook that plots daily forecasts in a single view.

FLOW-LEVEL DEPENDENCIES WITH @CONDA_BASE
Notice how listing 6.5 contains the following same set of dependencies for the `start` and `forecast` steps:

```
@conda(python='3.8.10', libraries={'sktime': '0.6.1'})
```

The `plot` step has only one additional library. As the number of steps increases, it may start feeling redundant to add the same dependencies to every step. As a solution, Metaflow provides a flow-level @conda_base decorator that specifies attributes shared by all steps. Any step-specific additions can be specified with a step-level @conda. The following listing shows an alternative version of ForecastFlow that takes this approach. The function bodies are equal to listing 6.5, so they are omitted for brevity.

Listing 6.6 Demonstrating @conda_base

```
@schedule(daily=True)
@conda_base(python='3.8.10', libraries={'sktime': '0.6.1'})      ⟵⎤ Uses @conda_base
class ForecastFlow(FlowSpec):                                        │ to define a common
                                                                     │ Python version and
    @step                                                            │ libraries
    def start(self):
        ...

    @step
    def forecast(self):
        ...                                                 Uses a step-level @conda
                                                            to add step-level additions
    @conda(libraries={'seaborn': '0.11.1'})   ⟵──┘         to the common base
    @step
    def plot(self):
        ...

    @step
    def end(self):
        ...
```

This concludes our exploration into dependency management for now. We will use and expand these lessons later in chapter 9, which presents a realistic machine learning application using pluggable dependencies. Next, we will address another important element of production deployments that is a common source of sporadic failures: human beings.

6.3 Stable operations

An intern, Finley, joins the company for the summer. Finley has a strong theoretical background in Bayesian statistics. Alex suggests that they could organize a fun internal competition to compare the performance of a Bayesian model created by Finley to a neural network model that Alex has wanted to build. Initially, Alex is overjoyed to see that the neural network model seems to be working better in the benchmark. However, as they validate the final results, they notice that Alex's prediction workflow had accidentally used Finley's model, so, in fact, Finley is the winner. If only Alex had been more careful in organizing the experiment, they could have spent more time perfecting the model instead of being misled by incorrect results.

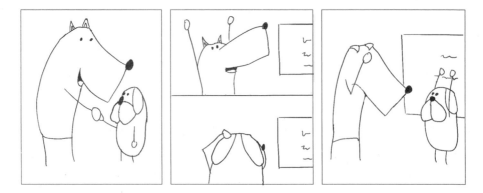

Imagine you have deployed a workflow to a production scheduler for the first time, as discussed in the previous sections. For most projects, this is merely the beginning, not the end. Increasingly often, the data scientists who develop workflows are also responsible for operating them in production. Hence, the data scientist has two responsibilities: first, keeping the production workflows running without interruptions, and second, continuing development on the workflow to improve results.

A challenge is that the two responsibilities have diametrically opposite goals: the production workflows need to be as stable as possible, whereas prototyping may require drastic changes in the project. The key to solving this dilemma is to keep production workflows clearly isolated from prototyping, so that no matter what happens in the prototyping environment, it can't affect production, and vice versa.

In a larger project, you may not have only a single prototyping version and a single production version. Instead, a team of data scientists can work on various prototypes concurrently. To test the experimental versions, they may be deployed to run side by side with a production version in a production-like environment. All in all, you can have any number of versions of a project running concurrently at different levels of maturity. All versions of the project must stay neatly isolated from each other to make sure that the results are clean from any interference.

To make this idea more concrete, imagine a data science application, say, a recommendation system, which is under continuous development by a team of data scientists. The team's mandate is to improve the system by pushing experiments through an *experimentation funnel*, depicted in figure 6.14.

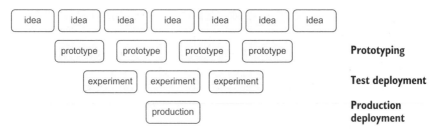

Figure 6.14   The experimentation funnel

At the top of the funnel, the team has tens or hundreds of ideas how the system could be improved. Members of the team can prototype and test a subset of prioritized ideas on their local workstations. Initial results from prototypes can help to determine which ideas warrant further development—it is expected that not all ideas will survive. Additional rounds of local development may follow.

Once you have a fully functional experimental workflow (or a set of workflows), often you will want to run an A/B experiment that compares the new version to the current production version in a live production environment. This requires that you have two or more test deployments running side by side. After some time, you can analyze the results to determine whether the new version should be promoted to be the new production version.

THE VERSIONING LAYER

The versioning layer helps to organize, isolate, and track all versions so it becomes feasible to manage even hundreds of concurrent versions and projects that are present at different levels of the experimentation funnel. In terms of our infrastructure stack, the versioning layer helps to determine *what versions of the code* are executed, as depicted in figure 6.15.

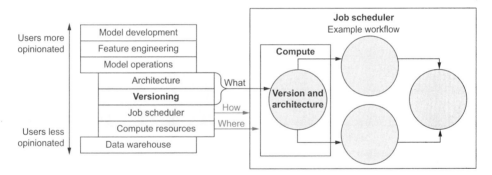

Figure 6.15   The role of the versioning layer: What code gets executed

Naturally the data scientist needs to write the code, that is, the actual business logic of the workflow in the first place. This is a concern of the (software) *architecture layer*, which we will discuss in chapter 8. It is hard to abstract away or generalize the business logic, which tends to be very specific to each project and use case, so we expect the data scientist to exercise a good deal of freedom and responsibility when it comes to developing it. Hence, it makes sense to place the architecture layer toward the top of the infrastructure stack where the infrastructure should be less constraining.

In contrast, the infrastructure can be more opinionated about versioning—keeping things neatly organized and versions clearly separated isn't a matter of personal preference but rather an organizational requirement. It is highly beneficial for everyone to use the same approach to versioning to facilitate collaboration and to avoid conflicts (like Alex and Finley's scenario earlier), which is another motivation for the infrastructure to provide a built-in versioning layer.

We can summarize the roles of the highlighted layers in figure 6.15, from the top down, as follows:

1 The data scientist designs and develops the business logic, that is, the architecture of the workflow (the architecture layer).
2 The infrastructure helps to manage multiple concurrently prototyped and deployed versions of the business logic (the versioning layer), to facilitate an experimentation funnel. Together, the architecture and the versioning layer determine *what* code is executed.
3 A robust production scheduler (the job scheduler layer), such as AWS Step Functions, determines *how* and *when* a particular workflow DAG is executed.
4 Finally, the compute layer is responsible for finding a server instance *where* each task of the workflow can be executed.

As discussed earlier, a major benefit of separating the "what, how, and where" is that we can design each subsystem independently. This section shows a reference implementation of the versioning layer as provided by Metaflow, but you could use another framework or approach to achieve the same goal: building and operating an experimentation funnel that allows a team of data scientists to iterate and test various versions of applications frictionlessly.

There isn't a single right way of building the funnel. We give you a set of tools and knowledge that help you design and customize an approach to versioning and deployments that work for your specific needs. For instance, many companies have developed their own custom wrapper scripts or CI/CD (continuous integration/continuous deployment) pipelines that leverage the mechanisms presented next. We begin the section by looking at versioning during prototyping and, after that, how to achieve safely isolated production deployments.

6.3.1 *Namespaces during prototyping*

Consider the scenario that Alex and Finley went through in the beginning of this section: both of them were prototyping alternative workflows for the same project. Accidentally, Alex analyzed Finley's results instead of his own. This highlights the need of staying organized during prototyping: each prototype should stay clearly isolated from others.

Metaflow has the concept of *namespaces* that help keep runs and artifacts organized. Let's demonstrate it with a simple workflow shown next.

> **Listing 6.7 A flow showing namespaces in action**

```
from metaflow import FlowSpec, step, get_namespace

class NamespaceFlow(FlowSpec):
```

```
    @step
    def start(self):
        print('my namespace is', get_namespace())    ◁───┐  Prints the current
        self.next(self.end)                                  namespace

    @step
    def end(self):
        pass

if __name__ == '__main__':
    NamespaceFlow()
```

Save the code in namespaceflow.py, and execute it as usual:

```
python namespaceflow.py run
```

You should see an output that mentions your username, for instance:

```
[1625945750782199/start/1 (pid 68133)] my namespace is user:ville
```

Now open a Python interpreter or a notebook, and execute the following lines:

```
from metaflow import Flow
Flow('NamespaceFlow').latest_run
```

This will print the run ID of the latest run *in the user's namespace.* In the case of the previous example, it will show the following:

```
Run('NamespaceFlow/1625945750782199')
```

Note how the run ID 1625945750782199 matches the latest executed run. You can also execute get_namespace() to confirm that the namespace is indeed the same as was used by the flow.

To show that latest-run works as expected, let's run the flow again, as follows:

```
python namespaceflow.py run
```

Now the Run ID is 1625946102336634. If you test latest_run again, you should see this ID.

Next, let's test how namespaces work when multiple users are working together. Execute the following command, which simulates another user, otheruser, running the flow concurrently:

```
USER=otheruser python namespaceflow.py run
```

Note that you are not supposed to set USER explicitly in real life. The variable is set automatically by your workstation. We set it here explicitly only to demonstrate how Metaflow behaves in the presence of multiple users.

For this run, the ID is 1625947446325543, and the namespace is user:otheruser. Figure 6.16 summarizes the executions in each namespace.

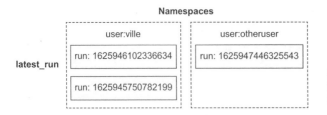

Figure 6.16 **Namespaces of two users, each with their own `latest_run`**

Now if you examine latest_run again, you will see that it still returns 1625946102336634, that is, Ville's latest run, and not the absolute newest run ID that was executed by otheruser. The reason is that the Client API respects the current namespace by default: it doesn't return the latest_run across all users but returns *your latest run.*

Built-in namespaces avoid situations like what Alex and Finley faced: It would be confusing if, say, your notebook that uses latest_run started showing different results because a colleague of yours executed the flow. By keeping metadata and artifacts namespaced, we can avoid such surprises.

Besides latest_run, you can refer to any specific run by their ID, like here:

```
from metaflow import Run
Run('NamespaceFlow/1625945750782199')
```

This will work because the specific run is in the current namespace. In contrast, try this:

```
from metaflow import Run
Run('NamespaceFlow/1625947446325543')
```

This will produce the following exception

```
metaflow.exception.MetaflowNamespaceMismatch: Object not in namespace
➡ 'user:ville'
```

because the requested flow doesn't exist in the current namespace—it belongs to otheruser. This behavior ensures that you don't accidentally refer to someone else's results, if, for example, you mistype a run ID.

> **NOTE** By default, the Client API allows you to inspect only runs and artifacts that you have produced. Actions taken by other users won't affect results returned by your Client API, unless you switch namespaces explicitly. In particular, a relative reference like latest_run is safe to use because it refers to the latest run in the current namespace and, hence, its return value can't change unexpectedly.

SWITCHING NAMESPACES

Namespaces are not a security feature. They are not meant to hide information; they just help in keeping things organized. You can inspect the results of any other user simply by switching the namespace. For instance, try the following:

```
from metaflow import Run, namespace
namespace('user:otheruser')
Run('NamespaceFlow/1625947446325543')
```

Use the `namespace` function to switch to another namespace. After a `namespace` call, the Client API accesses objects under the new namespace. Hence, it is possible to access a run by otheruser 1625947446325543. Correspondingly,

```
from metaflow import Flow
namespace('user:otheruser')
Flow('NamespaceFlow').latest_run
```

returns 1625947446325543. As you can expect, in this namespace you would get an error when accessing Ville's runs.

The `namespace` call is a convenient way to switch namespaces, for example, in a notebook. However, the Client API is also used inside flows to access data from other flows. For instance, remember `ClassifierPredictFlow` in chapter 3 that used the following lines to access the latest trained model:

```
@step
def start(self):
    run = Flow('ClassifierTrainFlow').latest_run
```

The Client API respects namespace also inside flows. The previous `latest_run` would return only models trained by your `ClassifierTrainFlow`. Now imagine that you wanted to use a model trained by your colleague, Alice. You could add a line, `namespace('user:alice')`, in the flow code to switch the namespace. However, what if the next day you want to try a model by another colleague, Bob? You could keep changing the code back and forth, but there's a better approach. Without changing anything in the code, you can switch namespaces on the command line with the `--namespace` option as follows:

```
python classifier_predict.py run --namespace user:bob
```

This makes it easy to switch between different inputs without having to hardcode anything in the code itself. Figure 6.17 illustrates the idea.

Switching namespaces changes only how the Client API *reads* data. It doesn't change how the results are stored—they are always attached to your username. Reading from any namespace is a safe operation in the sense that you can't accidentally overwrite or corrupt existing data. By limiting writes to your own namespace by default, you can be sure that your actions won't have unintended side effects for other users.

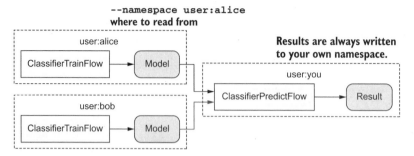

Figure 6.17   Switching between two namespaces

NOTE   Switching namespace with the `namespace` function or the `--namespace` option changes only the way the Client API reads results. It doesn't change the way results are written. They still belong to the current user's namespace by default.

GLOBAL NAMESPACE

What if you see a run ID like `NamespaceFlow/1625947446325543` in a log file, but you have no idea who started the run? You wouldn't know which namespace to use. In situations like this, you can disable the namespace safeguards by calling

```
namespace(None)
```

After this, you can access any object (runs, artifacts, etc.) without limitation. The `latest_run` will refer to the latest run executed by anyone, so its value may change at any time.

RECOMMENDATION   Don't use `namespace(None)` inside flows, because it exposes the flow to unintended side effects caused by other people (or even yourself, inadvertently) running flows. It can be a handy tool for exploring data, such as in a notebook.

6.3.2   *Production namespaces*

The previous section discussed namespaces during prototyping. In this context, it is natural to namespace runs by user, because, factually, there's always a single unambiguous user who executes the command `run`. But what about production deployments? There's no one executing a run, so whose namespace should we use?

Metaflow creates a new *production namespace* for each production deployment that is not attached to any user. Let's see what this means in practice by deploying the `namespaceflow.py` from listing 6.7 to AWS Step functions as follows:

```
python namespaceflow.py step-functions create
```

You should see an output like this:

```
Deploying NamespaceFlow to AWS Step Functions...
It seems this is the first time you are deploying NamespaceFlow to AWS Step
    Functions.
A new production token generated.
The namespace of this production flow is
    production:namespaceflow-0-fyaw
To analyze results of this production flow add this line in your notebooks:
    namespace("production:namespaceflow-0-fyaw")
If you want to authorize other people to deploy new versions of this flow to
    AWS Step Functions, they need to call
    step-functions create --authorize namespaceflow-0-fyaw
```

As the output indicates, a new unique namespace, `production:namespaceflow-0-fyaw`, was created for the deployment. As you can see, the namespace is not tied to a user, like `user:ville`, which we used during prototyping.

If you run `step-functions create` again, you will notice that the production namespace doesn't change. The deployment's namespace is tied to the flow name. It doesn't change unless you explicitly request a new namespace by executing

```
python namespaceflow.py step-functions create --generate-new-token
```

To see the namespace in action, let's trigger an execution on Step Functions like so:

```
python namespaceflow.py step-functions trigger
```

Wait for a minute or two for the execution to start. After this, open a notebook or a Python interpreter, and execute the following lines. Replace the namespace with the actual unique namespace that was output by `step-functions create`:

```
from metaflow import namespace, Flow
namespace('production:namespaceflow-0-fyaw')
Flow('NamespaceFlow').latest_run
```

You should see a `Run` object with a long ID prefixed with `sfn-`, like

```
Run('NamespaceFlow/sfn-72384eb6-2a1b-4c57-8905-df1aa544565c')
```

A key benefit of production namespaces is that your workflows can safely use the Client API, and relative references like `.latest_run` in particular, knowing the production deployments stay isolated from any prototyping that any users perform locally in their own namespace.

AUTHORIZING DEPLOYMENTS

Production namespaces include an important safeguard mechanism. Imagine a new employee, Charles, is getting used to Metaflow, and he explores various commands. As we discussed previously, local prototyping is always safe, because results are tied to

Charles's personal namespace. Charles might also test production deployments and execute the following:

```
python namespaceflow.py step-functions create
```

Charles's local version of namespaceflow.py might not be production ready, so by doing this, he might end up accidentally breaking the production deployment. We want to encourage experimentation, so we should make sure that new employees (or anyone else) don't have to be afraid of accidentally breaking anything.

To prevent accidents from happening, Metaflow prevents Charles from running step-functions create by default. Charles needs to know a unique *production token* that defines the production namespace to be able to run the command. In this case, if Charles really needs to deploy the flow to production, he would reach out to people who have deployed the flow previously, obtain the token, and execute the following:

```
python namespaceflow.py step-functions create --authorize namespaceflow-0-fyaw
```

The --authorize flag is only needed for the first deployment. After this, Charles can keep deploying the flow like anyone else. Note that --authorize is not a security feature. Charles can discover the token by himself, too, as we will see soon. It is only meant to act as an explicit confirmation for the action, which makes it a bit harder to cause damage inadvertently.

6.3.3   *Parallel deployments with @project*

When you run step-functions create, a flow is deployed to the production scheduler. The deployment is named automatically after the name of the FlowSpec class. In other words, by default there's exactly one production version attached to a flow name. You or your colleagues (after authorization) can update the deployment by running step-functions create again, but the newer version will overwrite the previous one.

As we discussed in the beginning of this section, larger projects may need multiple parallel but isolated production deployments, for example, to facilitate A/B testing of new experimental versions of the flow. Furthermore, a complex application may consist of multiple flows (like ClassifierTrainFlow and ClassifierPredictFlow in chapter 3), which should exist in the same namespace, so they can share artifacts among themselves safely. By default, when you deploy two flows with distinct names, a unique namespace will be generated for each one of them.

To address these needs, we can use a flow-level decorator called @project. The @project decorator doesn't do anything by itself, but it enables a flow, or multiple flows, to be deployed in production in a special way. The @project decorator is an optional feature that can help organize larger projects. You can start without it, have a single production version, and add it later as needs grow. Let's use a simple example shown in listing 6.8 to demonstrate the concept.

Listing 6.8   A flow with the @project decorator

```
from metaflow import FlowSpec, step, project

@project(name='demo_project')          ◁─┐   Annotates the flow with a project
class FirstFlow(FlowSpec):               │   decorator with a unique name

    @step
    def start(self):
        self.model = 'this is a demo model'
        self.next(self.end)

    @step
    def end(self):
        pass

if __name__ == '__main__':
    FirstFlow()
```

Save the code to firstflow.py. We annotated the flow with `@project`, which needs to be given a unique name. All flows with the same project name will use a single shared namespace.

Let's see what happens when you deploy it to Step Functions, as shown here:

```
python firstflow.py step-functions create
```

Thanks to the `@project` decorator, the flow isn't deployed with the name `FirstFlow` as usual. Instead, it is named `demo_project.user.ville.FirstFlow`. The `@project` is used to create parallel, uniquely named deployments. By default, the deployment is prefixed by the project name (`demo_project`) and the user who deployed the flow (`user.ville`). If another team member ran `step-functions create` with this flow, they would get a personal, unique deployment. This allows anyone to test their prototypes easily in a production environment without interfering with the main production version.

Sometimes experiments are not clearly tied to a single user. Maybe multiple data scientists collaborate on a joint experiment. In this case, it is natural to deploy the flow as a *branch*. Try this:

```
python firstflow.py --branch testbranch step-functions create
```

It will produce a deployment named `demo_project.test.testbranch.FirstFlow`—note that no username is present in the name. You can create any number of independent branches. Note that triggering respects `--branch` too. Try the following:

```
python firstflow.py --branch testbranch step-functions trigger
```

It will trigger an execution of `demo_project.test.testbranch.FirstFlow`.

By convention, if your project has a single blessed production version, you can deploy it with

```
python firstflow.py --production step-functions create
```

which will produce a deployment named demo_project.prod.FirstFlow. The --production option deploys a branched deployment like any other—there's no special semantics in --production. However, it can help to clearly distinguish the main production version from other experimental branches.

Besides allowing multiple parallel, isolated production deployments, the @project decorator is useful because it creates a single, unified namespace across multiple flows. To test the idea, let's create another flow for the same @project, shown in the following code listing.

Listing 6.9 Another flow in the same @project

```
from metaflow import FlowSpec, Flow, step, project

@project(name='demo_project')
class SecondFlow(FlowSpec):

    @step
    def start(self):
        self.model = Flow('FirstFlow').latest_run.data.model    ◁── Accesses an artifact in the same namespace
        print('model:', self.model)
        self.next(self.end)

    @step
    def end(self):
        pass

if __name__ == '__main__':
    SecondFlow()
```

Save the code in secondflow.py. You can test the flows locally by running the following:

```
python firstflow.py run
python secondflow.py run
```

Locally, the latest_run in SecondFlow refers to the latest run of FirstFlow in your personal namespace, in my case, user:ville. Let's deploy SecondFlow to our test branch as shown here:

```
python secondflow.py -branch testbranch step-functions create
```

This will deploy a flow named demo_project.test.testbranch.SecondFlow. Remarkably, both FirstFlow and SecondFlow share the same namespace, which in my case is named mfprj-pbnipyjz2ydyqlmi-0-zphk. The project namespaces are generated based on a hash of the branch name, the project name, and a unique token, so they will look a bit cryptic.

Now, trigger an execution on Step Functions as follows:

```
python secondflow.py --branch testbranch step-functions trigger
```

After a while, you can examine the results in a notebook or a Python interpreter like this:

```
from metaflow import namespace, Flow
namespace(None)
print(Flow('SecondFlow').latest_run['start'].task.stdout)
```

We use the global namespace, so we don't need to know the exact namespace used by our `testbranch`. However, this practice is a bit dangerous if other people are running `SecondFlows` simultaneously. Note that the flow name, `SecondFlow`, is still the same: the `@project` prefix is used only to name the flow for the production scheduler.

To see the power of `@project`, you can now make edits in `FirstFlow`, for instance, change the `model` string to something else. You can test changes locally as before, which won't impact the production deployment. After you are happy with the changes, you can deploy the improved `FirstFlow` as well as `SecondFlow` to a new branch, say, `newbranch`. The setup is visualized in figure 6.18.

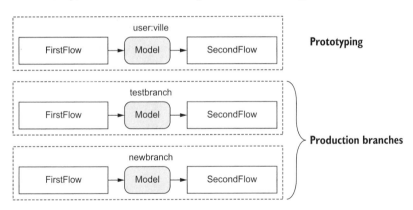

Figure 6.18   Three `@project` branches

When you execute them, only the pair of workflows deployed to `newbranch` is affected by the changes. The old version at `testbranch` is not affected. As depicted in figure 6.18, in this scenario we have three independent namespaces: the default user namespace used during prototyping and the two branches in production.

Let's summarize what we learned in this section in the context of an actual data science project. The project is developed continuously by multiple data scientists. They can generate hundreds of ideas on how to improve the project. However, we don't know which ideas work well without testing them in a realistic production environment. We visualized the process as an experiment funnel, depicted again in figure 6.19.

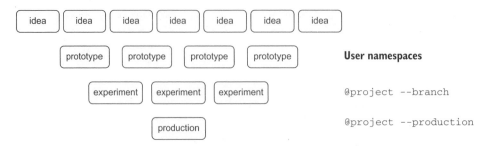

Figure 6.19   Facilitating the experimentation funnel using `@project`

Thanks to user namespaces, data scientists are able to prototype new versions and run them locally without fear of interfering with each other. Namespaces are enabled automatically to all Metaflow runs. Once they have identified the most promising ideas, they can deploy them to production as a custom `--branch` using `@project`. These custom branches can then be used to feed predictions to A/B experiments, for example. Finally, when an experiment has proven its value, it can be promoted to become the new main production version, deployed with `--production`.

Summary

- Using a centralized metadata server helps to track all executions and artifacts across all projects, users, and production deployments.
- Leverage a highly available, scalable production scheduler like AWS Step Functions to execute workflows on a schedule without human supervision.
- Use the `@schedule` decorator to make workflows run automatically on a predefined schedule.
- Metaflow's code packages encapsulate the user-defined code and supporting modules for cloud-based execution.
- Use containers and the `@conda` decorator to manage third-party dependencies in production deployments.
- User namespaces help isolate prototypes that users run on their local workstations, making sure that prototypes don't interfere with each other.
- Production deployments get a namespace of their own, isolated from prototypes. New users must obtain a production token to deploy new versions to production, which prevents accidental overwrites.
- The `@project` decorator allows multiple parallel, isolated workflows to be deployed to production concurrently.
- Use `@project` to create a unified namespace across multiple workflows.

Processing data

The past five chapters covered how to take data science projects from prototype to production. We have learned how to build workflows, use them to run computationally demanding tasks in the cloud, and deploy the workflows to a production scheduler. Now that we have a crisp idea of the prototyping loop and interaction with production deployments, we can return to the fundamental question: how should the workflows consume and produce data?

Interfacing with data is a key concern of all data science applications. Every application needs to find and read input data that is stored somewhere. Often, the application is required to write its outputs, such as fresh predictions, to the same system. Although a huge amount of variation exists among systems for managing data, in this context we use a common moniker, *data warehouse,* to refer to all of them. Given the foundational nature of data inputs and outputs, it feels appropriate to place the concern at the very bottom of the stack, as depicted in figure 7.1.

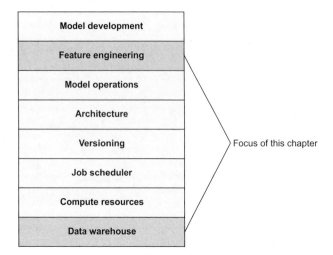

Figure 7.1   **The stack of effective data science infrastructure**

At the top of the stack resides another question related to data: how should the data scientist explore, manipulate, and prepare the data to be fed into models? This process is commonly called *feature engineering.* This chapter focuses on data at the bottom as well as the top of the stack, although we are biased toward the lower-level concerns, which are more clearly in the realm of generalized infrastructure.

Notably, this chapter is not about building or setting up data warehouses, which is a hugely complex topic of its own, covered by many other books. We assume that you have some kind of a data warehouse, that is, some way to store data, already in place. Depending on the size of your company, the nature of the data warehouse can vary widely, as depicted in figure 7.2.

If you are just prototyping, you can get going by using local files, for example, CSVs loaded using IncludeFile, which was featured in chapter 3. Most companies use a proper database such as Postgres to store their precious data assets. A medium-sized company might use multiple databases for different purposes, possibly accompanied by a federated query engine like Trino (aka Presto), which provides a unified way to query all data.

A large company might have a cloud-based data lake with multiple query engines, like Apache Flink for real-time data, Apache Iceberg for metadata management, and Apache Spark for general data processing. Don't worry if these systems are not familiar to you—we will give a high-level overview of the modern data architectures in section 7.2.1. In all these cases, data scientists face the same key question: how to access data in their workflows.

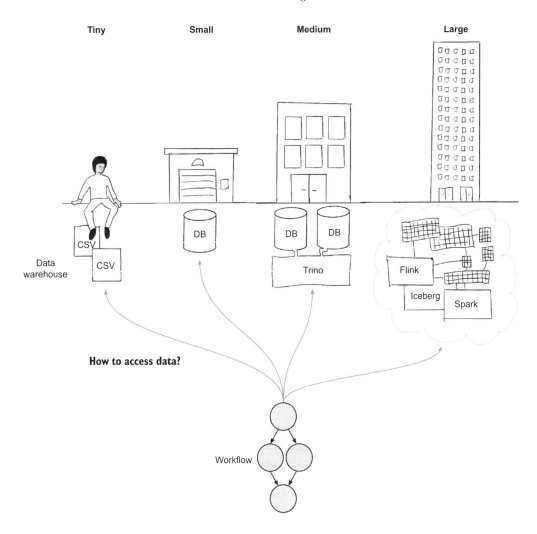

Figure 7.2 Various data infrastructures across companies from tiny to large

Besides having to integrate with different technical solutions, often the data science infrastructure needs to support different *data modalities* as well. The examples in this chapter mainly focus on *structured data*, that is, relational or tabular data sources, which are the most common data modality for business applications. In addition, the infrastructure may need to support applications dealing with *unstructured data*, like text and images. In practice, these days many real-world datasets are something in between—they are *semi-structured*. They contain some structure, such as columns strictly adhering to a schema, and some unstructured fields, for example, JSON or free-form text. This chapter focuses on data-related concerns that are common across data warehouses and data modalities, namely the following:

1   *Performance*—Given that data science applications tend to be data-intensive, that is, they may need to ingest large amounts of data, loading data can easily become a bottleneck in workflows. Having to wait for potentially tens of minutes or longer for data can make the prototyping loop quite painful, which we want to avoid. We will focus on this question in section 7.1.

2   *Data selection*—How to find and select subsets of data that are relevant for the task. SQL is the lingua franca of selecting and filtering data, so we need to find ways to interface with query engines like Spark that can execute SQL. These solutions can often be applied to semi-structured data, too, or for metadata referring to unstructured data. These topics are the theme of section 7.2.

3   *Feature engineering*—How to transform raw data to a format suitable for modeling, aka feature transformations. Once we have ingested a chunk of raw data, we need to address many concerns before the data can be input to models effectively. We will scratch the surface of this deep topic in section 7.3.

These foundational concerns apply to all environments. This chapter gives you concrete building blocks that you can use to design data access patterns, and maybe helper libraries of your own, which apply to your particular environment. Alternatively, you may end up using some higher-level libraries and products, such as *feature stores* for feature engineering, that abstract away many of these concerns. After learning the fundamentals, you will be able to evaluate and use such abstractions more effectively, as we will cover in section 7.3.

Another orthogonal dimension of data access is how frequently the application needs to react to changes in data. Similar to earlier chapters, we focus on *batch processing*, that is, applications that need to run, say, at most once in every 15 minutes. The topic of *streaming data* is certainly relevant for many data science applications that need more frequent updates, but the infrastructure required to do this is more complex. We will briefly touch on the topic in the next chapter. As we will discuss in section 7.2, surprisingly many data science applications that involve real-time data can be still modeled as batch workflows.

On top of all these dimensions we have *organizational concerns*: who should be responsible for data used by data science applications, and how are responsibilities divided between different roles—data engineers and data scientists in particular. Although the exact answers are highly company specific, we share some high-level ideas in section 7.2.

We will start the chapter with a fundamental technical question: how to load data efficiently in workflows. The tools introduced in the next section give a solid foundation for the rest of the chapter. You can find all code listings for this chapter at http://mng.bz/95zo.

7.1   Foundations of fast data

Alex developed a workflow that estimates the delivery time of cupcake orders. To train the estimator, Alex needs to ingest all historical cupcake orders from the company's main data warehouse. Surprisingly, loading the data from the database takes longer than building the model itself! After looking into the problem, Bowie realized that machine learning workflows need a faster way to access data than the previous path used mainly by dashboards. The new fast data path boosted Alex's productivity massively: it is now possible to train and test at least 10 versions of the model daily instead of just two.

When the author of this book did an informal survey of data scientists at Netflix, asking what the biggest pain point they face on a day-to-day basis is, a majority responded: finding suitable data and accessing it in their data science applications. We will come back to the question of finding data in the next section. This section focuses on the seemingly simple question: how should you load a dataset from a data warehouse to your workflow?

The question may seem quite tactical, but it has far-reaching, strategic implications. For the sake of discussion, consider that you couldn't load a dataset easily and quickly (or not at all) from a data warehouse to a separate workflow. By necessity, you would have to build models and other application logic *inside* the data warehouse system.

In fact, this has been the traditional way of thinking about data warehouses: bulk data is not supposed to be moved out. Instead, applications express their data processing needs, in SQL, for example, which the data warehouse executes, returning a tiny subset of data as results. Although this approach makes sense for traditional business intelligence, it is not a feasible idea to build machine learning models in SQL. Even if your data warehouse supports querying data with Python, for example, the fundamental issue is that the approach tightly couples the *compute layer*, which we discussed in chapter 4, with the data layer. This is problematic when workloads are very compute intensive: no mainstream database has been designed to run, say, on an autoscaling cluster of GPU-instances.

In contrast, if it is feasible to extract bulk data from the warehouse efficiently, it becomes possible to *decouple data and compute*. This is great for data science applications that tend to be both data- and compute-hungry. As advocated for in chapter 4, you can choose the best compute layer for each job, and, most important, you can let data scientists iterate and experiment freely without having to fear crashing a shared database. A downside is that it becomes harder to control how data is used—we will return to this question in the next section.

When considering the pros and cons of the coupled versus decoupled approach, it is good to remember that data science applications—and machine learning, in particular—behave differently than traditional analytics and business intelligence use cases. The difference is illustrated in figure 7.3.

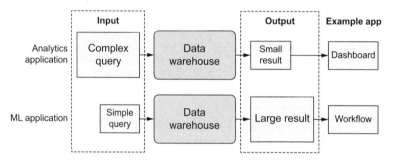

Figure 7.3   Contrasting data flows between analytics and ML applications

A traditional business analytics application, say, a Tableau dashboard, typically generates a very complex SQL query, which the data warehouse executes to return a small, carefully filtered result to the dashboard. In contrast, an ML application shows the opposite behavior: it presents a simple query to ingest, for instance, a full table of data, `select * from table`, which it feeds into an ML model.

Consequently, ML applications may hit two issues. First, the data warehouse may be surprisingly inefficient at executing simple queries that extract a lot of data, because they have been optimized for the opposite query pattern. Second, for the same reason, client libraries that are used to interface with the data warehouse are often rather inefficient at loading bulk data.

Although many real-world applications exhibit query patterns that lie somewhere between the two extremes, in many applications, loading data is the main performance bottleneck. The data scientist may need to wait for tens of minutes for the data to load, which seriously hurts their productivity. Removing productivity bottlenecks like this is a key goal of effective data science infrastructure, so in the subsequent sections, we will explore an alternative, extremely efficient way of accessing data. The approach works with many modern data warehouses and allows you to decouple data from compute, as well as define a clear division of work between data scientists and data engineers.

7.1.1 Loading data from S3

If you ask a data scientist how they would prefer accessing a dataset, assuming their personal productivity is the only consideration, a typical answer is "a local file." Local files excel at boosting productivity for the following reasons:

- *They can be loaded very quickly*—Loading data from a local file is faster than executing a SQL query.
- *The dataset doesn't change abruptly*—This is a key to effective prototyping. It is impossible to conduct systematic experimentation and iterations if the data underneath changes unannounced.
- *Ease of use*—Loading data doesn't require special clients, it doesn't fail randomly or become slow unpredictably when your colleagues are performing their experiments, and local files can be used by practically all off-the-shelf libraries.

Unfortunately, the downsides of local files are many: they don't work with production deployments or scaled-out experiments running in the cloud, and they need to be updated manually. Moreover, they make data warehouse administrators cringe because they fall outside the control of data security and governance policies.

Using a cloud-based object store like AWS S3 can provide the best of both worlds: keeping data in the cloud makes it compatible with cloud-based compute, deployment, and data governance policies. With some effort, as demonstrated next, we can make the user experience nearly as seamless as accessing local files. In particular, many people are surprised about this fact: loading data from a cloud-based object store like S3 can be faster than loading it from local files.

To showcase S3-based data in action and to see if the previous statement is really true, let's create a simple flow, shown in listing 7.1, to benchmark S3. The listing demonstrates a fundamental operation: loading data from files to memory of a Python process and comparing the performance of loading data from local files versus files in S3.

For testing, we use a sample of data from Common Crawl (commoncrawl.org), which is a public dataset consisting of random web pages. Details of the dataset don't matter. Notably, you can apply the lessons of this section equally well to unstructured data like images or videos or structured, tabular data. If you want, you can replace the dataset URL in the next listing with any other dataset that you can access in S3.

Listing 7.1 S3 benchmark

A public Common Crawl dataset available in S3

```
import os
from metaflow import FlowSpec, step, Parameter, S3, profile, parallel_map

URL = 
    's3://commoncrawl/crawl-data/CC-MAIN-2021-25/segments/1623488519735.70/wet/'

def load_s3(s3, num):          ⟵——— A helper function that loads data from S3
```

```
                  ┌─▷ files = list(s3.list_recursive([URL]))[:num]
  Picks the       │   total_size = sum(f.size for f in files) / 1024**3
  first num        │   stats = {}
  files in the     │   with profile('downloading', stats_dict=stats):  ◁──
  given S3         │       loaded = s3.get_many([f.url for f in files])  ◁──
  directory        │
                       s3_gbps = (total_size * 8) / (stats['downloading'] / 1000.)
                       print("S3->EC2 throughput: %2.1f Gb/s" % s3_gbps)
                       return [obj.path for obj in loaded]  ◁──

              class S3BenchmarkFlow(FlowSpec):
                  local_dir = Parameter('local_dir',
                                        help='Read local files from this directory')

                  num = Parameter('num_files',
                                  help='maximum number of files to read',
                                  default=50)

                  @step
                  def start(self):
                      with S3() as s3:  ◁──
                          with profile('Loading and processing'):
                  ┌─▷      if self.local_dir:
                  │            files = [os.path.join(self.local_dir, f)
                  │                     for f in os.listdir(self.local_dir)][:self.num]
                  │        else:
                  └─▷          files = load_s3(s3, self.num)

                          print("Reading %d objects" % len(files))
                          stats = {}
                          with profile('reading', stats_dict=stats):
                  ┌─          size = sum(parallel_map(lambda x: len(open(x, 'rb').read()),
                  └─▷ ⇒            files)) / 1024**3

                          read_gbps = (size * 8) / (stats['reading'] / 1000.)
                          print("Read %2.fGB. Throughput: %2.1f Gb/s" % (size, read_gbps))
                      self.next(self.end)

                  @step
                  def end(self):
                      pass

              if __name__ == '__main__':
                  S3BenchmarkFlow()
```

Annotations:
- **Picks the first num files in the given S3 directory** (points to line 1)
- **Collects timing information about the loading operation in stats** (points to `with profile('downloading', ...)`)
- **Loads files from S3 to temporary local files** (points to `loaded = s3.get_many(...)`)
- **Returns paths to temporary files** (points to `return [obj.path for obj in loaded]`)
- **The S3 scope manages the lifetime of temporary files** (points to `with S3() as s3:`)
- **If a parameter local_dir is specified, loads files from a local directory; otherwise, loads from S3** (points to the if/else block)
- **Reads local files in parallel** (points to the `size = sum(parallel_map(...)` line)

Save the code to a file called s3benchmark.py. If you are running it on your laptop, you can start by downloading a small amount of data as follows:

```
# python s3benchmark.py run --num_files 10
```

This downloads about 1 GB of data and prints statistics about the S3 throughput achieved.

The flow operates in two parts: first, if `--local_dir` is not specified, it calls the `load_s3` helper function to list the available files at the given URL and chooses the first num of them. After creating a list of files, it proceeds to download them in parallel using the get_many function of the Metaflow's built-in S3 client, metaflow.S3, which we cover in more detail in section 7.1.3. The function returns a list of paths to local temporary files that contain the downloaded data. The with S3 context manager takes care of clearing the temporary files after the context exits.

Second, the flow reads the contents of local files in memory. If --local_dir is specified, files are read from the given local directory that should contain a local copy of the files in S3. Otherwise, the downloaded data is read. In either case, files are processed in parallel using parallel_map, which is a convenience function provided by Metaflow to parallelize a function over multiple CPU cores. In this case, we simply count the number of bytes read and discard the file after reading it. This benchmark measures only the time spent loading data—we don't need to process the data in any way.

If you are curious to benchmark local disk performance using the --local_dir option, you can download files from S3 to a local directory as follows:

```
# aws s3 cp --recursive
➥ s3://commoncrawl/crawl-data/CC-MAIN-2021-25/segments/1623488519735.70/wet/
➥ local_data
```

Note that this is going to require 70 GB of disk space. Once the files have been downloaded, you can run the flow as follows:

```
# python s3benchmark.py run --num_files 10 --local_dir local_data
```

If you test the S3 downloading speed on your laptop, you end up mainly benchmarking the performance of your local network connection. A better option, as discussed in chapter 2, is to use a cloud-based workstation, which speeds up all cloud operations, regardless of your local bandwidth.

To get a better idea of realistic S3 performance, run the flow either on a cloud workstation or using a cloud-based compute layer like we discussed in chapter 4. You can run it, for instance, using AWS Batch as follows:

```
# python s3benchmark.py run --with batch:memory=16000
```

When running on a large EC2 instance, you should see results like this:

```
PROFILE: Loading and processing starting
S3->EC2 throughput: 21.3 Gb/s
Reading 100 objects
Read 11GB. Throughput: 228.2 Gb/s
PROFILE: Loading and processing completed in 5020ms
```

NOTE S3 buckets and the data therein are physically located in a certain region. It is advisable to run compute in the same region where the bucket is located for maximum performance and to avoid having to pay for the data transfer. For instance, the commoncrawl bucket used in this example is located in the AWS region us-east-1.

Figure 7.4 shows the performance as a function of the `--num_files` option.

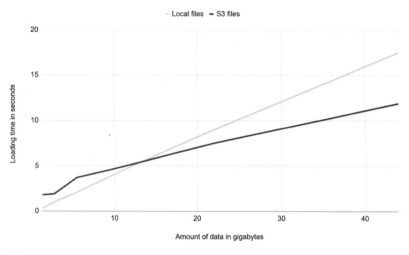

Figure 7.4   Loading time from local files vs. S3 as a function of the dataset size

The black line shows the total execution time when loading data from S3 and the gray line when loading data from local files. When the dataset is small enough, here, less than 12 GB or so, it is slightly faster to use local files. For larger datasets, loading data from S3 is indeed faster!

This result comes with an important caveat: the S3 performance is highly dependent on the size and type of the instance that executes the task. Figure 7.5 illustrates the effect.

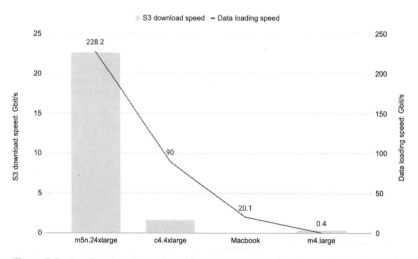

Figure 7.5   Loading data from S3 and from memory as a function of the instance size

A very large instance like `m5n.24xlarge` that comes with 384 GB of RAM and 48 CPU cores boasts massive throughput when loading data from S3: 20–30 gigabits per second, as shown by the gray bars. This is more than the local disk bandwidth on a recent Macbook laptop that can read up to 20 Gb/s. Medium-sized instances like `c4.4xlarge` show a fraction of the bandwidth, 1.5 Gbps, although still much more than what is achievable over a typical office Wi-Fi. A small instance like `m4.large` exhibits performance that's much slower than a laptop.

> **RECOMMENDATION** When dealing with data of nontrivial scale, it pays to use a large instance type. To control costs, you can use a medium-sized instance as a cloud workstation and run data-intensive steps on a compute layer like AWS Batch.

File size matters

If you try to reproduce S3 throughput figures with your own datasets but fail to see anything close to the previous numbers, the issue may be file sizes. Looking up an object in S3 is a relatively slow operation, which takes somewhere between 50–100 ms. If you have many small files, a lot of time is spent looking up files, which reduces throughput significantly. An optimal file size for S3 is at least tens of megabytes or more, depending on the amount of data.

KEEPING DATA IN MEMORY WITH THE DISK CACHE

To explain the black line in figure 7.5, let's dive deeper in the example. You may wonder if this benchmark makes any sense: the `load_s3` function downloads data to local temporary files, which we then read in the `start` step. Hence, we seem to be comparing loading data from temporary local files versus local files in a directory, which should be equally fast.

The trick is that when loading data from S3, the data should stay in memory, transparently stored in an in-memory *disk cache* by the operating system, without ever hitting the local disk, as long as the dataset is small enough to fit in memory. Figure 7.6 illustrates the logic.

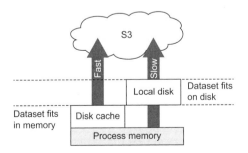

Figure 7.6 Loading data through the disk cache is fast compared to disk IO.

When the dataset size fits in memory, loading from S3 happens through the fast path depicted by the left arrow. When the dataset is larger than the available memory, some data spills onto the local disk, which makes loading data much slower. This is why S3 can be faster than local disk: when you run the flow, for example, with `--with batch:memory=16000`, the full 16 GB of memory on the instance is dedicated for the task. In contrast, many processes are fighting over the memory on your laptop, and as a result, it is often not feasible to keep all data in memory, at least when the dataset size grows as depicted by figure 7.4.

The black line in figure 7.5 shows how quickly data is read from either disk cache or local disk to the process's memory. The largest instance, `m5n.24xlarge`, keeps all data in the disk cache, so reading data is very fast, 228 Gbit/s. The data is just copied between memory locations in parallel. In contrast, the small instance, `m4.large`, is too small to keep the data in memory, so data spills on disk and reading becomes relatively sluggish, just 0.4 Gbit/s.

> **RECOMMENDATION** Whenever feasible, choose `@resources` that allow you to keep all data in memory. It makes all operations massively faster.

Let's summarize what we learned in this section:

- It is beneficial to use S3 instead of local files: data is easier to manage, it is readily available for tasks running in the cloud, and there can be only a minimal performance penalty, or even a performance improvement.
- We can load data very fast from S3 to the process's memory, as long as we use a large enough instance.
- Metaflow comes with a high-performance S3 client, `metaflow.S3`, which allows data to be loaded directly to memory without hitting the local disk.

These points form a foundation that we will build upon in the coming sections. In the next section, we will take these learnings closer to the everyday life of a data scientist and explore how to load large dataframes and other tabular data in tasks efficiently.

7.1.2 *Working with tabular data*

In the previous section, we were merely interested in moving raw bytes. The discussion applies to any data modalities from videos to natural language. In this section, we focus on a particular kind of data, namely structured or semi-structured data, which is often manipulated as dataframes. Data of this kind is extremely common in business data science—for instance, all relational databases hold data of this nature.

Figure 7.7 shows an example of a tabular dataset containing employee information. The dataset has three columns, name, age, and role, and three rows, a row for each employee.

As depicted in figure 7.7, we can store the dataset in different formats. In chapter 3, we talked about the CSV (comma-separated values) format, which is a simple text file containing a row of data in each line, with columns separated by commas. Alternatively,

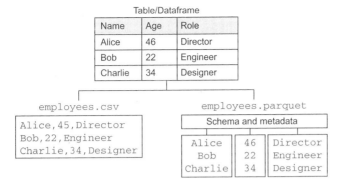

Figure 7.7 Storing tabular data as CSV vs. Parquet format

we can store the same data in the popular *Parquet* format, which is a *column-oriented storage format.*

In Parquet and other columnar formats, each column of data is stored independently. This approach offers a few benefits. First, with structured data, each column has a specific type. In this example, Name and Role are strings and Age is an integer. Each data type needs to be encoded and compressed in a specific way, so grouping data by column, that is, by type, is beneficial. Parquet files store an explicit schema and other metadata in the data file itself. In contrast, CSV files work around the issue by ignoring the schema altogether—everything becomes a string, which is a major downside of CSV.

Second, because each column is stored separately, it is possible to load only a subset of columns efficiently—imagine a query like SELECT name, role FROM table. Similarly, any operations that need to process a column like SELECT AVG(age) FROM table can be processed quickly because all relevant data is laid out contiguously in memory. Third, Parquet files are stored in a compressed binary format, so they take less space to store and are faster to transfer than plain CSV files.

READING PARQUET DATA IN MEMORY WITH APACHE ARROW

A major benefit of CSV files is that Python comes with a built-in module, aptly named csv, to read them. To read Parquet files, we will need to use a separate open source library called *Apache Arrow*. Besides being a Parquet file decoder, Arrow provides an efficient in-memory representation of data, which allows us to process data efficiently as well—more examples of this later.

Let's compare CSV and Parquet in practice. For testing, we use public trip data from New York City's Taxi Commission (http://mng.bz/j2rp), which is already available as public Parquet files in S3. For our benchmark, we use one month of data, which contains about 13 million rows, each representing a taxi trip. The dataset has 18 columns providing information about the trip.

The benchmark, shown in listing 7.2, compares the time spent loading data between CSV and two ways of loading Parquet using Arrow or pandas. The code works as follows:

1 The start step loads a Parquet file containing taxi trips from a public S3 bucket and makes it available as a local file, taxi.parquet. It uses pandas to convert the Parquet file to a CSV file, saving it to taxi.csv. We will use these two files to benchmark data loading in the subsequent steps.

2 After the start step, we split into three separate data-loading steps, each of which benchmarks a different way to load the dataset. Each step saves the time spent to load data in the stats artifact as follows:

  – The load_csv step uses Python's built-in csv module to loop through all rows, reading from the CSV file.

  – The load_parquet step loads the dataset in memory using PyArrow.

  – The load_pandas step loads the dataset in memory using pandas.

3 Finally, the join step prints the timings measured by the previous steps.

Listing 7.2   Comparing data formats

```
import os
from metaflow import FlowSpec, step, conda_base, resources, S3, profile

URL = 's3://ursa-labs-taxi-data/2014/12/data.parquet'       ◁——— One month of Taxi data,
                                                                 stored as a Parquet file
@conda_base(python='3.8.10',
        libraries={'pyarrow': '5.0.0', 'pandas': '1.3.2'})
  class ParquetBenchmarkFlow(FlowSpec):

      @step
      def start(self):                                    Loads the Parquet file in
          import pyarrow.parquet as pq                    memory using Arrow
          with S3() as s3:
              res = s3.get(URL)                           Moves the Parquet file to a
              table = pq.read_table(res.path)  ◁———       persistent location, so we
              os.rename(res.path, 'taxi.parquet')  ◁——    can load it later
          table.to_pandas().to_csv('taxi.csv')
          self.stats = {}                        ◁——  Stores profiling statistics in this dictionary
          self.next(self.load_csv, self.load_parquet, self.load_pandas)

      @step
      def load_csv(self):                                          Stores timing information
          with profile('load_csv', stats_dict=self.stats):  ◁—     in the dictionary
              import csv
              with open('taxi.csv') as csvfile:            Reads the CSV file using
                  for row in csv.reader(csvfile):  ◁——     the built-in csv module
                      pass                       ◁——
          self.next(self.join)                   Discards rows to avoid excessive
                                                 memory consumption
      @step
      def load_parquet(self):
          with profile('load_parquet', stats_dict=self.stats):   Loads the Parquet file
              import pyarrow.parquet as pq                        using Arrow. This time,
              table = pq.read_table('taxi.parquet')  ◁——          we time the operation.
          self.next(self.join)
```

Annotations (left margin):
- Downloads the Parquet file from S3 → res = s3.get(URL)
- Writes the dataset in a CSV file, so we can load it later → table.to_pandas().to_csv('taxi.csv')

```
    @step
    def load_pandas(self):
        with profile('load_pandas', stats_dict=self.stats):
            import pandas as pd
            df = pd.read_parquet('taxi.parquet')
    self.next(self.join)
```

◁─── **Loads the Parquet file using pandas**

```
    @step
    def join(self, inputs):
        for inp in inputs:
            print(list(inp.stats.items())[0])
        self.next(self.end)
```

◁─── **Prints timing statistics from each branch**

```
    @step
    def end(self):
        pass

if __name__ == '__main__':
    ParquetBenchmarkFlow()
```

Save the code in parquet_benchmark.py. For benchmarking purposes, this flow stores a Parquet file and a CSV file as local files, so this flow must be run on a laptop or a cloud workstation so all steps can access the files. Run the flow as follows:

```
# python parquet_benchmark.py --environment=conda run --max-workers 1
```

We use --max-workers 1 to force sequential instead of parallel execution of branches, which ensures more unbiased timings. Executing the start step takes a while, because it downloads a 319 MB compressed Parquet file from S3 and writes it to a local CSV file, which expands to 1.6 GB.

> **TIP** When iterating on a flow like ParquetBenchmarkFlow that has an expensive step in the beginning, such as start in this case, remember the resume command: instead of using run, which takes a while, you can use, for example, resume load_csv and keep iterating on later steps while skipping the slow beginning.

You should see an output like this, which shows the timings as milliseconds:

```
('load_csv', 19560)
('load_pandas', 1853)
('load_parquet', 973)
```

The results are also visualized in figure 7.8.

The load_parquet step is by far the fastest, taking less than a second to load 13 million rows of data! The load_pandas step takes twice as much time to read the Parquet file into a pandas DataFrame. We cheated a bit with the load_csv step, which takes almost 20 seconds, because it doesn't keep the data in memory like the other steps do. It simply iterates over the rows once. If we keep the data in memory—you

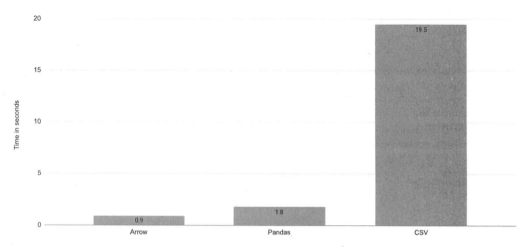

Figure 7.8 Comparing data loading times between Arrow, pandas, and CSV

can try it with `list(csv.reader(csvfile))`—the step takes 70 seconds and consumes nearly 20 GB of memory.

> **RECOMMENDATION** Whenever feasible, use the Parquet format to store and transfer tabular data instead of CSV files.

Hopefully these results convince you that using Parquet instead of CSV is almost always a win, the main exception being sharing small amounts of data with other systems and people who may not be able to handle Parquet. Also, Parquet files aren't as easy to inspect using standard command-line tools as simple textual CSV files, although tools exist that allow you to dump the contents of a Parquet file to a text file. Now that we know how to load tabular data stored as Parquet files, the next step is to consider the components on top of it.

7.1.3 *The in-memory data stack*

Using Parquet instead of CSV is a no-brainer, but how should one choose between Arrow and pandas? Luckily, you don't have to choose: the tools are often quite complementary. Figure 7.9 clarifies how the libraries forming the in-memory data stack fit together.

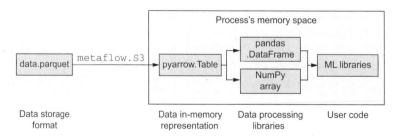

Figure 7.9 A modern stack for handling data in-memory

Parquet is a *data storage format*: it is a way to store and transfer data more efficiently than using CSV files. For instance, you can load Parquet files from S3 to your workflows very quickly using the `metafow.S3` library, as we have seen earlier. To use the data, we need to load and decode it from the Parquet files, which is the job of the Arrow library. Arrow supports multiple languages—its Python binding is called PyArrow. Arrow decodes data from Parquet files into an efficient *in-memory representation* of data, which can be used either directly or through another library, like pandas.

This is a superpower of Arrow: its in-memory representation has been designed in such a way that it can be leveraged by other *data processing libraries* like pandas or NumPy so that they don't have to make another copy of the data, which is a huge win when dealing with large datasets. This means that your *user code*, for example, a model-training step using an ML library, can read data managed by Arrow, possibly through pandas, in a very memory- and time-efficient manner. Notably, all data management is performed by efficient low-level code, not by Python directly, which makes it possible to develop extremely high-performance code in Python.

Whether to use pandas or NumPy or use the PyArrow library directly depends on the exact use case. A major benefit of pandas is that it provides many easy-to-use primitives for data manipulation, so if your task needs such functionality, converting from Arrow to pandas or using `pd.read_parquet` is a good option.

A major downside of pandas is that it can be quite memory-hungry, as we will see later, and it is not as performant as pure-Arrow operations. Hence, if you use an ML library that can accept Arrow data or NumPy arrays directly, avoiding conversion to pandas can save a lot of time and memory. We will see a practical example of this in section 7.3.

Why metaflow.S3?

If you have used Arrow or pandas previously, you may know that they support loading data from s3:// URLs directly. Why does figure 7.9 mention metaflow.S3, then? Currently, loading datasets consisting of multiple files can be much faster with metaflow.S3 than using the S3 interface built in Arrow and pandas. The reason is simple: metaflow.S3 aggressively parallelizes downloading over multiple network connections, which is required for maximum throughput.

It is likely that the libraries will implement a similar approach in the future. Once this happens, you can replace the `metaflow.S3` part in the diagram and code examples with a library-native approach. Everything else in the picture remains the same.

PROFILING MEMORY CONSUMPTION

When dealing with large amounts of in-memory data, memory consumption is often a bigger concern than execution time. In the previous examples, we have used the `with profile` context manager to time various operations, but what if we wanted to measure memory consumption similarly?

Measuring how memory consumption evolves over time is not as straightforward as looking at a timer. However, by leveraging an off-the-shelf library called memory_ profiler, we can create a utility function, in fact, a custom decorator, that you can use to measure peak memory consumption of any Metaflow step, as shown in the next listing.

Listing 7.3   Memory profiling decorator

Defines a Python decorator—a function that returns a function

```
from functools import wraps

def profile_memory(mf_step):
    @wraps(mf_step)
    def func(self):
        from memory_profiler import memory_usage
        self.mem_usage = memory_usage((mf_step, (self,), {}),
                                      max_iterations=1,
                                      max_usage=True,
                                      interval=0.2)
    return func
```

The @wraps decorator helps to make a well-behaving decorator.

Uses the memory_ profile library to measure memory consumption

Stores the peak memory usage in an artifact, mem_usage

If you haven't created decorators in Python before, this example may look a bit strange. It defines a function, profile_memory, which takes an argument, mf_step, that is the Metaflow step being decorated. It wraps the step in a new function, func, which calls the library memory_profiler to execute the step and measure its memory_ usage in the background. The profiler returns the peak memory usage, which is assigned to an artifact, self.mem_usage.

Save the code to a file, metaflow_memory.py. Now, in any flow, you can import the new decorator by writing from metaflow_memory import profile_memory at the top of the file. You must also make sure that the memory_profiler library is available, which you can do by adding 'memory_profiler': '0.58.0' to the libraries dictionary in @conda_base. Now you can decorate any step to be profiled with @profile_memory. For instance, you can enhance listing 7.3 by writing the following:

```
@profile_memory
@step
def load_csv(self):
    ...
```

Add the decorator to every branch. To print the memory consumption, you can use the following join step:

```
@step
def join(self, inputs):
    for inp in inputs:
        print(list(inp.stats.items())[0], inp.mem_usage)
    self.next(self.end)
```

To get a realistic read of the memory consumption of the CSV in the `load_csv` step, you should keep all rows in memory by using `list(csv.reader(csvfile))` instead of the `for` loop that discards rows. Note that this will require a workstation with more than 16 GB of RAM.

You can run parquet_benchmark.py as usual. In addition to timings, you will see peak memory consumption printed, which is illustrated in figure 7.10.

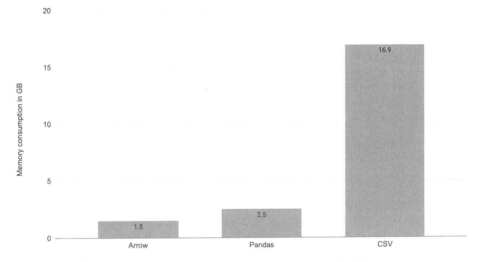

Figure 7.10   Comparing memory overhead between Arrow, pandas, and CSV

As expected, keeping all CSV data in memory as memory-inefficient Python objects is very costly—the `load_csv` step consumes nearly 17 GB of RAM, which is over 10× more than Arrow's efficient memory representation of the same data. pandas consumes a gigabyte more than Arrow, because it needs to maintain a Python-friendly representation of some objects, strings in particular.

> **RECOMMENDATION**   If memory consumption is a concern, avoid storing individual rows as Python objects. Converting to pandas can be costly as well. The most efficient option is to use Arrow and NumPy, if possible.

Thus far, we have developed building blocks that go from S3 to an efficient in-memory representation of data. Combined with high-memory instances (think `@resources (memory=256000)`), you can handle massive datasets efficiently in a single task. However, what if your dataset is larger than what can be handled on any reasonable instance? Or what if a suitable dataset doesn't exist but must be created by filtering and joining multiple tables together? In cases like this, it is best to rely on the rest of the data infrastructure, battle-hardened query engines in particular, to create suitable datasets for data science workflows from arbitrary amounts of raw data.

7.2   *Interfacing with data infrastructure*

Alex's delivery-time estimator turns out to be a success. As a result, the product team requests Alex build more fine-grained models for specific product categories. This requires more data preprocessing: Alex needs to extract the right subsets of data for each category as well as experiment with various combinations of columns that produce the best estimates for each category. Bowie suggests that Alex can do all the data preprocessing in SQL because databases should be good at crunching data. Alex counters the idea by pointing out that it is much faster to iterate on models and their input data using Python. Finally, they reach a happy compromise: Alex will use SQL to extract a suitable dataset and Python to define inputs for the model.

Data science workflows don't exist in a vacuum. Most companies have existing data infrastructure that has been set up to support various use cases from analytics to product features. It is beneficial that all applications rely on a consistent set of data, managed by a centralized data infrastructure. Data science and machine learning are not an exception.

Although data science workflows rely on the same input data, the same *facts* as discussed in section 7.3, the way workflows access and use data is often different from other applications. First, they tend to access much larger extracts of data—tens or hundreds of gigabytes—to, say, train a model, whereas a dashboard might show only a few kilobytes of carefully selected data at a time. Second, data science workflows tend to be much more compute-intensive than other applications, necessitating a separate compute layer, as discussed in chapter 4.

This section shows how you can integrate data science workflows into existing data infrastructure by leveraging techniques we learned in the previous section. Besides the technical concern of moving data around, we touch on an organizational question of how work can be divided between data engineers, who mainly work on the data infrastructure, and ML engineers and data scientists, who work on the data science infrastructure.

7.2.1 Modern data infrastructure

This book is about *data science* infrastructure, namely infrastructure required to prototype and deploy data-intensive applications that leverage optimization—or training—techniques of various kinds to build models to serve a diverse set of use cases. At many companies, the data science infrastructure has a sibling stack: the *data infrastructure* stack.

Because both stacks deal with data, and often both use DAGs to express workflows that transform input data to output data, one might wonder if there's actually any difference between the two stacks. Couldn't we just use the data infrastructure for data science, too? This book argues that activities related to data science are qualitatively

different from data engineering, which justifies a parallel stack. Model-building requires special libraries, typically more code, and definitely more computation than data engineering. However, it is beneficial to keep the two stacks closely aligned to avoid redundant solutions and unnecessary operational overhead.

To better understand how to integrate the stacks, let's start by considering the components of modern data infrastructure, as illustrated in figure 7.11. The figure is structured so that the most foundational components are at the center and more advanced, optional components in the outer layers.

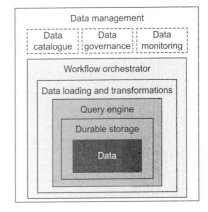

Figure 7.11 Components of the modern data infrastructure

- *Data*—At the very core, you have the data asset itself. This diagram doesn't illustrate how the data is acquired, which is a complex topic of its own, but we assume that you have some data that is stored, say, as CSV files, Parquet files, or as tables in a database.
- *Durable storage*—Although you could use a USB thumb drive for storage, it is preferable to rely on a more durable storage system like AWS S3 or a replicated database. One option is a modern *data lake*, that is, storing (Parquet) files on a generic storage system like S3 accompanied by a metadata layer like Apache Hive or Iceberg to facilitate access to data through query engines.
- *Query engine*—A query engine takes a query, such as a SQL statement, that expresses a subset of data through selects, filters, and joins. Traditional databases, such as Postgres, and *data warehouses*, like Teradata, couple the first three layers tightly together, whereas newer systems like Trino (formerly Presto) or Apache Spark are query engines that are more loosely coupled with the underlying storage system. For *streaming data*, systems like Apache Druid or Pinot can be used.

- *Data loading and transformations*—Extracting, transforming, and loading (ETL) data is a core activity of data engineering. Traditionally, data was transformed before it was loaded to a data warehouse, but newer systems, like Snowflake or Spark, support the extract-load-transform (ELT) paradigm where raw data is loaded to the system first and then transformed and refined as blessed datasets. Nowadays, tools like DBT (getdbt.com) are available to make it easier to express and manage data transformations. Data quality can be ensured using tools such as Great Expectations (greatexpectations.io).

- *Workflow orchestrator*—ETL pipelines are often expressed as DAGs, similar to the data science workflows we have discussed earlier in this book. Correspondingly, these DAGs need to be executed by a workflow orchestrator like AWS Step Functions or Apache Airflow, or Apache Flink for streaming data. From a workflow orchestrator's point of view, there is no difference between a data science workflow and a data workflow. In fact, it is often beneficial to use one centralized orchestrator to orchestrate all workflows.

- *Data management*—As the volume, variety, and demands for validity of data increases, yet another layer of data management components is often required. *Data catalogues*, such as Amundsen by Lyft, can make it easier to discover and organize datasets. *Data governance systems* can be used to enforce security, data lifetime, audits and lineage, and data access policies. *Data monitoring systems* help to observe the overall state of all data systems, data quality, and ETL pipelines.

It makes sense to start building the data infrastructure from the core outward. For instance, a grad student might care only about a dataset, stored in a CSV file on their laptop. A startup benefits from durable storage and a basic query engine, like Amazon Athena, which is featured in the next section. An established company with dedicated data engineers needs a solid setup for ETL pipelines as well. As the company grows to become a large multinational enterprise, they will add a robust set of data management tools.

Correspondingly, integrations between data and data science infrastructure grow over time. Figure 7.12 highlights the relationships. The layers that operate independently from data infrastructure are depicted with dotted lines. The dotted-line boxes highlight what makes data science special: we need a dedicated compute layer that is capable of executing demanding data science applications and models.

In contrast, the other layers often benefit from interfacing with data infrastructure as follows:

- *Data warehouse*—In the previous section, we learned effective patterns for interacting with raw data, stored as Parquet files, and a durable storage system, S3. In the next subsection, we will learn how to interface with a query engine.

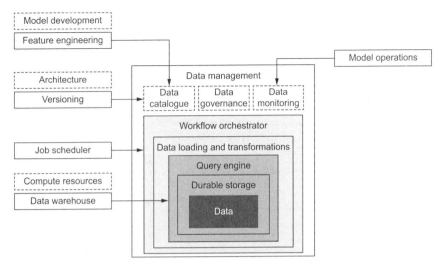

Figure 7.12 Interfacing the data science stack with data infrastructure

- *Job scheduler*—The workflow orchestration systems we covered in chapter 2 work equally well for data pipeline DAGs as well as data science DAGs. Because these DAGs are often connected—for instance, you may want to start a model training workflow whenever an upstream data updates—it is beneficial to execute them on the same system. For instance, you can use AWS Step Functions to schedule both data science as well as data workflows.

- *Versioning*—Assuming your data catalogue supports versioning of datasets, it can be beneficial to maintain data lineage all the way from upstream datasets to models built using the data. For instance, you can achieve this by storing a data version identifier, pointing to the data catalogue, as a Metaflow artifact.

- *Model operations*—Changes in data are a common cause for failures in data science workflows. Besides monitoring models and workflows, it can be beneficial to be able to monitor source data as well.

- *Feature engineering*—As we will discuss in section 7.3, when designing new features for a model, it is convenient to know what data is available, which is where a data catalogue can come in handy. Some data catalogues can double as feature stores as well.

Concretely, the integrations can take the form of Python libraries that encode the normative access patterns to data. Many modern data tools and services come with Python client libraries, such as *AWS Data Wrangler*, featured in the next section, which can be used for this purpose. Similar to data infrastructure in general, there is no need to implement all components and integrations on day one. You can add integrations over time as your needs grow.

DIVIDING WORK BETWEEN DATA SCIENTISTS AND DATA ENGINEERS

The larger the company, the longer the path from raw data to models. As the volume, variety, and requirements of validity of data grows, it is not reasonable to ask one person to take care of all of it. Many companies address the issue by hiring dedicated data engineers, who focus on all-things-data, and data scientists who focus on modeling.

However, the boundary between data engineers and data scientists is not clear. For instance, if three tables contain information that a model needs, who is responsible for creating a joined table or a view that can be fed into a data science workflow? From the technical point of view, the data engineer is an expert in developing even complex SQL statements and optimizing joins, so maybe they should do it. On the other hand, the data scientist knows the model and its needs most accurately. Also, if the data scientist wants to iterate on the model and feature engineering, they shouldn't have to bother the data engineer every time they need to make even a small change in the dataset.

The right answer depends on the exact needs of the organization, resourcing, and the skill set of data engineers and data scientists involved. Figure 7.13 suggests one proven way of dividing work, which demarcates responsibilities quite clearly between the two roles.

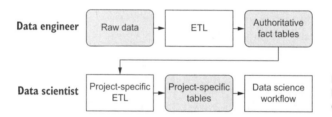

Figure 7.13 Defining an interface between the data engineer and the data scientist

The *data engineer* is responsible for data acquisition, that is, gathering raw data, data quality, and any data transformations that are needed to make the data available as widely consumable, authoritative, carefully curated datasets. In the case of structured data, the datasets are often tables with a fixed, stable schema. Notably, these upstream datasets should focus on *facts*—data that corresponds as closely as possible to directly observable raw data—leaving interpretations of data to downstream projects. The organization shouldn't underestimate the demands of this role or undervalue it. This role is directly exposed to the chaos of the real world through raw data, so they play a critical role in insulating the rest of the organization from it. Correspondingly, the validity of all downstream projects depends on the quality of upstream data.

The *data scientist* focuses on building, deploying, and operating data science applications. They are intimately familiar with the specific needs of each project. They are responsible for creating project-specific tables based on the upstream tables. Because they are responsible for creating these tables, they can iterate on them independently as often as needed.

The requirements for validity and stability can be looser for project-specific tables, depending on the needs of each project, because these tables are tightly coupled with a specific workflow that is also managed by the same data scientist or a small team of scientists. When dealing with large datasets, it is also beneficial that the data scientist can affect the layout and partitioning of the table, which can have massive performance implications when it comes to ingesting the table to the workflow, as discussed in the previous section.

Crucially, this arrangement works only if the data infrastructure, and the query engine in particular, is robust enough so to manage suboptimal queries. We can't assume that every data scientist is also a world-class data engineer, but it is still convenient to allow them to execute and schedule queries independently. Historically, many data warehouses broke too easily under suboptimal queries, so it wouldn't have been feasible to let non-experts run arbitrary queries. The modern data infrastructure should be able to isolate queries so that this isn't a problem anymore.

Details of data engineering are out of scope of this book. However, questions pertaining to the work of a data scientist are in scope, so in the next section, we will investigate how one can author project-specific ETL, interfacing with a query engine, as a part of a data science workflow.

7.2.2 Preparing datasets in SQL

In this section, we will learn how to use a query engine such as Trino or Apache Spark, or a data warehouse like Redshift or Snowflake, to prepare datasets that can be efficiently loaded in a data science workflow using the patterns we learned in the previous section. We will demonstrate the concept, illustrated in figure 7.14, using a managed cloud-based query engine, Athena, but you can use the same approach with other systems, too.

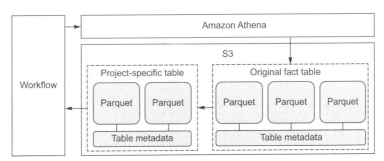

Figure 7.14 Using a query engine with an S3-based data lake

First, we will need to load data files to S3 and register them as a table with a suitable schema, stored in table metadata. Athena uses the popular Apache Hive format for its metadata.

After this, we can start querying the table. We will create a workflow that sends a SQL query to Athena, selecting a subset of the original fact table and writing the results as a new table. This type of query is called *Create Table as Select* (CTAS). CTAS queries work well for our needs, because they make it possible to download results from S3 using the fast data patterns we learned in the previous section.

We will use the open source library AWS Data Wrangler (https://github.com/awslabs/aws-data-wrangler) to interface with Athena. AWS Data Wrangler makes it easy to read and write data from various databases and data warehouses that AWS provides. However, it is not hard to adapt the examples to use other client libraries that provide similar functionality.

If you don't want to test a query engine at this moment, you can skip this subsection and move on to the next one. In the next subsection, we will see how we can postprocess data in a workflow.

SETTING UP A TABLE ON ATHENA

Amazon Athena is a serverless query engine, based on Trino, requiring no upfront setup. Just make sure that your IAM user or Batch role (`METAFLOW_ECS_S3_ACCESS_IAM_ROLE` in the Metaflow config) has a policy called `AmazonAthenaFullAccess` attached to it, which allows Athena queries to be executed. Also, make sure the AWS region is set in your configuration, for example, by setting the environment variable `AWS_DEFAULT_REGION=us-east-1`.

As a test dataset, we will use a subset of NYC Taxi Trip data, which we first used in listing 7.2. We will initialize a table with a year's worth of data, some 160 million rows, *partitioning* the table by month. In this case, partitioning simply organizes files as directories, allowing queries that read only a subset of months to finish much faster, because the query engine can skip whole directories of files. Partitioning requires a certain naming scheme, with directories prefixed with `month=`, which is why we copy files from their original location to a new S3 location that follows the desired naming scheme. The desired path structure looks like this:

```
s3://my-metaflow-bucket/metaflow/data/TaxiDataLoader/12/nyc_taxi/month=11/
➡ file.parquet
```

The prefix until `/nyc_taxi/` will look different in your case because it depends on your Metaflow config. The key part is the suffix after `nyc_taxi`, in particular `month=11`, which is used for partitioning.

To create a table, we need a predefined schema. We will create a schema specification by introspecting schema in the Parquet files. The table is registered with a data catalogue service called *AWS Glue*, which is tightly integrated with Athena. Listing 7.4 packs all these actions, downloading and uploading data in a desired hierarchy, schema definition, and table creation in a single Metaflow workflow. Here's how the code works:

- The `start` step takes care of two things:
  - It copies Parquet files to a partitioned directory hierarchy in S3. This requires the creation of new path names, which is accomplished with the utility function `make_key`. Note that by initializing the S3 client with `S3(run=self)`, Metaflow chooses a suitable S3 root for the files that is versioned with the run ID, allowing us to test different versions of the code safely without having to fear overwriting previous results. The root path of the resulting hierarchy is stored in an artifact called `s3_prefix`.
  - It inspects the schema of the Parquet files. We assume that all files have the same schema, so it suffices to look at the schema of the first file. The schema of the Parquet files uses slightly different names than the Hive format, which Athena uses, so we rename the fields based on the `TYPES` mapping using the `hive_field` utility function. The resulting schema is stored in an artifact, `schema`.
- Equipped with suitably laid-out Parquet files and a schema, we can set up a table in the `end` step. As an initialization step, we create a database in Glue, called `dsinfra_test` by default. The call will raise an exception if the database already exists, which we can safely ignore. After this, we can create a bucket for Athena to store its results and register a new table. The `repair_table` call makes sure that the newly created partitions are included in the table.

After these steps, the table is ready for querying!

Listing 7.4 Loading taxi data in Athena

Database name—you can choose any name

```
from metaflow import FlowSpec, Parameter, step, conda, profile, S3

GLUE_DB = 'dsinfra_test'
URL = 's3://ursa-labs-taxi-data/2014/'         ◁── NYC taxi data at a public bucket

TYPES = {'timestamp[us]': 'bigint', 'int8': 'tinyint'}   ◁── Maps some types in Parquet schema to Hive format used by Glue

class TaxiDataLoader(FlowSpec):

    table = Parameter('table',          ◁── Defines the table name, optionally
                      help='Table name',
                      default='nyc_taxi')

    @conda(python='3.8.10', libraries={'pyarrow': '5.0.0'})
    @step
    def start(self):
        import pyarrow.parquet as pq
                                         S3 object key (path) that conforms with our partitioning schema
        def make_key(obj):               ◁──
            key = '%s/month=%s/%s' % tuple([self.table] + obj.key.split('/'))
            return key, obj.path
```

```
          def hive_field(f):                      Maps Parquet types to Hive types, used by Glue
              return f.name, TYPES.get(str(f.type), str(f.type))

          with S3() as s3down:                              Downloads data and
              with profile('Dowloading data'):              generates new keys
                  loaded = list(map(make_key, s3down.get_recursive([URL])))
              table = pq.read_table(loaded[0][1])
              self.schema = dict(map(hive_field, table.schema))   Introspects schema
              with S3(run=self) as s3up:    #I                    from the first Parquet
                  with profile('Uploading data'):                 file and maps it to Hive
                      uploaded = s3up.put_files(loaded)
                  key, url = uploaded[0]
                  self.s3_prefix = url[:-(len(key) - len(self.table))]
              self.next(self.end)

          @conda(python='3.8.10', libraries={'awswrangler': '1.10.1'})
          @step
          def end(self):
              import awswrangler as wr
              try:
                  wr.catalog.create_database(name=GLUE_DB)
              except:
                  pass
              wr.athena.create_athena_bucket()
              with profile('Creating table'):
                  wr.catalog.create_parquet_table(database=GLUE_DB,
                                                  table=self.table,
                                                  path=self.s3_prefix,
                                                  columns_types=self.schema,
                                                  partitions_types={'month': 'int'},
                                                  mode='overwrite')
              wr.athena.repair_table(self.table, database=GLUE_DB)

      if __name__ == '__main__':
          TaxiDataLoader()
```

Annotations (reading left and right of the code):

- Uploads data to a Metaflow run-specific location
- Saves the new S3 location in an artifact
- Initializes a bucket for CTAS results
- Creates a new database in Glue and ignores failures caused by the database already existing
- Registers a new table with the new location and schema
- Requests Athena to discover newly added partitions

Save the code in taxi_loader.py. Running the flow will upload and download about 4.2 GB of data, so it is advisable to run it on Batch or on a cloud workstation. You can run the flow as usual:

```
# python taxi_loader.py --environment=conda run
```

On a large cloud workstation, the flow should take less than 30 seconds to execute.

Versioned data with metaflow.S3

Listing 7.4 uploads data to S3 without specifying a bucket or an explicit S3 URL. This is possible because the S3 client was initialized as S3(run=self), which tells Metaflow to refer to a *run-specific location* by default. Metaflow creates an S3 URL based on its datastore location, prefixing keys with a run ID.

This mode is useful when storing data in S3 that needs to be accessible by other systems (data that is internal to workflows can be stored as artifacts). Because data is stored relative to the run ID, any data you upload is automatically versioned, making sure that each run writes an independent version or copy of data without accidentally overwriting unrelated results. Afterward, if you need to track what data was produced by a run, you can find the data based on the run ID, allowing *data lineage* to be maintained.

After the run has completed successfully, you can open the Athena console and confirm that a new table, `nyc_taxi`, is discoverable under the database `dsinfra_test`. The console includes a convenient query editor that allows you to query any table in SQL. For instance, you can see a small preview of data by executing `SELECT * FROM nyc_taxi LIMIT 10`. Figure 7.15 shows what the console should look like.

Figure 7.15   Querying Taxi data on the Athena console

If you can see the table and its columns in the console, and the test query returns rows with values, the table is ready for use! Next, we will create a flow that executes CTAS queries against the table, which allows us to create arbitrary subsets of data to be consumed by workflows.

RUNNING CTAS QUERIES

How should a data scientist execute project-specific SQL queries? One option is to use tools provided by data infrastructure, following best practices used by data engineers. A downside of this approach is that the query is decoupled from the workflow that relies on it. A better approach might be to execute the query as a part of the workflow, as demonstrated next.

You could embed SQL statements as strings in your Python code, but to benefit from proper syntax highlighting and checking in IDEs, and to make the code more readable overall, we can store them as separate files. To test the idea, let's create a query that selects a subset of the newly created `nyc_taxi` table. The next code listing shows a SQL statement that selects taxi rides that start during business hours between 9 a.m. and 5 p.m.

Listing 7.5   SQL query to extract data for business hours

```
SELECT * FROM nyc_taxi
    WHERE hour(from_unixtime(pickup_at / 1000)) BETWEEN 9 AND 17
```

Save this SQL statement in a new subdirectory, sql, in a file sql/taxi_etl.sql. If you wonder about the time logic, `pickup_at / 1000` is required because timestamps in the dataset are expressed as milliseconds but `from_unixtime` expects seconds. Now we can write a flow that executes the query, shown next.

Listing 7.6   A flow with parameters

```
from metaflow import FlowSpec, project, profile, S3, step, current, conda

GLUE_DB = 'dsinfra_test'                    Attaches the flow to a project. This will
                                            come in handy in the next section.
@project(name='nyc_taxi')      ◁─────┘
class TaxiETLFlow(FlowSpec):
                                                Creates a result table name based
                                                on the ID of the current task
    def athena_ctas(self, sql):
        import awswrangler as wr
        table = 'mf_ctas_%s' % current.pathspec.replace('/', '_')    ◁────┘
        self.ctas = "CREATE TABLE %s AS %s" % (table, sql)
        with profile('Running query'):                           Submits the
            query = wr.athena.start_query_execution(self.ctas,   query to Athena
                                        ⇒ database=GLUE_DB)   ◁─┘
        output = wr.athena.wait_query(query)
        loc = output['ResultConfiguration']['OutputLocation']
        with S3() as s3:
            return [obj.url for obj in s3.list_recursive([loc + '/'])]

    @conda(python='3.8.10', libraries={'awswrangler': '1.10.1'})
    @step
    def start(self):
        with open('sql/taxi_etl.sql') as f:
            self.paths = self.athena_ctas(f.read())    ◁───── Formats and submits a
        self.next(self.end)                                   query, and stores the
                                                              URLs of the resulting
    @step                                                     Parquet files
    def end(self):
        pass

if __name__ == '__main__':
    TaxiETLFlow()
```

Annotations (left margin): Formats a CTAS SQL query and stores it as an artifact — Waits for the query to complete — Lists all Parquet files in the result set

`TaxiETLFlow` is a general-purpose flow that implements the pattern depicted in the beginning of this section in figure 7.14. It reads an arbitrary SELECT statement from a file, sql/taxi_etl.sql, converts it into a CTAS query by prefixing it with `CREATE TABLE`, submits the query, waits for it to finish, and stores the paths to the resulting Parquet files as an artifact, so they can be easily consumed by other downstream flows, an example of which we will see in the next section.

> **TIP** You can use the `current` object to introspect the currently executing run, as shown in listing 7.6. It can come in handy if you want to know the current run ID, task ID, or the user who is executing the run.

Save the code to taxi_etl.py. The flow needs an extra SQL file, so we use the `--package-suffixes` option, discussed in the previous chapter, to include all .sql files in the code package. Run the flow as follows:

```
# python taxi_etl.py --environment=conda --package-suffixes .sql run
```

After the run has completed, you can log in to the Athena console and click the History tab to confirm the status of the query, as shown in figure 7.16.

Figure 7.16   Query status on the Athena console

Because the run and task IDs are embedded in the table name, in this case, `mf_ctas_TaxiETLFlow_1631494834745839_start_1` in figure 7.16, it is easy to draw the connection between queries and runs. Vice versa, by storing the query to be executed as an artifact, `self.ctas`, and its results in another artifact, `self.paths`, we can form a full data lineage from the source data, the queries that process it, to the final output, for example, models, produced by workflows. Having this lineage can become extremely useful when debugging any issues related to the quality of predictions or input data.

> **RECOMMENDATION** Maintain data lineage between data infrastructure and data science workflows by including run IDs in the queries executed and by logging queries as artifacts.

As an exercise, you can adapt the example to work with another modern query engine. The same CTAS pattern works, for instance, with Spark, Redshift, or Snowflake. You can also schedule the ETL workflow to run periodically on a production-grade scheduler, possibly the same one used by the data engineering team, by using the techniques we learned in the previous chapter.

Regardless of what query engine you use, the general capability is what matters. Using this approach, a data scientist can include a project-specific data preprocessing step in their workflow and offload large-scale data crunching to a scalable query engine. In the next section, we will see how to access the results of even a large CTAS query by leveraging horizontal scalability and the fast data approach we learned earlier.

Cleaning old results

By default, the result tables produced by CTAS queries are persisted forever. This is beneficial for reproducibility and auditability, because you can examine any old results. However, it is a reasonable practice to delete old results after some period of time.

You can delete old data in S3 by using *S3 lifecycle policies*. Because results are just locations in S3, you can set a policy that deletes all objects at the location where CTAS results are written after a predetermined period, such as after 30 days. In addition, you want to delete table metadata from Glue.

You can delete Glue tables by executing `DROP TABLE` SQL statements with AWS Data Wrangler, or by using the following AWS CLI command:

```
aws glue batch-delete-table
```

with a list of tables to be deleted as arguments.

7.2.3 *Distributed data processing*

In section 7.1, we learned how to load Parquet files quickly from S3 to a single instance. This is a simple and robust pattern for datasets that can fit in memory. When combined with large instances with hundreds of gigabytes of RAM and efficient in-memory representations provided by Apache Arrow and NumPy, you can handle massive datasets, in some cases billions of data points, without having to resort to distributed computing and the overhead that comes with it.

Naturally this approach has its limits. Obviously, not all datasets fit in memory at once. Or, maybe doing complex processing of hundreds of gigabytes of data on a single instance is simply too slow. In cases like this, it is a good idea to fan out computation to multiple instances. In this section, we learn how to load and process data, such as tables produced by CTAS queries, in a distributed manner. As before, we will use Metaflow's `foreach` construct for distribution, but you can apply the same pattern with other frameworks that support distributed computation. The lessons learned in this chapter come in handy in the following two scenarios that are common in data science workflows:

1   *Loading and processing separate subsets of data in each branch*—For instance, in contrast to the K-means example in chapter 5, which used the same dataset to train all models, you can load a different subset, say, data specific to a country, in each `foreach` task.

2 *Efficient data preprocessing*—It is often convenient to do basic data extraction in SQL, followed by more advanced preprocessing in Python. We will use this pattern for feature engineering later in this chapter and in chapter 9.

A common characteristic in both of these cases is that we want to process *sharded,* or chunked, data, instead of all data at once. Figure 7.17 illustrates the high-level pattern.

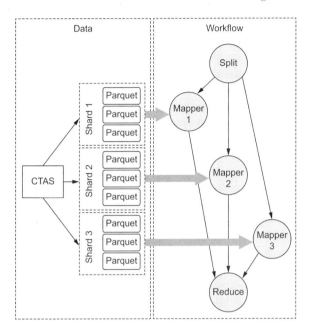

Figure 7.17 Processing sharded data in a workflow

A CTAS query produces a set of Parquet files that we can either partition by a column (e.g., by country) or we can divide them to roughly equal-sized shards. A workflow fans out a `foreach` over the shards, distributing data processing over multiple parallel steps. We can then combine the results in the `join` step. To highlight the similarity of this pattern to *the MapReduce paradigm* of distributed computing, figure 7.17 calls the `foreach` steps *Mappers* and the join step *Reduce.* To see how this pattern works in practice, let's work through a fun example: visualization of the taxi dataset.

EXAMPLE: VISUALIZING A LARGE DATASET

The following example works in two modes: it can either ingest an arbitrary subset of the taxi dataset produced by `TaxiETLFlow` (listing 7.6), or it can load raw data as-is. You can use the raw data mode if you didn't set up Athena in the previous section. In both cases, we will extract the latitude and longitude of the pickup location of each taxi trip and plot it on an image.

The task is made nontrivial by the fact that there are *many* trips in the dataset. In the raw mode, we process all trips in the year 2014, which amounts to 48 million data points. To demonstrate how large datasets like this can be processed efficiently, we perform preprocessing in parallel, as depicted in figure 7.17.

Let's start by writing a helper function that plots points on an image. Due to the scale of data, we'll use a specialized open source library, *Datashader* (datashader.org), that is tuned to handle millions of points efficiently. The helper function is shown in the next listing.

Listing 7.7   Plotting taxi trip coordinates

```
from io import BytesIO

CANVAS = {'plot_width': 1000,
          'plot_height': 1000,
          'x_range': (-74.03, -73.92),
          'y_range': (40.70, 40.78)}

def visualize(lat, lon):
    from pandas import DataFrame
    import datashader as ds
    from datashader import transfer_functions as tf
    from datashader.colors import Greys9
    canvas = ds.Canvas(**CANVAS)
    agg = canvas.points(DataFrame({'x': lon, 'y': lat}), 'x', 'y')
    img = tf.shade(agg, cmap=Greys9, how='log')
    img = tf.set_background(img, 'white')
    buf = BytesIO()
    img.to_pil().save(buf, format='png')
    return buf.getvalue()
```

Defines a bounding box for lower Manhattan → `'x_range': (-74.03, -73.92)`, `'y_range': (40.70, 40.78)}`

Accepts points as two arrays: latitude and longitude → `def visualize(lat, lon):`

Plots points, shading each pixel logarithmically

Saves the visualization as an artifact

Save the code to taxiviz.py, which we will import in the flow that follows. Note that the number of data points (up to 48 million) is much higher than the number of pixels (1 million) in the image. Hence, we will shade each pixel according to how many points hit it. We use a logarithmic color range to make sure that the faintest pixels don't wash away. Similar to the forecast plots in the previous chapter, we store the resulting image as an artifact, so it is versioned and stored in a run where it can be retrieved using the Client API and shown, for example, in a notebook.

Next, let's implement the flow itself—see the following listing. The flow implements the pattern depicted in figure 7.17. In the `start` step, we choose what input data to use: either the results of a CTAS query from a previously executed `TaxiETL-Flow` or raw data. We divide data into shards, each of which is processed by an independent `preprocess_data` task. The `join` step merges together data, arrays of coordinates, produced by each shard and plots the coordinates on an image.

Listing 7.8   A flow with parameters

Imports the helper function that we created earlier

```
from metaflow import FlowSpec, step, conda, Parameter,\
                     S3, resources, project, Flow
import taxiviz
URL = 's3://ursa-labs-taxi-data/2014/'
```

In the raw data mode, uses data from 2014 → `URL = 's3://ursa-labs-taxi-data/2014/'`

```
NUM_SHARDS = 4
```
A mapper function that preprocesses data for each shard

```
def process_data(table):
    return table.filter(table['passenger_count'].to_numpy() > 1)
```
As an example, we include only trips with more than one passenger.

```
@project(name='taxi_nyc')
class TaxiPlotterFlow(FlowSpec):
```
Uses the same project as TaxiETLFlow

```
    use_ctas = Parameter('use_ctas_data', help='Use CTAS data', default=False)
```
Chooses between the two modes: CTAS or raw data

```
    @conda(python='3.8.10')
    @step
    def start(self):
        if self.use_ctas:
            self.paths = Flow('TaxiETLFlow').latest_run.data.paths
        else:
            with S3() as s3:
                objs = s3.list_recursive([URL])
                self.paths = [obj.url for obj in objs]
        print("Processing %d Parquet files" % len(self.paths))
        n = round(len(self.paths) / NUM_SHARDS)
        self.shards = [self.paths[i*n:(i+1)*n] for i in range(NUM_SHARDS - 1)]
        self.shards.append(self.paths[(NUM_SHARDS - 1) * n:])
        self.next(self.preprocess_data, foreach='shards')
```
In the raw data mode, lists paths to raw data

In the CTAS mode, retrieves paths to CTAS results

Groups all paths into four roughly equal-sized shards

```
    @resources(memory=16000)
    @conda(python='3.8.10', libraries={'pyarrow': '5.0.0'})
    @step
    def preprocess_data(self):
        with S3() as s3:
            from pyarrow.parquet import ParquetDataset
            if self.input:
                objs = s3.get_many(self.input)
                orig_table = ParquetDataset([obj.path for obj in objs]).read()
                self.num_rows_before = orig_table.num_rows
                table = process_data(orig_table)
                self.num_rows_after = table.num_rows
                print('selected %d/%d rows'\
                      % (self.num_rows_after, self.num_rows_before))
                self.lat = table['pickup_latitude'].to_numpy()
                self.lon = table['pickup_longitude'].to_numpy()
        self.next(self.join)
```
Mapper step, processing each shard

Downloads data for this shard and decodes it as a table

Processes the table

Stores coordinates from the processed table

```
    @resources(memory=16000)
    @conda(python='3.8.10', libraries={'pyarrow': '5.0.0', 'datashader':
        '0.13.0'})
    @step
    def join(self, inputs):
        import numpy
        lat = numpy.concatenate([inp.lat for inp in inputs])
        lon = numpy.concatenate([inp.lon for inp in inputs])
        print("Plotting %d locations" % len(lat))
        self.image = taxiviz.visualize(lat, lon)
        self.next(self.end)
```
Visualizes and stores results as an artifact

Concatenates coordinates from all shards

```
    @conda(python='3.8.10')
```

```
    @step
    def end(self):
        pass

if __name__ == '__main__':
    TaxiPlotterFlow()
```

Save the code to taxi_plotter.py. If you ran `TaxiETLFlow` previously, you can run the flow like this:

```
# python taxi_plotter.py --environment=conda run --use_ctas_data=True
```

Otherwise, leave the option out to use the raw data directly. The flow runs for about a minute on a large instance. After the run has completed, you can open a notebook and type the following lines in a cell to see the results:

```
from metaflow import Flow
from IPython.display import Image
run = Flow('TaxiPlotterFlow').latest_run
Image(run.data.image)
```

The result should look something akin to one of the visualizations in figure 7.18. On the left, figure 7.18 shows the image of a full dataset. You can see the Midtown area being very popular (light shade). The image on the right was produced by a CTAS query that shows trips only during one hour between midnight and 1 a.m.—many areas outside the Midtown area are sparsely trafficked.

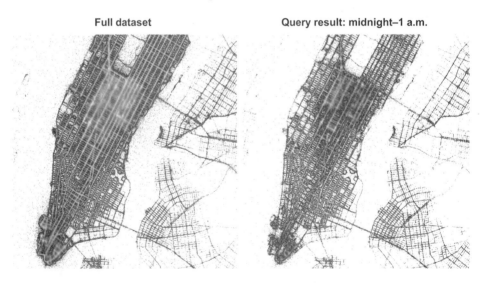

Full dataset   **Query result: midnight–1 a.m.**

Figure 7.18 Visualizing pickup locations in two different subsets of the taxi dataset

The code in listing 7.8 demonstrates the following three important concepts:

- Thanks to `@project`, we can safely separate an upstream data processing flow, `TaxiETLFlow`, from other downstream business logic like `TaxiPlotterFlow`. Crucially, `Flow('TaxiETLFlow').latest_run` points not at any random latest run of `TaxiETLFlow` but to the latest run that exists in the flow's own namespace, as discussed in chapter 6. This allows multiple data scientists to work on their own versions of the `TaxiETLFlow`→`TaxiPlotterFlow` sequence without interfering with each other's work.

- The `process_data` function demonstrates the mapper concept. After a raw dataset has been extracted with SQL in a CTAS query, the data scientist can further process data in Python, instead of having to pack all project-specific logic in the SQL query. Also, we avoid potentially memory-inefficient conversion to pandas.

    Think of `process_data` as an infinitely versatile user-defined function (UDF) that many query engines provide as an escape hatch to work around the limitations of SQL. Depending on the computational cost of `process_data`, the number of shards can be increased to speed up processing.

- We avoid storing the full dataset as an artifact, which is often inconveniently slow. Instead, we extract only the data we need—in this case, latitudes and longitudes—as space-efficient NumPy arrays and store them. Merging and manipulating NumPy arrays is fast.

This flow demonstrates that it is possible to handle even large datasets in Python using off-the-shelf libraries and a scalable compute layer. A major benefit of this approach is operational simplicity: you can leverage existing data infrastructure for the initial heavy lifting and SQL queries, and the rest can be handled by the data scientist autonomously in Python.

In the next section, we add the last step in the data path: feeding data into models. We will leverage the pattern discussed in this section to perform feature transformations efficiently.

An alternative approach: Dask or PySpark

As an alternative approach for distributed data processing, you could use a specialized compute layer like Dask (dask.org), which provides a higher-level interface for performing similar operations in Python. A benefit of Dask (or PySpark) is that the data scientist can operate on dataframe-like objects, which are automatically sharded and parallelized under the hood.

> **(continued)**
>
> A downside is the introduction of another, operationally nontrivial compute layer in your infrastructure stack. When a system like Dask or Spark works, it can boost productivity massively. When it doesn't work, either because of engineering issues or due to incompatibility with libraries that a data scientist wants to use, it can become a hard-to-debug headache.
>
> If you have a Dask cluster already available, you can easily offload data processing on it simply by calling it from your Metaflow steps. Equipped with this information about various approaches, you can make the right choice for your organization.

7.3 From data to features

Equipped with a powerful way to load data from the data warehouse to workflows, Alex can start getting more organized about how raw data is converted into matrices and tensors consumed by models. Alex would like to load various subsets of data from the data warehouse rapidly and define a set of custom Python functions—feature encoders—that convert the raw data to model inputs. The exact shape and size of the input matrices depends on the use case, so the system should be flexible enough to handle a wide variety of needs.

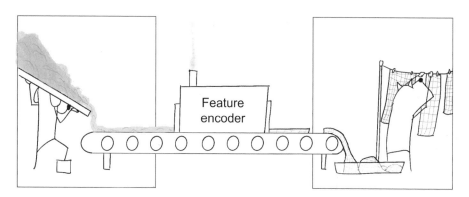

Thus far, we have discussed the low levels of data processing: how to access and process raw data efficiently. The discussion hasn't had anything to do with data science or machine learning specifically. Arguably, data science often involves generic data processing, so the focus is justified. This is also why we place *data* as the most foundational layer in our infrastructure stack.

In this section, we scratch the surface of the multifaceted question of how to think about the interface between data and models. This is a much higher-level concern with fewer universally applicable answers. For instance, a feature engineering approach that works for tabular data doesn't necessarily work for audio or time series.

A major part of the data scientist's domain expertise relates to feature engineering, so it is beneficial to let them experiment and adopt various approaches relatively freely. In this sense, feature engineering is a different kind of a concern than, say, the foundational topics of data discussed earlier in this chapter or the compute layer covered in chapter 4. The distinction is illustrated in figure 7.19, which was first presented in chapter 1.

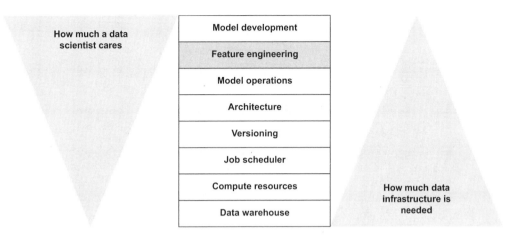

Figure 7.19 How much the data scientist cares about various layers of the stack

Instead of prescribing a one-size-fits-all solution to feature engineering, each domain can benefit from domain-specific libraries and services.

> **RECOMMENDATION** It is often a good idea to build, adopt, or buy domain-specific solutions for the feature layer, which can be tailored for the use case at hand. These solutions can sit on top of the foundational infrastructure, so they are complementary, not competing, with the rest of the stack.

We begin by defining the amorphous concept of *a feature*. Then we will provide a basic example that takes raw data, converts it into features, and feeds it into a model. Later, in chapter 9, we will expand the example to make it ever more featureful. This should give you a solid starting point in case you want to dig deeper, for instance, by reading a more modeling-oriented book that covers feature engineering in detail, and applying the lessons to your own infrastructure stack.

7.3.1 Distinguishing facts and features

It is useful to distinguish between *facts* and *features*. Besides providing conceptual clarity, this practice helps in dividing work between data engineers and data scientists. Let's use figure 7.20 to structure the discussion.

The figure is framed on a philosophical assumption that everything exists in an objective physical *reality* that we can partially observe to collect *facts*. Due to their observational nature, we can expect facts to be biased, inaccurate, or even incorrect occasionally. However, crucially, facts are as close to the objective reality as we can get.

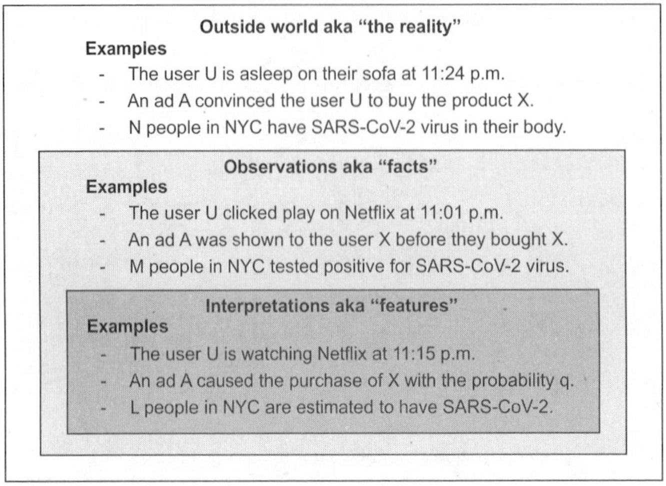

Figure 7.20   The nature of facts and features

From the engineering point of view, facts can be events collected from the product or data acquired from a third party. There shouldn't be much interpretation or ambiguity in them: for instance, someone clicking Play to watch *The Lion King* is a direct observation—a fact. Later, we may decide to interpret the Play event as a signal that the user prefers to watch this type of content, which might be a useful label—a *feature*—for a recommendation model. Countless other alternative interpretations exist for the Play event (maybe they fat-fingered a large banner on their mobile device) and, hence, many opportunities for feature engineering, although the underlying fact is unambiguous. The distinction between facts and features has important practical implications, some of which are outlined in table 7.1.

Table 7.1   Comparing and contrasting facts vs. features

	Features	Facts	Reality
Role	Data scientist	Data engineer	
Key activity	Define new features and challenge existing ones	Collect and persist reliable observations	
Speed of iteration	Fast—coming up with new interpretations is easy	Slow—starting to collect new data takes a lot of effort	
Can we control it?	Fully—we know and control all the inputs and outputs	Partially—we don't control the input, the reality that behaves in unpredictable ways	No, but we can make small interventions, such as A/B experiments
Trustworthiness	Varies, low by default	Aims to be high	The objective truth

As highlighted by the table, it is useful to have a role, often a data engineer, who is responsible for collecting and storing facts reliably. This is a complex undertaking by itself, because they need to interface directly with the constantly changing outside reality. After a reliable set of facts is available, another person, a data scientist, can take the facts, interpret and transform them into features, test them in a model, and iterate again with a new set of features to improve the model.

The key activities between the two roles are distinct. Optimally, the data scientist can iterate quickly because they have an infinite number of possible features to test. The more accurate and comprehensive the facts are, the better the models, which motivates data engineers to collect a wide variety of high-quality data. We can project these activities to the following patterns covered in this chapter:

- Data engineers maintain reliable *fact tables,* which are available for all projects.
- Data scientists can query the fact tables and extract interesting project-specific views of facts for their workflows, for instance, using the CTAS pattern.
- Data scientists can quickly iterate on features inside their workflow, in Python, using the MapReduce-style pattern we covered in the previous section.

In some cases, it can be useful to leverage off-the-shelf libraries and services like *feature stores* or *data labeling services* to aid with the last two steps, or you can create a custom library that answers to the specific needs of your company. In any case, it is prudent to start by considering a simple baseline solution that doesn't involve specialized tooling.

You can either use the baseline approach presented in the next section as-is, or you can use it as a foundation for your own domain-specific libraries. No matter what approach you take, it should be possible for data scientists to access facts easily and iterate on features quickly. It is highly beneficial to use a system like Metaflow to take care of versioning while doing this—otherwise, it is easy to lose track of what data and features yielded the best results.

7.3.2   Encoding features

The process that converts facts to features is called *feature encoding,* or *featurization.* A model takes a set of features, produced by sometimes tens or even hundreds of individual feature encoding functions, or *feature encoders.* Although you could interleave your featurization code with modeling code, especially in larger projects, it is very useful to have a consistent way of defining and executing feature encoders as a separate step.

Besides helping to make the overall architecture manageable, it is crucial that the same feature encoders are used both during training and inference to guarantee correctness of results. This requirement is often called *offline-online consistency,* where *offline* refers to periodic training of models as a batch process and *online* refers to on-demand predictions.

Another central requirement to feature pipelines is the management of *accurate train and test splits.* In many cases, like in our weather forecasting example in the previous chapter, historical data is used to predict the future. Models like this can be *back-tested* by taking a past point in time as a reference and treating data prior to it as history, which can be used for training, and data after it as a pretend future, which can be used for testing. To guarantee the validity of results, the training data must not contain any information past the reference point, often called *leakage*, which would count as obtaining information from the future.

A well-designed feature encoding pipeline can treat time as the primary dimension, which makes it easy to conduct backtesting while making sure that the time horizons are respected by feature encoders, preventing any kind of leakage. A feature encoding pipeline can also help to monitor *concept drift*, that is, the statistics of the target variable of the model changing over time. Some *feature stores*, which help with all these concerns, also present a UI that allows facts and features to be shared and discovered easily.

There isn't a single right or universal way to implement these concerns. Time is handled differently in different datasets, and maintaining online-offline consistency can be done in many different ways, depending on the use case—not all applications need "online" predictions. A tightly coupled data science team working on a project together can quickly communicate and iterate on feature encoders without a heavyweight technical solution.

A key contention is about flexibility and speed of iteration versus guaranteed correctness: you can devise (or acquire) a featurization solution that solves all the previous concerns, guaranteeing correctness, but makes it hard to define new features. For a sensitive, mature project, this might be the right tradeoff to make. On the other hand, imposing an overly rigid solution on a new project might make it hard to develop it rapidly, limiting its usefulness overall—the project may be 100% correct but also quite useless. A good compromise might be to start with a flexible approach and make it more rigid as the project matures.

Next, we will present an extremely simple feature encoding workflow, based on the `TaxiPlotter` workflow from the previous section. The example is on the flexible extreme of the spectrum: it doesn't address any of the previous concerns, but it lays the foundation that we will build on in chapter 9 that presents a more full-fledged featurization pipeline.

EXAMPLE: PREDICTING THE COST OF A TAXI TRIP

To demonstrate feature encoding—not our modeling skills—we build a simple predictor to estimate the cost of a taxi trip. We know that the price is directly correlated with the length of the trip, both in terms of time and space. To keep things simple, this example focuses only on the distance. We use simple linear regression to predict the amount paid given the distance traveled. We will make the example more interesting in chapter 9.

If this were a real task given to a data scientist, they would surely start by exploring the data, probably in a notebook. You can do it, too, as an exercise. You will find out that, as with any real-life dataset containing empirical observations, there is noise in data: a good number of trips have a $0 cost or no distance traveled. Also, a small number of outliers have a very high cost or distance traveled.

We start by making an interpretation, starting to turn facts into features, by assuming that these outlier trips don't matter. We use the function `filter_outliers` in the following code listing to get rid of trips that have values in the top or bottom 2% of the value distribution. The utility module also contains a function, `sample`, that we can use to uniformly sample rows from the dataset.

Listing 7.9 Removing outlier rows from an Arrow table

**Accepts a pyarrow.Table and a
list of columns to be cleaned**

```
def filter_outliers(table, clean_fields):
    import numpy
    valid = numpy.ones(table.num_rows, dtype='bool')
    for field in clean_fields:
        column = table[field].to_numpy()
        minval = numpy.percentile(column, 2)
        maxval = numpy.percentile(column, 98)
        valid &= (column > minval) & (column < maxval)
    return table.filter(valid)

def sample(table, p):
    import numpy
    return table.filter(numpy.random.random(table.num_rows) < p)
```

Processes all columns one by one

Starts with a filter that accepts all rows

Finds the top and bottom 2% of the value distribution

Includes only rows that fall between 2–98% of the value distribution

Returns a subset of the rows that match the filter

Samples a random p% of rows of the given table

Flips a biased coin on each row and returns the matching rows

Save the code in table_utils.py. It is worth noting that both the functions in listing 7.9, `filter_outlier` and `sample`, could be implemented in SQL as well. You could bake these operations in the SQL behind the CTAS query. Consider the following benefits of performing these operations in Python instead. First, expressing `filter_outliers` in SQL is somewhat nontrivial, especially when it is done over multiple columns. The resulting SQL would likely take more (convoluted) lines of code than the Python implementation.

Second, we are making major assumptions here: is 2% the right number? Should it be the same for all columns? A data scientist may want to iterate on these choices. We can iterate and test the code in Python much faster than what it takes to execute a complex SQL query.

Also note that both the functions are implemented without a conversion to pandas, which guarantees that the operations are both time- and space-efficient because they rely only on Apache Arrow and NumPy, both of which are backed by high-performance C and C++ code. It is quite likely that these operations are more performant in Python than they would be on any query engine. Listing 7.10 defines the functions that build a linear regression model and visualize it.

Listing 7.10   Training and visualizing a regression model

```
def fit(features):                           ◁──────  Accepts features as a
    from sklearn.linear_model import                 dictionary of NumPy arrays
     LinearRegression

    d = features['trip_distance'].reshape(-1, 1)
    model = LinearRegression().fit(d, features['total_amount'])    ┐ Builds a linear
    return model                                                     regression model
                                                                     using Scikit-Learn
def visualize(model, features):    ◁────── Visualizes the model
    import matplotlib.pyplot as plt

    from io import BytesIO
    import numpy
    maxval = max(features['trip_distance'])
    line = numpy.arange(0, maxval, maxval / 1000)   ┐ Plots a
    pred = model.predict(line.reshape(-1, 1))         regression line
    plt.rcParams.update({'font.size': 22})
    plt.scatter(data=features,
                x='trip_distance',
                y='total_amount',
                alpha=0.01,
                linewidth=0.5)
    plt.plot(line, pred, linewidth=2, color='black')
    plt.xlabel('Distance')
    plt.ylabel('Amount')
    fig = plt.gcf()
    fig.set_size_inches(18, 10)
    buf = BytesIO()              ┐ Saves the image
    fig.savefig(buf)               as an artifact
    return buf.getvalue()
```

Save the code to taxi_model.py. The `fit` function builds a simple linear regression model using Scikit-Learn. For details, you can see the documentation for Scikit-Learn (http://mng.bz/Wxew). The `visualize` function plots the features on a scatterplot and overlays the regression line on top of it.

The next code snippet shows the actual workflow, `TaxiRegressionFlow`, which is closely based on `TaxiPlotterFlow` from the previous section. It has the same two modes: you can either use preprocessed data from a CTAS query produced by `Taxi-ETLFlow`, or you can use the raw mode that accesses two months of unfiltered data.

Listing 7.11   From facts to features to a model

```
from metaflow import FlowSpec, step, conda, Parameter,\
                      S3, resources, project, Flow

URLS = ['s3://ursa-labs-taxi-data/2014/10/',    ◁─────
        's3://ursa-labs-taxi-data/2014/11/']            Uses two months of
NUM_SHARDS = 4                                          data in the raw mode
FIELDS = ['trip_distance', 'total_amount']
```

Samples the given percentage of data, 0.0–1.0.

Chooses between raw or CTAS mode, similar to TaxiPlotterFlow

```python
@conda_base(python='3.8.10')
@project(name='taxi_nyc')
class TaxiRegressionFlow(FlowSpec):
    sample = Parameter('sample', default=0.1)
    use_ctas = Parameter('use_ctas_data', help='Use CTAS data', default=False)

    @step
    def start(self):
        if self.use_ctas:
            self.paths = Flow('TaxiETLFlow').latest_run.data.paths
        else:
            with S3() as s3:
                objs = s3.list_recursive(URLS)
                self.paths = [obj.url for obj in objs]
        print("Processing %d Parquet files" % len(self.paths))
        n = max(round(len(self.paths) / NUM_SHARDS), 1)
        self.shards = [self.paths[i*n:(i+1)*n] for i in range(NUM_SHARDS - 1)]
        self.shards.append(self.paths[(NUM_SHARDS - 1) * n:])
        self.next(self.preprocess_data, foreach='shards')

    @resources(memory=16000)
    @conda(libraries={'pyarrow': '5.0.0'})
    @step
    def preprocess_data(self):
        from table_utils import filter_outliers, sample
        self.shard = None
        with S3() as s3:
            from pyarrow.parquet import ParquetDataset
            if self.input:
                objs = s3.get_many(self.input)
                table = ParquetDataset([obj.path for obj in objs]).read()
                table = sample(filter_outliers(table, FIELDS), self.sample)
                self.shard = {field: table[field].to_numpy()
                              for field in FIELDS}
        self.next(self.join)

    @resources(memory=8000)
    @conda(libraries={'numpy': '1.21.1'})
    @step
    def join(self, inputs):
        from numpy import concatenate
        self.features = {}
        for f in FIELDS:
            shards = [inp.shard[f] for inp in inputs if inp.shard]
            self.features[f] = concatenate(shards)
        self.next(self.regress)

    @resources(memory=8000)
    @conda(libraries={'numpy': '1.21.1',
                      'scikit-learn': '0.24.1',
                      'matplotlib': '3.4.3'})
    @step
    def regress(self):
        from taxi_model import fit, visualize
```

Cleans and samples each shard independently

Extracts clean columns as features

Merges feature shards by concatenating the arrays

```
                  ┌─▷ self.model = fit(self.features)
  Fits a          │   self.viz = visualize(self.model, self.features)   ◁─┐   Visualizes the model
  model           │   self.next(self.end)                                 │   and stores the image
                  └                                                       │   as an artifact

          @step
          def end(self):
              pass

if __name__ == '__main__':
    TaxiRegressionFlow()
```

Save the code in taxi_regression.py. If you ran `TaxiETLFlow` previously, you can run the flow like this:

```
# python taxi_regression.py –environment=conda run –use_ctas_data=True
```

Otherwise, leave the option out to use the raw data directly. It takes less than a minute to process a 10% sample of data on a large instance and about two minutes to process the full dataset without sampling. Figure 7.21 visualizes the regression line produced by the model as well as a scatterplot of raw data, as shown in a Jupyter notebook.

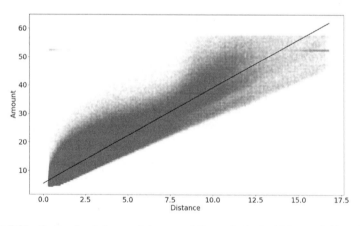

Figure 7.21   Regression between distance and the cost of a taxi trip, overlaid on data

This example expands the previous `TaxiPlotterFlow` example by demonstrating the following:

- The data scientist can use the MapReduce-style pattern to encode features.
- We can combine the best of both worlds by using SQL for data extraction and Python for feature engineering.

- It is possible to perform feature engineering in a performance-conscious manner in Python, thanks to libraries like Apache Arrow and NumPy, backed by C and C++ implementations.

In chapter 9, we will expand the example to include proper testing of the model, more sophisticated regression models using deep learning, and an extensible feature encoding pipeline.

This chapter covered a lot of ground, all the way from foundational data access patterns to feature engineering pipelines and model training, as summarized in figure 7.22.

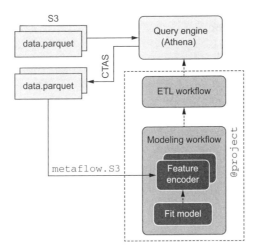

Figure 7.22 Summarizing the concepts covered in this chapter

We started with the fundamentals of moving data quickly from S3 to instances. We discussed efficient in-memory representation of data with Apache Arrow. After this, we showed how these techniques can be used to interface with query engines like Spark, Snowflake, Trino, or Amazon Athena, which are a core part of the modern data infrastructure.

We created a workflow that uses a query engine to process a dataset by executing a Create-Table-As-Select SQL query, the results of which can be downloaded quickly to a downstream workflow. Finally, we used this functionality to create a feature encoding pipeline that trains a model.

Combined with the lessons from the previous chapter, these tools allow you to build production-grade data science applications that ingest large amounts of data from a data warehouse, encode features in parallel, and train models at scale. For more computationally demanding feature encoders, you can leverage lessons from chapter 5 to optimize them, if necessary.

Summary

- Optimize downloading speed between S3 and EC2 instances by ensuring that data fits in memory and files are large enough and by using a large instance type.

- Use Parquet as an efficient format for storing tabular data and Apache Arrow to read and process it in memory.

- If memory consumption is a concern, avoid converting data to pandas. Instead, operate with Arrow and NumPy data structures.

- Leverage existing data infrastructure to extract and preprocess data for data science workflows and to connect them to ETL workflows.

- Use modern query engines like Spark, Trino, Snowflake, or Athena to execute SQL queries to produce arbitrary data extracts, stored in Parquet, for data science workflows.

- Organizationally, data engineers can focus on producing high-quality, reliable facts, whereas data scientists can iterate on project-specific datasets autonomously.

- Use the MapReduce pattern to process large datasets in Python in parallel. Libraries like Arrow and NumPy are backed by high-performance C/C++ code, making it possible to process data quickly.

- Leverage the foundational tools and patterns to build a solution that works for your particular use cases—feature engineering and feature pipelines tend to be quite domain-specific.

- When designing a feature pipeline, consider using time as the primary dimension to make it easy to backtest with historical data and to prevent leakage.

- In feature engineering pipelines, ensure that data scientists can access facts easily and iterate on features quickly.

Using and
operating models

This chapter covers

- Using machine-learning models to produce predictions that benefit real-world applications
- Producing predictions as a batch workflow
- Producing predictions as a real-time application

Why do businesses invest in data science applications? "To produce models" isn't an adequate answer, because models are just bundles of data and code with no intrinsic value. To produce tangible value, applications must have a positive impact on the surrounding world. For instance, a recommendation model is useless in isolation, but when connected to a user interface, it can lower customer churn and increase long-term revenue. Or a model predicting credit risk becomes valuable when connected to a decision-support dashboard used by human decision-makers.

In this chapter, we bridge the gap between data science and business applications. Although this is the second-to-last chapter of the book, in real-life projects, you should start thinking about the connection early on. Figure 8.1 illustrates the idea using the spiral diagram introduced in chapter 3.

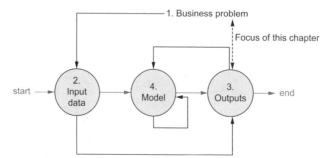

Figure 8.1 **Connecting outputs to surrounding systems**

In general, it is a good idea to begin by thoroughly learning about the business problem that needs to be solved. After this, you can identify and evaluate data assets that you can use to solve the problem. Before writing a line of modeling code, you can choose an architectural pattern that allows the results to be connected to a value-generating business application, which is the main topic of this chapter.

Frequently, thinking about inputs and outputs reveals issues, such as the lack of suitable data or technical or organizational difficulties in using the results, which can be addressed before any models have been built. Once it is clear how the application can be deployed in its environment, you can begin the actual modeling work. If the project is successful, such as personalized video recommendations at Netflix, the modeling work never ends: data scientists keep improving the models year after year.

Models can be used in production in countless ways. Companies are increasingly eager to apply data science to all aspects of business, resulting in a diverse spectrum of requirements. Theoretically, there's a well-defined way to produce predictions given a model. Technically, however, it is quite different from a system that produces real-time predictions in a high-speed trading system, say, populating a handful of predictions for an internal dashboard.

Note that we use the term *prediction* to refer to any output of a data science workflow. Strictly speaking, not all data science applications produce predictions—they can produce classifications, categorizations, inferences, and other insights as well. For brevity, we use *predictions* as an umbrella term to refer to any such outputs. Another commonly used term for activities like this is *model serving*—we want to make the model available, that is, serve the model, to other systems.

We begin the chapter by describing a number of common architectural patterns for using models to produce predictions. You can then choose and apply the most appropriate patterns to your use cases. We focus on two common patterns: precomputing results in advance, aka *batch predictions*, and doing the same in real-time through a web service, aka *real-time predictions*. These techniques are complementary to all the lessons we have learned in previous chapters.

The latter part of the chapter focuses on *model operations*, namely, how to ensure that the model keeps producing correct results over time. We learn about patterns for retraining and testing models continuously, as well as monitoring the performance of models. Similar to inference, there isn't a single right approach or a single right tool for implementing model operations, but learning about general patterns helps you to choose the right tool for each use case.

Figure 8.2 summarizes these topics on our infrastructure stack.

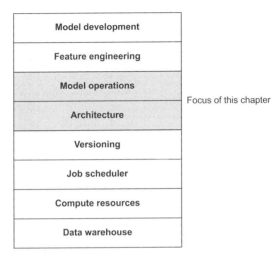

Focus of this chapter

Figure 8.2   The infrastructure stack

By placing the model operations and architecture high on the stack, we signal that these concerns can't be abstracted away from the data scientists—much less so than, say, the compute layer covered in chapter 4. The architecture of the overall data science application, and how it is operated in production, should follow the business problem being solved. Understanding how the application works end to end, from raw data to business results, allows the data scientist to use their domain knowledge and modeling expertise to the fullest. Naturally effective data science infrastructure should make it easy enough to apply various patterns without having to become a DevOps specialist. You can find all code listings for this chapter at http://mng.bz/8MyB.

8.1   Producing predictions

Encouraged by the efficiency gains produced by Alex's models, Caveman Cupcakes made a major investment in an industry-first, fully-automated cupcake factory. Alex and Bowie have been planning for months how to connect the outputs of Alex's machine learning models to the various control systems that power the facility. Some of the systems require real-time predictions, whereas others are optimized nightly. Designing a robust and versatile interface between the models and industrial automation systems wasn't trivial, but the effort was worth it! The well-designed setup allows Alex to develop and test better versions of the models as before, Bowie to observe the health of the production systems with full visibility, and Harper to scale the business dramatically.

Theoretically speaking, producing predictions should be quite straightforward. For instance, predicting with a logistic regression model is just a matter of computing a dot product and passing the result through a sigmoid function. Besides the formula being simple mathematically, the operations are not particularly costly computationally.

Challenges related to using models in real-life are practical, not theoretical. You need to consider how to manage the following:

- *Scale*—Although it might not take a long time to produce a single prediction, producing millions in a short enough time requires more thinking.
- *Change*—Data changes over time, and models need to be retrained and redeployed. Moreover, the application code will likely evolve over time, too.
- *Integrations*—To make a real-world impact, predictions need to be used by another system that is subject to challenges of scale and change on its own.
- *Failures*—The previous three issues are a rich source of failures: systems fail under load, change causes predictions to become incorrect over time, and integrations are hard to keep stable. Whenever something fails, you need to understand what failed, why, and how to fix it quickly.

Addressing any of these four points in isolation is a nontrivial engineering challenge by itself. Addressing all of them simultaneously requires significant engineering effort. Luckily, only a few data science projects require a perfect solution for all these concerns. Consider the following prototypical examples:

- A model to balance marketing budgets may require special integrations to marketing platforms, but the scale of data and the speed of change may be modest. Failures can also be handled manually without causing a major disruption.
- A recommendations model may need to handle millions of items for millions of users, but if the system fails sporadically, users won't notice slightly stale recommendations.
- A high-frequency trading system must produce a prediction in less than a millisecond, handling hundreds of thousands of predictions every second. Because the model is directly responsible for tens of millions of dollars of profit, it is cost effective to massively overprovision the infrastructure that hosts the models.

- A credit score model used by human decision-makers to underwrite loans has a modest scale and isn't subject to rapid change, but it is required to be highly transparent so humans can guard against any bias or other subtle failures.
- A language model trained to recognize place names isn't subject to rapid change. The model can be shared as a static file that is updated only sporadically.

A single cookie-cutter approach wouldn't solve all of these use cases. Effective data science infrastructure can provide a few different patterns and tools to gradually harden deployments, as discussed in chapter 6, making sure that each use case can be solved in the simplest possible manner. Due to the inherent complexity of using models to power real-life applications, it is critical to avoid introducing additional accidental complexity in the system. For instance, it isn't necessary or beneficial to deploy a scalable, low-latency model-serving system just to produce a modest number of predictions daily.

Your toolbox can also include off-the-shelf tools and products, many of which have emerged to address the previously described challenges over the past few years. Confusingly, no established nomenclature and categorization exist for these new tools, making it occasionally hard to understand how they should be used most effectively. Categories of tools, which are often grouped under the term *MLOps* (machine learning operations), include the following:

- *Model monitoring* tools that help address change, for example, by monitoring how the distribution of input data and predictions change over time, and failures by alerting when predictions drift outside an expected range.
- *Model hosting and serving* tools that help address scale and integrations by deploying models as a fleet of microservices that can be queried by outside systems, providing a solution for real-time predictions.
- *Feature stores* address change by providing a consistent way of dealing with input data, making sure that data is used consistently both during training time as well as for predictions.

Besides tools that are specific to machine learning and data science, it is often possible to leverage general-purpose infrastructure, such as a microservice platform to host models or a dashboarding tool to monitor models. This is a useful approach, especially when such tools are already installed in your environment.

In the following sections, we will introduce a mental framework that helps you to choose the best pattern for your use case. After this, we will walk through a hands-on example that shows the patterns in action.

8.1.1 Batch, streaming, and real-time predictions

When considering how to use a model effectively, you can start by asking the following central question: how quickly do we need a prediction after we know the input data? Note that the question is not how quickly the model can produce a prediction but rather what's the maximum amount of time we can wait until the prediction is used for something. Figure 8.3 illustrates this question of *input-response gap*.

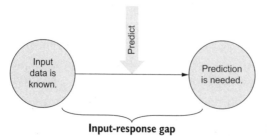

Input-response gap

Figure 8.3   The input-response gap

We can decide to produce predictions, depicted by the big arrow in figure 8.3, any time after the input data is known (obviously not before) and before the predictions are needed by outside systems. The longer the input-response gap, the more leeway we have to choose when and how to produce the predictions.

Why is this question important? Intuitively, it is clear that producing answers quickly is harder than producing them slowly. The narrower the gap, the harder the challenges of scale, change, integrations, and failures become. Although technically a system that can support a low latency can handle high latency as well, and, hence, it might be tempting to use a single low-latency system to handle all use cases, avoiding overengineering can make life much easier.

Depending on the answer, we can choose an appropriate infrastructure and software architecture for the use case. Figure 8.4 presents three common classes of model-serving systems based on the size of the gap: *batch*, where the gap is typically measured in tens of minutes and up; *streaming*, which can support gaps in the minute scale; and *real-time*, when responses are needed in seconds or milliseconds.

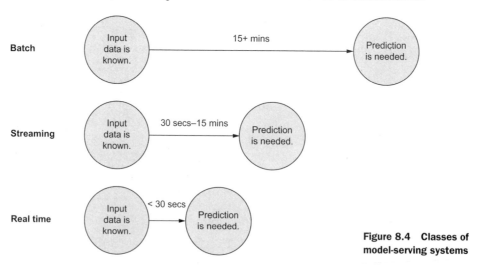

Figure 8.4   Classes of model-serving systems

The batch prediction approach is the easiest to implement—all systems have plenty of headroom to operate—but this approach is suitable only if you can afford waiting 15 minutes or more before using the predictions. In this case, you can aggregate all new input data in a big batch and schedule a workflow to run, say, hourly or daily, to produce predictions for the batch. The results can be persisted in a database or a cache where they can be accessed quickly by outside systems, providing a very low latency for accessing precomputed predictions.

It is not very practical to use a workflow scheduler to produce predictions much more frequently because a typical workflow scheduler is not optimized for minimal latency. If you need results faster, between 30 seconds and 15 minutes after receiving an input data point, you can use *a streaming platform* such as Apache Kafka, maybe with a streaming application platform like Apache Flink. These systems can receive data at scale and funnel it to data consumers in a few seconds.

An example of a streaming model might be a "watch next" recommendation in a video service. Let's say we want to show a personalized recommendation for a new video immediately when the previous one finishes. We can compute the recommendation while the previous show is playing, so we can tolerate a latency of a few minutes. This allows us to show a recommendation even if the user stops the show prematurely.

Finally, if you need results in less than a few seconds, you need a solution for *real-time model serving*. This is similar to any web service that needs to produce a response immediately, in tens of milliseconds, after the user clicks a button. For instance, companies powering internet advertising use systems like this to predict the most effective personalized banner ad for the user on the fly.

Another important consideration is how the predictions are going to be consumed by outside systems: is the workflow going to push results to a datastore, or are they going to be pulled from a service by a consumer? Figure 8.5 outlines these patterns—pay attention to the direction of the arrows.

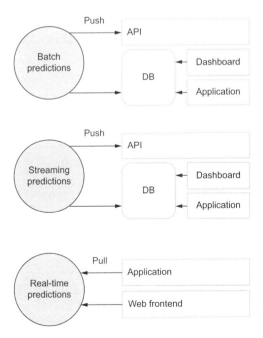

Figure 8.5 Patterns for sharing outputs

A workflow producing batch predictions can send the predictions to an external API or a database. It is then easy for other business applications, including dashboards, to access the predictions from the database. The same pattern applies to streaming predictions, with the crucial difference that predictions are refreshed more frequently. Note the direction of the arrows: batch and streaming push predictions to outside systems. Outside systems can't call them directly.

In contrast, a real-time model-serving system reverses the pattern: external systems pull predictions from the model. This approach is required when the input data becomes available just before the prediction is needed. For instance, consider a model generating targeted advertisements based on a list of websites the user has just visited. In this scenario, it is not feasible to precompute all possible combinations of websites in advance. The prediction must be computed in real-time.

The choice of the pattern has far-reaching implications, as described next:

- It is easy to develop and test batch predictions locally. You can use the same workflow system for batch predictions that is used to train the model, so no additional systems are needed. In contrast, developing and testing streaming and real-time predictions require additional infrastructure.
- Data processing for batch predictions, and sometimes in streaming, can follow the patterns outlined in chapter 7. It is relatively easy to make sure that features stay consistent across training and predictions because the same data processing code can be used on both sides. In contrast, real-time predictions need a datastore that supports low-latency queries as well as low-latency feature encoders.
- Scaling batch predictions is as easy as scaling training, using the compute layer outlined in chapter 4. Autoscaling streaming and real-time systems requires more sophisticated infrastructure.
- Monitoring models accurately and logging and managing failures are easier in batch systems. In general, ensuring that a batch system stays highly available incurs less operational overhead in contrast to a streaming or real-time system.

All in all, it is beneficial to start by considering whether the application, or parts of it, can be powered by batch predictions.

> **NOTE** Batch processing doesn't mean that predictions couldn't be accessed quickly when needed. In fact, precomputing predictions as a batch process and pushing the results to a high-performance datastore, like an in-memory cache, provides the fastest possible access to predictions. However, batch processing requires that inputs are known well in advance.

In the next sections, we will demonstrate the three patterns through a practical use case: a movie-recommendation system. We will begin with a short introduction on recommendation systems. We will then show how to use the recommendation model for batch predictions and, after this, how to use it to power real-time predictions. Finally, we will outline a high-level architecture for streaming predictions.

8.1.2 Example: Recommendation system

Let's build a simple movie-recommendation system to see how the patterns work in practice. Imagine that you work at a startup that streams videos online. The startup has no existing machine learning systems in production. You were hired as a data scientist to build a recommendations model for the company. However, you don't want to stop at the model. To make the model (and yourself) valuable, you would like to integrate the recommendations model you created to the company's live product, so it would power a new "recommended for you" feature in the UI.

Building such a system from scratch takes some effort. We lay out a project plan, shown in figure 8.6, which outlines the topics we will focus on in this section. We follow the spiral approach, so the first step would be to understand the business context of the feature in detail. For this exercise, we can skip the step (in real life you shouldn't!). We start by getting familiar with the data available and outlining a rudimentary modeling approach, which we can improve later if the project shows promise.

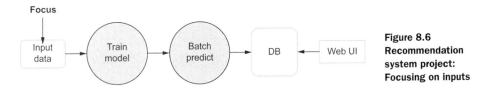

Figure 8.6 Recommendation system project: Focusing on inputs

We will develop the first version of the model using a well-known technique called *collaborative filtering*. The idea is straightforward: we know what movies existing users have watched in the past. By knowing a few movies that a new user has watched, we can find existing users similar to the new one and recommend movies that they had enjoyed. The key question for a model like this is to define what "similar" means exactly and how to calculate similarities between users quickly.

To train the model, we will use the publicly available MovieLens dataset (https://grouplens.org/datasets/movielens/). Download the full dataset with 27 million ratings from http://mng.bz/EWnj and unpack the archive.

Conveniently, the dataset includes a rich characterization of each movie, called the *tag genome*. Figure 8.7 illustrates the idea. In the figure, each movie is characterized by two dimensions: drama versus action and serious versus funny.

Our model represents movies in a similar vector space, but instead of two dimensions, the actual tag genome includes 1,128 dimensions, described in genome-tags.csv. The coordinates of each movie in this 1,128-dimensional space are listed in

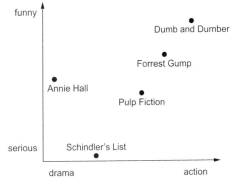

Figure 8.7 Movie tag genome

genome-scores.csv. To figure out the mapping between movie IDs and movie names, see movies.csv.

We know what movies each user has watched and the star rating they assigned for the movies. This information is contained in ratings.csv. We want to recommend only movies that users enjoyed, so we include only movies that the user has rated as four or five stars. Now we characterize each user based on the kinds of movies they like, in other words, a user (vector) is a sum of movie vectors they liked. Figure 8.8 illustrates the idea.

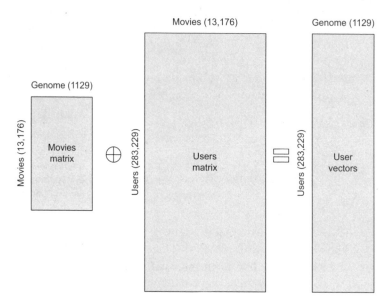

Figure 8.8   The three key matrices

To represent each user as a vector in the tag genome space, we take the *users matrix*, which tells us which movies the users liked, and use it to sum vectors from the *movies matrix*, which represents each movie. We can use the same method to represent any new user as a vector, if we know a few movies they have enjoyed. We normalize each user vector to unit length, because we don't want the number of movies watched to make any difference—only the nature of the movies should count.

The operations depicted in figure 8.8 are implemented in listing 8.1, which we use as a utility module. Most of the code in the listing is used for loading and transforming data from CSV files. The movies matrix is loaded in `load_model_movies_mtx` from a CSV that contains a `genome_dim` (1,128) number of rows for each movie. We chunk the file in fixed-sized vectors, stored in a dictionary keyed by movie ID.

The users matrix is a bit trickier to load because each user has watched a variable number of movies. Based on our learnings from chapter 5, which highlighted the performance of NumPy arrays, and chapter 7, which showed the power of Apache Arrow, we will use these two projects to handle the large dataset efficiently. We use Arrow's `filter` method to include only rows with a high rating. We use NumPy's `unique` method to count the number of movies watched by a user, chunk the rows accordingly, and store the resulting list of movie IDs watched by a user in a dictionary keyed by user ID.

Listing 8.1 Loading movie data

Loads the movies matrix

```
from pyarrow.csv import read_csv
import numpy as np

def load_model_movies_mtx():
    genome_dim = read_csv('genome-tags.csv').num_rows
    genome_table = read_csv('genome-scores.csv')
    movie_ids = genome_table['movieId'].to_numpy()
    scores = genome_table['relevance'].to_numpy()
    model_movies_mtx = {}
    for i in range(0, len(scores), genome_dim):
        model_movies_mtx[movie_ids[i]] = scores[i:i+genome_dim]
    return model_movies_mtx, genome_dim

def load_model_users_mtx():
    ratings = read_csv('ratings.csv')
    good = ratings.filter(ratings['rating'].to_numpy() > 3.5)
    ids, counts = np.unique(good['userId'].to_numpy(),
                            return_counts=True)
    movies = good['movieId'].to_numpy()
    model_users_mtx = {}
    idx = 0
    for i, user_id in enumerate(ids):
        model_users_mtx[user_id] = tuple(movies[idx:idx + counts[i]])
        idx += counts[i]
    return model_users_mtx

def load_movie_names():
    import csv
    names = {}
    with open('movies.csv', newline='') as f:
        reader = iter(csv.reader(f))
        next(reader)
        for movie_id, name, _ in reader:
            names[int(movie_id)] = name
    return names
```

Parses the dimensionality of the tag genome

Parses the movie genome file

Extracts the two columns we need as NumPy arrays

Extracts individual movie vectors from the long array

Loads the users matrix

Includes only watched movies that received four or five stars

Determines how many movies each user watched

Extracts individual user vectors from the long array

Loads the movie ID— movie name mapping

Save the code to a utility module, movie_data.py.

Finally, we create the user vectors in the next listing. The `make_user_vectors` function works by combining information from the user matrix and movie matrix. As a small optimization, we avoid creating a separate vector for each user, because we don't need to store the user vectors explicitly—more about that later. Instead, we reuse the same vector for each user sequentially.

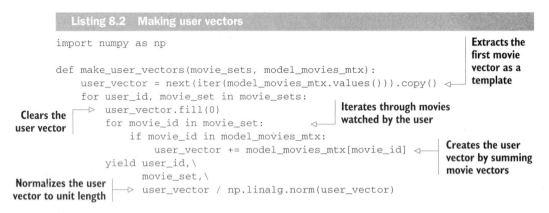

Listing 8.2   Making user vectors

```
import numpy as np                                              Extracts the
                                                               first movie
def make_user_vectors(movie_sets, model_movies_mtx):           vector as a
    user_vector = next(iter(model_movies_mtx.values())).copy()  template
    for user_id, movie_set in movie_sets:
        user_vector.fill(0)                      Iterates through movies
        for movie_id in movie_set:               watched by the user
            if movie_id in model_movies_mtx:
                user_vector += model_movies_mtx[movie_id]   Creates the user
        yield user_id, \                                    vector by summing
            movie_set, \                                    movie vectors
            user_vector / np.linalg.norm(user_vector)
```

Clears the user vector — points to `user_vector.fill(0)`

Normalizes the user vector to unit length — points to `user_vector / np.linalg.norm(user_vector)`

Save the code to a utility module, movie_uservec.py. We will use this soon in a training workflow.

TRAINING A RUDIMENTARY RECOMMENDATIONS MODEL

Figure 8.9 shows how our project is progressing. We are done with the input data part. Next, we sketch a rudimentary recommendation model as a placeholder for future work.

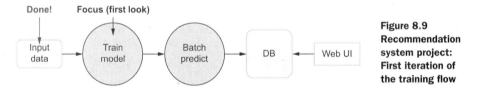

Figure 8.9
Recommendation
system project:
First iteration of
the training flow

To produce recommendations for a new user, we will find similar users by measuring the vector distance between the new user and all existing users and by picking the nearest neighbors. This would require hundreds of thousands of distance measurements just for a single set of recommendations, which is computationally very expensive.

Fortunately, highly optimized libraries exist to speed up the nearest neighbor search. We will use one such library, *Annoy*, that Spotify created for its music-recommendation system. Annoy will create an index, a model, of all user vectors, which we can save and use later to produce recommendations.

The code in listing 8.3 shows a workflow that trains a recommendation model. It uses the functions from `movie_data` to load the data, store them as artifacts, and produce user vectors, which it feeds to Annoy. Annoy will then produce an efficient representation of the user vector space.

Listing 8.3   Recommendation model training flow

```
from metaflow import FlowSpec, step, conda_base, profile, resources
from tempfile import NamedTemporaryFile
                                           Increases this parameter to improve
ANN_ACCURACY = 100                         the accuracy of the Annoy index
```

```
@conda_base(python='3.8.10', libraries={'pyarrow': '5.0.0',
                                         'python-annoy': '1.17.0'})
class MovieTrainFlow(FlowSpec):

    @resources(memory=10000)
    @step                              The start step stores
    def start(self):        ◁————————  movie data as artifacts.
        import movie_data
        self.model_movies_mtx, self.model_dim =\
        movie_data.load_model_movies_mtx()
        self.model_users_mtx = movie_data.load_model_users_mtx()
        self.movie_names = movie_data.load_movie_names()
        self.next(self.build_annoy_index)


    @resources(memory=10000)
    @step
    def build_annoy_index(self):
        from annoy import AnnoyIndex
        import movie_uservec
        vectors = movie_data.make_user_vectors(\
                    self.model_users_mtx.items(),
                    self.model_movies_mtx)
        with NamedTemporaryFile() as tmp:
            ann = AnnoyIndex(self.model_dim, 'angular')       Initializes an
            ann.on_disk_build(tmp.name)                       Annoy index
            with profile('Add vectors'):
                for user_id, _, user_vector in vectors:       Feeds user vectors
                    ann.add_item(user_id, user_vector)        to the index
            with profile('Build index'):
                ann.build(ANN_ACCURACY)  ◁——— Finalizes the index
            self.model_ann = tmp.read()
        self.next(self.end)

    @step
    def end(self):
        pass


if __name__ == '__main__':
    MovieTrainFlow()
```

Iterator that produces user vectors for all existing users — points to the `vectors = movie_data.make_user_vectors(...)` line.

Stores the index as an artifact — points to the `self.model_ann = tmp.read()` line.

Save the code to a file, movie_train_flow.py. To run the flow, make sure you have the MovieLens CSVs in the current working directory. Run the flow as follows:

```
# python movie_train_flow.py --environment=conda run
```

Building an index takes about 10–15 minutes. You can speed up the process at the cost of lower accuracy by lowering the ANN_ACCURACY constant. If you are curious to know how the constant affects the Annoy index, see the documentation of the build method at https://github.com/spotify/annoy. Alternatively, you can make things faster by running the code in the cloud as run --with batch.

After the index has been built, it is stored as an artifact. We will use this artifact in the next sections to produce recommendations, first as a batch workflow, then in real time.

8.1.3   *Batch predictions*

Now that we have a model, we can focus on the core of this chapter: using a model to produce predictions. How should we do it in practice? Let's consider how the discussion could play out in a business setting.

It is likely that the startup's systems are already organized as microservices, individual containers that expose well-defined APIs. Following the same pattern, it would feel natural to create the recommendation systems as another microservice (which we will do in the next section). However, during discussions with the engineering team, the following potential issues are identified with the microservice approach:

- The model takes much more memory and CPU power than existing lightweight web services. The company's container orchestration system would need to be changed to accommodate the new service.

- How should we scale the service? What if we get a surge of new users? The amount of compute power to produce thousands of recommendations per second is nontrivial.

- Isn't it wasteful to keep requesting recommendations every time the user refreshes the page? The recommendations don't change until the user has completed watching a movie. Maybe we should cache the recommendations somehow?

- Are you, the data scientist, going to be responsible for operating the new microservice? Engineers are responsible for their microservices, but operating them requires a sophisticated toolchain, which the data science team hasn't used before.

Also, you recognize *the cold start problem*: when a new user signs up, there's no data to produce recommendations for them. A product manager suggests that we could ask the user for a few movies they like as a part of the signup process to address the issue.

All of these points are valid concerns. After pondering the situation for a while, you come up with a radically different approach: what if, instead of a microservice, you produce recommendations for all the existing users as a big batch operation, structured as a workflow? For existing users, we can produce a long list of recommendations, so even after they have watched a movie, the list won't change drastically. You can refresh the list, say, nightly.

To solve the cold start problem, when a new user signs up, we can ask them to choose two movies they have enjoyed in the past, among, say, the top 1,000 most popular movies. Based on their initial choice, we can recommend other movies they might enjoy. A key observation is that we can precompute recommendations for all possible pairs of movies.

Figure 8.10 visualizes the situation. Conceptually, the user chooses a row corresponding to a movie and then a column corresponding to another movie. We exclude the diagonal—we don't allow the user to choose the same movie twice. Because the choice of (movie A, movie B) is equal to (movie B, movie A)—the order doesn't matter—we can also exclude one-half of the matrix. Hence, we need to precompute recommendations only for the upper triangle, the dark gray area in the matrix. You may remember the formula for determining the number of dark cells in matrix, that is, the number of 2-combinations $\binom{1000}{2}$, which equals 499,500.

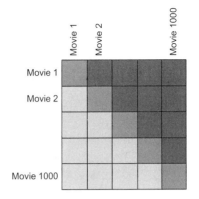

Figure 8.10 Producing recommendations for all pairs of movies (the dark triangle)

In other words, we can handle any choice made by the user by precomputing about half a million recommendations, which is quite doable! We gain many benefits by doing this: we can write the recommendations to a database that the engineering team manages with no performance concerns, no scalability concerns, no need to cache anything, and no new operational overhead. Batch predictions seem like a great approach for this use case.

PRODUCING RECOMMENDATIONS

Per the spiral approach, we should consider how the results will be consumed by outside systems before we spend too much time in producing them. We will start by thinking through how we can use the model to produce recommendations to better understand the shape of the results. We will focus on sharing the results and then come back to finalize the batch prediction flow. Figure 8.11 shows our progress.

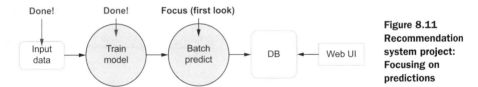

Figure 8.11 Recommendation system project: Focusing on predictions

The Annoy index produced by `MovieTrainFlow` allows us to find nearest neighbors for a new user vector quickly. How should we go from similar users to actual movie recommendations? A simple policy is to consider what other movies the neighbors have enjoyed and recommend them.

Figure 8.12 illustrates the idea. Imagine we have a vector for a new user, depicted by the large gray circle. Using the Annoy index, we can find its neighbors, bounded by the oval. Based on the users matrix, we know what movies the neighbors have enjoyed, so we can simply count the frequencies of movies in the neighborhood, exclude the ones that the user has watched already, and return the remaining highest frequency movies as recommendations. In the figure, all the neighbors have watched the movie *Alien*, so it has the highest frequency and, hence, becomes our recommendation. If the user had already watched all the movies in the neighborhood, we can increase the size of the neighborhood until we find valid recommendations.

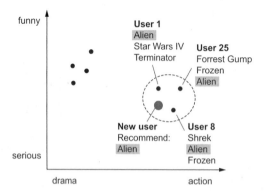

Figure 8.12   Neighborhood of similar users (the dashed circle)

Listing 8.4 shows a utility module that implements the logic. The `load_model` function is used to load the Annoy index from an artifact. Annoy wants to read the model from a file, so we have to write the model first to a temporary file. The `recommend` function produces recommendations for a set of users, represented by sets of movie IDs they have watched (`movie_sets`). It increases the size of the neighborhood until new movies are found. The `find_common_movies` returns the `top_n` most commonly watched movies in the neighborhood, excluding movies that the user has already seen.

Listing 8.4   Producing recommendations

```
from collections import Counter
from tempfile import NamedTemporaryFile
from movie_uservec import make_user_vectors          ◁── Uses the same function to
                                                          create vectors as training

RECS_ACCURACY = 100        ◁── Lower this value for faster,
                               less accurate results.

def load_model(run):            ◁── Loads an Annoy index
    from annoy import AnnoyIndex     from an artifact
    model_ann = AnnoyIndex(run.data.model_dim)
    with NamedTemporaryFile() as tmp:        Allows Annoy to read
        tmp.write(run.data.model_ann)        the index from a file
        model_ann.load(tmp.name)
    return model_ann,\
            run.data.model_users_mtx,\
            run.data.model_movies_mtx


def recommend(movie_sets,
              model_movies_mtx,
              model_users_mtx,
              model_ann,               Returns recommendations
              num_recs):        ◁──   for the given users
    for _, movie_set, vec in make_user_vectors(movie_sets,              Produces
                                    model_movies_mtx):   ◁──           user vectors

        for k in range(10, 100, 10):        ◁──
            similar_users =\                      Increases the neighborhood size
                model_ann.get_nns_by_vector(vec,  until recommendations are found
```

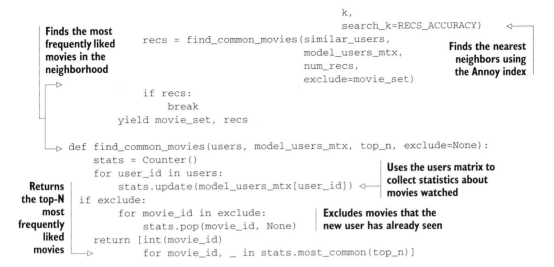

Finds the most frequently liked movies in the neighborhood

Finds the nearest neighbors using the Annoy index

Uses the users matrix to collect statistics about movies watched

Excludes movies that the new user has already seen

Returns the top-N most frequently liked movies

```
                                        k,
                                        search_k=RECS_ACCURACY)
            recs = find_common_movies(similar_users,
                                       model_users_mtx,
                                       num_recs,
                                       exclude=movie_set)
            if recs:
                break
        yield movie_set, recs

def find_common_movies(users, model_users_mtx, top_n, exclude=None):
    stats = Counter()
    for user_id in users:
        stats.update(model_users_mtx[user_id])
    if exclude:
        for movie_id in exclude:
            stats.pop(movie_id, None)
    return [int(movie_id)
            for movie_id, _ in stats.most_common(top_n)]
```

Save the code to a file movie_model.py. We will use the module soon.

Note that we use the same make_user_vectors function both to train the model (build an index) as well as produce predictions. This is very important because models must use the same feature space for training and predictions. Remember how in chapter 7 we discussed how feature encoders turn facts into features. Although we can't guarantee that facts stay stable over time—facts changing is called *data drift*—at least we can guarantee that the feature encoders, here make_user_vectors, are used consistently.

> **IMPORTANT** Place data processing and feature encoding code in a separate module that you can share between training and prediction flows, ensuring that features are produced consistently.

Now that we have a good idea of how to produce recommendations, let's consider how we can share them with outside systems effectively.

SHARING RESULTS ROBUSTLY

Let's build an integration with a database that is used by a web application showing recommendations. Figure 8.13 shows our progress. In a real-life project, you would most likely use a library specific to your data warehouse or database to store the results. Here, to demonstrate the idea, we write the results to a SQLite database, which is conveniently built into Python.

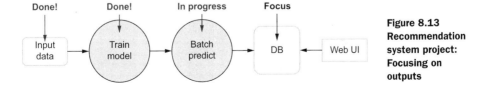

Figure 8.13 Recommendation system project: Focusing on outputs

Listing 8.5 shows a function, save, which creates a database (stored in a file) with two tables: movies, which stores information about movies (movie ID, name, and whether they should be shown during the signup process), and recs which stores a list of recommended movies for each pair of movies chosen during signup.

> **Listing 8.5   Storing recommendations**

```python
import sqlite3

def recs_key(movie_set):          # Makes a canonical key out of two
    return '%s,%s' % (min(movie_set), max(movie_set))    # movie IDs. The order doesn't matter.

def dbname(run_id):               # Returns a versioned database name
    return 'movie_recs_%s.db' % run_id

def save(run_id, recs, names):
    NAMES_TABLE = "CREATE TABLE movies_%s("\
                "    movie_id INTEGER PRIMARY KEY,"\       # SQL to create a
                "    is_top INTEGER, name TEXT)" % run_id   # movies table
    NAMES_INSERT = "INSERT INTO movies_%s "\
                "VALUES (?, ?, ?)" % run_id
    RECS_TABLE = "CREATE TABLE recs_%s(recs_key TEXT, "\   # SQL to create a
                "    movie_id INTEGER)" % run_id           # recommendations
                                                           # table
    RECS_INSERT = "INSERT INTO recs_%s VALUES (?, ?)" % run_id
    RECS_INDEX = "CREATE INDEX index_recs ON recs_%s(recs_key)" % run_id  # SQL to create
                                                           # an index to
                                                           # speed up
    def db_recs(recs):                                     # querying
        for movie_set, user_recs in recs:
            key = recs_key(movie_set)
            for rec in user_recs:
                yield key, int(rec)

    name = dbname(run_id)
    with sqlite3.connect(name) as con:
        cur = con.cursor()
        cur.execute(NAMES_TABLE)
        cur.execute(RECS_TABLE)
        cur.executemany(NAMES_INSERT, names)
        cur.executemany(RECS_INSERT, db_recs(recs))
        cur.execute(RECS_INDEX)
    return name
```

- **SQL to insert movies in the table**
- **SQL to insert recommendations in the table**
- **Makes recommendations compatible with our SQL statement**
- **Creates and populates a database with recommendations**
- **Returns the versioned database name**

Save the code to a file movie_db.py. We will use the module soon. Note an important detail about the save function: it versions the database and the tables with a Metaflow run ID. Versioning the outputs is crucial, as it allows you to do the following:

- *Operate multiple parallel versions safely.* You can have multiple versions of recommendations in production, for example, using the @project decorator we discussed in chapter 6. For instance, this is required if you want to A/B test recommendation variants with live traffic. Thanks to versioning, the variants can never interfere with each other.

- *Separate publishing of results, validation, and promotion to production.* Using this pattern, you can safely run a batch prediction workflow, but its results don't take effect until you point the consumers at the new table, making it possible to validate the results first.

- *Write all results as an atomic operation.* Imagine the workflow fails while writing results. It would be very confusing if half of the results were new and half old. Many databases support transactions, but not all, especially if results span multiple tables or even multiple databases. The versioning approach works with all systems.

- *Experiment safely.* Even if someone runs the workflow on their laptop during prototyping, there won't be an adverse effect on production systems automatically.

- *Aid debugging and auditing.* Imagine a user reports unexpected or incorrect predictions. How do you know what they were seeing exactly? Versioning makes sure that you can backtrack a full lineage of predictions from the UI back to model training.

- *Clean up old results efficiently.* In particular, if you version the whole tables of results, you can quickly clean old results with a single DROP TABLE statement.

We will discuss these topics in more detail in section 8.2 about model operations.

RECOMMENDATION   Always include a version identifier in all results you write to external systems.

Now that we have the two key ingredients, a module to produce recommendations and a module to share them, we can develop a flow that precomputes all recommendations needed during the signup.

PRODUCING A BATCH OF RECOMMENDATIONS

Next, we will implement the last piece: producing hypothetical user profiles and generating recommendations for them. We will do this in a flow that will use the latest model produced by MovieTrainFlow. Figure 8.14 shows our progress.

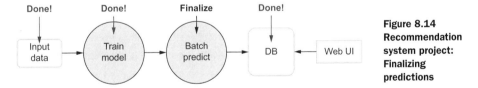

Figure 8.14 Recommendation system project: Finalizing predictions

Having a separate model to train a model and batch-produce predictions is useful because it allows you to schedule the two flows independently. For instance, you could retrain the model nightly and refresh recommendations hourly.

A key challenge with batch predictions is scale and performance. Producing hundreds of thousands of recommendations takes many compute cycles, but it shouldn't take hours or days to complete a run. Luckily, as shown in the following listings, we can use familiar tools and techniques to address the challenge: horizontally scaling workflows from chapter 3, scalable compute layers from chapter 4, performance tips from chapter 5, and patterns for large-scale data processing from chapter 7. Once finished, we can deploy the workflow to production using the lessons from chapter 6.

Figure 8.15 shows a general architecture of batch prediction workflows. We start by fetching data that we want to predict with. We split the data to multiple batches that can be processed in parallel. Finally, we send the results to an outside system.

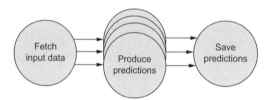

Figure 8.15   Typical structure of a batch prediction workflow

In this example, we produce recommendations only for hypothetical new users who pick two of their favorite movies during the signup process. In a real product, we would update recommendations for existing users as well, fetching their user profiles every time the flow runs.

As discussed in the beginning of this section, we limit the number of movies new users can choose to limit the number of combinations we have to precompute. To increase the likelihood that a new user is able to find their favorites, we pick the top K most popular movies. The next listing shows a function, top_movies, that finds the subset of popular movies.

We will produce all combinations of popular movies, resulting in about 500,000 pairs for the top-1,000 movies. We can produce recommendations for these 500,000 hypothetical user profiles in parallel. We split the list of pairs to chunks of 100,000 profiles using a utility function, make_batches.

Listing 8.6   Utilities for batch recommendations

```
from collections import Counter
from itertools import chain, groupby
                                              Splits a list to fixed-size chunks
def make_batches(lst, batch_size=100000):  ⟵  and returns a list of chunks
    batches = []
    it = enumerate(lst)
    for _, batch in groupby(it, lambda x: x[0] // batch_size):
        batches.append(list(batch))
    return batches
                                       Counts all movie IDs in the user matrix and
                                       returns the top K most popular ones
def top_movies(user_movies, top_k):  ⟵
    stats = Counter(chain.from_iterable(user_movies.values()))
    return [int(k) for k, _ in stats.most_common(top_k)]
```

Save the code to a file, movie_recs_util.py. It will be used in the following flow. Listing 8.7 puts all the pieces together. It generates all movie pairs in the start step, produces recommendations for batches of user profiles in parallel in the batch_recommend step, and aggregates and stores the results in the join step, following the pattern depicted in figure 8.15 above.

Listing 8.7 Batch recommendations flow

```
from metaflow import FlowSpec, step, conda_base, Parameter,\
                      current, resources, Flow, Run
from itertools import chain, combinations

@conda_base(python='3.8.10', libraries={'pyarrow': '5.0.0',
                                        'python-annoy': '1.17.0'})
class MovieRecsFlow(FlowSpec):

    num_recs = Parameter('num_recs',
                         help="Number of recommendations per user",
                         default=3)
    num_top_movies = Parameter('num_top',
                               help="Produce recs for num_top movies",
                               default=100)

    @resources(memory=10000)
    @step
    def start(self):
        from movie_recs_util import make_batches, top_movies
        run = Flow('MovieTrainFlow').latest_successful_run
        self.movie_names = run['start'].task['movie_names'].data
        self.model_run = run.pathspec
        print('Using model from', self.model_run)
        model_users_mtx = run['start'].task['model_users_mtx'].data
        self.top_movies = top_movies(model_users_mtx,
                                     self.num_top_movies)
        self.pairs = make_batches(combinations(self.top_movies, 2))
        self.next(self.batch_recommend, foreach='pairs')

    @resources(memory=10000)
    @step
    def batch_recommend(self):
        from movie_model import load_model, recommend
        run = Run(self.model_run)
        model_ann, model_users_mtx, model_movies_mtx = load_model(run)
        self.recs = list(recommend(self.input,
                                   model_movies_mtx,
                                   model_users_mtx,
                                   model_ann,
                                   self.num_recs))
        self.next(self.join)

    @step
    def join(self, inputs):
        import movie_db
```

Fetches the latest model

Produces a list of the most popular movies

Produces hypothetical user profiles: pairs of popular movies

These steps are run in parallel.

Loads the Annoy index

Produces recommendations for this batch

```
        self.model_run = inputs[0].model_run
        names = inputs[0].movie_names
        top = inputs[0].top_movies
        recs = chain.from_iterable(inp.recs for inp in inputs)
        name_data = [(movie_id, int(movie_id in top), name)
                     for movie_id, name in names.items()]
        self.db_version = movie_db.save(current.run_id, recs, name_data)
        self.next(self.end)

    @step
    def end(self):
        pass

if __name__ == '__main__':
    MovieRecsFlow()
```

Aggregates recommendations across all batches

Saves recommendations to the database

Save the code to a file, movie_recs_flow.py. Run the flow as follows:

```
# python movie_recs_flow.py --environment=conda run
```

By default, only the top 100 movies are considered. You can add the option --num_top=1000 (or higher) to precompute recommendations for more movies. After the run has finished, you should find a SQLite database file, prefixed with movie_recs_, in the current working directory. The database containing recommendations for 500,000 users (hypothetical user profiles) is about 56 MB—there is clearly room for growth! If you want to run this flow in the cloud, you can change the @resources decorators to @batch to run just the start and batch_recommend steps remotely. You need to run the join step locally because we will need the SQLite database stored in a local file soon.

Note how we use the expression Flow('MovieTrainFlow').latest_successful_ run to access the model produced by MovieTrainFlow. This call operates in the same namespace as MovieRecsFlow, meaning each user can experiment with flows freely without interfering with each other's work. As discussed in chapter 6, namespacing works with the @project decorator, too, so you can safely deploy various variants of the flows in production concurrently.

You can use the sqlite3 command-line tool to open the database and query it. However, this chapter is all about producing actual business value using models, so we can take a step further and view the results on a web UI!

USING RECOMMENDATIONS IN A WEB APP

In a real-life business setting, your responsibility as a data scientist would probably end at writing the results to a database. Another engineering team can easily read the recommendations from the database and build an application around them. Figure 8.16 shows the final step.

Although usually you can rely on other engineering teams when it comes to web application development, it is occasionally useful to be able to build a quick application prototype to see the results in action. Fortunately, powerful open source frameworks exist that make it easy to build simple dashboards in Python. Next, we will use

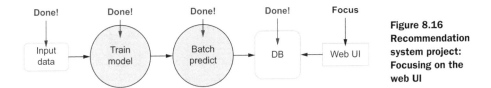

Figure 8.16 Recommendation system project: Focusing on the web UI

one such framework, Plotly Dash (https://plotly.com/dash/), to build a simple UI to simulate the signup flow with recommendations.

First, let's create a simple client library to fetch recommendations from the SQLite database. We need only two functions: get_recs, which returns precomputed recommendations given two movies, and get_top_movies, which returns a list of top movies that we have recommendations for. The next listing shows the client.

> ### Listing 8.8 Accessing recommendations

```
import sqlite3
from movie_db import dbname, recs_key

class MovieRecsDB():
    def __init__(self, run_id):            ← Opens a versioned
        self.run_id = run_id                 database given a run ID
        self.name = dbname(run_id)
        self.con = sqlite3.connect(self.name)
                                           Fetches recommendations for
                                           a hypothetical user profile
                                           consisting of two movies
    def get_recs(self, movie_id1, movie_id2):   ←
        SQL = "SELECT name FROM movies_{run_id} AS movies "\
              "JOIN recs_{run_id} AS recs "\
              "ON recs.movie_id = movies.movie_id "\
              "WHERE recs.recs_key = ?".format(run_id=self.run_id)
        cur = self.con.cursor()
        cur.execute(SQL, [recs_key((movie_id1, movie_id2))])
        return [k[0] for k in cur]
                                       Returns a list of top movies
    def get_top_movies(self):      ←
        SQL = "SELECT movie_id, name FROM movies_%s "\
              "WHERE is_top=1" % self.run_id
        cur = self.con.cursor()
        cur.execute(SQL)
        return list(cur)
```

Save the code to a file, movie_db_client.py. Next, install Plotly Dash by running the following:

```
# pip install dash
```

Plotly Dash allows you to build a whole web application, both the user interface running in the browser and the web server backend in a single Python module. You can refer to its documentation and tutorials to learn the tool in detail. Next, we use it to put together a small, self-explanatory prototype UI, shown in figure 8.17.

Listing 8.9 shows the Dash app that produces the web UI from figure 8.17. The app has two main parts: the layout of the app is defined in `app.layout`, including a list of movies in dropdowns that we fetch from the database. The function `update_output` is called by Dash whenever the user clicks the button. If the user has chosen two movies, we can fetch the corresponding recommendations from the database.

Choose two movies you like

1st movie
Select...
2nd movie
Select...

Recommend!

Choose movies to see recommendations

Figure 8.17   Web UI for our example recommendation system

Listing 8.9   Recommendations web app

```
import sys
from dash import Dash, html, dcc
from dash.dependencies import Input, Output, State
from movie_db_client import MovieRecsDB

RUN_ID = sys.argv[1]                                         Specifies the version of the database
movies = [{'label': name, 'value': movie_id}                as a command-line argument
          for movie_id, name in MovieRecsDB(RUN_ID).get_top_movies()]

app = Dash(__name__)                                         Fetches a list of top
app.layout = html.Div([                                      movies from the database
    html.H1(children="Choose two movies you like"),
    html.Div(children='1st movie'),
    dcc.Dropdown(id='movie1', options=movies),
    html.Div(children='2nd movie'),
    dcc.Dropdown(id='movie2', options=movies),
    html.P([html.Button(id='submit-button', children='Recommend!')]),
    html.Div(id='recs')
])

@app.callback(Output('recs', 'children'),
              Input('submit-button', 'n_clicks'),
              State('movie1', 'value'),
              State('movie2', 'value'))                      Function that is called
def update_output(_, movie1, movie2):                        when the button is clicked
    if movie1 and movie2:
        db = MovieRecsDB(RUN_ID)
        ret = [html.H2("Recommendations")]
        return ret + [html.P(rec) for rec in db.get_recs(movie1, movie2)]
    else:
        return [html.P("Choose movies to see recommendations")]

if __name__ == '__main__':          Starts the                Fetches
    app.run_server(debug=True)      web server                recommendations
                                                              from the database
```

Defines the UI components (annotation pointing to `app.layout`)

Save the code to a file, movie_dash.py. To start the server, you need a database produced by `MovieRecsFlow` in the current working directory. Once you have a database, you can point the server at it by specifying a run ID as follows:

```
# python movie_dash.py 1636864889753383
```

The server should output a line like

```
Dash is running on http://127.0.0.1:8050/
```

You can copy and paste the URL into your browser, which should then open the web app. Now you can choose any pair of movies and get recommendations personalized to your taste! Figure 8.18 shows two example results.

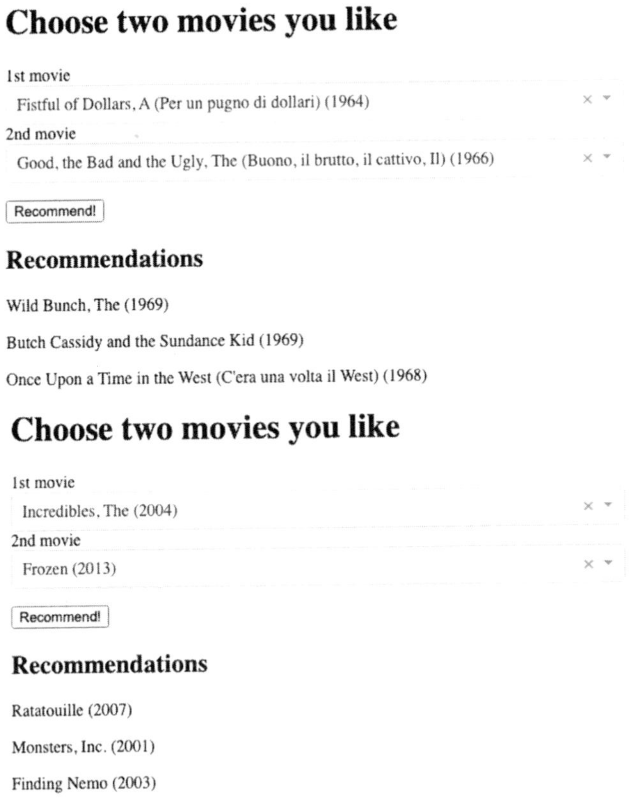

Choose two movies you like

1st movie

Fistful of Dollars, A (Per un pugno di dollari) (1964)   × ▾

2nd movie

Good, the Bad and the Ugly, The (Buono, il brutto, il cattivo, Il) (1966)   × ▾

[Recommend!]

Recommendations

Wild Bunch, The (1969)

Butch Cassidy and the Sundance Kid (1969)

Once Upon a Time in the West (C'era una volta il West) (1968)

Choose two movies you like

1st movie

Incredibles, The (2004)   × ▾

2nd movie

Frozen (2013)   × ▾

[Recommend!]

Recommendations

Ratatouille (2007)

Monsters, Inc. (2001)

Finding Nemo (2003)

**Figure 8.18   Examples
of recommendations**

Notice how the UI is perfectly snappy. There is no noticeable delay in producing the recommendations, resulting in a pleasant user experience. This is a major benefit of batch predictions: there isn't a faster way of producing predictions than not computing anything at all on the fly.

Congratulations for developing a fully functional recommendations system, from raw data all the way to a functional web UI! In the next section, we will see how the same model could be used to produce recommendations on the fly, which is useful for situations where we don't know the input data in advance.

8.1.4   *Real-time predictions*

Remember figure 8.4 from the beginning of the chapter? As shown again in figure 8.19, if you have at least 15 minutes from the moment you know the input data to the time when predictions are actually needed, you can consider batch predictions. The previous section demonstrated an extreme case of this: we could pregenerate all input data, pairs of top movies, long before predictions were needed.

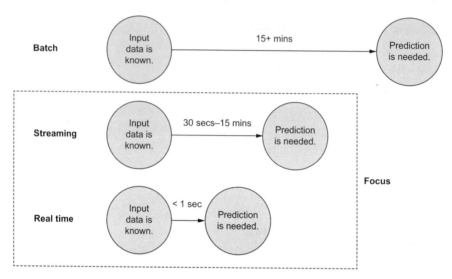

Figure 8.19   Focusing on streaming and real-time predictions

Clearly, we don't always have the luxury of time. For instance, we may want to recommend movies or other products a few minutes or seconds after the user has viewed them. Although ideally, it would be convenient to have a system that can work the same way regardless of the time scale, in practice, one needs to make tradeoffs to produce predictions quickly. For example, if you need answers in seconds, there's not enough time to spin instances up and down on the compute layer on the fly. Or, there's not enough time to download a large dataset from S3 as a whole.

Hence, systems that need to produce answers quickly need to be built differently. In the context of machine learning, such systems are often called *model-serving* or *model-hosting systems*. Their operating principle at the high-level is simple: first, you need a model (file), which is typically produced by a batch workflow, such as by Metaflow. Often, the model is accompanied by functions for preprocessing incoming data, for example, to convert incoming facts to features, and functions for postprocessing results in the desired format. The bundle of a model and supporting code can be packaged as a container, which is deployed on a microservice platform that takes care of running the containers and routing requests to them.

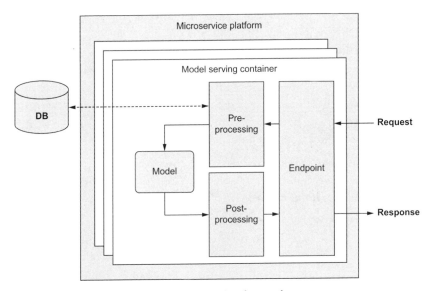

Figure 8.20   Architecture of a typical model-hosting service

Figure 8.20 illustrates the high-level architecture of a model hosting service:

1 A real-time prediction is produced by sending a request, such as over HTTP, to *a hosting endpoint*, which is hosted at an address like http://hosting-service/predict.
2 The endpoint decodes and validates the request and forwards it to a preprocessing function.
3 A preprocessing function is responsible for converting facts included in the request to features used by the deployed model. Often, the request itself doesn't contain all the required data, but additional data is looked up from a database. For instance, the request may contain just a user ID, and the latest data related to the user is fetched from the DB.
4 A feature vector/tensor is fed to the model, which produces a prediction. Sometimes, a model may be an ensemble of multiple models or even a complex graph of models.
5 The prediction is processed by a postprocessing function to convert it to a suitable response format.
6 A response is returned.

Note that the architecture of a model-hosting service is not that different from a typical microservice that is not related to machine learning. You just need a container with a service that can receive requests, process some code on the fly, and return a response. For some data science use cases, it is quite feasible to use an existing microservice platform, such as Fargate on AWS or even Google App Engine for model serving.

However, the following additional concerns may make it necessary to use a specialized model-serving platform or layer additional services on top of a general-purpose platform:

- The models may be computationally demanding and require a lot of memory and specialized hardware like GPUs. Traditional microservice platforms may have a hard time accommodating such heavyweight services.
- Models and their inputs and outputs need to be monitored in real time. Many *model-monitoring* solutions exist to help with this use case.
- You want to use a *feature store* to take care of converting facts to features in a consistent manner. In figure 8.20, the feature store would replace or integrate to the preprocessing function and the database.

If you need a specialized platform, all major cloud providers provide model-serving solutions like Amazon Sagemaker Hosting or Google AI Platform. Or you can leverage open source libraries like Ray Serve (ray.io) or Seldon (seldon.io).

EXAMPLE: REAL-TIME MOVIE RECOMMENDATIONS

Let's practice real-time predictions using a minimal model-hosting service. This example expands our previous movie recommendation system by allowing recommendations to be produced based on a list of movies that can be updated in real time. For instance, you could use this system to produce real-time recommendations based on all movies that the user has been browsing recently.

The example is not meant to be production ready as such. Instead, it will demonstrate the following key concepts of a model-serving system, as outlined in figure 8.20:

- A service endpoint that is accessible over HTTP
- A preprocessing function that uses the same featurization module as the training code
- Loading and using a model trained with a batch workflow
- Postprocessing the predictions in a decided output format

We will use a popular Python web framework, Flask (flask.palletsprojects.com), to wrap the logic as a web service. The example can be easily adapted to any other web framework as well. The following code sample lists a fully functional model-hosting service.

Listing 8.10   Model-hosting service

```
from io import StringIO
from metaflow import Flow
from flask import Flask, request
from movie_model import load_model, recommend    Uses helper modules from
from movie_data import load_movie_names           the previous section

class RecsModel():    ◁——— The model helper class              Fetches the
    def __init__(self):                                        latest model
        self.run = Flow('MovieTrainFlow').latest_successful_run  ◁┘ ID
        self.model_ann,\
        self.model_users_mtx,\
        self.model_movies_mtx = load_model(self.run)    Loads the
        self.names = load_movie_names()                 model
```

```
        def get_recs(self, movie_ids, num_recs):                    ⟵───┐ Generates
            [(_, recs)] = list(recommend([[None, set(movie_ids))],       │ recommendations
                                    self.model_movies_mtx,
                                    self.model_users_mtx,
                                    self.model_ann,          Produces
                                    num_recs))         ⟵─── recommendations for
                                                           one set of movies
            return recs

        def get_names(self, ids):
            return '\n'.join(self.names[movie_id] for movie_id in ids)

        def version(self):        ⟵─── Returns the model version
            return self.run.pathspec

    print("Loading model")       Loads the model (this     Preprocess
    model = RecsModel()      ⟵─── may take a few minutes)   function to
    print("Model loaded")                                   parse
    app = Flask(__name__)                                   information
                                                            from the       Outputs
    def preprocess(ids_str, model, response):      ⟵─── request          a version
        ids = list(map(int, ids_str.split(',')))                          identifier of
        response.write("# Model version:\n%s\n" % model.version())  ⟵───┘ the model
        response.write("# Input movies\n%s\n" % model.get_names(ids))
        return ids
                                              Postprocess function
                                              to output response
    def postprocess(recs, model, response):        ⟵───┘
        response.write("# Recommendations\n%s\n" % model.get_names(recs))

    @app.route("/recommend")   ⟵─── Flask endpoint specification
    def recommend_endpoint():                                        Processes
        response = StringIO()                                        input from
        ids = preprocess(request.args.get('ids'), model, response)  ⟵───┘ the request
        num_recs = int(request.args.get('num', 3))
        recs = model.get_recs(ids, num_recs)   ⟵─── Produces recommendations
        postprocess(recs, model, response)   Finalizes and outputs response
        return response.getvalue()
```

A helper function to map IDs to movie names

Parses integer IDs from a comma-separated string

Save the code to movie_recs_server.py. To run the server, you need an execution environment that includes the libraries needed by the model. Because this is not a Metaflow workflow but a Flask app, we can't use @conda as in earlier examples. Instead, you can create a suitable Conda environment manually by executing the following:

```
# conda create -y -n movie_recs python-annoy==1.17.0 pyarrow=5.0.0 flask
  metaflow
# conda activate movie_recs
```

Once the environment has been activated, you can execute the service locally as follows:

```
# FLASK_APP=movie_recs_server flask run
```

It will take a minute or more to load the model and start the server. Once the server is up and running, you will see next output:

```
Model loaded
 * Running on http://127.0.0.1:5000/ (Press CTRL+C to quit)
```

After this, you can start querying the server. To send an HTTP request to the server, open another terminal window where you can send requests to the server using the command-line client `curl`. You can browse movies.csv for interesting movie IDs and then query recommendations as follows:

```
# curl 'localhost:5000/recommend?ids=4993,41566'
```

It takes about 50–100 ms to produce a response that looks like this:

```
MovieTrainFlow/1636835055130894
# Input movies
Lord of the Rings: The Fellowship of the Ring, The (2001)
Chronicles of Narnia: The Lion, the Witch and the Wardrobe, The (2005)
# Recommendations
Lord of the Rings: The Two Towers, The (2002)
Lord of the Rings: The Return of the King, The (2003)
Harry Potter and the Sorcerer's Stone (2001)
```

You can use the `num` parameter to produce more recommendations:

```
# curl 'localhost:5000/recommend?ids=16,858,4262&num=10'
# Model version:
MovieTrainFlow/1636835055130894
# Input movies
Casino (1995)
Godfather, The (1972)
Scarface (1983)
# Recommendations
Goodfellas (1990)
Godfather: Part II, The (1974)
Donnie Brasco (1997)
Léon: The Professional (1994)
Bronx Tale, A (1993)
Taxi Driver (1976)
Raging Bull (1980)
Departed, The (2006)
No Country for Old Men (2007)
American Gangster (2007)
```

Congratulations! You have created a web service that produces recommendations in real time. Although the service works, you should consider a number of improvements to make the service fully production ready. First, on the infrastructure side consider the following:

- The service should be packaged in a Docker container so it can be deployed to a microservice platform.
- This service is able to handle only a single request at a time. You should consult the Flask documentation to learn how to deploy the app so that multiple requests can be handled in parallel.
- If even more scale is needed, you can run multiple containers in parallel. This requires a load balancer to route traffic to individual containers.
- It is a good idea to capture logs and basic metrics about requests volumes, for which many off-the-shelf tools are available.

Second, on the modeling side, consider adding the following:

- A model monitoring solution to track model metrics in real time
- A solution to track data quality in requests to detect changes in the input data distribution
- A service to manage A/B experiments

Most ML-specific tooling required by model deployments relate to debuggability and the quality of results. Imagine that a prediction returned by the service looked odd. The first question is, what model produced the predictions? To answer the question, we included the model version in each prediction response. Without a model version identifier, it would be impossible to know where the prediction originated, especially in a complex environment that may have multiple model versions deployed concurrently.

Figure 8.21 illustrates the idea of model lineage.

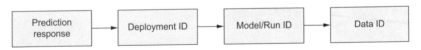

Figure 8.21 Backtracking model lineage from predictions to raw data

By using an architecture as shown in figure 8.21, we can track the lineage of predictions all the way back to the source data:

- Each prediction response should contain an ID denoting what deployment produced the response.
- Each deployment, for example, a container running a certain version of the model, should get a unique ID.
- The container should know the ID of the model and the run that produced the model.
- Knowing the run ID, we can trace back to the data that was used to train the model.

You are now well equipped to make informed choices between real-time or precomputed batch prediction, and the frameworks to support them. When in doubt, steer toward the simplest possible approach that works.

Summary

- To produce value, machine learning models must be connected to other surrounding systems.

- There isn't a single way to deploy a data science application and produce predictions: the right approach depends on the use case.

- Choose the right infrastructure for predictions, depending on the time window between when the input data becomes known and when predictions are needed.

- Another key consideration is whether surrounding systems need to request predictions from the model, or whether the model can push predictions to the surrounding systems. In the latter case, batch or streaming predictions are a good approach.

- If the input data is known at least 15–30 minutes before predictions are needed, it is often possible to produce predictions as a batch workflow, which is the most straightforward approach technically.

- It is important to attach a version identifier in all model outputs, both in batch and real-time use cases.

- Real-time predictions can be produced either using a general-purpose microservice framework or a solution that is tailored to data science applications. The latter may be the best approach if your models are computationally demanding.

- Make sure your deployments are debuggable by investing in monitoring tools and lineage. It should be possible to track every prediction all the way to the model and a workflow that produced it.

Machine learning with the full stack

This chapter covers

- Developing a custom framework that makes it easier to develop models and features for a particular problem domain
- Training a deep learning model in a workflow
- Summarizing the lessons learned in this book

We have now covered all layers of the infrastructure stack, shown in figure 9.1, except the topmost one: model development. We only scratched the surface of the feature engineering layer in chapter 7. Isn't it paradoxical that a book about machine learning and data science infrastructure spends so little time talking about the core concerns of machine learning: models and features?

The focus is deliberate. First, many excellent books already exist about these topics. Mature modeling libraries like TensorFlow and PyTorch come with a plethora of in-depth documentation and examples. As depicted in figure 9.1, these topics tend to be the core areas of expertise of professional data scientists and machine learning engineers, whereas the lower layers are not. To boost the day-to-day productivity of

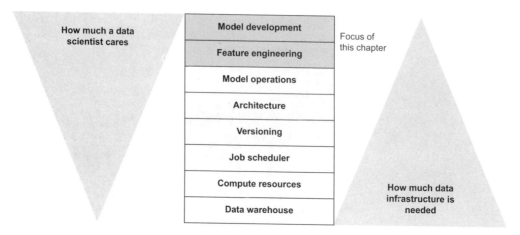

Figure 9.1   Infrastructure stack with the data scientist's areas of interest

data scientists effectively, it makes sense to help them where help is needed the most: the lower layers of the stack.

Also, the topmost layers tend to be very application-specific in contrast to the lower layers. For instance, the models and features required by a computer vision application are very different from those used for balancing marketing budgets. However, they both can use the same approach for accessing data from the cloud, running and orchestrating containers, and versioning and tracking projects.

Out of the four Vs discussed in chapter 1—volume, velocity, validity, and variety—it is the last one that's hardest to address with a standardized solution. If the infrastructure addresses the first three Vs well, it becomes feasible to develop and deploy a wide variety of use cases, even when each project comes with its own data pipelines, bespoke models, and custom business logic.

Going back to another theme discussed in chapter 1, we can minimize accidental complexity caused by boilerplate code that deals with data, compute, and orchestration by providing a common, low-overhead solution to the lower layers of the stack. At the same time, we can accept the fact that real-world use cases come with some amount of inherent complexity, which the top layers need to manage. Not everything can be abstracted away.

Building on what you have learned in this book, you can design your own libraries that support modeling and feature engineering for your specific use cases, which further helps to keep complexity in check. In the same way that traditional software leverages features and services provided by an operating system like OS X or Linux, your libraries can treat the lower layers of the stack as an operating system for any data-intensive applications. However, you don't need to rush into doing this. It is a good idea to build a few applications without any special abstractions to better understand if and where common patterns exist that would benefit from extra support and standardization.

To show how all these concepts work together, including a custom library to support model development, the next section walks through a realistic project that touches all layers of the stack. After the comprehensive example, we conclude the book by summarizing the lessons learned throughout the book. You can find all code listings for this chapter at http://mng.bz/N6d7.

9.1 Pluggable feature encoders and models

This section will expand the taxi-trip cost prediction example we started in chapter 7. Our original version was very naive. We used linear regression to predict the price based on one variable: the distance traveled. You can probably spot at least one glaring issue in this model: the duration of the trip matters in addition to the distance.

Let's imagine predicting trip prices accurately is a real business challenge. What would a realistic solution look like? For starters, it is unlikely that you would know the optimal solution to a real-life business problem from the get-go. To find a working solution, you have to experiment with a number of models and features, testing their performance through multiple iterations. You would certainly use more than one variable for prediction, so you would likely spend a good amount of time designing and implementing suitable features. Likely, you would test the features with different model architectures, too.

Also, real-life data is often lacking. As shown by the example in chapter 7, you can get reasonably good results with a simple model when high-quality features, like the actual distance of the trip, are available. What if our application doesn't have access to the taxi meter or the car's odometer but only to the rider's smartphone? Maybe we know only the location of pick-up and drop-off, and we have to predict the price without knowing the exact distance traveled, which we will practice later.

In this section, we will develop a more advanced model in a more realistic setting. Because we know we will need to iterate on multiple models and features—maybe we have a team of data scientists working on the problem—we standardize the model development setup by implementing a simple framework that allows us to plug in custom feature encoders and test various models flexibly.

Using the framework, we develop features that use geographic locations to predict the price. To make this possible, we upgrade our model from the 1950s-style linear regression to a 2020s-style deep learning model built with Keras and TensorFlow. To validate our model, we put together a benchmark that compares the performance of various modeling approaches. As before, we access the raw data directly from a public S3 bucket.

9.1.1 Developing a framework for pluggable components

We have a few different ideas for the kinds of models and features that might perform well for the price-prediction task. We want to quickly prototype and evaluate them to determine the most promising approach. Technically, we could implement each idea as a separate workflow from scratch, but we would likely notice that many approaches for the task follow a similar pattern: they all load raw data, split it to train and test sets, run feature encoders, train a model, and evaluate it using the test data. The implementation of the model and the feature encoders varies but not the overall structure of the workflow.

To make the model development process more efficient, we implement the common pattern as a shared workflow, which allows different feature encoders and models to be plugged in easily. The approach is similar to how we compared various algorithms for computing a co-occurrence matrix in chapter 5. Figure 9.2 illustrates the approach.

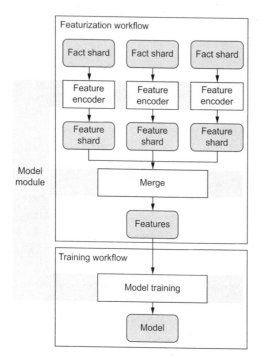

Figure 9.2   **Pluggable models and feature encoders (light gray) inside a shared workflow**

To implement a new modeling approach, the scientist needs to develop three components, shown as light gray boxes in figure 9.2: first, feature encoders that turn raw input data, facts, to features. To make featurization efficient, we can parallelize it over multiple shards of data. Second, after all shards have been processed, we can merge the feature shards into an input dataset for the model. You may recognize this approach as the MapReduce pattern we introduced in chapter 7. Third, we need a set of functions to train a model.

These three components can be implemented as pluggable modules. We develop two separate workflows to execute the plugins: one to process the features, and another to train a model. By keeping the data and training separate, we make it possible to schedule them independently. For instance, you can use the shared featurization workflow to produce data for a batch prediction workflow, if you want to follow the batch prediction pattern introduced in chapter 8. Following this pattern, you could, say, retrain a model daily and price new data hourly.

In Python, we typically define various implementations of the same interface as separate classes. Let's start by defining the interfaces of the three components: *encoder*, *merge*, and *model training*. A feature encoder needs to implement two methods: encode, which converts a shard of input data—that is, a fact shard—represented as a PyArrow table, to a feature shard. The shards are then provided to another method, merge, which merges the shards into a dataset that can be processed by a model. Figure 9.3 illustrates the role of the two functions.

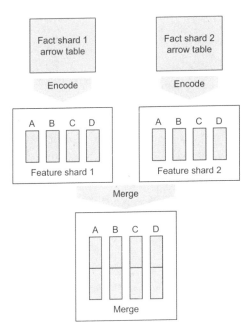

Figure 9.3 Encoding sharded input data first to features and then to a merged dataset

An encode function can output multiple named features, shown as A–D in figure 9.3, which are output as a dictionary where the key is a feature name and the value is a data structure, chosen by the encoder, which stores the features. Our current code expects that all shards produce the same set of features, but as an exercise, you can change the code to relax that requirement. The merge function gets all feature shards as its inputs and chooses how to combine them to produce a final dataset.

DEFINING A FEATURE ENCODER

Many models can read data efficiently as NumPy arrays, so we start by defining a template for encoders that output NumPy arrays. The next listing shows a general-purpose superclass—a class that specific encoders can derive from—that expects that the encode function outputs a NumPy array. It takes care of merging NumPy arrays produced in shards without being opinionated about what the arrays contain exactly.

Listing 9.1 Feature encoder superclass that handles NumPy arrays

**Defines the methods as class methods, so they
can be used without instantiating the class**

```
class NumpyArrayFeatureEncoder():
    @classmethod
    def encode(cls, table):
        return {}

    @classmethod
    def merge(cls, shards):
        from numpy import concatenate
        return {key: concatenate([shard[key] for shard in shards])
                for key in shards[0]}
```

**Accepts
a shard
of facts as
a PyArrow
table**

**Encoders will override this
method to produce NumPy
arrays with features.**

**Accepts a list of
feature shards**

**Concatenates
feature shards
into one large
array**

Loops through all features

We will be creating a number of small modules, so let's create a dedicated directory for them, taxi_modules. Save the code in taxi_modules/numpy_encoder.py.

Next, let's define a feature encoder that uses the NumpyArrayFeatureEncoder we just created. The encoder shown in the next listing will work as a baseline: it grabs the trip_distance column and the actual trip price, total_amount, from the dataset as-is, allowing us to compare the quality of our predictions that don't use the distance feature directly.

Listing 9.2 Baseline feature encoder

**Reuses the merge method from
NumpyArrayFeatureEncoder**

```
from taxi_modules.numpy_encoder import NumpyArrayFeatureEncoder

class FeatureEncoder(NumpyArrayFeatureEncoder):
    NAME = 'baseline'
    FEATURE_LIBRARIES = {}
    CLEAN_FIELDS = ['trip_distance', 'total_amount']

    @classmethod
    def encode(cls, table):
        return {
            'actual_distance': table['trip_distance'].to_numpy(),
            'amount': table['total_amount'].to_numpy()
        }
```

**Sets the
encoder
name**

**Defines extra software
dependencies for this encoder**

**Returns two
features as
NumPy arrays**

**Defines what
columns in the
fact table should
be cleaned**

Save the code in taxi_modules/feat_baseline.py. We will prefix all feature encoder modules with a feat_ prefix, so we can discover them automatically. The encoder defines a few top-level constants as follows:

- NAME—Identifies this feature encoder.
- FEATURE_LIBRARIES—Defines what extra software dependencies this encoder needs.
- CLEAN_FIELDS—Determines what columns of the facts table need to be cleaned.

The role of these constants will become more clear as we start using them. Next, let's create a utility module that loads the plugins like the one defined earlier.

PACKAGING AND LOADING PLUGINS

It should be possible to create a new feature or a model simply by adding a file in the taxi_modules directory. Based on the filename, we can determine whether the module is a feature encoder or a model. The following listing walks through all files in the taxi_modules directory, imports modules with an expected prefix, and makes them available through shared dictionaries.

> **Listing 9.3 A flow with parameters**

Maps model names to model classes

```
import os
from importlib import import_module

MODELS = {}
FEATURES = {}
FEATURE_LIBRARIES = {}
MODEL_LIBRARIES = {}

def init():
    for fname in os.listdir(os.path.dirname(__file__)):
        is_feature = fname.startswith('feat_')
        is_model = fname.startswith('model_')
        if is_feature or is_model:
            mod = import_module('taxi_modules.%s' % fname.split('.')[0])
            if is_feature:
                cls = mod.FeatureEncoder
                FEATURES[cls.NAME] = cls
                FEATURE_LIBRARIES.update(cls.FEATURE_LIBRARIES.items())
            else:
                cls = mod.Model
                MODELS[cls.NAME] = cls
                MODEL_LIBRARIES.update(cls.MODEL_LIBRARIES.items())
```

- **Maps feature encoder names to feature encoder classes**
- **Records the libraries needed by encoders**
- **Walks through all files in the taxi_modules directory**
- **Records the libraries needed by models**
- **Checks the file prefix**
- **Imports the module**
- **Populates dictionaries containing encoders and models**

Save the code in taxi_modules/__init__.py. Note that the module needs to reside in the same directory with the feature encoders and models for the file discovery to work correctly. The filename __init__.py has a special meaning in Python: having an __init__.py file in a directory tells Python that the directory corresponds to a *Python package*. A Python package is a collection of modules that can be installed and imported as a unit. Read more about packages at http://mng.bz/Dg8a.

Currently, our taxi_modules package (directory) contains the following files:

```
taxi_modules/__init__.py
taxi_modules/feat_baseline.py
taxi_modules/numpy_encoder.py
```

We will be adding many more throughout the chapter. A benefit of arranging modules in a Python package is that you could publish and share it as a package that can be installed as any other Python package—imagine `pip install taxi_modules` or `conda install taxi_modules`. You can refer to https://packaging.python.org/ for detailed instructions. You could then include the package in your Metaflow projects using, say, the `@conda` decorator.

However, it is not necessary to publish the package. A simpler approach is to make sure that the package directory is adjacent to your flow scripts. For instance, a data science team could have a Git repository of the following structure:

```
taxi_modules/__init__.py
taxi_modules/...
flow1.py
flow2.py
flow3.py
```

In this case, flow1, flow2, and flow3 all have access to the shared `taxi_modules` package automatically, thanks to the fact that Metaflow packages all subdirectories automatically as described in chapter 6.

> **RECOMMENDATION**   If you have a relatively stable package that data scientists don't have to modify as they work on their flows, you can package and publish it as a normal Python package, which can be included in flows like any other third-party library using `@conda`. If data scientists are expected to iterate rapidly on the contents of the package as a part of their projects, like in the case of feature encoders of this example, you can make the prototyping loop much smoother by including the package as a subdirectory, which Metaflow versions automatically.

9.1.2   *Executing feature encoders*

We are almost ready to start executing feature encoders. Before defining a flow to do that, we need two more utility modules. First, to preprocess facts, we use the utility functions from `table_utils.py`, which we introduced in chapter 7. The next code sample shows the module again.

Listing 9.4   Removing outlier rows from an Arrow table

Accepts a pyarrow.Table and a list of columns to be cleaned

```
def filter_outliers(table, clean_fields):
    import numpy
    valid = numpy.ones(table.num_rows, dtype='bool')      # Starts with a filter that accepts all rows
    for field in clean_fields:                             # Processes all columns one by one
        column = table[field].to_numpy()
        minval = numpy.percentile(column, 2)               # Finds the top and bottom 2% of the value distribution
        maxval = numpy.percentile(column, 98)
        valid &= (column > minval) & (column < maxval)     # Includes only rows that fall between 2–98% of the value distribution
```

```
          return table.filter(valid)
```

Returns a subset of the rows that match the filter

```
def sample(table, p):
    import numpy
    return table.filter(numpy.random.random(table.num_rows) < p)
```

Samples a random p% of rows of the given table

Flips a biased coin on each row and returns the matching rows

Save the code in taxi_modules/table_utils.py. For more details about how these functions work, refer to chapter 7.

Second, we define a helper module that executes the feature encoders. Listing 9.5 shows a module with two functions: execute preprocesses the facts table by cleaning all fields listed in CLEAN_FIELDS. It also takes a sample of input rows, if sample_rate is smaller than 1.0. After this, it executes all the discovered feature encoders, supplying them with the fact table. The merge function takes two lists of shards, features for training and testing separately, and merges each feature using the merge function specified by its encoder.

Listing 9.5 Executing feature encoders

Imports discovered features

```
from itertools import chain
from taxi_modules.table_utils import filter_outliers, sample
from taxi_modules import FEATURES

def execute(table, sample_rate):
    clean_fields = set(chain(*[feat.CLEAN_FIELDS
                               for feat in FEATURES.values()]))
    clean_table = sample(filter_outliers(table, clean_fields), sample_rate)
    print("%d/%d rows included" % (clean_table.num_rows, table.num_rows))
    shards = {}
    for name, encoder in FEATURES.items():
        print("Processing features: %s" % feat)
        shards[name] = encoder.encode(clean_table)
    return shards

def merge(train_inputs, test_inputs):
    train_data = {}
    test_data = {}
    for name, encoder in FEATURES.items():
        train_shards = [inp.shards[name] for inp in train_inputs]
        test_shards = [inp.shards[name] for inp in test_inputs]
        train_data[name] = encoder.merge(train_shards)
        test_data[name] = encoder.merge(test_shards)
    return train_data, test_data
```

Applies feature encoders to the fact table

Produces a set of fields that need to be cleaned

Cleans and samples facts

Iterates over all encoders

Executes an encoder

Merges training and test data separately

Iterates over all features

Merges feature shards for a feature

Save the code in taxi_modules/encoders.py. Now we have the machinery ready for pluggable feature encoders!

We can put together a workflow, shown in listing 9.6, that discovers data, produces features for shards of data in parallel, and finally merges a final dataset. The structure of the workflow is similar to TaxiRegressionFlow from chapter 7, except that this time, we don't hardcode features in the workflow itself but let plugins specify them. This way, data scientists can reuse the same workflow—making sure all results are comparable—and focus on developing new feature encoders and models.

In this example, we will use two months of taxi trip data that was introduced in chapter 7, September and October 2014. To test model performance, we use data from November. We will handle each month of data as a separate shard using foreach.

Listing 9.6   Workflow that executes pluggable feature encoders

```
from metaflow import FlowSpec, step, conda, S3, conda_base,\
                      resources, Flow, project, Parameter
from taxi_modules import init, encoders, FEATURES, FEATURE_LIBRARIES
from taxi_modules.table_utils import filter_outliers, sample
init()
TRAIN = ['s3://ursa-labs-taxi-data/2014/09/',         ←┐ Use two months of
         's3://ursa-labs-taxi-data/2014/10/']          │ data for training
TEST = ['s3://ursa-labs-taxi-data/2014/11/']   ←┐
                                                 │ Tests with one
                                                 │ month of data
@project(name='taxi_regression')
@conda_base(python='3.8.10', libraries={'pyarrow': '3.0.0'})
class TaxiRegressionDataFlow(FlowSpec):
    sample = Parameter('sample', default=0.1)

    @step
    def start(self):                         ┌ Persists the set of features as
        self.features = list(FEATURES)   ←┘ artifacts for later analysis
        print("Encoding features: %s" % ', '.join(FEATURES))
        with S3() as s3:
            self.shards = []
            for prefix in TEST + TRAIN:
                objs = s3.list_recursive([prefix])
                self.shards.append([obj.url for obj in objs])   ←┐ Discovers
        self.next(self.process_features, foreach='shards')        │ data shards

    @resources(memory=16000)                      ┌ Ensures that libraries needed
    @conda(libraries=FEATURE_LIBRARIES)   ←┘ by encoders are available
    @step
    def process_features(self):
        from pyarrow.parquet import ParquetDataset
        with S3() as s3:
```
Downloads and decodes a shard ⎨
```
            objs = s3.get_many(self.input)
            table = ParquetDataset([obj.path for obj in objs]).read()
        self.shards = encoders.execute(table, self.sample)   ←┐
        self.next(self.join_data)                              │ Executes
                                                               │ encoders
                                                               │ for a shard
    @resources(memory=16000)
    @conda(libraries=FEATURE_LIBRARIES)
    @step
    def join_data(self, inputs):                    ┌ Ensures the features artifact is
        self.features = inputs[0].features   ←┘ available after the join step
```

```
        self.train_data,\
        self.test_data = encoders.merge(inputs[1:], [inputs[0]])
        self.next(self.end)
```

Merges shards separately for train and test data

```
    @step
    def end(self):
        pass

if __name__ == '__main__':
    TaxiRegressionDataFlow()
```

Save the code in taxi_regression_data.py next to (not inside) the taxi_modules directory. At this point, the directory structure should look like this:

```
taxi_regression_data.py
taxi_modules/__init__.py
taxi_modules/feat_baseline.py
taxi_modules/numpy_encoder.py
taxi_modules/encoders.py
taxi_modules/table_utils.py
```

You can now test the workflow as follows:

```
# python taxi_regression_data.py --environment=conda run
```

It should print Processing features: baseline three times, once for each shard. If you are curious, you can open a notebook to inspect the train_data and test_data artifacts, which we will put in use soon.

If you have a compute layer like AWS Batch set up as discussed in chapter 4, you can execute the workflow in the cloud. For instance, you can try this:

```
# python taxi_regression_data.py --environment=conda run --with batch
```

As discussed earlier, this way you can scale the workflow to handle much larger datasets and produce the features faster, if needed.

Pluggable encoders are the main exciting thing about this workflow. Let's test how they work by creating another encoder. This time we create a feature that doesn't depend on the trip_distance field in the input data—let's assume our application doesn't have it available or we don't trust the taxi meter reading. Instead, we determine the distance traveled based on the coordinates of the pick-up and drop-off locations that are available in the fact table.

Our new feature, called Euclidean and defined in the next listing, measures the distance as a Euclidean distance between the locations. This is obviously inaccurate: taxi trips in a city are longer than a straight-line distance, and the earth is round, so we can't use the simple Euclidean formula over long distances. However, as it is often the case, a simple approach with known deficiencies allows us to get started quickly.

Listing 9.7   Encoding Euclidean trip distance as a feature

```
from taxi_modules.numpy_encoder import NumpyArrayFeatureEncoder

class FeatureEncoder(NumpyArrayFeatureEncoder):
    NAME = 'euclidean'
    FEATURE_LIBRARIES = {}
    CLEAN_FIELDS = ['pickup_latitude', 'pickup_longitude',
                    'dropoff_latitude', 'dropoff_longitude']

    @classmethod
    def encode(cls, table):
        import numpy
        plon = table['pickup_longitude'].to_numpy()
        plat = table['pickup_latitude'].to_numpy()
        dlon = table['dropoff_longitude'].to_numpy()
        dlat = table['dropoff_latitude'].to_numpy()
        euc = numpy.sqrt((plon - dlon)**2 + (plat - dlat)**2)
        return {'euclidean_distance': euc}
```

Extracts coordinates from the fact table

Computes the Euclidean distance between the coordinates

Converts coordinates to NumPy arrays

Save the code in taxi_modules/feat_euclidean.py. Note that the encoder performs all math using NumPy arrays, avoiding conversion to individual Python objects, which makes the encoder very performant—following the advice from chapter 5.

After this, run the workflow again as follows:

```
# python taxi_regression_data.py --environment=conda run
```

This time, you should see both `Processing features: baseline` and `Processing features: euclidean`. Adding a new feature was just a matter of writing the definition of the feature in listing 9.7—no changes in the workflow were needed. You can imagine multiple scientists collaborating and creating new features and models over time, which get evaluated and benchmarked using a shared workflow, ensuring the validity of results.

The modules in the taxi_modules directory demonstrated a useful pattern: we use the underlying general-purpose infrastructure and abstractions around it, like Metaflow, as the foundation. On top of it, we created a custom, domain-specific library, which makes it easier to iterate on a specific application—in this case, the trip price prediction. Figure 9.4 illustrates the pattern.

This pattern allows you to handle a wide variety of use cases effectively. The general-purpose infrastructure can focus on foundational concerns, data, compute, orchestration, and versioning, whereas higher-level, domain-specific libraries can codify policies on how individual applications should be developed. It is also feasible to evolve the domain-specific libraries quickly as the needs of applications change while keeping the foundations stable.

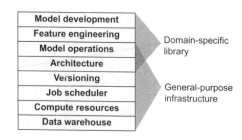

Figure 9.4   A domain-specific library on top of the foundational infrastructure stack

RECOMMENDATION Use domain-specific libraries to codify application-specific policies and general-purpose infrastructure to handle low-level concerns. This way, you don't need to optimize the whole stack for the needs of a specific use case.

Now that we have a train and test datasets available, we can start benchmarking models. Similar to feature encoders, we want to be able to define new models easily as pluggable modules.

9.1.3 Benchmarking models

For this project, we define a model as a combination of model architecture and training code, as well as a set of features. This allows us to test different model variants that use different feature sets easily. Similar to feature encoders, we define a common interface that all models must implement. The interface defines the following methods:

- `fit(train_data)` trains the model given the training data.
- `mse(model, test_data)` evaluates the `model` with `test_data` and returns the mean squared error measuring prediction accuracy.
- `save_model(model)` serializes the model to bytes.
- `load_model(blob)` deserializes the model from bytes.

The last two methods are required to persist the model. By default, as described in chapter 3, Metaflow uses Python's built-in serializer, Pickle, to serialize objects to bytes. Many machine learning models include their own serialization methods, which work more reliably than Pickle, so we allow model classes to use a custom serializer. Notably, the resulting bytes are still stored as a Metaflow artifact, so models are stored and accessed as any other workflow result.

We start by defining a naive linear regression model that predicts the price using the actual distance, like the one we used in chapter 7. We can compare other models that don't rely on the `actual_distance` feature against this baseline. We will define code for a general-purpose regressor soon, but we start with a model specification, shown here.

Listing 9.8 Baseline linear regression model

```
from taxi_modules.regression import RegressionModel      ◁——  Leverages a general-
                                                                purpose regression model
class Model(RegressionModel):
    NAME = 'distance_regression'          ◁——  Model name
    MODEL_LIBRARIES = {'scikit-learn': '0.24.1'}    ◁——  Uses Scikit-Learn as
    FEATURES = ['baseline']                               the modeling library
    regressor = 'actual_distance'    ◁——
```

Requires a baseline feature encoder (points to `FEATURES = ['baseline']`)

Uses the actual_distance variable to predict the price (points to `regressor = 'actual_distance'`)

Save the code in taxi_modules/model_baseline.py. Remember that listing 9.8 loads models from files that have the model_ prefix. The role of the FEATURES and regressor attributes becomes clearer in the context of the RegressionModel base class, which is defined in the next code sample.

Listing 9.9   Superclass for linear regression models

```
class RegressionModel():

    @classmethod
    def fit(cls, train_data):
        from sklearn.linear_model import LinearRegression
        d = train_data[cls.FEATURES[0]][cls.regressor].reshape(-1, 1)
        model = LinearRegression().fit(d, train_data['baseline']['amount'])
        return model

    @classmethod
    def mse(cls, model, test_data):
        from sklearn.metrics import mean_squared_error
        d = test_data[cls.FEATURES[0]][cls.regressor].reshape(-1, 1)
        pred = model.predict(d)
        return mean_squared_error(test_data['baseline']['amount'], pred)

    @classmethod
    def save_model(cls, model):
        return model

    @classmethod
    def load_model(cls, model):
        return model
```

Fits a single-variable linear regression model using Scikit-Learn

Tests a single-variable linear regression model using Scikit-Learn

Uses standard Python Pickle to serialize the model; nothing custom needed

---

Save the code in taxi_modules/regression.py. The module defines a simple linear regression model using Scikit-Learn, which uses a single variable, defined in the regressor attribute, to predict the trip price, stored in the amount variable. We use Scikit-Learn's mean_squared_error function to measure the model accuracy in the mse method. Nothing special is needed to serialize and deserialize the model in save_model and load_model, because Scikit-Learn models work well with Pickle.

MODEL WORKFLOW

Let's define a workflow to run the models. We allow each model to define the features they expect to be available. Only models that have all their features available are enabled. This way, models don't fail randomly when you remove and add feature encoders during prototyping. The list of eligible models is determined in the start step. Figure 9.5 shows the structure of the workflow.

Each model, depicted by hypothetical models A, B, and C, are handled by a separate foreach branch. First, in the train step, we train a model using the train_data dataset produced by TaxiRegressionDataFlow. Then, in the eval step, we evaluate

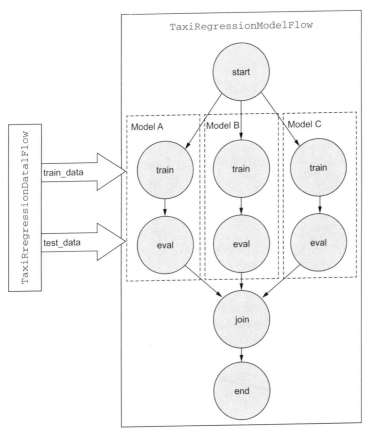

Figure 9.5 The relationship between the two taxi workflows: Data and models

the model performance using `test_data`. In the `join` step, a summary of model evaluations is printed out. The next listing shows the code.

Listing 9.10 Workflow that executes pluggable models

```
from metaflow import FlowSpec, step, conda, S3, conda_base,\
                     resources, Flow, project, profile
from taxi_modules import init, MODELS, MODEL_LIBRARIES
init()
@project(name='taxi_regression')
@conda_base(python='3.8.10', libraries={'pyarrow': '3.0.0'})
class TaxiRegressionModelFlow(FlowSpec):

    @step
    def start(self):
        run = Flow('TaxiRegressionDataFlow').latest_run
        self.data_run_id = run.id
        self.features = run.data.features
```

> Accesses input data
> from the latest run of
> **TaxiRegressionDataFlow**

> Records features used by this run

```
        self.models = [name for name, model in MODELS.items()
                       if all(feat in self.features\
                              for feat in model.FEATURES)]
        print("Building models: %s" % ', '.join(self.models))
        self.next(self.train, foreach='models')
```

**Determines which models
can be executed based on
their input features**

```
    @resources(memory=16000)
    @conda(libraries=MODEL_LIBRARIES)
    @step
    def train(self):
        self.model_name = self.input
        with profile('Training model: %s' % self.model_name):
            mod = MODELS[self.model_name]
            data_run = Flow('TaxiRegressionDataFlow')[self.data_run_id]
            model = mod.fit(data_run.data.train_data)
            self.model = mod.save_model(model)
        self.next(self.eval)
```

**Trains the
model**

**Accesses
training data**

**Saves the model in an artifact
using a model-specific serializer**

```
    @resources(memory=16000)
    @conda(libraries=MODEL_LIBRARIES)
    @step
    def eval(self):
        with profile("Evaluating %s" % self.model_name):
            mod = MODELS[self.model_name]
            data_run = Flow('TaxiRegressionDataFlow')[self.data_run_id]
            model = mod.load_model(self.model)
            self.mse = mod.mse(model, data_run.data.test_data)
        self.next(self.join)
```

**Loads the
model and
deserializes it**

**Evaluates
the model
performance**

```
    @step
    def join(self, inputs):
        for inp in inputs:
            print("MODEL %s MSE %f" % (inp.model_name, inp.mse))
        self.next(self.end)
```

Prints a summary of model scores

```
    @step
    def end(self):
        pass


if __name__ == '__main__':
    TaxiRegressionModelFlow()
```

Save the code in taxi_regression_model.py. Because this flow accesses results produced by TaxiRegressionDataFlow, make sure you have run that flow first. At this point, the directory structure should look like this:

```
taxi_regression_data.py
taxi_regression_model.py
taxi_modules/__init__.py
taxi_modules/feat_baseline.py
taxi_modules/feat_euclidean.py
taxi_modules/model_baseline.py
taxi_modules/regression.py
```

```
taxi_modules/numpy_encoder.py
taxi_modules/encoders.py
taxi_modules/table_utils.py
```

You can run the flow as usual:

```
# python taxi_regression_model.py --environment=conda run
```

You should see these lines in the output: `Training model: distance_regression` and `Evaluating distance_regression`. The final evaluation should look roughly as follows:

```
MODEL distance_regression MSE 9.451360
```

To make things more interesting, let's define another regression model that uses the Euclidean distance feature we defined earlier. See the next code listing.

Listing 9.11 Regression model that uses the Euclidean distance feature

```
from taxi_modules.regression import RegressionModel

class Model(RegressionModel):
    NAME = 'euclidean_regression'
    MODEL_LIBRARIES = {'scikit-learn': '0.24.1'}
    FEATURES = ['euclidean']
    regressor = 'euclidean_distance'
```

Save the code in taxi_modules/model_euclidean.py, and run the workflow again as follows:

```
# python taxi_regression_model.py --environment=conda run
```

This time, you should see two models being trained and evaluated in parallel: `distance_regression` and `euclidean_regression`. The output will look like the following:

```
MODEL euclidean_regression MSE 15.199947
MODEL distance_regression MSE 9.451360
```

Not surprisingly, the mean squared error is higher for the model that uses Euclidean distance between the pick-up and drop-off locations to predict price, compared to the baseline model that uses the actual distance traveled. With these two models, we have established a solid baseline for future models. A more sophisticated model should be able to easily beat the performance of `euclidean_regression`. It would be great to get close to the performance of `distance_regression` just by relying on the location features. In the following section, we will build a much more sophisticated model to answer the challenge.

9.2   *Deep regression model*

If you have ever ridden in a taxi in a big city, you know that the Euclidean distance between two locations and even the actual route length can be bad predictors of the actual time it takes to complete the trip. Some locations are prone to traffic jams or are otherwise slow to travel through. A smart model would learn to recognize such slow spots based on historical data and estimate the price of the trip accordingly.

Let's start by thinking how we can construct features that capture the notion of travel time and distance as a function of two locations. The first realization is that we don't need an arbitrarily accurate location. The distance difference of a few city blocks typically doesn't cause a systematic difference in price. Hence, instead of using exact coordinates, we can use a map grid, visualized in figure 9.6, to encode start and finish locations.

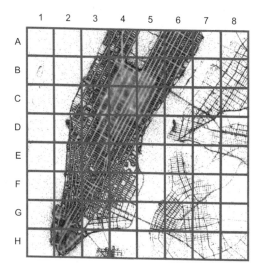

Figure 9.6   Hypothetical map grid over Manhattan

For instance, using the grid in figure 9.6, you can encode a trip between two locations as pairs of grid coordinates, such as A4–F2 and G7–B6. Naturally a real-world application would use a more fine-grained grid than the one illustrated in the figure.

How would you encode location pairs like this as features? We can treat grid locations like A4 and F2 as tokens or words, like we did with Yelp review clustering in chapter 5. We could have a high-dimensional vector that represents each grid location as a separate dimension. We could then apply *multi-hot encoding* to mark the pick-up and drop-off locations as 1s and the other dimensions as 0s to produce a sparse trip vector. Figure 9.7 illustrates the idea.

An inconvenient detail about this approach is that we have to fix the dimensions, that is, the map grid, in advance. If we make the grid too small, we can't handle trips outside the area. If

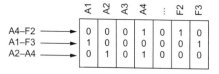

Figure 9.7   Taxi trips encoded as multi-hot binary vectors

we make it too big, the data becomes very sparse and possibly slow to process. Also, we must maintain a mapping between grid locations and the dimensions.

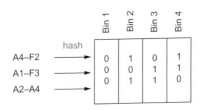

Figure 9.8 **Applying feature hashing to trip vectors**

The same problem exists with any high-cardinality categorical variables. A well-known solution to the problem is *feature hashing*: instead of having a named dimension for each possible value, we produce a hash of each value and place them in a bin accordingly. Crucially, many fewer bins exist than distinct values originally. As long as the hash function stays consistent, the same value always ends up in the same bin, producing a multi-hot-encoded matrix with a fixed, lower dimensionality compared to the first approach. Figure 9.8 illustrates the idea.

In figure 9.8, we assume that hash(A4) = bin 2, hash(F2) = bin 4, and so forth. Notice that we could enlarge the grid and add, say, a coordinate A99 without affecting existing data, which is a benefit of the hashing approach. Also, we don't have to explicitly store the mapping between coordinate labels and dimensions, making the implementation a bit simpler.

When using hashing, we have no guarantee that two distinct values would always end up in distinct bins. It is possible that two distinct values end up in the same bin, causing random noise in the data. Despite this deficiency, feature hashing tends to work well in practice.

Let's assume that we want to test the idea of using a matrix of hashed grid-coordinate features, as shown in figure 9.8. How should we encode and store the matrix in practice? We could build a feature encoder producing a suitable matrix without considering what model is going to consume it, but it doesn't hurt to think through the problem end to end. Let's look at the modeling problem at hand. Our model will be as follows:

- *High-dimensional*—To keep the model reasonably accurate, grid cells should be in the range of hundreds of meters or less. Hence, an area of 100 square kilometers requires 10,000 grid cells, that is, 10,000 input dimensions.
- *Large-scale*—We have tens of millions of trips in our input data that we can use to train the model.
- *Nonlinear*—The relationship between the pick-up and drop-off locations and price is a complex function of various variables that we want to model.
- *Sparse*—Trips are not spread uniformly over the map. We have limited data for some areas and plenty for others.
- *Categorical regression model*—We use categorical variables, discrete locations on the map grid, to predict a continuous variable, the trip price.

Given these characteristics, we may need something more powerful than a linear regression model. The scale and nonlinearity of the problem suggest that a deep learning model might be a suitable tool for the job. We choose to use Keras, an easy-to-use, popular package for deep learning, which is included in the TensorFlow package.

Following the widely used nomenclature in the world of deep learning, we call the input matrices *tensors*. In this example, tensors behave pretty much like any other arrays, like NumPy arrays we have used earlier, so don't let the fancy-sounding word scare you. In general, tensors can be thought of as multidimensional arrays that can be manipulated through well-defined mathematical operations. If you are curious, you can read more about them at https://www.tensorflow.org/guide/tensor.

Developing a high-quality deep neural network model involves art and science, as well as many rounds of trial and error. We trust that these topics are familiar to professional data scientists already, but if not, a plethora of high-quality online materials and books are already available. Hence, details of deep learning are out of the scope of this book. The goal of this book is to support data scientists who develop these models with effective infrastructure, like the scaffolding we have developed so far.

9.2.1   *Encoding input tensors*

Let's create a feature encoder that implements the previous idea. Our encoder should perform the following tasks:

1 Convert coordinates to grid locations. We can use an off-the-shelf *geohashing* library, such as `python-geohash`, to accomplish this. Given a latitude and longitude pair, it produces a short string geotoken denoting the corresponding grid location. For more details about geohashes, see the Wikipedia article about the topic (https://en.wikipedia.org/wiki/Geohash).
2 Hash the geotokens to a fixed number of bins.
3 Multi-hot-encode the bins to produce a sparse tensor.
4 Merge and store feature shards, encoded as tensors, for subsequent use.

You can tune the following two parameters in the encoder to adjust the resource consumption-accuracy tradeoff:

- `NUM_HASH_BINS`—Determines the number of bins for feature hashing. The smaller the number, the more hash collisions and, hence, noise there will be in the data. On the other hand, a higher number will require a larger model, which is slower and more resource-consuming to train. You can experiment with a number that produces the best results—there isn't a single right answer.
- `PRECISION`—Determines the grain of the geohashes, that is, the grid size. The higher the number, the more accurate the locations are, but a higher number will require a higher `NUM_HASH_BINS`, too, to avoid collisions. Also, the higher the number, the more sparse the data will be, potentially hurting accuracy. The default `PRECISION=6` corresponds to about 0.3×0.3–mile grid.

The encoder is implemented in the next listing.

Listing 9.12   Encoding hashed trip vectors as features

```
from metaflow import profile          Hashes geolocations
NUM_HASH_BINS = 10000                  to 10,000 bins
```

```
PRECISION = 6                        ⟵──── Grid granularity

class FeatureEncoder():
    NAME = 'grid'
    FEATURE_LIBRARIES = {'python-geohash': '0.8.5',
                         'tensorflow-base': '2.6.0'}
    CLEAN_FIELDS = ['pickup_latitude', 'pickup_longitude',
                    'dropoff_latitude', 'dropoff_longitude']

    @classmethod
    def _coords_to_grid(cls, table):
        import geohash                  ⟵
        plon = table['pickup_longitude'].to_numpy()
        plat = table['pickup_latitude'].to_numpy()
        dlon = table['dropoff_longitude'].to_numpy()
        dlat = table['dropoff_latitude'].to_numpy()
        trips = []
        for i in range(len(plat)):
            pcode = geohash.encode(plat[i], plon[i], precision=PRECISION)
            dcode = geohash.encode(dlat[i], dlon[i], precision=PRECISION)
            trips.append((pcode, dcode))    ⟵
        return trips

    @classmethod
    def encode(cls, table):
        from tensorflow.keras.layers import Hashing, IntegerLookup
        with profile('coordinates to grid'):
            grid = cls._coords_to_grid(table)
        hashing_trick = Hashing(NUM_HASH_BINS)
        multi_hot = IntegerLookup(vocabulary=list(range(NUM_HASH_BINS)),   ⟵
                                  output_mode='multi_hot',
                                  sparse=True)
        with profile('creating tensor'):
            tensor = multi_hot(hashing_trick(grid))
        return {'tensor': tensor}

    @classmethod
    def merge(cls, shards):
        return {key: [s[key] for s in shards] for key in shards[0]}
```

Converts coordinates to grid locations ⟶ `def _coords_to_grid(cls, table):`

Uses the geohash library to produce grid locations

Loops through all trips in the input table ⟶ `for i in range(len(plat)):`

Produces a pair of geohashes for each trip

Stores the pairs in a list

Uses the Keras hashing layer to perform feature hashing ⟶ `hashing_trick = Hashing(NUM_HASH_BINS)`

Produces a tensor ⟶ `tensor = multi_hot(hashing_trick(grid))`

Uses the Keras IntegerLookup layer to perform multi-hot encoding

Merges tensors from feature shards into a large tensor ⟶ `return {key: [s[key] for s in shards] for key in shards[0]}`

Save the code in taxi_modules/feat_gridtensor.py. For details about the Keras layers, Hashing and IntegerLookup, refer to the Keras documentation at keras.io. In essence, they implement the hashing and multi-hot encoding ideas that we discussed earlier. In the case of tensors, the merge method can simply collate the shards in a dictionary. There's no need to merge them in a large tensor, because we will feed the tensor to the model through a custom data loader, shown next.

DATA LOADER

How to feed data into deep learning models efficiently is a deep topic of its own. A key challenge is that we may want to use GPUs to train the model, but a typical GPU doesn't have enough memory to hold the whole dataset in GPU memory at once. To work around the limitation, we must feed data to the GPU in small batches.

The next listing shows a simple data loader that accepts features shards as `tensor_shards`, produced by the `merge` method defined earlier. For training, we can specify a `target` variable, in our case a NumPy array containing the trip price, which is sliced and returned alongside the training data to the model.

Listing 9.13 Data loader for a Keras model

```python
BATCH_SIZE = 128
def data_loader(tensor_shards, target=None):
    import tensorflow as tf
    _, dim = tensor_shards[0].shape
    def make_batches():
        if target is not None:
            out_tensor = tf.reshape(tf.convert_to_tensor(target),
                                    (len(target), 1))
        while True:
            row = 0
            for shard in tensor_shards:
                idx = 0
                while True:
                    x = tf.sparse.slice(shard, [idx, 0], [BATCH_SIZE, dim])
                    n, _ = x.shape
                    if n > 0:
                        if target is not None:
                            yield x, tf.slice(out_tensor, [row, 0], [n, 1])
                        else:
                            yield x
                        row += n
                        idx += n
                    else:
                        break
    input_sig = tf.SparseTensorSpec(shape=(None, dim))
    if target is None:
        signature = input_sig
    else:
        signature = (input_sig, tf.TensorSpec(shape=(None, 1)))
    dataset = tf.data.Dataset.from_generator(make_batches, \
                    output_signature=signature)
    data.prefetch(tf.data.AUTOTUNE)
    return input_sig, dataset
```

Annotations:
- **Defines the target variable for training; no target for testing** → `def data_loader(tensor_shards, target=None):`
- **Increase this value to speed up training.** → `BATCH_SIZE = 128`
- **Number of hash bins in input tensors** → `_, dim = tensor_shards[0].shape`
- **Generates input batches with optional target vectors** → `def make_batches():`
- **Loops forever. Training code will stop when needed.** → `while True:`
- **Converts the NumPy array to a tensor** → `out_tensor = tf.reshape(tf.convert_to_tensor(target), (len(target), 1))`
- **Resets the target index after each epoch** → `row = 0`
- **Loops over all feature shards** → `for shard in tensor_shards:`
- **Resets the shard index** → `idx = 0`
- **Extracts batches from the shard until no more rows are left** → `while True:`
- **Slices a batch from the shard** → `x = tf.sparse.slice(shard, [idx, 0], [BATCH_SIZE, dim])`
- **Gets the number of rows in the batch** → `n, _ = x.shape`
- **If the batch is non-empty, yields it; otherwise, moves to the next shard** → `if target is not None:`
- **Slices a vector from the target array** → `yield x, tf.slice(out_tensor, [row, 0], [n, 1])`
- **If no target is specified, just returns input data** → `yield x`
- **Increments row indices to the next batch** → `row += n` / `idx += n`
- **Specifies the type of the input tensor** → `input_sig = tf.SparseTensorSpec(shape=(None, dim))`
- **For testing, the dataset contains only input tensors.** → `signature = input_sig`
- **For training, the dataset also contains target vectors.** → `signature = (input_sig, tf.TensorSpec(shape=(None, 1)))`
- **Produces a dataset object wrapping the generator** → `dataset = tf.data.Dataset.from_generator(make_batches, output_signature=signature)`
- **Optimizes data access** → `data.prefetch(tf.data.AUTOTUNE)`

Save the code in taxi_modules/dnn_data.py. A slight complication is caused by the fact that the target is one large NumPy array, whereas training data is stored in multiple sparse tensor shards. We must make sure that features from both sources stay aligned. Figure 9.9 illustrates the situation.

Figure 9.9 illustrates three feature shards on the left and the target array on the right. Note how the last batch at the end of each shard, batches 5, 8, and 10, are smaller than the others. The sizes of feature shards are arbitrary and, hence, not always divisible by BATCH_SIZE. Listing 9.13 maintains two index variables: row to keep

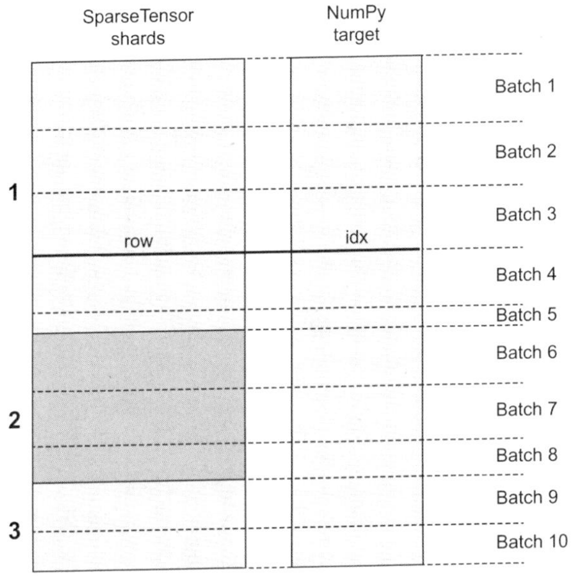

Figure 9.9   **Aligned batches between sharded tensors and a single NumPy target array**

track of the row in the current shard, and idx to keep track of the index in the target array. The row index resets at each shard, whereas idx increments across shards.

Batches are returned by a generator function, data_loader, which loops over data forever. In the context of machine learning, one iteration over the whole dataset is commonly called an *epoch*. The training procedure runs over multiple epochs, optimizing the parameters of the model. Eventually, the training procedure hits a stopping condition, such as reaching a predefined number of epochs, and stops consuming data from the data loader.

The generator function is wrapped in a TensorFlow Dataset object that our Keras model is able to consume. We must manually specify the data types contained in the dataset. For training, the dataset contains tuples of a sparse sensor and a target variable. For testing, the dataset contains only sparse tensors.

Note the BATCH_SIZE parameter at the top of the file. Adjusting the batch size is one of the key knobs you can turn to fine-tune training performance: higher values will result in faster training, especially on GPUs, but the accuracy of the model may be hurt. In general, lower values lead to better accuracy at the cost of slower training time. Another small detail worth highlighting is the dataset.prefetch call at the end: this call instructs TensorFlow, which Keras uses under the hood, to load the next batch to GPU memory while a previous batch is being computed, giving a small boost to training performance.

Now we have the machinery for producing input tensors that can be consumed by a custom data loader. The next step is to develop the model itself.

9.2.2 Defining a deep regression model

To give you an idea of what a realistic model for our price-prediction task looks like, we define and train a deep neural network model in Keras. We show how to feed it with data, run it on GPUs, monitor its training, and evaluate its performance against other models. The example resembles the process that any data scientist developing a similar model would go through.

For starters, we take care of some mundane bookkeeping matters. We start by defining two utility functions, load_model and save_model, which can be used to persist any Keras model. The KerasModel helper class we define in listing 9.14 allows you to store models as artifacts, working around the fact that Keras models can't be pickled by default.

The class leverages the built-in Keras functions to save and load a model to and from a file. We can't use the Keras functions as-is, because local files won't work across compute layers, for example, when you run –with batch. Also, we want to leverage Metaflow's built-in versioning and datastore to keep track of models, which is easier than keeping local files organized manually.

Listing 9.14 Superclass for Keras models

```
import tempfile

class KerasModel():
    @classmethod
    def save_model(cls, model):
        import tensorflow as tf                          Saves the model to
        with tempfile.NamedTemporaryFile() as f:         a temporary file
            tf.keras.models.save_model(model, f.name, save_format='h5')
            return f.read()
```

Reads bytes representing the model from the temporary file

```
    @classmethod
    def load_model(cls, blob):
        import tensorflow as tf
        with tempfile.NamedTemporaryFile() as f:
            f.write(blob)
            f.flush()
            return tf.keras.models.load_model(f.name)
```

Writes bytes to a temporary file

Asks Keras to read the model from the temporary file

Save the code in taxi_modules/keras_model.py. We can use these methods to handle any Keras model that subclasses KerasModel, like the one we define later.

Next, we will define a model architecture for our nonlinear regression task in listing 9.15. Although the listing presents a reasonable architecture, many others likely perform even better for this task. The process of finding an architecture that yields robust results involves a good amount of trial and error, the speeding up of which is a key motivation for data science infrastructure. As an exercise, you can try to find a better performing architecture, both when it comes to training speed as well as accuracy.

Listing 9.15   A flow with parameters

**Accepts the input tensor type
signature as an argument**

```
def deep_regression_model(input_sig):
    import tensorflow as tf
    model = tf.keras.Sequential([
        tf.keras.Input(type_spec=input_sig),
        tf.keras.layers.Dense(2048, activation='relu'),
        tf.keras.layers.Dense(128, activation='relu'),
        tf.keras.layers.Dense(64, activation='relu'),
        tf.keras.layers.Dense(1)
    ])
    model.compile(loss='mean_squared_error',
                  steps_per_execution=10000,
                  optimizer=tf.keras.optimizers.Adam(0.001))
    return model
```

**The input layer is shaped based
on the input data signature.**

**Defines the
hidden layers**

**Target
variable
(trip price)**

**Minimizes
mean
squared
error**

Accelerates processing on GPUs

Save the code in taxi_modules/dnn_model.py. The model in listing 9.15 consists of a sparse input layer matching our input features, three hidden layers, and a dense output variable, representing the trip price we want to predict. Note that we compile the model with mean squared error as our loss function, which is the metric we care about. The steps_per_exeuction parameter speeds up processing on GPUs by loading multiple batches for processing at once. Next, we will specify a model plugin by putting together all the pieces we have developed this far as follows:

- The model subclasses KerasModel for persistence.
- Use data_loader from the dnn_data module to load data.
- Load the model itself from the dnn_module module.

The following code listing shows the model module.

Listing 9.16   Model definition for the Keras model

**Number of training epochs. Increase
for more accurate results.**

```
from .dnn_data import data_loader, BATCH_SIZE
from .keras_model import KerasModel
from .dnn_model import deep_regression_model
EPOCHS = 4

class Model(KerasModel):
    NAME = 'grid_dnn'
    MODEL_LIBRARIES = {'tensorflow-base': '2.6.0'}
    FEATURES = ['grid']

    @classmethod
    def fit(cls, train_data):
        import tensorflow as tf
        input_sig, data = data_loader(train_data['grid']['tensor'],
                          train_data['baseline']['amount'])
        model = deep_regression_model(input_sig)
```

**Change this to
{'tensorflow-gpu': '2.6.2'} if
you want to leverage GPUs.**

Initializes a data loader

**Creates
a model**

Monitors progress with TensorBoard

```
monitor = tf.keras.callbacks.TensorBoard(update_freq=100)
num_steps = len(train_data['baseline']['amount']) // BATCH_SIZE
model.fit(data,
          epochs=EPOCHS,
          verbose=2,
          steps_per_epoch=num_steps,
          callbacks=[monitor])
return model
```

Trains the model   **Number of batches**

Computes the mean squared error between predictions and correct prices

```
@classmethod
def mse(cls, model, test_data):
    import numpy
    _, data = data_loader(test_data['grid']['tensor'])
    pred = model.predict(data)
    arr = numpy.array([x[0] for x in pred])
    return ((arr - test_data['baseline']['amount'])**2).mean()
```

Initializes a data loader in testing more; no target variable

Converts the result tensor to a NumPy array

Save the code in taxi_modules/model_grid.py. The final directory structure should look like this:

```
taxi_regression_data.py
taxi_regression_model.py
taxi_modules/__init__.py
taxi_modules/feat_baseline.py
taxi_modules/feat_euclidean.py
taxi_modules/feat_modelgrid.py
taxi_modules/model_baseline.py
taxi_modules/model_euclidean.py
taxi_modules/model_grid.py
taxi_modules/regression.py
taxi_modules/numpy_encoder.py
taxi_modules/encoders.py
taxi_modules/table_utils.py
taxi_modules/keras_model.py
taxi_modules/dnn_model.py
taxi_modules/dnn_data.py
```

This is starting to look like a real data science project! Luckily, each module is small, and the overall structure is quite understandable, especially when accompanied by documentation. We are now ready to start training the model.

9.2.3 *Training a deep regression model*

Let's begin with a word of warning: training a deep neural network model is a very compute-intensive procedure. Whereas the linear regression models we defined earlier in this chapter train in seconds, the deep regression model we defined above can take hours or even days to train, depending on your hardware.

In general, it is a good idea to start with a quick round of smoke testing—does the workflow even complete successfully?—before spending hours to train an untested model. We start by testing the end-to-end workflow quickly, making sure that everything is working correctly. You should be able to complete the smoke test on any hardware, including your laptop, in a few minutes.

SMALL-SCALE TRAINING

The easiest way to make training fast is to reduce the amount of data. Hence, we start the smoke test by creating a tiny 1% sample of our full dataset. Run the data workflow, which we defined in listing 9.6, to create a sample as follows:

```
# python taxi_regression_data.py --environment=conda run -sample 0.01
```

Now, we can run the model workflow:

```
# python taxi_regression_model.py --environment=conda run
```

Assuming all the three model plugins exist in the taxi_modules directory, the `start` step should print the following line:

```
Building models: euclidean_regression, grid_dnn, distance_regression
```

With a 1% sample, the workflow should execute for about 5–10 minutes, depending on your hardware. The result of the model benchmark is output in the `join` step. It is expected to look something like this:

```
MODEL euclidean_regression MSE 15.498595
MODEL grid_dnn MSE 24.180864
MODEL distance_regression MSE 9.561464
```

As expected, the `distance_regression` model that uses the actual distance performs the best. Sadly but expectedly, our deep regression model, `grid_dnn`, performs worse than the model using the Euclidean trip distance when trained with a small amount of data. It is widely known that traditional machine learning methods often beat deep learning when the amount of data is limited. However, if you saw results like these, you should celebrate: the whole setup works end to end!

LARGE-SCALE TRAINING

For a more realistic, large-scale training, you can adopt a few best practices:

- Use a GPU to speed up training. You can do this in the following ways:
  - You can leverage GPUs on your laptop or desktop, if you have such hardware available.
  - You can launch a GPU instance as a cloud workstation and execute the examples on the instance. Make sure you use an instance image (AMI) that includes CUDA kernel libraries, such as AWS Deep Learning AMI (https://aws.amazon.com/machine-learning/amis/).
  - You can set up a remote compute layer, for example, Batch compute environment, with GPU instances.
- Make sure that your workstation doesn't terminate during training (e.g., your laptop runs out of battery or the SSH connection to the workstation dies). If you use a cloud workstation, it is advisable to use a terminal multiplexer like

screen or tmux to make sure the process stays running, even if the network connection dies. See, for example, http://mng.bz/lxEB for instructions. Alternatively, if you use a GPU-powered compute layer, you can deploy the workflow to a production scheduler like AWS Step Functions, as discussed in chapter 6, which takes care of running the workflow reliably.

- Use a monitoring tool like TensorBoard, which is an open source package and service provided by Google for free, to monitor progress. Although this is not required, it gives peace of mind to see that the training task is making progress.

If you want to leverage a GPU for training, replace this line

```
MODEL_LIBRARIES = {'tensorflow-base': '2.6.0'}
```

in model_grid.py with

```
MODEL_LIBRARIES = {'tensorflow-gpu': '2.6.2'}
```

to use a GPU-optimized version of TensorFlow.

After your workstation is ready to go, create a larger dataset by executing, for example:

```
# python taxi_regression_data.py --environment=conda run -sample 0.2
```

You can test training with up to a 100% sample, depending on your hardware and patience. If you are executing the command on a cloud workstation, make sure to run these commands inside screen or tmux, so you can reattach to the process if your SSH session dies. You can start a training run as follows:

```
# python taxi_regression_model.py --environment=conda run -max-workers 1
```

Note that we specify -max-workers 1, which limits the foreach to run only one process at a time. This ensures that the heavyweight GPU task doesn't need to compete with other processes running on the workstation simultaneously.

Because we enabled logging to TensorBoard in model_grid.py already, we can simply run TensorBoard in another terminal window to monitor progress. Open another terminal session and navigate to the directory where you started the run. Then, install TensorBoard by running the next code:

```
# pip install tensorboard
```

If you are running training on a local machine, you can open TensorBoard locally by executing the following:

```
# tensorboard --logdir logs
```

It should print out an URL like http://localhost:6006/, which you can copy and paste to a browser window. If you are running a cloud workstation, it might be easier to rely on a publicly hosted TensorBoard at https://tensorboard.dev for monitoring. To use the service, simply execute the following:

```
# tensorboard dev upload --logdir logs
```

When you run the command for the first time, it asks you to authenticate and save a token locally. After doing this, it should print out a URL that looks like https://tensorboard.dev/experiment/UeHdJZ7JRbGpN341gyOwrnQ/, which you can open with a browser.

Both the local as well as the hosted TensorBoard should look like the screenshot in figure 9.10. You can reload the page periodically to see the training making progress. If all goes well, the loss curve should trend downward as shown in the figure.

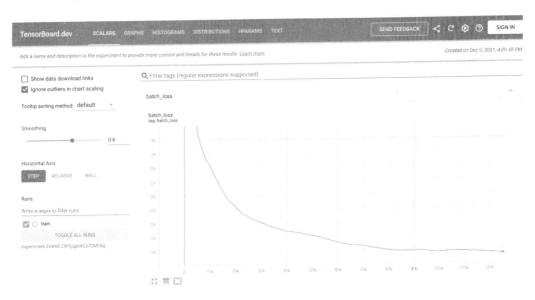

Figure 9.10   Screenshot of tensorboard.dev showing model convergence

Another handy command that may be available on a GPU-powered system is nvidia-smi, which shows statistics about GPU utilization. It should show all GPUs available in your system and a utilization figure that's above 0%, if a GPU is being used by the training process.

On a powerful GPU instance (p3.8xlarge), training the model with a full dataset (100% sample) over four epochs takes about eight hours. If you want to attempt speeding up the training, you can experiment with different variants of the model as follows:

- You can decrease the value of NUM_HASH_BINS and precision in feat_gridtensor .py to make the input tensors small. Or experiment changing with only one of those parameters to change the hashing behavior.
- You can change the model architecture in dnn_model.py. For instance, you can remove hidden layers or make them smaller.
- You can increase BATCH_SIZE to a very high number, say, 10,000, to make the model train much faster. You can use TensorBoard to monitor the effect of the batch size to model loss.
- You can make EPOCHS smaller to reduce the number of training iterations. Or you can change other parameters but increase EPOCHS.

A rewarding element of model development is that the results are perfectly quantifiable. You can experiment with the previous parameters and see the effect on model performance as soon as the training finishes. As a baseline for your experiments, training the models with a full dataset produces the following results:

```
MODEL euclidean_regression MSE 15.214128
MODEL grid_dnn MSE 12.765191
MODEL distance_regression MSE 9.461593
```

Our efforts are not in vain! When trained with a full dataset, the deep regression model handily beats the naive Euclidean model, approaching the performance of the actual distance measurement. In other words, it is possible to build a model that predicts the trip price relatively accurately by considering only the pick-up and drop-off locations, and such a model performs better than a model that considers only a straight-line distance between the locations.

As an exercise, you can try to improve the model: you can include, for example, time of day as a feature, which surely affects traffic patterns. You can also test different variations of the model architecture or try to improve the performance of the data loader. After a few rounds of improvement, you should be able to beat the performance of the baseline model.

However, this chapter is not about optimal models for price predictions. More important, we learned how to design and develop a simple domain-specific framework that allows a data scientist to define new features and models to solve this particular business problem effectively and test the performance of the new variants consistently. Although this example was a rather simple one, you can use it as an inspiration for your own, more sophisticated frameworks that stand on the shoulders of the full infrastructure stack.

9.3   *Summarizing lessons learned*

We began the book with a picture, shown again in figure 9.11, illustrating the full life cycle of a data science project. We promised to cover all parts of the life cycle, so your organization can increase the number of projects that are executed simultaneously (volume), speed up the time to market (velocity), ensure that the results are robust

Figure 9.11 The full life cycle of a data science project

(validity), and make it possible to support a wider variety of projects. To summarize the book, let's see how the chapters we covered map to the figure.

1 Models shouldn't be built in isolation. We emphasized the importance of focusing on the business problem on a number of occasions. We introduced the idea of a spiral approach in chapter 3 and applied it to example projects throughout the book.

2 What tooling should data scientists use to develop projects effectively, and where and how to use the tooling? The entirety of chapter 2 was dedicated to the topic of notebooks, IDEs, cloud workstations, and workflows. We introduced a particular framework, Metaflow, in chapter 3, which addresses many of these concerns in a user-friendly manner. Also in this chapter, we demonstrated how custom libraries built on top of the stack can boost productivity in particular problem domains.

3 How do we benefit from off-the-shelf libraries without exposing projects to random breakage and performance degradation? We discussed the performance implications of libraries in chapter 5 and dug deeper into the question of dependency management in chapter 6. We used a variety of open source ML libraries in examples, culminating in a deep neural network model showcased in this chapter.

4 How should we discover, access, and manage data? All of chapter 7 was dedicated to this broad and deep topic.

5 Machine learning projects tend to be very compute heavy—open-ended experimentation, model training, and large-scale data processing all need compute power. How should one provision and manage compute resources? Chapter 4 dove deep in the world of compute layers and modern container orchestration systems.

6 Once the results become available, how can they be connected to surrounding business systems? Crucially, production deployments should run reliably without human intervention, as discussed in chapter 6. Chapter 8 discussed how the results can be leveraged in various contexts from relatively slow batch processes to millisecond-range real-time systems.

7 Finally, the fruits of the data science project get used in practice. If the consumers of the project find the results promising, the cycle starts again because there's an appetite to make the results even better. If the response is negative, the cycle starts again as the data scientist moves on to a new project.

The fact that the cycle never stops is the ultimate justification for investing in an effective data science infrastructure. If the cycle ran only once, any working solution would suffice. However, because the cycle repeats over multiple projects and multiple teams, each of which keeps improving applications they own, the need for a common, shared foundation becomes apparent.

Hopefully this book succeeded in giving you a solid understanding of the foundational layers, data, compute, orchestration, and versioning, in the context of data science projects. Using this knowledge, you are able to evaluate the relative merits of various technical systems and approaches, make informed decisions, and set up a stack that makes sense in your environment.

Although the foundation can be shared, the diversity of applications and approaches at the top of the stack will increase over time as data science is applied to new domains of life. When it comes to solving particular business problems, there's no replacement for human creativity and domain expertise. A foundation is just a foundation: it is now your turn to grab a sketchpad, experiment, and start building new and exciting, well-tailored data science applications on top of the stack.

Summary

- The top layers of the stack, model development and feature engineering, tend to be domain specific. You can create small, domain-specific libraries on top of the foundational infrastructure stack to address the needs of each project.

- Models and feature encoders can be implemented as pluggable modules, enabling quick prototyping and benchmarking of ideas.

- Use a common workflow to load data, produce train and test splits, and execute feature encoders and models, making sure results are consistent and comparable between models.

- Modern deep learning libraries work well with the infrastructure stack, particularly when executed on a compute layer that supports GPUs.

- Use off-the-shelf monitoring tools and services like TensorBoard to monitor training in real time.

appendix
Installing Conda

The Conda package manager was introduced in chapter 5. Follow these instructions to install Conda on your system:

1   Open the home page of *Miniconda* at http://mng.bz/BM5r.
2   Download a Miniconda installer either for Mac OS X or Linux (Metaflow doesn't currently support Windows natively).
3   Once the package has been downloaded, execute the installer on a terminal as follows:

```
bash Miniconda3-latest-MacOSX-x86_64.sh
```

Replace the package name with the actual package name you downloaded.

4   When the installer asks, "Do you wish the installer to initialize Miniconda3," answer Yes.
5   After the installation completes, restart your terminal for the changes to take effect.
6   In a new terminal, run the following:

```
conda config --add channels conda-forge
```

This will make community-maintained packages at conda-forge.org available in your installation.

That's it! The @conda decorator in Metaflow will take care of installing packages using the newly installed Conda.

index

RELATED MANNING TITLES

Machine Learning Engineering in Action
by Ben Wilson

ISBN 9781617298714
576 pages, $59.99
March 2022

Deep Learning with Python, Second Edition
by François Chollet

ISBN 9781617296864
504 pages, $59.99
October 2021

Data Science Bookcamp
Five real-world Python projects
by Leonard Apeltsin

ISBN 9781617296253
704 pages, $59.99
October 2021

For ordering information, go to www.manning.com